Teaching the Bible

TEACHING THE BIBLE

The Discourses and Politics of Biblical Pedagogy

Fernando F. Segovia
and
Mary Ann Tolbert,
Editors

ORBIS BOOKS

Maryknoll, New York 10545

The Catholic Foreign Mission Society of America (Maryknoll) recruits and trains people for overseas missionary service. Through Orbis Books, Maryknoll aims to foster the international dialogue that is essential to mission. The books published, however, reflect the opinions of their authors and are not meant to represent the official position of the society.

Manufactured in the United States of America

Library of Congress Cataloging-in-Publication Data

Teaching the Bible : the discourses and politics of biblical pedagogy
/ Fernando F. Segovia and Mary Ann Tolbert, editors.
    p.   cm.
Includes bibliographical references and index.
ISBN 1-57075-202-8 (pbk.)
    1. Bible—Study and teaching.   2. Bible—Study and teaching—History.
I. Segovia, Fernando F.   II. Tolbert, Mary Ann, 1947–

BS600.2.T44   1998
220'.071—dc21   98-25987
                                                                      CIP

CONTENTS

v

PART II
Social Location and Biblical Pedagogy in the United States

PART III
Social Location and Biblical Pedagogy in Global Perspective

PART IV

Biblical Interpretation: Pedagogical Practices

PREFACE

The present volume represents the second phase of a multidimensional project on the relationship between biblical interpretation and the social location of the interpreter. The first phase, *Reading from This Place,* consisted of two volumes, both published by Fortress Press in 1995. These volumes examined this relationship from a national and a global perspective, respectively. This second phase, *Teaching the Bible,* focuses on the implications and ramifications of this relationship for the teaching of biblical studies—the rhetoric and politics of biblical pedagogy—both in itself and within the context of theological education.

The volume gathers together papers from a broad variety of voices in biblical criticism and theological studies, from both the United States and abroad. The papers have been divided into four major sections, in keeping with their major concerns and aims: (1) Biblical Interpretation and Theological Education; (2) Social Location and Biblical Pedagogy in the United States; (3) Social Location and Biblical Pedagogy in Global Perspective; and (4) Biblical Interpretation: Pedagogical Practices. The volume also includes an introduction by one of the co-editors, Fernando F. Segovia.

As in the case of the previous volumes, this work is meant as a further contribution to the fundamental question regarding the role of the interpreter in the light of a very different world within biblical criticism—a world of increasing and irreversible diversity and pluralism, the world of the twenty-first century.

ACKNOWLEDGMENTS

The editors would like to express their profound gratitude to all those individuals and institutions who have made this volume possible:

First, to the Lilly Endowment and Dr. Craig Dykstra, vice president for religion; and to the Association of Theological Schools in the United States and Canada and Dr. Gail Buchwalter King, Associate Director, for their strong support of this second phase of the project and the generous funding that made it possible.

Second, to Dr. Joseph C. Hough, Jr., dean of the Divinity School at Vanderbilt University, for his kind assistance in all areas and dimensions of the project.

Third, to Mr. Robert Ellsberg, editor-in-chief of Orbis Books, who gave his full backing to the volume, and to the editorial staff of Orbis Books who brought it to completion under their expert and gracious supervision.

Fourth, to Mr. W. Gregory Carey and Ms. Leticia Guardiola-Sáenz, both students in the area of New Testament and early Christianity within the graduate department of religion at Vanderbilt University, who assisted in the task of editing and formatting the papers for publication.

Finally, to all those scholars and friends who kindly accepted our invitations to take part in this project. To them we are specially indebted.

INTRODUCTION:
PEDAGOGICAL DISCOURSE AND
PRACTICES IN CONTEMPORARY
BIBLICAL CRITICISM

Toward a Contextual Biblical Pedagogy

Fernando F. Segovia

In previous analyses of the course of biblical criticism in the twentieth century, I have portrayed the world of contemporary biblical criticism as consisting of four main and competing paradigms or umbrella models of interpretation, each with its own distinctive mode of discourse and broad spectrum of interpretive positions.[1] These four paradigms I have identified as follows: historical criticism; literary criticism; cultural criticism; and cultural studies.[2]

I have also argued that these umbrella models of interpretation presently find themselves, at the turn of the century, at different levels of competitiveness in the public arena of the discipline, as a result of the particular path of development or "plot" I have charted for the discipline as a whole. Such varying states of readiness I have described as follows: First, a much-weakened historical criticism (as *traditionally* conceived and practiced), thoroughly displaced from its former position of near-absolute hegemony and left rather at a loss, still, for a vigorous and informed defense regarding its own methodological strategies and theoretical grounds.[3] Second, the two original would-be pretenders to the throne, literary criticism and cultural criticism, which have become, since their sharp and successful challenge to historical criticism, quite entrenched in the discipline, quite sophisticated in method and theory, and quite vibrant in interdisciplinary dialogue and exchange. Finally, a still nascent cultural studies, essentially a child of mixed parentage: on the one hand, a product of the profound methodological and theoretical shifts introduced into the discipline by both literary and cultural criticism; on the other hand, and above all, the result of certain crucial demographic and sociocultural changes at work in the discipline, as in all other classical theological disciplines—an ever-growing presence of outsiders (Western women; non-Western critics and theologians; and non-

Western minorities residing in the West) in the discipline, who now entered what had been a thoroughly clerical, male, and Western domain.[4] I should specify that such an evaluation of the competitive dynamics among these four paradigms reflects more accurately the situation in Western North America than in Europe; indeed, in many ways, though with some outstanding exceptions here and there, the "Old World" is only now beginning to struggle with issues that many in the United States have already engaged and moved beyond.[5]

I have further undertaken to surface and unpack a number of fundamental presuppositions at work in the construction and employment of each umbrella model of interpretation by means of a comparative analysis of six basic elements or principles operative, in one way or another, in all four paradigms: location of meaning; reading strategy; theoretical foundations; role of the reader; theological presuppositions; and pedagogical implications. A principal aim of such an exercise in metatheory was to outline as starkly as possible the manifold options and choices facing, at every step of the way, contemporary professional practitioners of the discipline today—choices and options, it should go without saying, that signal in turn immediate and inevitable consequences for any critic's conception and practice of the discipline.

In effect, as I have further argued, the situation has become radically different now, at the turn of the century, than it was in the mid-1970s. To wit: Methodological diversity within a dominant paradigm (historical criticism), involving overall consensus regarding the same basic mode of discourse, has yielded to: (1) diversity of paradigms, with widely different modes of discourse; (2) diversity of methods and theories within each paradigm, of a sort far more difficult to manage and transcend than that present in the previously dominant paradigm; and (3) ever-increasing diversity of interpreters, bringing to the fore issues of ideology across all paradigms. Quite aside from the question of whether such a shift has been beneficial or harmful to the discipline—in the end, a highly personal and contextualized judgment—the fact remains that its implications and ramifications impinge upon all critics at every step of the way. As a result, such questions as the following now call for explicit and sustained consideration:

• How are ancient texts—indeed "antiquity" itself—to be approached and why?

• What is precisely the role of the biblical critic as critic?

• What is the relationship of biblical criticism to the other theological disciplines as well as to other disciplines in the humanities and the social sciences?

• What is the relationship of the biblical critic not only to the church but also to other religious traditions and their own forms of criticism regarding such traditions?

• What is the relationship of the biblical critic to the broader society as well as to the world at large?

- What are the ethical, social, and ideological responsibilities of biblical interpretation?

- How is the teaching of the discipline to be undertaken in this day and age?

For any critic who wishes to reflect self-consciously on these matters, there is really no choice but to proceed step by step, question by question, given the magnitude and significance of each question. In this study, therefore, I should like to focus on the last question—the question of pedagogy—and hence on the last of the six basic principles mentioned above that I have already surfaced and unpacked in all four critical paradigms. I shall do so in two stages.

First, I shall examine in a more sustained and systematic fashion the pedagogical discourse and practices proper to each of the first three paradigms: historical criticism, literary criticism, and cultural criticism. It should be made clear from the start that the proposed analysis faces a significant though not insurmountable obstacle: the question of pedagogy has rarely, if ever, been raised, much less addressed, explicitly in any of these three paradigms. This means of course that the proposed analysis can only proceed by rendering explicit what has remained largely implicit throughout, that is to say, by bringing to the surface the pedagogical discourse and practices presupposed within each paradigm. At the same time, however, such analysis is not entirely an exercise in deduction; it is also an exercise in recollection. In other words, I approach this question neither as a complete stranger nor as a participant observer, but as a cognizant insider—as someone who, given the coincidence between such disciplinary developments and my own engagement with the discipline, has both resided in and worked from within each of the paradigms in question.

I shall pursue this mixture of deduction and recollection by means of a conversation with a number of individuals who not only embody in a very distinctive way the ideals and goals of each paradigm, but who also have captured in writing such ideals and goals in a very precise way—in other words, individuals whom I regard as both key representatives of and outstanding spokespersons for their respective crafts. In so doing, I would emphasize, my aim is not to engage in scorched-earth tactics, slashing and burning, tearing down, and destroying—a regrettable and still much-too-common dimension of our discipline, I am afraid, due in large part to its emergence alongside Western capitalism and expansionism, with its credo of a ruthless "virile" competition; my aim rather is to engage in critical dialogue with a number of individuals from whom I have learned a great deal and with whose work I happen to be thoroughly familiar.

Second, I shall then proceed to examine, in a similar type of conversation, a number of voices that have, in recent times and within the ambit of the cultural studies paradigm, begun to call for new directions in the teaching of the discipline, with specific reference to its expanding methodological and theoretical apparatus and, above all, the growing phenomenon of globalization at work within it. My aim in such an exercise is to analyze the various diagnoses offered for the discipline—the overall perception of its present state of affairs—as well as any corresponding prescriptions for change.

Such a twofold analysis and engagement, in itself a central component of intercultural criticism as I have defined it,[6] has two basic purposes in mind: to reveal the direction and tenor of the pedagogical discussion in the discipline in the face of a new century; to set the stage for a constructive pedagogical proposal of my own from the perspective of cultural studies.

PEDAGOGICAL DISCOURSE AND PRACTICES
IN HISTORICAL, LITERARY, AND CULTURAL CRITICISM

Historical Criticism

In my initial assessment of the pedagogical model underlying historical criticism, I made a number of observations with regard to its basic principles and implications:[7] First, the model involved learned impartation and passive reception. In keeping with its corresponding demand for a universal and informed reader-construct, the model argued that the proper dissemination and acquisition of the right methodological tools could turn student/readers, regardless of sociocultural moorings or theological persuasion, into informed and universal teacher/critics. Second, given such emphasis on learned impartation, the model was at heart highly pyramidal and authoritative, quintessentially patriarchal, with competing claims to honor advanced in terms of academic genealogy (who begat whom: where one studied and with whom) and critical sociolect (proper versus improper approximations to the text). Third, quite in keeping once again with the universal and informed reader-construct, the model further entailed a process of dehumanization as a key component in its rite of initiation for all would-be practitioners and devotees. Student/readers would become teacher/critics by learning how not to read themselves as readers, except for the purpose of surfacing theological presuppositions so that these could be properly identified and duly obviated. In the end, I concluded, this was a model for which student/readers remained dependent on teacher/critics for an account of the text and its meaning. Only the voice of reason, properly activated and cultivated through a concomitant acquisition of scientific tools and divestment of sociocultural vagaries, could speak ex cathedra on matters interpretive.

As interlocutor in historical criticism, I turn to the work of Prof. Joseph A. Fitzmyer, S.J., by way of an article on historical criticism that he contributed some years ago to a special issue of *Theological Studies* devoted to the question of contemporary biblical criticism.[8] The study represents a succint, pointed, and spirited defense of historical criticism[9] in the light of four perceived challenges: (1) integrism within Roman Catholic circles: the method is captive to modernism and underplays the character of the Bible as "Word of God"; (2) liberalism within Roman Catholic circles: the method represents the end of traditional, folk catholicism; (3) theological criticism: the method shows no concern for the final text—its literary features, canonical setting, and theological meaning; (4) fundamentalism within Protestant circles: the method forsakes the fundamentals of Christian doctrine by bypassing the inspiration of the text and the authority of the written Word. Interestingly enough, however, despite the date in question (1989), no challenge from within the tradition of academic criticism is entertained.[10]

The defense itself is broadly mounted, touching upon such various facets of the method as historical trajectory, reading strategy, ideological presuppositions, and ecclesiological role. It is further undertaken from the perspective of the critic as historian of religion and Christian theologian—a perspective that includes a view of criticism as involving both historical reconstruction and theological propaedeutics (Bible as ancient record and Word of God) and thus a view of Christian doctrine and life as subject to the guidance and judgment of the Word of God and of this Word as accessible only through the channel of historical criticism. The defense also makes a fundamental distinction between method and presuppositions.

The method itself, which is said to consist of a basic core and subsequent refinements, is characterized as "neutral," that is to say, as without "presuppositions."[11] Classical philology constitutes the core: at the heart of the method, therefore, lie questions of both a textual (the establishment of the text) and a historical nature (authenticity; integrity; date and place; content; occasion or purpose of writing; background).[12] Beyond this core one finds a series of refinements that, strictly speaking, do not form part of historical criticism but that have become associated with it over time: literary criticism (structure; style; form); source criticism; form criticism; and redaction criticism. From the point of view of historical criticism as philology, therefore, the Bible represents an ancient record and, as such, must be approached and analyzed like any other ancient record—paying close attention to the different historical backgrounds, contemporary contexts, and original languages of the texts in question—if one is to arrive at the meaning intended by the authors themselves.

Given its neutral character, the method can be pursued with different presuppositions in mind: while some are said to "taint" the method unduly (e.g., the rationalistic analysis or challenges of the nineteenth century; the demythologizing, existentialist approach of Rudolf Bultmann), one in particular is described as "exegesis" proper, what Fitzmyer calls "philology plus."[13] Such exegesis—defined from the perspective of the Roman Catholic Church—calls for a view of the Bible, of the ancient record, as the Word of God set forth in human words, a position that entails a number of further presuppositions as well: composed under the guidance of the Spirit; authoritative for the Jewish-Christian heritage; given by God to God's people for edification and salvation; properly expounded only within the context of the tradition that has emerged from it "within the communal faith-life" of the people. From the point of view of historical criticism as exegesis, therefore, God has spoken historically and uniquely in the Bible, and thus it takes a combination of historical criticism and faith presuppositions to ascertain its proper and correct meaning as Word of God in human words.

In the end, Fitzmyer hints at the pedagogical implications of this approach: while the method does impose a "heavy burden" on readers, it alone allows, as suggested by the Bible itself (2 Pet 3:15–17 and Acts 8), for proper reading and interpretation to take place. The pedagogical model at work is thus unmistakable and confirms all the preliminary observations listed above:

• First, student/readers need to master the principles of classical philology and the techniques of its later refinements in order to become critic/teachers; further, student/readers also need to possess the proper faith presuppositions to become exegetes. On the one hand, therefore, student/readers must acquire an extensive knowledge of the period and area under consideration, an expertise involving original languages, contemporary contexts, and historical backgrounds. On the other hand, student/readers must also possess extensive familiarity with regard to the exegetical tradition as such, the various presuppositions at work in such a tradition, and the faith presuppositions of proper exegesis.

• Second, given their mastery of such principles and techniques and their possession of such knowledge and expertise, teacher/critics hold the key to the meaning of the Bible as an ancient record; likewise, given their familiarity with presuppositions and their grounding in faith presuppositions, teacher/exegetes also hold the key to the meaning of the Bible as Word of God.

• Third, such mastery and such learning render critics objective and impartial in their research, lifting them above social location and ideology and allowing them to recover the original meaning of the text (the ancient record) intended by the authors; similarly, such familiarity and such grounding give proper direction to their historical research, placing it within a sound context and agenda and rendering them able to retrieve the full meaning of the text (the Word of God) intended by the sacred authors.

What emerges thereby is a pedagogical model that is highly pyramidal, patriarchal, and authoritative; a model where the teacher/critic, as the voice of reason, collects and disseminates the historical mysteries of the text as ancient record to student/readers; and the teacher/exegete, as the voice of faith, unveils and discloses the theological mysteries of the text as Word of God to student/readers—a model where teacher/critics rise above social location and ideology to arrive at the meaning of the text and where teacher/exegetes locate themselves within a specific context and agenda to arrive at the full meaning of that text.

Literary Criticism

With respect to the pedagogical model underlying literary criticism, I noted in my initial assessment that its basic principles and implications were not unlike those of historical criticism.[14] First, the model again involved sophisticated impartation and passive acquisition. Given its call at first for a universal and informed reader-construct and later on for a more specific and formal reader-construct, the model took it for granted that all student/readers, regardless of sociocultural moorings or theological persuasion, could become teacher/critics, provided that the right theoretical and methodological apparatuses were properly propagated and learned. Second, given the continued emphasis on sophisticated impartation, the model remained at heart highly pyramidal and authoritative, typically patriarchal, with competing claims to honor now offered in terms of literary sociolect (which particular critical stance to follow) and external authority (which critics to read). Third, regardless of the reader-construct at work, whether that of the universal and informed reader or that of the specific and formal reader, the model continued to abstain, in its rite of initiation for all would-be practitioners and devotees, from any reading of real readers. The model clearly clung thereby to the ideal of dehumanization: real student/readers would become teacher/critics by learning how not to read themselves. I concluded by stating that this was a model in which student/readers continued to be ultimately dependent on teacher/critics for an account of the text and its meaning, although, to be sure, such a position gradually eroded as more and more attention was placed on the possibility of multiple interpretations and the role of the reader in the act of reading.

As interlocutor in literary criticism, I shall have recourse to the work of Mark Allan Powell, in particular the introductory volume on narrative criticism that he authored for the *Guides to Biblical Scholarship* series published by Fortress Press.[15] This is a work that sets out to explain the ways, aims, and consequences of one particular strand of literary criticism—narrative criticism—in the light of both historical criticism and other approaches within literary criticism itself.[16] In so doing, the work adopts a tone of comparative exposition rather than formal apologia, no doubt due to the fact that, by the time of composition (1990), literary criticism—and certainly narrative criticism—had already become well entrenched in the discipline. As such, its primary aim is not justification but differentiation.[17] This exercise in differentiation is further undertaken from the perspective of the critic as both historian of religion and Christian theologian—a perspective that includes a view of criticism as involving both literary analysis and theological propaedeutics (the Bible as literature and Word of God).

Powell begins by distinguishing literary criticism from traditional criticism: while historical criticism sought to explain the texts in terms of historical circumstances, literary criticism focuses on the literary qualities of the texts as such.[18] As a result, a number of basic differences between the two approaches can be readily outlined. In effect, literary criticism: (1) concentrates on the present text in its finished form—rather than on its process of formation; (2) emphasizes the unity and coherence of the text as a whole—rather than its lack of flow and unintelligibility; (3) views the text as an end in itself—rather than as a means toward some type of historical reconstruction; and (4) opts for a communications model of interpretation—rather than for an evolutionary or excavative model. Despite such differences and the different insights they generate regarding the text, Powell argues for a relationship of complementarity rather than opposition between the two approaches: literary criticism does not question the legitimacy of historical criticism but simply suspends the question of historicity in order to study the text as literature.[19] In fact, Powell goes on to argue, narrative criticism must have knowledge of the social and historical circumstances assumed by the narrative in order to be truly effective. One could say, therefore, that for Powell literary criticism functions as a sort of climax to historical criticism, insofar as it brings the final text to the fore for analysis.

Powell then proceeds to distinguish narrative criticism from other "ways of reading" within literary criticism itself—structuralism, rhetorical criticism, and reader-response criticism.[20] It is the aim of narrative criticism to read the text in terms of its "implied" reader—the reader presupposed by, present in, and reconstructed from the text. As such, narrative criticism can be readily distinguished from the other strands of literary criticism: (1) structuralism argues for a "competent" reader—a reader who understands the deep structures and codes undergirding the text; (2) rhetorical criticism opts for the "intended" reader—the reader to whom the text was first addressed; (3) reader-response criticism favors a first-time reader—a reader who encounters the text in sequential order. Again, despite such differences and the different insights generated with regard to the text, Powell tacitly argues for a relationship of complementarity rather than opposition among the various approaches: while clearly favoring the reading offered by way of the "implied" reader, narrative criticism does not call into question the modes of reading at work in the other approaches.[21] One could add, therefore, that for Powell, once the final text is brought to the fore for analysis, it can be subjected to a number of different "ways of reading."

It is clear from both exercises in differentiation that literary criticism, including narrative criticism, involves a set of presuppositions as well as a method.[22] Its key methodological principle is clear: to read the text as the implied reader would. Such a mode of reading may be further described as follows. First, the implied reader—the reader constructed and addressed by the implied author—is reconstructed from the text on the basis of clues provided by the text itself.[23] Second, such reading requires that the reader know everything that the text assumes the reader to know, while bypassing everything that the text does not assume the reader to know. In other words, such reading pursues only those questions that the text assumes its reader will ask and no others. Third, such reading does not necessarily require a first-time reader but may actually call for a multiple reader of the text. Finally, such reading must follow the various narrative devices deployed in the text by the implied author. These devices have to do with story or the content of the narrative (events, characters, settings, plot) as well as discourse or the rhetoric of the narrative (point of view; levels of narration; symbolism and irony; narrative patterns). Consequently, the aim of such reading is to understand the story as presented by the implied author in and through the text. In the end, therefore, the concept of the implied reader does set definite criteria for interpretation: any proposed reading of a text must be justified in terms of the dictates and expectations to be found within the text itself.

Given Powell's view of the Bible as both literature and Word of God, such reading has a further aim: to read the text as Scripture in story form.[24] In so doing, the benefits of narrative criticism for believers are clear. First, such reading remains focused throughout on the Bible itself—not on its history or prehistory. Second, such reading also remains focused thereby on the canonical text, the authoritative text for Christian communities—not on sources and traditions. Third, such reading is very much in line as well with the Christian doctrine of the Spirit, insofar as it allows for revelation to take place not just in the past but also in the present, in the process of engaging the story of the text. Finally, through this focus on story, such reading opens the door to personal and social transformation. Consequently, in shedding light on the literary features of the text, narrative criticism activates the socioreligious and spiritual dimensions of the text as well—its revelatory and transformative character as Scripture.

On the whole, Powell shows only intermittent, limited concern with the pedagogical implications of this approach. Still, the pedagogical model at work is not at all difficult to unravel and confirms the various preliminary observations noted above:

• First, although the method is said at one point to bring professional and nonprofessional readers closer together, in the end there is no question that student/readers not only need to master the principles and techniques of literary criticism, and narrative criticism in particular, in order to become teacher/critics, but they also need to acquire extensive knowledge of the social and historical circumstances assumed by the texts. At the same time, there is no need for student/readers to possess a faith stance in order to become teacher/critics, although for those who do the method is described as most beneficial. Thus, while in a certain sense the method may be said to be much more effective for those who look upon the Bible as both literature and Word of God, it is clear that, in order to read the Bible as literature, one need not regard it as Scripture.

• Second, given their mastery of the principles and techniques of narrative criticism as well as their familiarity with the social and historical circumstances presupposed by the texts, teacher/critics do retain the key—allowing for a certain measure of ambiguity present within the text itself—to the meaning of the Bible, whether perceived as a work of literature or as the Word of God. Through such mastery and such familiarity, teacher/critics are able to follow the devices and intentions of the implied author and attain thereby a proper understanding of the text—again, allowing for a certain range of meaning within the parameters set by the text itself.

• Third, the combination of such mastery and such familiarity allows for objectivity and impartiality in research, placing teacher/critics beyond all consideration of social location and ideology and allowing them to recover—within the measure of ambiguity introduced by the text itself—the original meaning of the text intended by its implied author. At the same time, for those operating out of a faith stance, such research also bears immediate fruit from both a socioreligious and a spiritual angle: in the extended process of engaging the story of the text and deciphering the meaning intended by the implied author, there is ample opportunity for the revelation of the Spirit as well as for personal and social transformation.

The result is a pedagogical model that is, once again, highly pyramidal, patriarchal, and authoritative: a model where the teacher/critic, as the voice of the informed and universal (implied) reader, grasps the literary mysteries of the text and discloses it to student/readers, mysteries which also have profound spiritual as well as socioreligious consequences for members of faith communities; a model where teacher/critics move beyond social location and ideology to arrive at the original meaning of the text.

Cultural Criticism

In my initial assessment of the pedagogical model underlying cultural criticism, I pointed out that its basic principles and implications were quite similar to those of historical criticism.[25] First, the model involved, once again, learned impartation and passive reception. In the light of its call for either an informed and universal reader-construct or an informed and committed reader-construct, the model argued that all student/readers, regardless of sociocultural location or theological persuasion, could become teacher/critics, if the right methodological tools and theoretical apparatus were properly taught and acquired. Second, given the abiding emphasis on learned impartation, the model was likewise highly pyramidal and authoritative, patriarchal to the core, with competing claims to honor advanced in terms of disciplinary sociolect (which particular discipline to follow) and external authority (which writers or tradition) to read. Third, as part of its rite of initiation for would-be practitioners and devotees, the model, depending on the dominant reader-construct at work, either continued to abstain from any reading of real readers, or engaged in a broad reading of real readers (but only for the purpose of surfacing and obviating sociocultural presuppositions and establishing crosscultural communication), or called for a circumscribed reading of real readers in terms of social class. Aside from this last option, dehumanization still prevailed as an ideal: student/readers were still expected to become teacher/critics by learning how not to read themselves, except for the purpose of bringing to the fore sociocultural presuppositions. Within the last option, all student/readers would have to learn how to read themselves, but only according to the categories of oppressors and oppressed. In the end, I concluded, this was yet another model in which student/readers looked to teacher/critics for an account of the text and its meaning, although with some erosion of the position due to the increasing focus placed on sociocultural as well as socioeconomic characteristics.

As partner in dialogue with respect to cultural criticism, I turn to the work of Bruce J. Malina. More specifically, I have in mind a study of his that served as an introduction to his first major venture into what he eventually would come to call social scientific criticism.[26] This early study amounts to a formal apologia for the introduction of cultural anthropology into biblical criticism in the light of the traditional questions brought by historical criticism to the texts—the sort of questions outlined by Joseph Fitzmyer in his own defense of historical criticism years later.[27] Although questions of a "literary" sort are mentioned, it is clear that what Malina has in mind in this regard—despite the time of writing (1981)—are the traditional questions of historical criticism regarding literary forms and style, not the more recent questions introduced by literary criticism, by then very much on the rise.[28]

The thrust of the apologia is not that the concepts and models of cultural anthropology have much to offer biblical studies, but rather that the basic question raised by cultural anthropology constitutes not only the climax but also the sine qua non of the discipline. While traditional criticism pursues the important questions of what, who, when, where, historical how, and literary how, cultural anthropology addresses the question of why: the fundamental question of meaning in culture. Without this particular perspective provided by cultural anthropology, therefore, traditional criticism can only deal with this question in highly impressionistic fashion and thus remains constantly exposed to the twin perils of ethnocentrism and anachronism. The apologia itself is undertaken from the perspective of the biblical critic as historian of religion, not as Christian theologian. What is sought is a more sophisticated exercise in the history of religion by way of a focus on the sociocultural dimensions of the texts. Thus, the main concern is not with the Bible as Word of God but with the Bible as a cultural record of antiquity. Consequently, the goal of the exercise is to allow for a more accurate understanding of these texts as "foreign" texts from "a distant place and a distant time." For Malina, therefore, biblical criticism represents, first and foremost, an exercise in crosscultural understanding, and such understanding proves impossible without recourse to cultural anthropology.[29] In the end, it would be quite proper to describe the proposed undertaking as an attempt to perfect historical criticism.

The desired crosscultural understanding involves presuppositions—not all of which are properly recognized as such[30]—as well as a method. The line of argumentation may be traced as follows. First, an accurate understanding of the texts "on their own terms" is possible. Contemporary readers can cross the cultural and historical divide between the world of today and the world of antiquity. Second, the meaning of a text as embodied in its wording is derived from the social system out of which the text emerges. Consequently, an accurate understanding of texts requires an understanding of the social system behind the texts. Third, in order to understand the social system behind these texts, it is necessary to understand the cultural story—the cultural scripts, cues, and models—at work in such a world, the world of the first-century Mediterranean Basin. Fourth, to understand this cultural story across the cultural and historical divide, it is necessary to have recourse to crosscultural models of interpretation. Such models make it possible for the differences between cultural stories to be sharply outlined and differentiated, so that one can avoid reading one's own cultural story into that of the biblical text and thus read the cultural story of the biblical texts "on their own terms." Lastly, human beings are capable of constructing such models as a result of several factors: (1) their ability to think abstractly, to make models of experience, and to compare the various models in question; (2) their awareness that they themselves change; and (3) their ability to take on the role of another empathetically.[31] In sum, only cultural anthropology can supply such crosscultural models for biblical studies, and thus only cultural anthropology can provide the key for an accurate understanding of these texts.

Throughout, Malina is concerned with the pedagogical implications of social scientific criticism. Indeed, the driving question here is how to make it possible for contemporary student/readers to achieve an accurate and fair reading and interpretation of these "foreign" texts and of the "foreigners" behind them. The resultant pedagogical model is quite clear and follows the initial observations listed above:

- First, student/readers need not only master the principles and techniques of historical criticism, so that they can continue to ask all of the important questions characteristic of traditional criticism, but also familiarize themselves thoroughly with concepts and models of cultural anthropology—especially those derived from the study of contemporary Mediterranean society or other similar societies—so that they can proceed to raise the fundamental question of meaning: the why question. Student/readers need not, however, possess a correct faith stance to become teacher/critics. In effect, whether they look upon these texts as Scripture or as cultural remains of the past, student/readers must develop extensive expertise in both the study of first-century Mediterranean society and the anthropological study of contemporary Mediterranean society and other cultural analogues. Only then will they be able to test the crosscultural models of cultural anthropology against the reality of the ancient texts, to establish a fit between data and models, and to attain fair and adequate understanding of these texts.

- Second, given their mastery of the principles and techniques of historical criticism as well as their familiarity with the concepts and models of cultural anthropology, teacher/critics still retain the key to the meaning of the Bible, whether perceived as the Word of God or as a record of antiquity. Through such mastery and familiarity, teacher/critics attain an accurate and fair understanding of the texts as well as of the social system and cultural story behind the texts.

- Third, this combined grasp of historical criticism and cultural anthropology allows teacher/critics to read themselves in terms of their own social system and cultural story, rescues them from the mire of ethnocentrism and anachronism, and renders them objective and impartial in their own understanding—across the historical and cultural divide—of the texts as well as of the social system and cultural story behind these texts. In effect, the humanization of student/readers may be said to serve as a tool for dehumanization: by surfacing and bracketing their own social system and cultural story, student/readers become teacher/critics, beyond social location and ideology, able to read "foreigners" in both present and past, accurately and empathetically.

The result is a pedagogical model that is, yet again, highly pyramidal, patriarchal, and authoritative; a model where the teacher/critic, as the voice of the informed, universal, and self-enlightened reader, captures the sociocultural mysteries of the text and mediates it to student/readers; a model where teacher/critics rise above social location and ideology through self-knowledge to arrive at the meaning of the text.

RECENT CALLS FOR CHANGE: CULTURAL STUDIES

Such then are the pedagogical implications of historical criticism, literary criticism, and cultural criticism for the discipline. I should now like to turn to a number of studies published in the last few years that argue—from a variety of different perspectives—for fundamental changes in such practices and discourses. Given the already extensive and constantly expanding volume of the literature in question, one must of necessity be selective with respect to the voices chosen for analysis and dialogue. In what follows, therefore, I have opted for a series of representative studies that assess the discipline in general in the light of recent developments, especially of the sociocultural sort, and with a strong focus on teaching and education. Furthermore, given my own situation of diaspora in the West, I have concentrated by and large on the emerging discussion within the United States, although such a discussion could be easily expanded into a conversation of global dimensions.[32] Finally, I have arranged the studies in question in chronological fashion, so as to provide a sense of the evolving discussion.

African Americans and the Academy—W. H. Myers (1991)

Pride of place in this regard should go, without a doubt, to William Myers's analysis of the hermeneutical dilemma confronting African Americans in biblical studies, in itself part of a more comprehensive and highly successful volume dealing with the question of African-American interpretation of the Bible.[33] The diagnosis is laid out from the start: biblical interpretation—and Myers has historical criticism specifically in mind—is profoundly eurocentric, whether in terms of the hermeneutical motifs chosen, the methodological concerns pursued, or the events highlighted in the history of interpretation. Such eurocentrism has immediate consequences: the exaltation of a particular worldview above all others; the confining of the task of interpretation by and large to the past, while the burning issues of the day remain unaffected; the exclusion of other traditions of interpretation from consideration. This eurocentric hold on the Bible and its interpretation further reflects the broader eurocentric control exercised over the political, economic, and social systems of a culture, including its charter documents and the norms for their interpretation.

From the point of view of the African-American critic, therefore, to enter the world of biblical interpretation is to enter not only a foreign world, a world of eurocentric questions and concerns, but also a world that does not see itself as foreign, a world that presents itself as normative and hence without cultural bias. The result is a fundamental dilemma. Anchored in a very different tradition of interpretation altogether, a tradition not considered valid within the discipline as such, the critic is at a loss: wondering, on the one hand, about the relevance of such an approach for the African-American community—an oppressed community in need of liberation, for which the Bible has functioned as a traditional and powerful tool in this regard; acquiring, on the other hand, a certain measure of appreciation for the contributions of the eurocentric approach to the interpretive task.

This dilemma, Myers continues, is accentuated by the eurocentric character of theological education in general, characterized as it is by the predominance of eurocentric curricula, a paucity of African-American colleagues, the lack of alternative models and sources, a thorough resistance to change, and the profound identification of a tradition with an interpretive approach. To be sure, the dilemma extends outside African-American circles as well. Indeed, from the point of view of the Third World and minorities in the First World, the traditional approach can only be regarded as inadequate, insofar as it fails to take into account how other peoples interpret the texts.[34] For all those outside eurocentric boundaries, therefore, the diagnosis amounts to an ongoing dilemma.

For Myers, the remedy to be prescribed is not yet altogether clear at this point, given the differences of opinion among African Americans themselves with regard to proper strategies for change. In the end, Myers limits himself to a few guiding principles: the solution (1) must come from within the ranks of African-American scholars; (2) will probably represent a combination of contextual research and interdisciplinary accord; (3) will probably entail the adoption of a variety of methodologies held in balanced tension; (4) should include dialogue with critics from Europe, Euro-America, and the Third World; and (5) must involve a restructuring of pedagogical content and academic venues.

More specifically, Myers calls for a broader conception of canon, not so much in terms of its final form but rather of the process and functions of the final form,[35] so that the notion of canon can be extended to include the approaches to it of different believing communities—such as sermons, spirituals, testimonials, conversion narratives, and call narratives among African Americans. In this way, he argues, the eurocentric grip on texts and their interpretation as well as the hermeneutical dilemma faced by all outsiders to eurocentrism will begin to give way, slowly but surely.

Biblical Studies in the Third World—P. J. Hartin (1992)

This study, which appeared a year later, deals with the challenges that the Third World, as seen through the particular optic of South Africa (a South Africa still engaged at the time of writing in the process of dismantling the system of apartheid), brings to bear on the teaching of biblical studies, specifically within the context of a large state university with a vast majority of black students as its primary constituency.[36] Diagnosis and remedy are immediately identified: a discipline that has been taught in undifferentiated fashion throughout the world, including South Africa, must now begin to take into account the needs and contexts of the students in question, which, in the case of South Africa, involves the reality of a multicultural and multireligious society.

Such a reality calls for a type of instruction that is twofold in nature: on the one hand, instead of focusing on the dissemination and absorption of information about the Bible, it calls for the Bible to speak to the lives of students; on the other hand, instead of imposing a particular approach or cultural understanding on the biblical text, it calls for allowing the text to speak for itself. Its goal is to produce students who are "competent" or "responsible" students of the Bible. Such competency has two distinct foci, therefore: students and texts. First, from the point of view of students, competency requires a knowledge of African traditional religions, given their influence upon the students. Second, from the point of view of texts, competency demands the acquisition of tools and methods proper to the sciences used to analyze the texts. Third, from the point of view of both students and texts, competency calls for a commitment to postmodernism, with its view of reality as highly fragmented. Such adherence to postmodernism serves a variety of purposes. With regard to students, it is meant to rule out the dogmatizing of any one cultural understanding of the Bible, to underline the difficult nature of understanding across different perspectives, and to yield respect for the viewpoints of other peoples and cultures. With regard to the texts, it is meant, once again, to rule out the dogmatizing of any one approach to the Bible.

Such competency, moreover, is to be imparted and acquired by means of a "hands-on" approach to the biblical text. Thus, the focus of instruction throughout is the biblical text, which is used as a point of entry into the various areas of inquiry within the discipline. These areas of study are organized in turn around the major components of the standard model in communications theory: from a horizontal perspective, the sequence of author (production), text, and reader (reception); from a vertical perspective, the relationship of text and reference. The sequence of instruction proceeds as follows: (1) a beginning focus on the student as reader—a close reading of the text from the student's own context; (2) a focus on the text, both in terms of production and reference; (3) a focus on the reception of the text by other readers, in the past or in the present. In the end, the result should be the production of a "competent" reading alongside other such readings from both past and present, but now from the perspective of the students' own lives within a multicultural and multireligious society.

The ultimate aim behind such competency is socioreligious as well as sociopolitical. To begin with, competency allows the Bible to inspire the imagination, that is, allows students to recontextualize the images and stories of the Bible within their own cultures and contexts, so that events in their own lives and worlds are formulated and communicated through the terms, stories, and narratives of the Bible.[37] The result should be a similar imaginative retelling on the part of a broad variety of different groups and cultures, all of which would have recourse to the same language and message but would express it in a variety of ways.[38] In so doing, therefore, competency further uses the Bible as a way of bringing together different peoples and cultures by way of certain common values—human dignity, justice, and peace. For Hartin, such a situation would represent a possible and much-desired solution for the travails of South Africa.

Feminism and Colonialism—K. O'Brien Wicker (1993)

This study, though brief, is important, insofar as it raises the question of culture—of class, ethnicity, and race—from within the context of the feminist movement; published a year later, it forms part of the landmark two-volume feminist introduction to and commentary on the Bible.[39] The diagnosis of the discipline here is actually twofold, as the study looks backward and forward at the same time.

A first level is presupposed: a view of the discipline as profoundly patriarchal, both in terms of the texts studied and the history of the interpretation of these texts. The prescription, already in effect as well, calls for a pedagogical strategy that reflects the broader scholarly discourse of women's and feminist studies, with a specific emphasis on women in the biblical texts and women's or gendered readings of the biblical texts. A second level, newly awakened by means of a sojourn in Zimbabwe, is envisioned: a view of the discipline as profoundly Western, not only in terms of patriarchy but also in terms of feminism itself. The prescription demands the development of a feminist pedagogical strategy that takes into consideration issues of class, ethnicity, and race. In other words, as a result of a crosscultural experience in Africa, O'Brien Wicker comes to realize that the discipline has been profoundly colonialist as well, and that in such colonialism, Western women find themselves as thoroughly implicated as Western men. The prescription, therefore, requires a feminism that goes beyond the concerns and issues of middle- or upper-class Western women, a feminism that takes an international perspective to heart, a feminism that is postcolonial in nature.[40]

Such an approach to biblical studies, developed in opposition to the traditional colonial mode of education and biblical studies,[41] adheres to the following principles: (1) rejection of the patriarchal worldview, the claims of the inherent superiority of men over women, and the hegemony of the public over the private sphere; (2) condemnation of Christian anti-Semitism as unwarranted and unjustified; and (3) resistance to other historical expressions of Christian imperialism, such as those at work in the process of colonization.[42] Its fundamental goal, variously exercised, is to see how a text like the Bible can not only prove liberating for women, but also promote the full humanity of women and men of all races, ethnic backgrounds, and classes.[43]

For O'Brien Wicker the crucial step taken by feminism remains caught in the Western project of colonization and thus must be taken a step further by going beyond a consideration of gender, of woman as woman, to include a consideration of race, ethnicity, and class. As such, the discipline must acquire a global perspective if it is not to remain fundamentally Western in orientation and practice.

Global Outlook—J. R. Levison and P. Pope-Levison (1995)

Within the context of a volume on method and hermeneutics in New Testament studies, the authors contributed an article on the subject of global hermeneutics.[44] The beginning rationale for the inclusion of such an unusual study in the collection provides a sharp diagnosis of the discipline. This diagnosis is twofold. On the one hand, from the point of view of the First World, the traditional view of the critic—the critic as someone who uncovers the "original meaning" of the Bible by "jettisoning all bias"—has been rendered untenable, insofar as "prejudgments" arising from the critic's own context are now widely accepted as influencing the understanding of any text. On the other hand, from the point of view of the Third World, a rapid shift in the center of gravity of Christianity, not only in terms of numbers but also in terms of vitality, is taking place, toward the Third World and away from the First World. Given the central importance of context in interpretation, therefore, the discipline must develop a global outlook, if it is not to remain woefully inadequate for the present day and age.

The prescription recommended is Western-inspired: the dialectical hermeneutics of Hans-Georg Gadamer, which is seen as having replaced the traditional model described above.[45] The effects and implications of such a move are described as follows. First, instead of focusing on the original meaning of the Bible or the contemporary context of the interpreter, the model emphasizes the conversation between the ancient text and the present-day interpreter, in the course of which the latter brings specific questions to the Bible arising from his or her context. Second, the goal behind such a conversation is to bring about a fusion of two horizons—that of the text and that of the interpreter—in a way that is both true to the past and relevant to the present. Third, given the present spread of Christianity, no First-World interpretation of the Bible can exhaust the meaning of a text, since it ignores contexts that bring their own questions into the process of interpretation; consequently, the conversation with the Bible must proceed on a global scale.

What such a global perspective means for the discipline is immediately made clear: from the point of view of Latin America, a focus on class struggle, integral liberation, and the relationship between politics and religion; from the point of view of Asia, a focus on popular traditions, religious traditions, and economics; from the point of view of Africa, a dominant focus on a hermeneutics of resonance with the Bible. At the same time, a critique of such new Third-World contributions is appended: (1) despite the emphasis on the importance of readings from grassroots communities, there are few examples of such popular interpretations available; (2) the fusion of horizons can lead to a collapse of the distinction between text and context; (3) interpretations of the New Testament frequently contain a negative portrayal of Second Temple Judaism, furnishing thereby the seeds for anti-Semitism. The elements of the critique are thus quite varied in nature and import: (1) the first is not a theoretical challenge but a basic call for more research; (2) the second represents a theoretical challenge, but is presented only as a possibility and with a remedy attached—proper use of social-scientific criticism as a way of allowing for parallels while keeping the two horizons properly distinct; (3) the third is also a theoretical challenge, now based on fact and with a remedy supplied: greater use of research showing the rich diversity of Second Temple Judaism.

For the authors, therefore, the discipline has no option but to become global, in the light of developments within both the First and the Third Worlds. In this regard the hermeneutics of the West—the fusion of horizons à la Gadamer—is taken as pointing the way and as a correction to any actual or possible deficiencies or excesses present in the biblical interpretation of either world. Indeed, one finds no critique of the conversational model as such.[46]

Center and Margins—B. Blount (1995)

The full-fledged proposal by this African-American scholar calls for a fundamental reorientation of New Testament criticism along the lines of cultural interpretation—a mode of reading that both takes into account the context of readers with regard to the meaning of texts and admits of a variety of responsible readings.[47] Blount contends that traditional biblical studies—primarily understood in terms of historical criticism—have followed a single interpretive ideology: biblical texts have been interpreted according to the perspective of standard eurocentric values.[48] As a result, any group outside this normative value system not only finds its own interpretive perspective excluded from consideration as unscientific but also finds itself expected to assimilate the interpretive practices and underlying values of the dominant group. Such a diagnosis of the discipline Blount traces to his own origins and experiences in the Black Church, where he recalls facing the inability of the traditional methods to bring the text to life in the black community as well as the external criticism of black interpretation as prejudiced. Such a diagnosis, however, could also have come from any group at the margins of the eurocentric perspective, yielding thereby a center–margins type of discourse.[49]

Two fundamental differences distinguish these two interpretive perspectives. On the one hand, while the center highlights issues of christology and soteriology—the question of religious salvation, the margins emphasize social and political issues—the question of inequity. On the other hand, while the center focuses on textual and conceptual issues in the text (the question of the meaning back-then), the margins emphasize the issue of interpersonal interaction between text and reader (the question of the meaning for-today). For Blount the answer lies not in a reverse enthronement of the marginal optic—a move that would simply yield a different type of single interpretive ideology, ultimately as restrictive as that of eurocentrism—but rather in a type of reading that brings together the two perspectives: a reading that sees texts as both religious and social, and interpretation as involving all three concerns (the textual, the ideational, and the interpersonal). Only such a reading, with its corresponding view of interpretations as complementary rather than alternative, can yield a fuller picture of the meaning of a text. Blount develops this type of reading, cultural interpretation, on the basis of two theoretical discourses—sociolinguistics of the functionalist type and sociology of the liberationist type.[50]

From functionalist sociolinguistics Blount takes the basic insight that context shapes the creation and use of language—that people in different sociological environments operate with different linguistic forms—and that meaning derived from language is also shaped by context.[51] What is true of language, Blount argues, is also true of reading.[52] From the point of view of biblical studies, therefore, interaction between different sociolinguistic perspectives—such as those of the center and the margins—and the language of a text inevitably yields different understandings of the meaning and power of that text.[53] Thus, if a sociolinguistic perspective is to become more comprehensive, it must attempt to see the text from the other perspective. In the end, however, Blount cautions that functionalist sociolinguistics fails to address the crucial issue of sociopolitical power—the fact that one community's sociolinguistic perspective can dominate and devalue those of other communities.

From liberationist sociology, therefore, Blount borrows the missing sociopolitical dimension: not only does one's spatial location in life determine what one sees, but also that perspective espoused by those who hold political and numerical superiority emerges as the official one, with all others lacking in power and legitimation. This is true of society and politics as well as of science and scholarship.[54] It is also true, Blount adds, of reading. From the point of view of biblical studies, therefore, the sociolinguistic perspective represented by traditional biblical studies has effectively enthroned itself as the official perspective, looking upon all those outside its boundaries as unacceptable and calling instead for assimilation unto itself. Hence, if one is to avoid such an ideological position, one must recognize the validity of all points of view and analyze texts from a perspective that includes both center and margins.[55] Such a task, however, cannot originate with the center, given the latter's inability to surmount its own ideology to begin with; rather, change must come from the outside, and thus the task lies with the margins.

It is precisely this task that Blount sets for himself in his agenda of cultural interpretation: to bring the sociolinguistic perspective from the margins fully into the discussion and hence into contact with the center; in so doing, to challenge the entire agenda of biblical studies and force a change in its traditional eurocentric perspective.[56] The vision that emerges is that of a far more inclusive discipline, where there is no such thing as a final and definitive meaning, where readings must work within the confines of textual and ideational elements, and where all interpreters are similarly influenced by and must come to terms with the interpersonal dimension of interpretation.

CONCLUDING COMMENTS

A summary of how these representative voices look upon the present state of affairs in the discipline and what they call for by way of pedagogical changes and innovations is in order:

1.   The diagnoses of the discipline offered prove to be remarkably similar: biblical criticism is described as profoundly eurocentric or Western. Such eurocentrism is said to match the patriarchal nature of the discipline and to reflect not only the broader eurocentric character of theological education in general but also the strong eurocentric control over culture. Its characteristics are variously identified as follows: (a) confinement of the task of interpretation to the past; (b) focus on the discovery of the original meaning of the text, the meaning back then; (c) emphasis on the impartation and absorption of information; (d) insistence on a particular method or cultural understanding; (e) predilection for christological and soteriological questions, such as the issue of religious salvation; (f) a view of instruction as universal and undifferentiated. In the end, such a view of the discipline is regarded as profoundly ironic: a worldview that is highly cultural in nature—Western or eurocentric—presents itself as without cultural bias and hence as normative, as the center, resulting in the exaltation of a particular worldview above all others.

2.   Such a state of affairs is seen as having consequences for all outsiders to eurocentrism and the West, for those in the margins; and the descriptions of

such consequences turn out to be quite similar as well: such individuals and groups find themselves in a foreign world. In other words, the discipline constitutes a world where their own traditions of interpretation are excluded from consideration as inadequate, where their own concerns and contexts are ignored as irrelevant, and where they are expected to conform to the traditions and dictates of the normative position.

3.   The remedies prescribed for such a situation represent variations of the same principle: the need to take into account the lives and contexts of "the other." Among such remedies one finds: (a) a broader conception of the canon, including not only the biblical texts but also the various approaches to these texts emanating from different communities; (b) a different view of textual meaning, with a two-fold focus on both texts and interpreters, the past and the present, the meaning back-then and the meaning for-today; (c) taking into account the lives and contexts of communities from around the globe, especially of those in the margins, whether in the West or in the Third World, especially given the shift in Christianity away from the West, both in terms of numbers and vitality; (d) a commitment to a view of reality as fragmented, not only in terms of gender but also in terms of class, ethnicity, and race; (e) recourse to a broad range of methodologies and the recognition of multiple readings, so that no one approach or interpretation is enthroned as a result; (f) a view of texts as both religious and social documents, concerned as much with questions of religious salvation as with questions of inequity.

4.   The goals and hopes behind such remedies are in keeping with the fundamental diagnosis advanced: the need for the discipline to become less eurocentric or Western. Such goals and hopes are variously described as follows: (a) an awareness of Christianity as a global religion and of the different questions brought to the text by different groups and cultures of the world; (b) dialogue among all such groups and cultures, now reading the texts from the point of view of their own contexts and lives; (c) use of the Bible as a point of unity for diverse groups and cultures, with a stress on the values of human dignity, peace, and justice; (d) the liberation of women and men of all classes, races, and ethnicities.

   With such diagnoses and prescriptions, such goals and hopes, I would argue, the tenor and direction of the pedagogical discussion in the discipline leave behind altogether the parameters observed earlier in historical, literary, and cultural criticism and begin to move instead well within the ambit of the cultural studies paradigm as I conceive it, given the emphasis placed, first and foremost, on the diversity of readers and contexts as well as on the diversity of methods and readings. The implications for the discipline, its pedagogical discourse and practices—though still very much in the making—will no doubt prove enormous, perhaps amounting in the end to a complete reconception and reconfiguration of the discipline, in line with the twenty-first century now almost upon us.

NOTES

1. F. F. Segovia, "'And They Began to Speak in Other Tongues': Competing Modes of Discourse in Contemporary Biblical Criticism," in *Reading from This Place*. Volume 1: *Social Location and Biblical Interpretation in the United States,* ed. F. F. Segovia and M. A. Tolbert (Minneapolis: Fortress Press, 1995), 1–32; and "Cultural Studies and Contemporary Biblical Criticism: Ideological Criticism as Mode of Discourse," in *Reading from This Place*. Volume 2: *Social Location and Biblical Interpretation in Global Perspective,* ed. F. F. Segovia and M. A. Tolbert (Minneapolis: Fortress Press, 1995), 1–17.

2. For other ways of looking at the recent path and present state of the discipline, see, e.g., E. Schüssler Fiorenza, "'For the Sake of Our Salvation . . . ,' Biblical Interpretation and the Community of Faith," in *Bread Not Stone: The Challenge of Feminist Biblical Interpretation* (Boston: Beacon Press, 1984), 23–42; A. C. Thiselton, "New Testament Interpretation in Historical Perspective," in *Hearing the New Testament: Strategies for Interpretation,* ed. J. B. Green (Grand Rapids: William B. Eerdmans, 1995), 10–36; The Bible and Culture Collective, "Introduction," *The Postmodern Bible* (New Haven-London: Yale University Press, 1995), 1–19.

3. I always insist on describing this first umbrella model in terms of *traditional* historical criticism, and I do so not only to refer to that particular approach to texts that governed the discipline for so long and according to which so many generations were trained—and indeed continue to be trained, in Europe to be sure but also in the United States and Canada—but also to highlight the fact that, as a paradigm, such criticism failed to establish any sort of sustained critical dialogue with developing currents within the field of historiography itself, its home base since the nineteenth century. In other words, I use the adjective "traditional" to signify both a particular historical phenomenon in the discipline and a particular theoretical stance within historiography. I would add that, from my point of view, such lack of dialogue with historiography and such inability to mount a proper defense on its own behalf are closely related.

4. On the nature and ramifications of this development, see my "Racial and Ethnic Minorities in Biblical Studies," *Ethnicity and the Bible,* in *Biblical Interpretation Series,* ed. M. G. Brett (Leiden: E. J. Brill, 1996), 470–92.

5. In my opinion two factors have played a significant role in this regard: (a) the persistent character of biblical criticism in Europe as thoroughly clerical, male, and Western; (b) an evident lack of interdisciplinary dialogue with the humanities, in itself highly ironic given the riches available in poststructuralist and postmodernist currents and movements within Europe itself.

6. See my "Toward a Hermeneutics of the Diaspora: A Hermeneutics of Otherness and Engagement," in *Reading from This Place,* 1:57–73; and "Toward Intercultural Criticism: A Reading Strategy from the Diaspora," in *Reading from This Place,* 2:303–30.

7. Segovia, "'And They Began to Speak in Other Tongues,'" 13.

8. J. A. Fitzmyer, "Historical Criticism: Its Role in Biblical Interpretation and Church Life," *Theological Studies* 50 (1989): 244–59. The venue is a Roman Catholic journal of theology published by the theological faculties of the Society of Jesus in the United States. The issue included articles on U.S. Catholic biblical scholarship, the social sciences, feminist hermeneutics, narrative criticism, New Testament theology, and contemporary translations of Scripture into English.

9. For other recent presentations of historical criticism, see: J. Reumann, "After Historical Criticism, What? Trends in Biblical Interpretation and Ecumenical, Interfaith Dialogues," *Journal of Ecumenical Studies* 29 (1992): 55–86; Monika Fander, "Historical-Critical Methods," in *Searching the Scriptures*. Volume 1: *A Feminist Introduction,* ed. Elisabeth Schüssler Fiorenza (New York: Crossroad, 1993), 205–24; J. Maxwell Miller, "Reading the Bible Historically: The Historian's Approach," in *To Each Its Own Meaning: An Introduction to Biblical Criticisms and Their Application,* ed. S. L. McKenzie and

S. R. Haynes (Louisville: Westminster/John Knox Press, 1993), 11–28; Jon D. Levenson, "The Hebrew Bible, the Old Testament, and Historical Criticism" and "Historical Criticism and the Fate of the Enlightenment Project," in Jon D. Levenson, *The Hebrew Bible, the Old Testament, and Historical Criticism: Jews and Christians in Biblical Studies* (Minneapolis: Fortress Press, 1993), 1–32 and 106–26, respectively.

10. The reason is clear. For Fitzmyer ("Historical Criticism," 255) "new modes" of interpretation can only serve to correct or refine the "basic" method of historical criticism; they can neither substitute for nor be allowed to replace this "fundamental" approach. In other words, traditional historical criticism is represented as theoretically unassailable: it may be refined but it cannot be contested. As a result, the metatheoretical character of the disciplinary discussion already at work at the time of composition is altogether bypassed if not dismissed in principle.

11. This "neutral" method reveals, however, all sorts of unspoken and unexamined theoretical presuppositions, such as the following: (a) critical objectivity—the method itself has no presuppositions and thus practitioners can lay claim to impartiality in research; (b) objectivist understanding of meaning—meaning is contained in the texts themselves; (c) authorial intention—such meaning represents what the author intended to write; (d) texts as historico-social capsules—such meaning further reflects the world of the text; (e) a hermeneutics of discovery—meaning and reality are out there, beyond readers, and can be properly retrieved through the use of the right scientific methods; (f) exclusive validity—meaning can be retrieved only by way of this method and none other.

12. On the origins, development, and presuppositions of classical philology, see M. Olender, *The Languages of Paradise: Race, Religion, and Philology in the Nineteenth Century* (Cambridge: Harvard University Press, 1992). On the origins, development, and presuppositions of archaeology, see B. Kurlick, *Puritans in Babylon: The Ancient Near East and American Intellectual Life, 1880–1930* (Cambridge: Harvard University Press, 1996).

13. The theoretical edifice comes close to collapse at this point. If the historical method is indeed neutral as claimed, then it should follow that all those who employ it should come to the same historical conclusions, regardless of the "presuppositions" at work in its use or application. The admission that the soundness of the results varies according to the "presuppositions" of different practitioners should serve as a warning signal that something is very much amiss, that the proposed fundamental division between "method" and "presuppositions" has to be thoroughly re-examined.

14. Segovia, "'And They Began to Speak in Other Tongues,'" 19.

15. M. A. Powell, *What Is Narrative Criticism?* in *Guides to Biblical Scholarship: New Testament Series* (Minneapolis: Fortress Press, 1991). See also his "Narrative Criticism," in *Hearing the New Testament*, 239–55.

16. For other recent presentations of literary criticism, see: C. Clifton Black, "Rhetorical Criticism," and Kevin J. Vanhoozer, "The Reader in New Testament Interpretation," in *Hearing the New Testament*, 256–77 and 301–28, respectively; S. E. Porter, "Literary Approaches to the New Testament: From Formalism to Deconstruction and Back," and D. L. Stamps, "Rhetorical Criticism of the New Testament: Ancient and Modern Evaluations of Argumentation," in *Approaches to New Testament Study: Journal for the Study of the New Testament Supplementary Series*, 120, ed. S. E. Porter and D. Tombs (Sheffield: Sheffield Academic Press, 1995), 77–128 and 129–69, respectively. For a more developed summary of rhetorical criticism, see: Burton L. Mack, *Rhetoric and the New Testament* in *Guides to Biblical Scholarship: New Testament Series* (Minneapolis: Fortress Press, 1990).

17. It should be noted, however, that no such differentiation is undertaken with regard to cultural criticism in any of its various formations, a critical movement well on the way by this time as well.

18. Powell, "Scripture as Story," in *What Is Narrative Criticism?*, 1–10.

19. This irenic view of the relationship between the two approaches is quite problematic—despite Powell's protestations to the contrary (ibid., 92)—in the light of the basic

opposition posited with respect to the present status of the text. In other words, how can the perception of unity and coherence in the text favored by literary criticism be reconciled with the view of lack of flow and unintelligibility in the text espoused by historical criticism? There has to be a point of no return, a point at which the perceived unevennesses of the text can no longer be subsumed under the principles of unity and coherence . . . unless of course one takes the road of deconstruction.

20. Powell, "Ways of Reading," in *What Is Narrative Criticism?*, 11–21.

21. This irenic view of the relationship among the various approaches within literary criticism is severely called into question by Powell's own reference (ibid., 20–21) to the critique of the implied reader of narrative criticism advanced by certain reader-response critics. The critique is presented as twofold: (a) from a formalist perspective, it is argued that no reader is able to grasp all the complex interrelationships that occur within a text, as called for by the concept of the implied reader; (b) from a hermeneutical perspective, it is argued that the concept of the implied reader will differ according to the particular interests and contexts of real readers. In response, Powell deals only with the formalist dimension of the critique: while the goal of reading "as the implied reader" may be unattainable, it remains a worthy goal nonetheless. The hermeneutical challenge, however, is much more fundamental and remains unanswered: how can the perception of the implied reader in the text as favored by narrative criticism be reconciled with a view of the implied reader as reflecting the interests and contexts of the real readers as advocated by a number of reader-response critics?

22. In addition to the theoretical presuppositions identified, a number of others remain unacknowledged: (a) critical objectivity—the method allows for the literary features of the text to surface and thus allows for impartiality and accuracy in research; (b) objectivist understanding of text and meaning—the literary features are in the text, come from the hand of the implied author, and serve as a guide to a proper understanding of the text and its meaning; (c) authorial intention—such meaning represents what the implied author actually wrote; (d) hermeneutics of discovery—the literary features and the meaning of the text are out there, beyond readers, and can be properly retrieved through the use of the right methods; (e) privileged validity—despite the argument for the complementarity of different approaches, it is clear that through its dependence on the concept of the implied reader, narrative criticism does provide criteria for interpretation, insofar as it deals with what is in the text itself. To be quite fair to Powell, however, one should point out that he does acknowledge a measure of ambiguity throughout in narrative criticism: within the parameters set by the text itself, there may be differences in interpretation.

23. To be sure, the implied author is also reconstructed by the reader from the text, constitutes the perspective from which the text must be interpreted, and thus serves as the interpretive key to the text. In other words, to read as the implied reader would read is to read according to the dictates and expectations of the implied author.

24. Powell, "Story as Scripture," in *What Is Narrative Criticism?*, 85–101.

25. Segovia, "'And They Began to Speak in Other Tongues,'" 26–27.

26. B. J. Malina, "Bible Study and Cultural Anthropology," in *The New Testament World: Insights from Cultural Anthropology* (Atlanta: John Knox Press, 1981), 1–24 . In the second edition of this volume (*The New Testament World: Insights from Cultural Anthropology*, rev. ed. [Louisville: Westminster/John Knox Press, 1993], 1–17), this chapter was reproduced with only minor variations, including the addition of a subtitle: "Bible Study and Cultural Anthropology: Interpreting Texts Fairly." (References will be to this second edition.) In the intervening years between these two editions, a number of the basic ideas contained in this study were taken up again and expanded in B. J. Malina, "Reading Theory Perspective: Reading Luke-Acts," in *The Social World of Luke-Acts*, ed. J. H. Neyrey (Peabody, MA: Hendrickson Publishers, 1991), 3–23.

27. For other recent presentations of cultural criticism, see: S. C. Barton, "Historical Criticism and Social-Scientific Perspectives in New Testament Study," in *Hearing the New Testament*, 10–36; P. F. Esler, "Social Worlds, Social Sciences and the New Testament," in

The First Christians in Their Social Worlds: Social-Scientific Approaches to New Testament Interpretation (Minneapolis: Fortress Press, 1990), 1–19; P. F. Esler, "Introduction: Models, Context, and Kerygma in New Testament Interpretation," in *Modelling Early Christianity: Social-Scientific Studies of the New Testament in Its Context,* ed. P. F. Esler (London-New York: Routledge, 1995), 1–20; B. Holmberg, "Sociology and New Testament Studies," in *Sociology and the New Testament. An Appraisal* (Minneapolis: Fortress Press, 1990), 1–20. For a more developed summary, see J. B. Elliott, *What Is Social-Scientific Criticism?* in *Guides to Biblical Scholarship* (Minneapolis: Fortress Press, 1992).

28. It should be noted that in his later reformulation of this apologia ("Reading Theory Perspective"), literary criticism has replaced historical criticism as the main point of reference. This reorientation is clear from the start, as Malina argues against any view of meaning as residing in language, in "wording," rather than in the social systems embodied in and conveyed by language, in "meanings" (3–8). The remainder of the article confirms this shift. All reading, Malina declares, involves an intrapersonal or individual dimension, best explored by psycholinguistics, as well as an interpersonal or social dimension, best explored by sociolinguistics (8–12). With regard to the former, Malina argues (12–17), the model employed by literary criticism in general—the propositional model (the text as "a sort of supersentence") at work in "contemporary structural, semiotic, deconstructionist, 'Marxist,' and aesthetic literary criticism"—is completely off target, insofar as it is unverifiable by actual research into reading. With regard to the latter, Malina continues (17–22), the model followed by most of literary criticism—decontextualized reading (from "the print itself") as in the case of "the effort to read the Bible as literature" and "much of the reader-response approach to literature"—is neither fair nor just, since it dismisses the social dimensions of author, original audience, and text in question.

29. Malina does address, briefly, the importance and relevance of cultural anthropology for Christian believers, for all those who accept the Bible as the Word of God ("Bible Study and Cultural Anthropology," 17-18). First, the incarnation of the Word of God signifies the enculturation of God's Word. In other words, the life of the Word of God and the written accounts of or reflection on that life cannot but follow the cultural story of the period in question. Second, as a result, the only way to understand the Word of God today is to do so from within the context of that cultural story of the past—the cultural story of first-century Palestinian and Mediterranean culture. At the same time, Malina adds (25), such understanding yields a cultural story that is radically different from that of contemporary readers. Indeed, the following hermeneutical principle is offered: an accurate interpretation of these texts is more likely to be one in which the "differences" between the world of the reader and the world of the text are too great, the "variance" between moral judgments too disturbing, and the "focus" between religious concerns too distant. What Malina does not do, however, is to address himself to the implications and ramifications of such profound differences for the theological task of believing Christians. In the end, he remains the historian of religion.

30. Among those not recognized as such are the following: (a) critical objectivity—the method allows for sociocultural presuppositions to come to the fore and thus for impartiality and accuracy in research; (b) objectivist understanding of meaning—meaning is contained in the texts themselves; (c) texts as historico-social capsules—the meaning contained in the texts derives from the world of the text; (d) hermeneutics of discovery—meaning and reality are out there, beyond readers, and can be properly retrieved through the use of the right scientific methods; (e) exclusive validity—accurate meaning can only be had through the use of this particular approach. A number of other presuppositions are not mentioned at all: (a) Social systems or cultures as monolithic: a view of meanings as universally imparted, shared, and utilized. In other words, there is one cultural story, and all individuals and texts reflect that story, whether in the past or in the present. (b) Social systems or cultures as all-encompassing: it is possible to speak, for example, of first-century Mediterranean culture. (c) Social systems or cultures as fixed and unchanging: it is possible

to use models derived from contemporary anthropological research on Mediterranean culture to apply to first-century Mediterranean culture. (d) Models as neutral: the question of the ideological orientation of the models and their creators is never raised. (e) Communication within social systems or cultures as unproblematic: meanings are readily conveyed and received across all segments of society.

31. For Malina, therefore, the models of cultural anthropology are indispensable insofar as they are both scientific and crosscultural. On the one hand, as "abstract, simplified representations of more complex real-world objects and interactions," such models allow for "adequate" understanding insofar as they are subject to a scientific process of validation ("Bible Study and Cultural Anthropology," 19–20). Once formulated, the models can be tested against the "real world" experience to which they relate and are either validated or modified in the case of any errors of omission or commission detected in the process of testing. On the other hand, such models allow for "adequate" understanding of other cultures insofar as they deploy a comparative perspective (that of the text and that of the reader) and call upon the cultural trait of empathetic understanding of the other. Malina's vision (25) for the use of cultural anthropology in biblical criticism, therefore, is to borrow crosscultural models from anthropological research on either Mediterranean society or other societies "similar" to those reflected in the biblical texts and to test these models against the evidence of the texts themselves. If a fit exists between model and data, then the model is validated and adequate understanding—accurate understanding—of the "foreign" biblical texts results.

32. For an overview, see R. S. Sugirtharajah, "The Margin as a Site of Creative Revisioning" and "Cultures, Texts and Margins: A Hermeneutical Odyssey," in *Voices from the Margin: Interpreting the Bible in the Third World*, ed. R. S. Sugirtharajah; rev. ed. (Maryknoll: Orbis Books, 1995), 1–8 and 457–75, respectively. For works from the Two-Thirds World in general, see: (a) From an African perspective: C. S. Banana, "The Case for a New Bible," in *"Rewriting" the Bible: The Real Issues*, ed., J. L. Cox, I. Mukonyora and F. J. Verstraelen (Gweru: Mambo Press, 1993), 17–32; I. J. Mosala, "The Use of the Bible in Black Theology" in *Biblical Hermeneutics and Black Theology in South Africa* (Grand Rapids: William B. Eerdmans, 1989), 13–42. (b) From an Asian perspective: G. Soares-Prabhu, "The Historical Critical Method: Reflections on Its Relevance for the Study of the Gospels in India Today," in *Theologizing in India*, ed. M. Amaladoss (Bangalore: Theological Publications in India, 1981), 214–49; R. S. Sugirtharajah, "Introduction, and Some Thoughts on Asian Biblical Hermeneutics," in *Biblical Interpretation* 2 (1994): 251–63; Kwok Pui-lan, *Discovering the Bible in the Non-Biblical World* (Maryknoll: Orbis Books, 1995). (c) From a Latin American Perspective: J. S. Croatto, "Biblical Hermeneutics in the Theologies of Liberation," in *Irruption of the Third World: Challenge to Theology*, ed. V. Fabella and S. Torres (Maryknoll: Orbis Books, 1983), 140–68; P. Richard, "The Hermeneutics of Liberation: Theoretical Orientation for a Communitarian Reading of the Bible," chapter 15, this volume.

33. W. H. Myers, "The Hermeneutical Dilemma of the African American Biblical Student," *Stony the Road We Trod: African American Biblical Interpretation*, ed. C. H. Felder (Minneapolis: Fortress Press, 1991), 40–56.

34. Myers (ibid., 45–47) sees the eurocentric approach as under challenge from a number of different quarters, not only outside but also inside the West. The discussion, however, is far more cultural than methodological in character, developed almost exclusively from the point of view of groups alien to the eurocentric perspective.

35. At this point, Myers is drawing on the discussion regarding canonical criticism between Brevard Childs (*Biblical Theology in Crisis* [Philadelphia: Westminster Press, 1970]; *Introduction to the Old Testament as Scripture* [Philadelphia: Fortress Press, 1979]; *The New Testament as Canon* [Philadelphia: Fortress Press, 1985]; *Biblical Theology of the Old and New Testaments* [Minneapolis: Fortress Press, 1993]), with its focus on final form, and James Sanders (*Torah and Canon* [Philadelphia: Fortress Press, 1972]; *Canon and*

Community [Philadelphia: Fortress Press, 1984]; *From Sacred Story to Sacred Text* [Philadelphia: Fortress Press, 1987]), with its focus on the functions of the final form. For a recent overview of canonical criticism, see Robert W. Wall, "Reading the New Testament in Canonical Context," in *Hearing the New Testament*, 370–93.

36. P. J. Hartin, *Third World Challenges in the Teaching of Biblical Studies: Occasional Papers* 25 (Claremont: The Institute for Antiquity and Christianity, 1992). From a geopolitical point of view, Hartin describes South Africa as a "Third-World country" insofar as it fulfills the various characteristics common to such countries: survival on the basis of external help; exploitation of resources by foreign nations; almost complete lack of infrastructure; absence of basic services for large segments of the population; poverty and illiteracy. From a socioeducational point of view, Hartin describes the University of South Africa, which carries out its mission through distance education and comprises around 120,000 students, as a secular institution. Within such a context, he further describes instruction in biblical studies as follows: it is not in the service of the church, much less any particular Christian church; it approaches the Bible as literature, as a classic; and, in so doing, it has recourse to a variety of scientific approaches.

37. Needless to say, despite the emphasis on the secular character of biblical studies at the university and the approach to the Bible as a classic of literature within such a setting, one finds a very high theological conception of the Bible at work in this pedagogical program, best expressed perhaps in Hartin's concluding hopes (ibid., 19) for the future of South Africa: the use of the Bible in problem-solving, specifically with regard to the future of South Africa, with the Bible "as a means by which different cultures are able to share their understandings," yielding in the end "an even richer culture illuminated by the possible worlds opened up by the Bible."

38. In formulating this view of biblical instruction, Hartin relies heavily on the work of Paul Ricoeur (ibid., 10–13), with its well-known threefold sequence of (a) naïve understanding—a guess at the meaning of the text; (b) explanation—validation of the guess by attention to the text as a written inscription, now distanced from the life of its author and leading a life of its own; and (c) understanding by appropriation—making the text (the direction opened up by it, the imagination of new possible worlds) one's own. It is this final dimension of interpretation, therefore, that should be the goal of biblical studies: to allow the text to speak "on its own" to the lives of students, wherever they find themselves.

39. K. O'Brien Wicker, "Teaching Feminist Biblical Studies in a Postcolonial Context," in *Searching the Scriptures*. Volume 1: *A Feminist Introduction*, ed. Elisabeth Schüssler Fiorenza (New York: Crossroad, 1993), 367–80.

40. Following the lead of Laura E. Donaldson (*Decolonizing Feminisms: Race, Gender, and Empire-building* [Chapel Hill and London: University of North Carolina Press, 1992]), O'Brien Wicker (ibid., 368) distinguishes between *historical* colonialism, the historical fact of political and geographic conquest, and *discursive* colonialism, the actualization of metaphors in experience. On the one hand, feminism represents a reaction to the discursive colonization of patriarchy. On the other hand, however, feminism also constitutes a form of discursive colonization, insofar as it has attempted to speak in the name of all women, to universalize itself. Consequently, feminism must be decolonized, must become postcolonial.

41. The colonial model of education is represented in terms of a number of basic strategies: (a) education of the native for a subordinate role; (b) integration of the native into the culture of the colonial power; (c) privileging of males, their thoughts and deeds. Its counterpart in biblical studies is represented in terms of the following assumptions: (a) acceptance of the patriarchal perspective as divinely validated, with corresponding rejection of nonpatriarchal readings; (b) affirmation of the inherent superiority of men over women, the public sphere over the private; (c) a view of Christianity as the only true religion or as superior to all other religious traditions; (d) acceptance of political assertions made in the text; (e) use of the categories of orthodoxy and heresy to invalidate certain interpretations

of the tradition; (f) decontextualization of biblical texts in ways that absolutize injunctions addressed to particular situations. See ibid., 369, 371–72.

42. More concretely, such an approach reveals the following characteristics (ibid., 374–75): (a) reflection on experiences that relate to the ideas or issues under study, with an emphasis on the diversity of voices and hence on race, ethnicity, and class—as opposed to an assimilation of "truth" without regard for experience; (b) alternative feminist readings of texts—as a way of resisting claims to absolute truth, respecting differences, and rejecting the impulse to create artifical unities; (c) critical reflection on the presuppositions regarding stances toward the revelatory nature of the texts, the implications of such presuppositions, and the feminist claim on the priority of experience in interpretation—as a way of showing that all interpretations are necessarily interpretive.

43. Ibid., 372–73. It is clear in this regard that O'Brien Wicker adopts a variation of the strategy of suspicion (see "Feminist and Womanist Criticism," *The Postmodern Bible* [The Bible and Culture Collective; New Haven and London: Yale University Press, 1995], 225–71, esp. 247–51). Rather than abandoning the Bible as a hopelessly patriarchal and colonialist text, therefore, the call is for a variety of strategies of subversion meant to weaken or displace its system of oppression as well as bring to the fore liberating visions of a different and fully inclusive system.

44. J. R. Levison and P. Pope-Levison, "Global Perspectives on New Testament Interpretation," in *Hearing the New Testament*, 329–48.

45. The authors take their cue from David Tracy's discussion in Part Two of R. M. Grant with D. Tracy, *A Short History of the Interpretation of the Bible* (Minneapolis: Fortress Press, 1984), 153–87. For Gadamer himself, see H.-G. Gadamer, *Truth and Method*, 2nd ed. (New York: Crossroad, 1990). On the rise and development of the "new hermeneutics," see V. B. Leitch, "Hermeneutics," in *American Literary Criticism from the Thirties to the Eighties* (New York: Columbia University Press, 1988), 182–210.

46. A critique undertaken, in a highly sympathetic vein, by Tracy himself (*Interpretation of the Bible*, 160–66).

47. B. K. Blount, *Cultural Interpretation: Reorienting New Testament Criticism* (Minneapolis: Fortress Press, 1995), esp. 1–23 (Chap. 1: "A Contextual Approach"), 89–96, and 175–94 (chap. 11: "Beyond Interpretative Boundaries").

48. For Blount, it should be noted, the term "ideology" is pejorative, indicating a restrictive rather than inclusive perspective, whether deployed from the center (as in the case of traditional biblical studies) or from the margins (as in the case of liberation hermeneutics); the goal, therefore, is to develop a "non-ideological" method, that is, a method that takes into account a variety of perspectives, from center and margins alike. See ibid., 3–4.

49. As such, the discussion proceeds throughout at a much broader level than was the case with William Myers, taking into consideration to be sure—indeed as a point of departure—the African-American experience but going beyond it as well to encompass a wide variety of other groups and experiences in the margins.

50. With regard to functionalist sociolinguistics, Blount follows the model of M. A. K. Halliday, *Explorations in the Functions of Language* (London: Edward Arnold, 1973); with regard to liberationist sociology, he adopts, with modifications, the model of Enrique Dussel, *Philosophy of Liberation* (Maryknoll: Orbis Books, 1985).

51. The model entails a number of presuppositions. First, it sees language as oriented toward and structured according to its use in acts of communication, so that meaning involves both the internal makeup of language and its use. Second, it has recourse to three categories of text-linguistic inquiry: (a) the textual, which considers language as it functions grammatically—the components of language as structured syntactically to establish meaning; (b) the ideational, which considers the conceptual implications behind lexical terms and phrases—the conceptual references signified by those terms and phrases; (c) the interpersonal, which considers the role played by sociolinguistic factors—the sociocultural

environment of the language user. Third, since language is seen as functioning interactively, it argues that the meaning of language can be comprehended only by taking all three variables into account. See Blount, *Cultural Interpretation*, 8–14.

52. While Halliday's model is elaborated from the perspective of the producer of the text, Blount develops it from the standpoint of the reader of the text, with the latter bringing a new contextual element to the interpersonal phase. By itself, therefore, a text is said to possess "meaning potential"—a range of possible meanings open to individual interpreters and made concrete by readings from different sociolinguistic frameworks. See ibid., 15–16.

53. The meaning potential of a text, while vast, is not unlimited, since the textual and ideational factors set parameters for the interpersonal dimension, "unequivocally stating what the material cannot mean." For Blount, therefore, a text cannot be interpreted in any way that a community chooses; rather, readings must be meaningful or responsible, that is, must have "linguistically accurate and contextually appropriate conclusions," conclusions that "fit within this textual-ideational boundary" and "simultaneously interact beyond this boundary with the interpersonal context of the reader. . . ." At the same time, meaning is not static but expansive: as the interpersonal dynamics change, so do the meaningful and responsible readings. Ibid., 27–28, 84–86, 89–92.

54. Such a model presupposes a scientific process in which a centrist totality is positioned in dialectical fashion against an exterior totality: adjustments to the center, therefore, are carried out within a totalistic framework that coopts rather than accepts input from the periphery. Ibid., 18–20.

55. Such a model calls for an analectical moment in the scientific process: not just the dialectical recognition by the center of an exterior totality, which it proceeds to meet by way of confrontation, but an effective interchange between totalities, with an analysis of reality from that marginal perspective. Such analysis, moreover, poses a threat to any system upholding a centrist view of the social system, insofar as it recognizes that the opposites may work to create a new whole. Ibid., 20–22.

56. It should be noted that Blount (ibid., 177–84) does criticize Dussel's model on two counts: (a) it focuses only on two approaches—the traditional and the Latin American; (b) it sees the analectical moment as yielding a new and complete reference for meaning. For Blount, the full spectrum of meaning in a text can only come about by allowing a multitude of communal interpretations to engage one another analectically; further, this spectrum of meaning is never final or complete, but always expanding, sometimes in explosive fashion. While having recourse to the language of center and margins, therefore, it is clear that Blount also looks upon both center and margins as consisting of a wide array of individual and communal interpretations.

Part I

Biblical Interpretation and Theological Education

I

THEOLOGICAL EDUCATION
IN A NEW CONTEXT

*Reflections from the Perspective
of Brazilian Theology*

Paulo Fernando Carneiro de Andrade

In the course of the present century, Catholic Theology has been imparted in a number of macrocontexts that were substantially different from one another from a cultural point of view. These macrocontexts marked the theological paradigms of each period as well as the corresponding modes of theological education, although this fact has not always been properly acknowledged, especially during the first half of the century, when the manualistic tradition in theology presented itself as a universal rather than contextual theology.

Among Catholics, the first explicit call for a contextual "academic" theology, issued by a group of priests from Haiti and Africa, dates from around 1955.[1] Despite such a call, the hegemony of manualistic theology, the predominant model of theological education at the time, continued at least until the Second Vatican Council. This type of theology, based on paradigms derived from traditional European culture, survived into the 1960s, due above all to the prevalence within the Catholic context of an anti-modernist impulse, which made it difficult, if not impossible, to introduce certain fundamental questions of modernity into Catholic thought, despite the efforts of a number of important theological sectors in this regard.

It is Vatican II, therefore, that marks the encounter of Catholicism with modernity. Thus, for Karl Rahner the fundamental meaning of the Council was to render visible, in a new way quite unknown until then, the universal character of the Catholic Church.[2] One could say that for Rahner it was only at this point that the Catholic Church discovered itself as a truly global church, since prior to this time the work of the Church had resembled much more that of an

---

This is a translation by Fernando F. Segovia of the original manuscript in Portuguese, "Ensinar teologia em um novo contexto: Algumas reflexões a partir da Teologia Brasileira."

export firm, whose business it was to disseminate European religion and culture throughout the world.[3] According to Rahner, therefore, the Council brings to a close this period of the Catholic Church as a European church, bringing about a rupture that can only be compared to that which marked the transition from Jewish Christianity to Gentile Christianity under the influence of Paul.[4]

Within this context, the importance of the dialogical perspective at the Council should be underlined as well. Thus, between the second and third sessions of the Council, Pope Paul VI issued—on August 6, 1964—the programmatic encyclical *Ecclesiam Suam* ("On the Church"),[5] which dealt primarily with the "problem of the Church's dialogue (*colloquium*) with the modern world" (*Ecclesiam Suam* 14). For Paul VI, "the Church must enter into dialogue with the world in which it lives" (*Ecclesiam Suam* 65). Such dialogue is understood by the Pontiff as "a recognized method of the apostolate . . . a way of making spiritual contact" (*Ecclesiam Suam* 81). The dialogical perspective introduced by this encyclical, at a time when such conciliar documents as *Nostra Aetate*, *Ad gentes*, and *Gaudium et Spes* were being prepared, permeates these documents and becomes fundamental for the post-conciliar Church.[6]

This juxtaposition of the Church's self-discovery as a global rather than European church with the emergence of a dialogical perspective led to a major encounter, not only with the culture of Western modernity and its sciences, but also with the different local cultures and, in time, with the major world religions as well, setting the stage thereby for the beginning of interreligious dialogue. It should be noted that the Church's approach to local cultures took place in a rather complex way, given the coming together of a number of different factors. On the one hand, the valorization of local churches as a result of an ecclesiology of church-communion—be it as a corollary of the fundamental meaning of the Council or of the dialogical perspective—and the rapprochement with modernity, whose paradigms point toward a respect for diverse subjects seen as an autonomous source of value, called for a valorization of other cultures. On the other hand, the social sciences to which both the Church and theological thinking now had recourse furnished new means for the understanding of other cultures. One should remember in this regard the critique of ethnocentrism emerging out of cultural anthropology.[7]

CONTEXT FOR THE EMERGENCE AND TEACHING OF LIBERATION THEOLOGY

With the valorization of cultural diversity and the affirmation of the local church, the formulation of contextual theologies began to take place, even before the conclusion of the Council itself, in a brand new way and with a force completely without precedent in the last few centuries. From the point of view of Latin America, the first meeting of Latin American theologians, which took place in Petrópolis, Brazil, in March of 1964, represents a good example of such developments. The text of the letter of invitation sent to the participants presented the following as one of the objectives for such a meeting:

To awaken in the different theological faculties, professors of theology, etc., by means of this group an attitude of active interest, opening up new horizons and identifying issues for investigation of interest to Latin Americans. The goal is to have this meeting serve as a point of departure for a theological research agenda regarding the problematic of the Latin American Church.[8]

This meeting—which was attended by, among others, Juan Luis Segundo, Lucio Gera, and Gustavo Gutiérrez—may be regarded as the first step in the effort to create a Latin American theology.

With respect to theological education, a two-fold development can be observed: (1) the creation of a number of strong theological centers in universities, such as the department of theology at the Catholic Pontifical University of Rio de Janeiro (established as a Pontifical Ecclesiastical School in 1972); (2) the launching of a number of centers for theological formation located in the midst of the people, such as those of João Pessoa (Northeast), under the leadership of José Comblin; Acre (Legal Amazon), under the leadership of Clodovis Boff; and Recife and Fortaleza (Northeast).

In an article published in 1981, José Comblin—who was at the time in charge of the formation program for seminarians in the rural zone of the Diocese of João Pessoa—sets forth the kind of theological education necessary for such a formation program and the relationship between this type of theological education and its immediate context.[9] Comblin notes that European academic theology continues to be part of the formation of Latin American priests. As such, despite their attempt to adapt European theology to the Latin American situation, most professors find it difficult to do so, given the fact that they received their most important theological training in Europe.[10]

According to Comblin, contemporary academic theology is basically a critical theology. Such a theology creates more problems than it solves. Thus, in making use of the human sciences, which are also critical sciences, such a characteristic becomes even more pronounced. When faced with fundamental questions, this type of theology points above all to the diversity of possible responses and the range of inquiries that can be undertaken. As such, it fails to prepare seminarians for the pastoral task. It produces uncertainty and ambiguity rather than action.[11] For Comblin, such a situation is a direct result of the fact that theology, despite the efforts of Latin American theologians to do so, has not yet been placed at the service of evangelization.[12]

Comblin is also of the opinion that, ever since the appearance of Paul VI's Apostolic Exhortation *Evangelii Nuntiandi* in 1975, it has become impossible to ignore the relationship that exists between culture and evangelization, to the point that cultural diversity conditions evangelization. Thus, Comblin states, "it is impossible to train a priest without reference to the culture that he is going to evangelize."[13] Indeed, for him, even within Europe itself one must take into consideration the cultural difference that exists between the middle classes and the working classes. In other words, a priest who is destined to work among the middle classes cannot be trained in the same way as a priest whose labor will be among the working classes. In Latin America, Comblin points out, such differences are much more radical. In effect, besides a similar difference between a working-class culture and a middle-class culture, one finds as well the presence of a traditional peasant culture, with indigenous as well as African American variations. Consequently, it is impossible to use the same type of theological education to train the clergy for evangelization in such diverse contexts.[14]

Comblin further regards the study of philosophy as absolutely necessary for the study of theology. Indeed, philosophy cannot be replaced by the human sciences, given their partial and abstract character.[15] At the same time, the philosophy in question is not at all the "philosophia perennis"—that is to say, Greek philosophy—but rather the perennial philosophy (the wisdom) of each people and culture. As such, it is necessary for the priest to learn the conception of the world and of human beings, as well as the human wisdom to be found in the people to be evangelized, as communicated in the everyday actions of the people in question. Since the philosophy of a people is by no means homogeneous but varies according to the different cultures to be found within such a people, the evangelizer must become acquainted with the specific philosophy of the segment to be evangelized. No theological concept should be learned without dialogue with the philosophy of the people in question.[16]

The contextualization of theological education is pursued thereby in at least two intersecting ways: first, through a reorientation of theology itself, now taught as being at the service of evangelization; second, through a theological formation grounded in philosophy, by which is meant the worldview and wisdom of the people. To learn this philosophy, it is necessary to know and to share in the culture of the people to whom it belongs, while being aware at all times of the fact that within any one people there are different cultures to be found (working classes and middle classes; countryside and city; Iberian American, indigenous, African American; and so forth).

In the case of Latin America, the search for a contextualized theology that takes seriously into account fundamental pastoral questions ultimately resulted in the birth of Liberation Theology, which emerged toward the end of the 1960s and which continued to develop throughout the 1970s and 1980s. This theology sought to reinterpret the entire tradition of the Church as well as the Sacred Scriptures from the point of view of the following central question: how is it possible to be a Christian in a continent of exploited and oppressed poor? Liberation Theology arose out of a socioeconomic context of oppression and marginalization and took the side of the poor. This position on behalf of the poor eventually became known as the "option for the poor" and came to characterize not only Latin American theology but also its pastoral practice, giving way to the creation of Base Christian Communities. Different religious communities were formed among the people, mostly by a few individuals who wished to share the life of the poor and to be of assistance in organizing them. The centers for theological formation mentioned above—including that of Paraíba, where Comblin was working at the time—located as they were within the context of the people, had as their goal a theological education for seminarians and religious who were going to work with the popular classes, a resounding majority at the time. Living together with the oppressed poor and sharing their living conditions would allow these students to become acquainted with the philosophy of the poor; in this way, they would learn a contextualized theology and would truly prepare themselves for the pastoral task.

The question that can be raised at this point is whether this Latin American context of the 1960s through the 1980s still endures today, or whether a new context has by now emerged, which would imply the formulation of new theological paradigms and thus the need to search for a new mode of theological education in Latin America.

From a socioeconomic point of view, the Latin American context of the 1960s through the 1980s, especially in Brazil, is marked by a consolidation of the process of industrialization. Beginning with the years after World War II, the West embarked on a process of rapid industrialization. In the case of Brazil, the 1950s were characterized by enormous transformations in the country as well as by the expansion of its industrial base. In the course of this decade, the Gross National Product (GNP) grew by about 20 percent per capita, while the urban population increased from 39 to 46 percent. Such development continued through the following decades, as a result of heavy investment in science and technology.[17]

The rapid expansion of the Brazilian industrial base as a result of the growth in the GNP did not take place in such a way as to benefit the entire population. Indeed, from the 1960s through the 1980s, the gulf between the rich and the poor grew wider. In effect, the wealthiest 20 percent of the population secured an increasing percentage of the GNP, leading to a progressive decrease for the poorest 20 percent. At the same time, the agricultural sector declined, producing a large wave of migration to the cities and the creation of jobs tied to the industrial and civil construction sectors. Consequently, the wealth created by the workers, as reflected in the growth of the GNP, was transferred to the dominant economic class.

From a political point of view, the decades of the 1960s through the 1980s were characterized in Latin America, and specifically in Brazil, by the emergence of military dictatorships, set up to ensure the process of capitalist industrialization as well as to repress the self-organization of the popular sector, guaranteeing in the process the socio-economic model of strong concentration of income at the top. As a result, a new type of hegemonic poverty emerged: the poverty of urban and rural workers, exploited by the capitalist structures of production, within a framework of a process of accumulation à la Ford (Fordism)—a poverty different from that of the masses of the rural and urban poor of yesteryear, the result of a process of pre-capitalist exploitation or marginalization.[18] It is this new type of poverty that Latin American Theology encountered in the 1960s and to which it pointed in its "preferential option for the poor."[19]

From the point of view of cultural macrocontext, the culture of modernity, grounded in the Enlightenment, became gradually hegemonic from the 1950s on, replacing in the process the traditional culture of pre-modernity. This culture of Enlightenment-based modernity has as its driving force the conviction that human reason, impelled as it is by ultimate values that give meaning to life, possesses an unlimited capacity to orient human behavior and actions toward the construction of an always better future through a progressive process of self-illumination (enlightenment), carried out by means of an encounter with the world and with itself. Such a culture entails an almost absolute confidence in human reason, which, overcoming all obstacles, is capable of conducting all men and women toward progress and hence toward happiness.[20] This cultural matrix underlined the process of capitalist industrial modernity as much as its critique and opposition did, in terms of the economic model of real socialism.

In the course of the dialogue between Christianity and the modern world, certain sectors of the Catholic Church as well as of other Christian churches leaned toward a modernity of the capitalist-Enlightenment type. Other sectors, however, declared their solidarity with those oppressed by the modern-industrial-capitalist project and ended up in conversation with theories critical of this project and thus, at times, with Marxism. One should note in this regard, however, that such theories were similarly grounded in the modernity of the Enlightenment.

It was then as a result of this encounter between theological reflection and theories critical of the economic model of industrial capitalism—theories which were said to provide the best explanation for the Latin American poor, the object of the option for the poor, as well as the best praxis for overcoming such a situation—that Liberation Theology was born. The new modes of theological education that were developed at the time must be placed within this overall framework, even in their determination to establish a constant link between praxis and theory, most evident in the institutes and formation centers established among the people.

EMERGENCE OF A NEW CONTEXT

The 1980s signaled the emergence of a new context, which came to the fore for the most part during the 1990s. This new context has to do with the beginning of a new phase in the global economy, made possible in part by new technologies emerging in the fields of computer science and microelectronics. This new phase is characterized by the phenomenon of globalization and the expansion of the financial and service sectors of the economy, which, in the light of their new role, lead one to believe that industrial society is giving way to post-industrial society.

Post-Industrial Society and the Phenomenon of the Global Economy

This globalization or "worldlification" of the economy can be seen in part as an evolution of a type of market that began in the period after World War II, namely, the development of multinational companies. Yet, there is something quite new altogether in the globalization phenomenon of the 1990s: in effect, an economic interpenetration beyond borders, whether in the process of production, in commerce, in financing, or in research-development.[21] This phenomenon, which underwent rapid acceleration after the demise of the socialist regimes of Eastern Europe, means, on the one hand, an unprecedented geographical expansion of the market, and, on the other hand, the transformation of a variety of human demands and needs, now taken over by the market. Thus, the market expands geographically as well as qualitatively, leading to the universalization of the logic present in the law of value: everything everywhere becomes a commodity.[22]

This evolution in the process of globalization coincides with the erosion of three main pillars of the post-war economy: (1) the Fordism model (*fordismo*) of the industrialized countries of the West; (2) the Soviet model (*sovietismo*) of Eastern Europe; and (3) the developmental model (*desenvolvimentismo*) of the countries of the Third World.[23] Indeed, one should underline with regard to this last point the end of the hegemonic project at work from the 1950s through the 1980s—the push toward an industrialization that would replace imports as the basis for economic development.[24]

The process of economic globalization coincides as well with the process of transition from an industrial to a post-industrial economy. To be sure, such a transition does not signify a decline in industrial production, just as the earlier transition from an agricultural to an industrial economy did not result in a decline in agricultural production. In fact, the development of new technologies has made possible a process of unprecedented automatization, with an enormous increase in productivity and a corresponding decrease in the cost of production of industrial goods. This process has freed human and material resources, which have in turn been shifted to the production of new services whose creation was also in part made possible by new technologies in the fields of communications and transportation.[25]

The result is the formation of a society based on advanced technology, widely computerized and with an abundant supply of goods and services. From within such a context, then, a phenomenon quite new in form and extension comes to the fore: the condition of exclusion. In effect, different human groups fail to have, for different reasons, their needs supplied by the expanding market. Such groups are therefore placed at the margins of the market or even completely outside of it, giving rise thereby to a new form of poverty, in many cases absolute.

These economic transformations have a broad effect on the labor market. First, there is a strong decline in manufacturing and, in general, in any type of work directly tied to the industrial sector. Second, there is growth in the managerial sector, and, through the use of intermediaries, the classic work pattern of industrial societies begins to be replaced by tasks assigned to autonomous or self-employed individuals. Finally, there is an increase in unemployment as well as in the informal sector of the economy. In fact, this latter sector becomes increasingly important, either by absorbing the surplus labor supply or by responding rapidly, in a flexible and dynamic way, to the new demands placed upon the omnipresent market.[26]

Modernity in Crisis

The transformation of the industrial economy into a post-industrial economy, accompanied as it is by its corollary of globalization, is linked to a profound crisis in the hegemonic culture associated with an industrial economy: the culture of modernity grounded in the Enlightenment. As industrial society is left behind, the culture that functioned as both its expression and its moving force comes to an end.

In fact, just as the crises of the 1970s (the oil crisis; the rise of totalitarian regimes in the West, especially in Latin America; the Vietnam War; the discovery of ecological limits on development; the widening of the North-South gulf; and so on) called into question, in a very clear way, the idea of progress and the universal value of modern reason, so now the very formation of a post-industrial economy calls for a break with the logic of Enlightenment-based modernity, for the most part linear and homogenizing in nature. This culture, already contested in the 1960s by a variety of different sectors of society (such as, for example, the hippie movement), becomes less and less plausible after the 1980s.[27]

This crisis of Enlightenment-based modernity represents a crisis for the paradigm as such, as well as for all those historical projects traditionally associated with it. Within modernity, a historically determined discourse about God, human beings, and the world is mistakenly identified with reality and exclusive truth. This exclusive access to the truth, vindicated by reason, ultimately turns into a reductionistic and impoverished perspective, giving rise to a contradiction at the heart of modernity. On the one hand, Enlightenment-based modernity represents a rupture with a culture based on authority and tradition, as it introduces the critical method and generates in this way freedom and the demand for equality. On the other hand, reason itself, which modern culture identifies with the truth, excludes all truth that does not fit within its framework and flattens differences in order to claim universality for itself. Thus, instrumental rationality ends up, by subordinating all other rationalities to itself, giving rise to new mechanisms of domination.

In this way, Enlightenment-based modernity, despite its significant advances in the direction of a liberating project, fails to bring it to fulfillment. A number of questions, regarded today as fundamental, did not find an adequate response, or more accurately, did not succeed many times in even being understood as questions. Such was the case with both the question of ecology and the question of subjectivity.[28]

The constant search for progress was conducted for the most part within a model of exploitation-domination. Modernity affirms the value of the individual through its espousal of an anthropocentric perspective. However, a reductionistic form of anthropocentrism tied to rationalism ends up by devaluing nature and other forms of life, giving rise to the idea of a presumed right on the part of rational humanity to dominate and subjugate without limits what is not rational. It seemed as if progress could be expanded indefinitely and as if reason itself could undertake to resolve whatever obstacle should arise in its path. The energy crisis of the 1970s, brought about by the actions of the oil-producing nations, placed in evidence the ecological limits of this model of development, bringing to the fore thereby the ecological question already raised at an earlier time by a number of social movements.

The affirmation of the individual, made in terms of a reduction of the individual to the rational level, signified at the practical level the negation of subjectivity. Affectivity, the passions, mysticism, and spirituality were to be subordinated to reason in the name of human happiness itself. The reduction of all truth to the rational level leads to a consideration of all that is not rationalizable and subject to control by modern reason as false or, at the very least, as inferior. The process of civilization is then understood as a process of progressive rationalization, in the course of which men and women become ever more human as they enlighten themselves through the critique of reason and the control of their subjectivity.[29]

As a result of this process, the world is deprived of its sense of enchantment, and religion is considered, in certain sectors, a matter of simple superstition. The question of values and ethics is avoided through the control of instrumental rationality, which bears within it its own justification. Within this perspective, progress and the power of reason that leads to such progress become the highest values and are readily identified with the liberating project present within modernity, even though in practice such values may result in domination and inequality.[30]

The crisis of the industrial development model in the 1970s, which took place just as a new phase in the world economy was about to break out, gave way to the crisis of modernity, which was intimately tied to this model. If up to this time the critique of modernity was confined to certain groups, from this point on this critique undergoes a significant expansion, with at least three major tendencies in evidence:

1. The first tendency is to be found in neofascist and fundamentalist movements, which represent a retreat in the face of modernity based on different experiences of frustration with its accomplishments.

2. The second tendency may be identified with the emergence of a hedonistic and nihilistic culture. This particular tendency fails to offer a real alternative to modernity. It is a reaction to it, not a retreat as in the first tendency, since its goal is to advance certain specific values of modernity. Within this tendency, still present today, the driving force of Cartesianism, "I think, therefore I am," becomes "I feel, therefore I am." Thus, sensation replaces reason and leads to an explosion of subjectivity.[31] This tendency, moreover, denies any possibility that modern reason may lead men and women to happiness. The goal rather is an individualism of the most radical kind, wherein the human being turns upon himself or herself, since outside nothing is sure, objective, or non-ambiguous. This exacerbation of subjectivity at the cost of objectivity leads in some cases to a total dissociation between the public and the private spheres, with attribution of value only to the private sphere and a corresponding disregard for politics and the concept of representation.[32] Such radical individualism and such negation of the value of modern rationality ultimately result in the creation of a fragmented identity and a perception of society as devoid of any historicity, with no interest in the past or in the future, only in the present.

A further aspect of this tendency is a total relativization of values and ideas. If nothing makes sense, everything goes, and tolerance is transformed thereby into indifference: where no debate is worth the trouble, no idea bears discussion, and no argument has any value—only feelings and affections, which are mistakenly identified as sensations.[33] Along with the disregard for reason comes a disregard for learning and scientific knowledge, a loss of the social role of the intellectual, and a disregard for formal education and the traditional institutions of learning. The most tragic aspect of such a development is that, in the final instance, indifference and the refusal to search for meaning and significance in human life and experience ultimately result in existential degradation, with a corresponding impoverishment of the ability to wonder, to show enthusiasm, to orient a life with an ideal in mind, to love or to enjoy intensely.[34] This existential degradation ultimately brings about, quite paradoxically, an increasing loss in the ability to have sensations and to produce feelings. At that point, a contradiction results: a search for ever-stronger sensations, capable of producing some type of emotion in a benumbed subject.

Within such a context, the traditional institutions of socialization in modernity—the bourgeois family and the modern school system—lose their ability to transmit or to reproduce images of the world, values, models for action, and community feelings.[35] The "mass media" in turn become more important as a factor in socialization—contributing for the most part, however, to the formation of this hedonistic tendency as well as leading to a destructuralization of time and the creation of a fragmented conscience, polarized in the present. Historical processes and situations, as in the case of the Gulf War, tend to be presented in personalized fashion, in an emotional and spectacular way, almost as an item for ready consumption, as was the case with the coverage of this event by the CNN television network.[36]

One should note as well the process of emptying that takes place within this tendency with regard to two institutions typical of modernity: work and marriage.[37] First, with the dissociation between the public sphere and the private sphere, work loses its vocational character. Since it is precisely this dimension that allows for a connection between the private and collective spheres, with its configuration of work as both service and fulfillment, work becomes simply a means for supplying the needs of the individual and a profession. At the same time, love and marriage are regarded only as a source of personal gratification and, given their dissociation from family and children, cease to be lived as a matrix for social relations. Love loses its dimension as a significant decision for a life full of ramifications and responsibilities as well as new possibilities, becoming instead ephemeral and banal.[38]

3. Besides these two tendencies at the heart of the crisis of Enlightenment-based modernity, there is a third. This last tendency has to do with the emergence of a new type of culture—a culture that seeks to go beyond the first modernity but without proposing a new form of retreat or a new form of reductionism.

Toward a New Culture

One of the most distinctive traits of this new culture still in formation, besides the two already mentioned above, is the emergence of a new form of subjectivity. This culture has as its anthropological base an understanding of the human being not only as a rational being but also as a being of sentiments, affections, passions, intuitions, and mysticism—in sum, as a pluridimensional being. Human subjectivity is thus looked upon as a value in itself, not to be reduced to or dominated by objective rationality. Modern reason is no longer understood exclusively as the source of and the way to happiness. Rather, happiness itself is also sought in the satisfaction of those human dimensions that go beyond scientific reason, now regarded as one "reason" among others.[39]

The different logics or "reasons" are no longer placed in a hierarchical system ordained by instrumental reason; on the contrary, differences are valued and in the process a new sensibility emerges with respect to freedom. As a result, the concept of freedom becomes more expansive, now including the right of every human being to live according to his or her convictions and sensibilities, quite independently of their rational justification, and to have such choices respected. Within this culture, there is an attempt to live the pluridimensionality of the human being not in fragmented fashion but as a unity. Within such a context, there is a search for new and creative syntheses of human knowledge and experience, which in turn give way to a reformulation, in a different key, of the question of interdisciplinarity.

In the transition from a linear logic toward a logic that may be characterized more as a net or a matrix, a purely progressive notion of time also comes to an end, as does a mechanistic view of the world, whether with respect to nature or to society. The understanding of space is affected as well, resulting in a new mixture of the local with the universal, in such a way that the new phenomenon of globalization is no longer conceived in terms of simple uniformity but rather in terms of a possible affirmation and promotion of local culture. Thus, just as "fast food" spreads throughout the world, so does the regional cuisine from diverse parts of the world find a place in the major cities of the globe. Local customs do not disappear but rather combine with international customs to find new modes of linkage and synthesis.[40]

A new sensibility with regard to life, conceived in terms of solidarity, comes to the fore as well. The human being is seen as a part of a greater whole, with duties and responsibilities toward nature and other forms of life. Within this context, there is interest in the ecological question as well as in the different models of development. In the formation of this vision, solidarity emerges as a fundamental value, calling for a personal response vis-à-vis the suffering and the needs of concrete others as well as with reference to different forms of life.[41]

On the basis of these new paradigms, a further redefinition of the public and private spheres takes place, thus including within the overall discussion the question of the state as well. In effect, the identification between the public realm and the realm of government breaks down, giving rise to new forms of property and new forms of organisms under communitarian rather than governmental control. The attribution of exclusive responsibility to the state with regard to the resolution of all problems in the social, cultural, economic, and political spheres gives way to the realization that there are limits to the measures a government can take with respect to the grave and complex challenges present in each of these sectors. Moreover, with the reformulation of the question of solidarity, the responsibility of each citizen with regard to the resolution of national or local problems is affirmed, as is the fact that certain concrete gestures can be of help in the resolution of such problems, calling forth thereby what has come to be known as "people power" (*ação cidadã*). Such power is seen as neither displacing nor supplanting but rather as complementing that of government. Such power, moreover, goes beyond traditional forms of charitable aid, given not only its communitarian rather than individualistic character, but also its clear perception of the political dimensions of the problems it seeks to confront. At the same time, people power rejects any type of explicit partisanship with regard to its proposals as well as any centralization of its activities, opting instead for a model more along the lines of a cooperative network.[42]

All of these new elements outlined above seem to point toward the creation of a new culture that can go beyond that of Enlightenment-based modernity without rejecting the positive values of the latter. In highlighting these three tendencies, my intention is not to exhaust the cultural possibilities that are emerging today as the result of the crisis of modernity or to affirm that such tendencies already constitute well-structured or alternative options. Rather, it is better to see them as possibilities that present themselves today as major tendencies and that can even be combined with one another.

CONSEQUENCES FOR LIBERATION THEOLOGY AND ITS TEACHING

The process of economic transformation of the 1980s and 1990s, and the crisis of modernity, point to the need for the construction of new paradigms in theology in general and in Liberation Theology in particular.

1. The question of gender, largely bypassed by the Liberation Theology of the 1960s through the 1980s, has become increasingly important and leads to the incorporation of new perspectives, new goals, new methods, and new results.[43]

2. The sense of everyday life as a theological and political locus and time deprives the future of its character as the only possessor and conveyor of meaning, capable of justifying either the present or the past. As a result, there is need to reconceive the nature of utopian thinking. In fact, the unlimited confidence placed in instrumental reason, which makes it possible to believe in the ability to plan the ideal future with precision and thus to establish in a univocal and apodictic way the road for humanity to follow in the pursuit of such a goal, is in the process of breaking down. Such developments signify neither the end of all hope nor the absence of any roads to follow, with their corresponding consecration of the present as a time without a future. Indeed, it is faith itself that provides the certainty of the historical possibility of constructing a future that is more just.[44] Such a future is a future built not only on the basis of great movements and deeds but also on the basis of everyday actions and diverse struggles of a local and partial nature. The fundamental values of the faith continue to function as

a compass for guiding the way and for making possible movement in the direction of a goal thus partially conceived. Utopia is thereby displaced from the end to the process itself. The means now construct the end. The future is constructed on the way.

3. Affectivity and subjectivity become a theological locus as well. The question regarding the happiness of concrete human beings in the here and now gains in importance from both a theological and a pastoral point of view. Any theology that fails to make a contribution to human happiness and wellbeing, that fails to lead to affective integration, loses plausibility.

4. The sense of mysticism and celebration, linked to a liberating praxis, can no longer be relegated to second place. The paradigms associated with the emerging new culture demand a rethinking of the space previously assigned to mysticism and celebration within a secularized context, where the fundamental aspects of the faith and of religious experience were looked upon, at times, as alienating.

5. Popular culture itself is also seen from a new point of view. Previously, the need to become acquainted with popular culture, with the "philosophy" of the poor, revealed at times a rather instrumental impulse. The goal was to get to know this culture not because of its own intrinsic value but rather for the purpose of evangelization and internal critique. The new paradigms, however, lead to a valorization of popular culture as such, no longer opposed and subordinated to modern culture. The wisdom of the people, with its very different logic from that of Enlightenment-based modernity, becomes thereby a new theological locus, leading to a new experience of God and a different way of talking about global reality.

All of these observations, which are in no way exhaustive, point to a number of the new paradigms to be incorporated into Liberation Theology, as part of the new economic and cultural context of the 1990s. Furthermore, as the paradigms change, so should the modes of theological education associated with such paradigms. As a result, it becomes imperative to rethink the very nature of the centers for theological formation, so that they find themselves in harmony rather than in contradiction with these new paradigms.

NOTES

1. See Marcel Chappin, "Theologies in Context," in *Dictionary of Fundamental Theology*, ed. René Latourelle and Rino Fisichella (New York: Crossroad, 1994), 1097–1102, esp. p. 1098.

2. K. Rahner, "Interpretazione teologica fondamentale del Concilio Vaticano II," *Sollicitudine per la Chiesa* (Nuovi Saggi VIII; Rome: Paoline, 1982), 343–61.

3. Ibid., 345.

4. Ibid., 355.

5. For the English text, from which the following quotations are taken, see *The Papal Encyclicals. Volume 5: 1958–1981*, ed. Claudia Carlen Ihm (Raleigh: Pierian Press, 1990), 135–60.

6. See Jacques Dupuis, "Dialogo Interreligioso nella Missione Evangelizzatrice della Chiesa," *Vaticano II. Bilancio e prospettive, venticinque anni dopo (1962–1987),* ed. René Latourelle (Assisi: Cittadella Editrice, 1987), 1234–56.

7. See Claude Lévi-Strauss, *Race and History* (Paris: Unesco, 1968; orig. French edition: 1952).

8. For the document, see Roberto Oliveros Maqueo, *Liberación y teología. Génesis y crecimiento de una reflexión (1966-1976)* (Lima: Centro de Estudios y Publicaciones, 1977), 52.

9. J. Comblin, "Algumas reflexões sobre a formação sacerdotal hoje," *Revista eclesiástica brasileira* 41 (1981): 320–45.

10. Ibid., 327–28.

11. Ibid., 329.

12. Ibid., 330.

13. Ibid., 331.

14. Ibid.

15. Ibid., 332.

16. Ibid., 333.

17. See Felipe Herrera, *O Desenvolvimento da América Latina e seu Financiamento* (Rio de Janeiro: Análise e Perspectiva Económica, 1968).

18. See Krishan Kumar, *From Post-Industrial to Post-Modern Society. New Theories of the Contemporary World* (Cambridge: Blackwell, 1995).

19. See CNBB [Conferência Nacional dos Bispos do Brasil], *Justiça e Paz se Abraçarão* (São Paulo: Editora Salesiana Dom Bosco, 1995), 59–60.

20. See Leszek Kolakowski, *Tratado sobre la mortalidad de la razón* (Caracas: Monte Avila, 1969), 253–325; Jürgen Habermas, "Dogmatism, Reason, and Decision: On Theory and Praxis in Our Scientific Civilization," in J. Habermas, *Theory and Praxis* (Boston: Beacon Press, 1973), 253–82.

21. See François Houtart, editorial in *Alternatives Sud* 1 (1994): 7–18.

22. See Samir Amin, "La nouvelle mondialization capitaliste. Problèmes e perspectives," *Alternatives Sud* 1 (1994): 19–44.

23. Ibid., 21.

24. Ibid., 34–36.

25. See David Harvey, *The Condition of Postmodernity: An Enquiry into the Origins of Cultural Change* (Oxford-New York: Blackwell, 1989), 119–97.

26. See Peter F. Drucker, *Post-Capitalist Society* (New York: HarperBusiness, 1993).

27. See Steven Best and Douglas Kellner, *Postmodern Theory and Critical Interrogations* (London: Macmillan, 1991).

28. See Stanley Aronowitz, "Pós-modernismo e política," *Pós-modernismo e política,* ed. H. Buarque de Hollanda (Rio de Janeiro: Rocco, 1991), 151–75.

29. See Remo Bodei, *Geometria delle passioni. Paura, speranza, felicità: filosofia e uso politico* (Milan: Feltrinelli, 1991).

30. Best and Kellner, *Postmodern Theory,* 34–75.

31. See Christopher Lasch, *The Culture of Narcissism: American Life in an Age of Diminishing Expectations* (New York: Norton, 1978).

32. It should be noted in this regard that within the context of modernity the public realm and the private realm were separated but not dissociated. See I. Vacanti, "La condizione 'postmoderna': una sfida per la cultura cristiana," *Aggiornamenti Sociali* 2 (1990): 119–35, esp. 123.

33. See José Mardones, *Postmodernidad y cristianismo. El desafío del fragmento* (Santander: Sal Terrae, 1988), 68–72.

34. Vacanti, "La condizione 'postmoderna,'" 122.

35. See in this regard Allan Bloom, *The Closing of the American Mind: How Higher*

Education Has Failed Democracy and Impoverished the Souls of Today's Students (New York: Simon & Schuster, 1987), for an excellent critical analysis of the North American university system; see also Brigitte Berger and Peter Berger, *The War Over the Family: Capturing the Middle Ground* (Garden City, NY: Anchor Press/Doubleday, 1983), for a study of the relationship between the crisis of the bourgeois family and the crisis of modernity.

36. Vacanti, "La condizione 'postmoderna,'" 128; Mardones, *Posmodernidad y cristianismo*, 64–68, 75–77.

37. Vacanti, "La condizione 'postmoderna,'" 122–23.

38. Ibid., 124.

39. See Harvey, *Condition of Postmodernity*, 10–118.

40. Ibid., 201-307.

41. See Agnes Heller and Ferenç Fehér, *The Postmodern Political Condition* (New York: Columbia University Press, 1988), 74–88.

42. See Alberto Melucci, *Sistema politico, partiti e movimenti sociali* (Milan: Feltrinelli, 1990).

43. See *Teologia na Ótica da Mulher* (Rio de Janeiro: Pontifícia Universidade Católica do Rio de Janeiro, Departamento de Teologia, Núcleo de Estudos sobre a Mulher, 1990).

44. See João Batista Libânio, *Fé e Política: Autonomias específicas e articulações mútuas* (São Paulo: Loyola, 1985).

2

CONSTRUCTIVE THEOLOGY
AND BIBLICAL WORLDS

Peter C. Hodgson

THE DRAINING OF THEOLOGY
OUT OF BIBLICAL STUDIES

In remarks to the Society of Biblical Literature on "How My Mind Has Changed," Wayne Meeks recounts how he entered the graduate program at Yale University in the late 1950s under the impression that he would be studying something called "biblical theology."[1] At the time two sorts of biblical theology were mainly available, one inspired by Karl Barth and the ecumenical movement, with an emphasis on "God acting in history," the other by Rudolf Bultmann who sharply criticized the "history of salvation" model and offered in its place an existentialist interpretation.

There were heated debates between these two approaches. Meeks aligned himself with the Bultmannians and for a few years was an ardent existentialist, but then a strange thing happened: he found that theology began to drain out of his way of studying the Bible. The reasons he identifies for this fateful shift are interesting. In the first place, a major change occurred in the academic teaching of religion in North America with the Supreme Court decision of 1963, which, while banning school prayer, also specified that the U.S. Constitution erects no barrier to the objective teaching about religion in public schools. This was a catalyst for establishing departments of religious studies in public universities, and the "religious studies model" quickly came to dominate the field and its professional societies. Basically there was no place for "theology" in the religious studies curriculum, if theology meant a confessional embrace of and advocacy for normative truth claims. Theology did not meet the test of objective teaching about religion, and teachers of religion were quite prepared to abandon it in exchange for recognition by and funding from the state (or the administrators of secular universities).

In the second place, Meeks found himself growing increasingly uncertain about Bultmann's existentialist reconstruction of Christian theology. Not only

46

did it lead into the "quicksand of subjectivism," but also his demythologizing interpretation of the Gospel of John finally did not seem to work as an historical explanation. Meeks was also struck by the astonishing variety of ways in which the Pauline letters had been interpreted in the history of Western religious thought. "I discovered," he writes, "that nineteen centuries of interpretation of Paul by theologians, many of whom were much smarter than I, had not succeeded in producing a coherent and transparent way of reading the letters as theology." Meeks thus seems to have been led to the conclusion that theological questions are intrinsically undecidable and that it is better to refocus one's energies in an arena where modest results can at least be obtained. In his case, this led to a career-long inquiry into "the social world of early Christianity"—an enterprise in which those who were involved had the sense of being "in quest of something real." Theology, by implication, was preoccupied with something ideal, fictitious, imaginary, poetic.

A third factor, not mentioned by Meeks, also contributed to the draining of theology out of not only biblical studies but also church history, the history of religions, ethics, and ministerial practice—all the disciplines that were at one time unified under the rubric of "theological studies." This was the impact of postmodern modes of thought, which, in Edward Farley's helpful summation,[2] are "historical, contextual, particularistic, ethnic, gender-related, praxis-oriented, antifoundational, pluralistic, antimetaphysical, and very much focused on discourse, language, and symbolism." Insofar as theology makes "totalizing" claims about metaphysical realities on the basis of nonhistorically conditioned foundations, it seems to be intrinsically incompatible with the postmodern temper. In this situation the impulse of many has been either to abandon theology completely or to adhere uncompromisingly to its (pre)modern forms; relatively few have attempted to reconstruct it in light of the challenges of postmodern culture. The latter is the most difficult yet fruitful course. If it can be accomplished, a revisioned theology might have a place not merely alongside but *within* biblical, historical, ethical, and practical studies. Indeed, without theology, these disciplines experience a strange sort of lack. They avoid discourse about the very thing that is at the heart of religious experience, the transformative presence of God in the world, however that is to be understood.

Wayne Meeks is not unaware of the lack. He would have liked not merely to understand history but to have changed it. He notes that his work has left little time and energy to address some larger questions, such as, "*Who cares* about the historical beginnings of Christianity?"[3] He has had to bracket the kinds of interpretative issues that brought him into the profession in the first place. He does not regret this since it was necessary, having to do "with the division of labor." Yes—but as in the economic arena so also in the academic, the division of labor comes with a price. The price of academic "specialism," as Farley describes it, is the growth of hubris with respect to one's own methods and viewpoint, the loss of any larger sense of unity and purpose in academia, and the preempting of education as "paideia"—education that orients life and existence to truth about reality in humanizing, moral, and interpersonal ways.[4]

CONSTRUCTIVE THEOLOGY
AS CRITICAL PRAXIS CORRELATION

The Word of God theologies regnant in the first two-thirds of our century have indeed become problematic. They directed attention away from the hermeneutical interplay of text and context, of writing and reading, to a transtextual referent. For Barth this referent, the Word of God incarnate in Christ, had an objective, authoritative, suprahistorical status; for Bultmann it was existentially connected with human subjectivity in the immediacy of faith. The discursive strategies of texts and the social location of readers were downplayed. As dogmatics, theology set forth the objective credo of the church; as existentialist interpretation, it focused on the transcendental structures of human existence. In neither case was it recognized to be an overtly constructive activity, a product of human imagination arising out of engagement with texts read with specific interests in ever-changing contexts—yet oriented to something that discloses itself in the texts and their reading. This recognition is now commonplace among revisionist theologians, including some of the leading voices in North America today: David Tracy, Gordon Kaufman, Langdon Gilkey, Schubert Ogden, John Cobb, Rosemary Radford Ruether, Edward Farley, Sallie McFague, Marjorie Suchocki, Francis Schüssler Fiorenza, Rebecca Chopp, Elizabeth Johnson.

My own contribution to the revisionist project and its hermeneutics may be summarized as follows: theology is a constructive activity that correlates root revelatory experiences, traditioned textual expressions, and contemporary social locations through the interaction of critical-interpretative and practical-appropriative thinking.[5] Root experiences are events in which a revelation or disclosure of ultimate being/truth occurs. Exodus, Sinai, Golgotha, Easter, and Pentecost are prime biblical examples, but such experiences occur in the lives of communities and individuals throughout history.[6] It is important in my view to distinguish root experiences from the texts/traditions by which they are expressed and mediated. As I shall argue more fully below, the theological meaning of a text does not reside *behind* the text (in the mind of its author or in its original setting) or *in* it (in its linguistic structure and semantic relations), but rather *in front of* it, in an experience of truth or a way of being in the world that is shared by both text and interpreter and that is always constituted anew in the act of interpretation. Thus, there are three elements in the hermeneutical circle, not two: there is a fore-text as well as a text and a con-text, a disclosive and redemptive happening as well as a source and a situation. The ontological status of the fore-text (or "happening") is elusive in the sense that we never have access to it directly but only as mediated through interpreted texts. A revelatory experience *is* insofar as it is expressed, but it is not reducible to its expressions. I know that postmodernity is skeptical about such claims: for it the revelatory fore-text is a mere pretext, and thus for it everything collapses into text or context, that is, into linguistic systems and localized interests. My position is not that revelation is a datum, a *tertium quid,* to be added on to text and context, but rather that it comes forth in the interaction between text and context.

The element of context or situation introduces another dimension of experience into the hermeneutical process—the personal and social experience of interpreters as distinct from root experience. There is a sense in which interpretation goes between experience and experience—the immediate experience that generates interpretation and the root experience that is the object of interpretation. The latter does not always, or even usually, show itself as *root* experience. The *radical, root* character of experience is usually concealed in the mundaneness of everyday existence, as is the potentially revelatory power of experience. Nevertheless, the ultimate object of every interpretative act is precisely this dimension of radicality. It remains for the most part hidden in historical, aesthetic, and literary interpretation; it becomes more explicit in philosophical and especially theological interpretation. In religion the potential radicality of all experience is thematized in central root experiences by which everything else is illumined.

The model I am proposing identifies two movements or ways of thinking that connect the three elements and come together to form a "critical praxis correlation." The first, which I am calling *critical-interpretative thinking*, entails a backward, questioning movement from the interpreter through the textual media to the root or revelatory experience, which is established as an object of critical scrutiny, a meant object. It is a movement of critical distancing and analysis, of explanation by means of concepts, of interpretative judgments. It entails cognitive initiative on the part of the interpreter, by which a range of experience is taken apart and constituted before the mind as an object of knowledge. It involves a flow of meaning from the interpreter through the medium to the experience. But then, in the case of *root* experiences at least, a strange thing happens: a *reversal* in the flow of meaning occurs, so that now experience discloses itself on its own terms and by its own power, through its own primary symbols, rather than having a constructed meaning imposed upon it.

This gives rise to the second way, that of *practical-appropriative thinking*, which entails a forward, answering movement from the root experience through the media to the interpreter, a movement to which we as interpreters belong and in which we experience something like a disclosure. We both appropriate this movement, make it our own, *and* are appropriated by it, caught up in it. This is a movement of application, of participatory praxis, which not only is oriented to concrete worldly situations, but also helps to shape the preunderstandings that are the fundamental source of the conceptuality that makes critical thinking possible. No matter where we enter the circle of understanding, whether at the point of critical theory or of participatory praxis, we are in the middle of things, something is always presupposed, something always follows, and we must work our way through the circuit in disciplined fashion.

This situation of being in the midst of a swirling critical praxis correlation has led me to suggest that the hermeneutical circle of theology might also be thought of as a hermeneutical *ship*.[7] The ship has no foundation other than itself, no permanent port. It sails on the open seas and is subject to the force of highly fluid elements (wind, water). What supports it is solely its own structural integrity, the interplay of its elements (masts, sails, hull, tiller, fittings, crew). There is no Atlas god who carries the ship on his shoulders. This is why everything is always and only a matter of interpretation. The ship is a powerful antifoundationalist metaphor, but using it is by no means a counsel of despair or an embrace of conceptual relativism. On board the ship meaningful and ordered life goes on, purposes are accomplished, goals attained. Life on board the ship can be one of adventure, joy, fulfillment. But it is an illusion to think that the ship will someday arrive at a mythic island of paradise or absolute truth. The only truth we know is the truth we create as we sail the seas, and our earthly voyage is endless. This is why it should not surprise us, as it apparently did Wayne Meeks, that nineteen centuries have produced no agreement on the theological interpretation of Paul. Theology is a voyage without end, one that must be charted anew by each generation.

I have said that theology is a *constructive* activity. In the postmodern context the word "constructive" is a more appropriate adjective to describe the sort of activity that theology engages in than the words "systematic" or "dogmatic."[8] Without fully elaborating this point, it should be evident that every theological system is a *construct* that has the purpose of promoting coherence and wholeness in thinking critically and practically about the discourses of faith and their root experiences, the multifaceted revelation of God. It is not an account of that revelation as such. Systems are the work of theologians, not of God. We need systems to think about the interrelations of things, but it is easy to forget their limited, fragmentary, situation-dependent character. This is where the word "constructive" has certain advantages over "systematic." Etymologically it means arranging or piling things up that have been scattered or strewn about. To construe is to strew things together, to fashion a meaningful arrangement, to bring a semblance of order out of chaos. Moreover (as the etymology reminds us), what is strewn about and piled up is *straw*. Thomas Aquinas knew that everything produced by human beings is like straw, but he also knew that we *can* and *must* build things of it. Without the work of building, construing, constructing, we could not dwell humanly in the world. But we must not forget that in order to construct something new, something old must be deconstructed (namely the materials out of which the new is built), and that whatever we build is, in the words of Job, like "straw before the wind." An element of tragedy is present in every great construction, for it is fated to become, in Hegel's vivid image, "the ruins of excellence."

Constructive theology can be likened to a work of fiction or poetry. It is a product of human imagination whose subject matter is not an empirical object or a factual occurrence. Like good fiction and poetry, however, it is oriented to reality and is a construal of the real—a construal that highlights possibilities and perceptions, depths and dimensions hidden from ordinary experience but there nonetheless for those with eyes to see. The theologian "invents" but not simply out of his or her subjective fantasy. Rather the inventions are based on multiple resources ranging from ancient texts to communally shared experiences, and they elicit the root, radical dimension of these texts and experiences, namely a revelatory encounter with ultimate reality. Theological fiction has an experimental quality: one is invited to enter into its imaginative world, try out its construals, test and modify them in light of one's own experience. Good theology stands up against such tests: it proves its value, its veracity, in a community of discourse over space and time.

THEOLOGY AND THE "WORLD" OF BIBLICAL TEXTS

The division of labor that has come to characterize theological and religious studies can be understood in a hermeneutical rather than a disciplinary way. In my version of the critical praxis correlation,[9] both historical studies and the disciplines associated with the "science of religion" (sociological, psychological, linguistic, literary, comparativist) attend most directly to the texts and traditions by which the discourses of faith have been given expression, the first oriented more to their history over time, the second to their structural features. Practical or ministerial studies are most directly concerned with the appropriation, enactment, and practice of faith in the diversity of situations and locales in which believers find themselves. And constructive studies make the direct object of their concern neither the praxis of faith nor the texts of faith but the experience that gives rise to faith—a revelatory experience having as its source and referent God.

The primary thing I want to stress is the interdependence of these dimensions. In the case of biblical studies, which employs the methods of both history and the science of religion, the very purpose of the critical analysis and interpretation of texts, diachronically and synchronically, is to enable the experience to which those texts bore witness to become alive for us today, and this is accomplished by constructing distinctive narrative accounts of what has happened, or meaningful patterns of linguistic, literary, or social relationships. Thus biblical studies, like the human and social sciences in general, have an inherently practical and ethical dimension, which for the most part remains concealed. They are also based in one way or another on a worldview, a religious commitment, a theological construal of the meaning and truth of reality. Recent discussions in the philosophy of history have made the case that every work of historical interpretation entails a narrative construction that has both ethical implications and metahistorical roots.[10] A similar ethical and metascientific dimension is implicit in the use of science-of-religion methods.

In the case of practical studies, while application is paramount, interpretation is also requisite, and practical theology is not a direct practice but a theory of a practice. Practice is not simply the application of theory but theory's own originating and self-correcting foundation. Practice provides the preunderstandings, values, and criteria in terms of which critical theories are constructed. At the same time, theological theory is not a speculative flight of fancy but the foundation of practice in the sense of offering an interpretation or construction of the events that point to the ultimate source of all practice, namely God.

Finally, constructive theology has access to its distinctive subject matter, *theos,* not directly but only through the root experiences of faith as mediated by the discourses of faith. And its purpose is to let the revelatory event come to expression anew, issuing in redemptive transformations of the world in which we live. Thus constructive studies mediate between historical-scientific studies and practical-ministerial studies, drawing upon both and contributing to both; and in theological construction the critical and practical ways of thinking attain some kind of balance.

Because the concern of constructive theology is with the interpretation of revelatory experience expressed in the symbols of faith, its tendency is to reduce the multiplicity of the symbols and textual forms to an intelligible unity. It is seeking to develop doctrines or teachings on the basis of symbols, and moreover to order these doctrines into a coherent whole on the basis of a thematic focus furnished by the cultural and religious situation of a particular interest or time. Its quest is for unity and coherence, whereas the responsibility of the historian or sociologist is to display variety and disparity. The tensions between the two directions are both inevitable and fruitful. Constructive theologians must remember that their unity has the character of a construct, and historians must remember that sheer diversity is unintelligible. Each in fact relies upon the other. Theological constructs must have some sort of reality referent anchored in determinate historical traditions, and historical analysis takes on the character of a narrative construction. In brief, the boundaries between the disciplines are really crossing points, not barriers.

The time has come to bring theology out of the religious studies closet, argues Frank Reynolds,[11] and to recognize it as an integral component within the whole—a whole that is composed of *Religionswissenschaft* (theories of religion, methods of comparison, interpretations of religious experience), historical studies of particular traditions, and theological/ethical reflection. These three primary areas of study should have very porous boundaries, permitting a variety of interactions, and Reynolds believes that most faculty and students should have competence in at least two of them. Reynolds does not elaborate on what the distinctive contribution of theology and ethics to the whole might be, but a clue is provided by Edward Farley in the paper cited earlier: theological/ethical thinking contributes to "paideia," which is a "sense for truth and reality as they pertain to life in the everyday world." More specifically, education as paideia accomplishes three things in Farley's scenario: the mediation of "world-awareness" (a sense of truth, reality); the creation and maintenance of the "good society"; and the promotion of "thinking" as the response to a summons from a mysterious presence. Thinking, or what Hans-Georg Gadamer calls "truth," is clearly distinct from method even though it may and must avail itself of methodological procedures as part of its self-disciplining. It ought to occur not simply alongside the other arenas of religious studies but also *within* them, just as they ought to be internalized by it.

The implications of this sort of interpenetration, if carried through in a serious way, are large and complex. I want to explore just one aspect, namely what might be accomplished by reintroducing theological reflection into biblical studies. To do this, I shall elaborate on my earlier proposal that the theological meaning of a text does not reside behind it or in it, but in front of it. Theological meaning resides in an experience of truth or a way of being in the world that is shared by both text and interpreter, one that is always constituted anew in the act of interpretation, through what Gadamer calls a "fusion of horizons"—i.e. the horizons of text and interpreter.[12]

Paul Ricoeur has developed this Gadamerian insight and applied it to biblical hermeneutics in a particularly helpful way.[13] What Gadamer refers to as the *Sache* of the text, Ricoeur names "the world of the text," and he elaborates on the theological implications of this category in the following way. First, "it frees biblical hermeneutics from the temptation to introduce prematurely existential or existential categories of understanding"—which, we should recall, was Meeks's primary objection to Bultmann's biblical theology.

> The necessary stage between structural explanation and self-understanding is the unfolding of the world of the text; it is the latter that finally forms and transforms the reader's being-a-self in accordance with his or her intention. . . . The primary task of a hermeneutics is not to bring about a decision in the reader but first to allow the world of being that is the "thing" of the biblical text to unfold. In this way, above feelings, dispositions, belief, or unbelief is placed the proposal of a world, which, in the language of the Bible, is called a new world, a new covenant, the kingdom of God, a new birth. These are realities that unfold before the text, unfolding to be sure for us, but based on the text. This is what can be called the "objectivity" of the new being projected by the text.[14]

Second, by focusing on the world of the text, the problem of the inspiration and revelation of scripture is shifted to an entirely new ground. It is not a matter of "the insufflation to an author of a meaning that is projected in the text," such that it might be said that it is God who speaks, even dictates, the words of scripture. Rather, "the Bible is revealed to the extent that the new being that is in question is itself *revealing* with respect to the world, to all of reality, including my existence and my history. . . . Revelation . . . is a feature of the biblical *world*."[15]

Third, because what is involved in the new way of being that unfolds before the text is precisely a world, a global horizon, a totality of significations, it is inappropriate to privilege personal address or the I-thou aspect of divine-human relations.

> The biblical world has aspects that are cosmic (it is a creation), communal (it involves a people), historicocultural (it concerns Israel, the kingdom of God), as well as personal. Human beings are implicated in their varied dimensions—cosmological, historical, and worldly, as well as anthropological, ethical, and personalist.[16]

This has enormous implications for a theology that is revisioned in the postmodern context, with its ecological, political, socio-economic, psychological, sexual, ethnic, and dialogical concerns. A transformed way of being human in the world involves all these dimensions, and the new world imaged in the *basileia*, in "God's project,"[17] is that of a community of inclusive wholeness and mutuality of recognition in which all the established economies of domination are broken, overturned in principle.

Finally, the world of the biblical text, like that of any literary text, is "a projected world, one that is poetically distanced from everyday reality." Thus, the new being makes "its way through the world of ordinary experience, despite the closedness of this experience." Ordinary experience is not negated, as in certain gnostic visions, but transformed by the power of projection, which is able to make a break, a new beginning, in the midst of the old and familiar. The reality status of what is poetically envisioned is that of the *possible*.[18] The possible is not the illusory, a product of wishful thinking, nor is it the merely ideal in the sense of a mental fantasy; rather, it is the *real transfigured, fulfilled as to its possibilities so that it becomes actual*. This speaks to the desire of Meeks and other social historians to be involved in the "quest of something real." Theology engages the real just as much as sociology, but it is the poetically real, not the empirically real, with which it is concerned. Imagination is its principal cognitive tool, not science.

Perhaps the same can be said of theology's language about God. God does not appear as an empirical object anywhere in the biblical texts or human experience. Yet it is the power of God that constitutes the power of projection by which the new comes into being and the possible is envisioned. The being of God is that of poetic possibility rather than of prosaic reality. Using a Hegelian distinction, we might say that God is "actual" but not "real"—or better, that God encompasses the real within the divine actuality, which is the actuality of possibility. God can never be the *object* of predication but is rather the *power of new predication*. In this sense God "speaks" and "acts" in the Bible and is its sole "subject." I think Ricoeur is getting at something like this when he writes that

> the referent "God" is at once the coordination of these diverse [biblical] discourses and the vanishing point, the index of incompletion, of these partial discourses.... [It] gather[s] together all the significations produced by the partial discourses and open[s] up a horizon that escapes the closure of discourse.[19]

This means that God cannot be circumscribed by the hermeneutical circle of which we have been speaking, cannot be located at any one of its points, whether that of the fore-text, the text, or the context. Rather, God appears in their *interaction*—an interaction by which new meanings and new ways of being are unfolded—and thus God is a hermeneutical event. Invoking once again my sailing metaphor,[20] we could say that God is not on board the hermeneutical ship, but that God propels it, draws it forward, is the wind blowing into its sails. On most points of sail, the wind is ahead of the ship, pulling it forward through the vacuum—a negative force—generated on the leeward side of the sails. God is not an objectifiable, controllable object but blowing/living spiritual power, always ahead of theology, drawing and driving it. Yet without the ship of theology, the wind would not be "caught," its redemptive power would blow for nature but not for humans. Wind or moving air is the root metaphor present in the word "spirit," so to think of God as the wind blowing into the sails is to understand God as Spirit. Like the wind, the Spirit of God generates a mysterious, attracting-propelling power in the world. God's power is not predominantly that of a positive force. Rather, like a vacuum, it is the power of negation or emptiness, the power of powerlessness— which proves to be the greatest power of all. I believe this is one way of approximating the elusive mystery of Paul's theology, which is a theology of crucifixion and spiritual presence. Such is the power and wisdom of God, which is foolishness and weakness in the eyes of the world.

Yet the Pauline world, in all its complexity, is only one of many biblical worlds. It is appropriate that we should speak not simply of the "world" of the text but of "worlds": postmodernity reminds us of the pluralism that is present in the Bible as well as among ourselves. As I read the contributions to the first volume of *Reading from This Place* and prepared remarks for the closing session of the first conference, I was struck by both the diversity of readings and the makings of a fragile consensus. I asked the contributors: How do we know that the truth about human beings has something to do with freedom, justice, dignity, and mutual recognition rather than with hierarchy, patriarchy, and colonization?[21] Why do we surmise that reality is neither unitary nor a set of binary oppositions, neither monistic nor dualistic, but holistic?[22] What gives us the confidence to suggest that Sophia-God is an eros toward reconciliatory emancipation?[23] The biblical texts are certainly not unambiguously clear about these things, nor are our contexts. The texts are often more of a barrier than a help.[24] The predominant hegemonic culture is a severe barrier, and our localized contexts can all too easily fall into rivalry and self-serving agendas.[25] How does it come about that a plurality of readings from mostly marginalized, countercultural, and intercultural settings might be converging toward a broad consensus on these matters? I agree that reading from *multiple perspectives* is what is liberating.[26] That it should be so is astonishing—or perhaps it is the work and witness of the Spirit in our time, unfolding a new kind of world in which *we* can dwell.

NOTES

1. W. A. Meeks, "How My Mind Has Changed," Society of Biblical Literature, 20 November 1994 (unpublished paper).

2. E. Farley, "Re-Thinking Graduate Theological Education," unpublished paper for the Auburn Center Working Group on Theological Doctoral Study, 1994.

3. Vincent Wimbush raised a similar question at the first of the "Reading from This Place" conferences (January 22–24, 1993): "*Why* do we read biblical texts at all?" See his "Reading Texts as Reading Ourselves: A Chapter in the History of African-American Biblical Interpretation," in *Reading from This Place.* Volume 1: *Social Location and Biblical Interpretation in the United States*, ed. F. F. Segovia and M. A. Tolbert (Minneapolis: Fortress Press, 1995), 95–108.

4. See n. 2 above. See also E. Farley, *Theologia: The Fragmentation and Unity of Theological Education* (Philadelphia: Fortress Press, 1983).

5. See my *Winds of the Spirit: A Constructive Christian Theology* (Louisville: Westminster/John Knox Press, 1994), 10–16. Here and elsewhere in this essay I have drawn on material from this book in revised form.

6. The concept of "root experiences" derives from Emil Fackenheim, who regards Auschwitz as a root experience of modern Judaism, posing in a radical way the command not to deny the God of Israel in face of the Holocaust. See *God's Presence in History: Jewish Affirmations and Philosophical Reflections* (New York: New York University Press, 1970). Increasingly Auschwitz is being recognized as a root experience of post-modernity as such.

7. Hodgson, *Winds of the Spirit*, 13.

8. Ibid., 38–41.

9. Ibid., 31–36.

10. See H. White, *Metahistory: The Historical Imagination in Nineteenth Century Europe* (Baltimore: Johns Hopkins University Press, 1973), chap. 1.

11. F. E. Reynolds, "Theology, Religious Studies and the Challenge of Religious Pluralism," unpublished paper presented at Vanderbilt University, November 1991, and discussed by the Auburn Center working group on the future of doctoral theological studies in 1994.

12. H.-G. Gadamer, *Truth and Method*, 2nd ed., trans. rev. by Joel Weinsheimer and Donald G. Marshall (New York: Crossroad, 1989), 265–324, 341–79.

13. The theme is found in a number of Ricoeur's essays. I am drawing on "Philosophical Hermeneutics and Biblical Hermeneutics," in *From Text to Action: Essays in Hermeneutics, II*, trans. Kathleen Blamey and John B. Thompson (Evanston: Northwestern University Press, 1991), 89–101.

14. Ibid., 95–96.

15. Ibid., 96.

16. Ibid., 96.

17. For this expression, see S. H. Ringe, "Solidarity and Contextuality: Readings of Matthew 18:21–35," *Reading from This Place*, 209.

18. Ricoeur, *From Text to Action*, 96–97.

19. Ibid., 97–98.

20. Hodgson, *Winds of the Spirit*, 36.

21. This was a common theme in the contributions of Justo González, Chan-Hie Kim, Sharon Ringe, Abraham Smith, Norman Gottwald, Ada María Isasi-Díaz, Fernando Segovia, and Vincent Wimbush to the conference discussion. See their respective papers in the first volume of *Reading from This Place*.

22. Mary Ann Tolbert emphasized this in the conference discussion as well as in her paper, "Reading for Liberation," and "Afterwords: The Politics and Poetics of Location," *Reading from This Place*, 263–76 and 305–17, respectively.

23. See the essay by Antoinette Clark Wire, "The God of Jesus in the Gospel Sayings Source," *Reading from This Place*, 277–303.

24. This was pointed out in the essays and conference discussion by Amy-Jill Levine, Randall Bailey, Tina Pippin, and Mary Ann Tolbert.

25. Thus Levine.

26. Thus Tolbert.

3

GLOBALIZATION IN
THEOLOGICAL EDUCATION

Joseph C. Hough, Jr.

Globalization in theological education has been a theme in the discussions sponsored by the Association of Theological Schools (ATS) for more than a decade now. In 1980 at its biennial meeting, the ATS scheduled an open and intensive examination of a series of new challenges to theological education. The discussions were meant to determine what, if any, course of action was required by the association and its member schools. After vigorous debate about the sorts of issues that needed to be addressed and the terminology that should be used to describe the changes in question, agreement was reached to appoint a special committee to define the issues represented by the "globalization" of theological education and to make further recommendations for action by the ATS.

This committee, headed by Donald Shriver of Union Theological Seminary in New York, deliberated for about six years. In 1986, at the recommendation of the Shriver Committee, the ATS formed a Task Force on Globalization charged to prepare theological schools for a "decade of globalization" during the 1990s. Under the leadership of William E. Lesher and Robert J. Schreiter, the task force set about its agenda with a sense of urgency. Between 1990 and 1994, some of the most creative persons in theological education were commissioned to do papers in an effort to clarify both conceptual issues and the very practical issues of the changes in curriculum, faculties, and constituencies needed to meet the challenges posed by the congeries of forces impinging on theological education. The fruits of these efforts have been made available to all member schools of the ATS in five special issues of its journal, *Theological Education.*[1]

CONTEXT AND IMPACT OF GLOBALIZATION

These actions by the ATS are, at least in part, responses to the broader changes that are transforming the intellectual, political, and economic life of the entire world. For example, it is almost a cliché these days to refer to the rapid globalization of economic life. The capacity for rapid movement of capital; the accel-

erating transfer of manufacturing bases from locations within the earlier industrialized nations to the newly industrializing nations; the transformation of corporations from national firms to worldwide conglomerates—all of these
developments and hundreds of others are indicative of the growing economic
interdependence of most of the nations of the world. According to John Cobb,
these changes also signal the end of the political and economic hegemony of the
Western nations. Although there has never been a time when the nations of the
West seemed to be more powerful than now, Japan and China as well as a number of smaller Asian nations are emerging as significant political and economic
players on the global scene, while the poorer nations of the world's Southern
Hemisphere are beginning to claim a larger share of the manufacturing base,
the wealth, and the associated political power formerly situated in the West.[2]

Politically, not only is the relative balance of power between nations shifting at a rapid pace, but major changes have also taken place in the relative
power of minorities and women within the United States and many of the
other Western democracies. A growing body of national and local legislation
has struck down legal barriers to voting, employment, housing, and education
based on race and gender. While no one claims that racial and gender equality
has been achieved, significant gains have been made, and those gains are being
reflected in the visibility of both minorities and women in all areas of political
and economic life.

The changes presently shaping intellectual life in the universities and in the
broader culture as well are usually referred to as "postmodernism." Included
in the notion of the postmodern is the existence of diverse perspectives on literature, art, architecture, and philosophy; but for some writers the sweep of
postmodernism is much broader. A number of challenges to the range of conceptual tools developed during the Enlightenment have emerged during the
last century. The first signal that major changes in the conceptual apparatus of
Western thought were in the offing was the collapse of support for Newtonian
physics. Gradually, it became apparent that the existing conceptual basis for
physics that had prevailed since Isaac Newton simply no longer provided a
coherent view of the universe.[3] These persisting challenges to Enlightenment
thinking have developed over time and have converged with developments in
anthropology, linguistic studies, literary criticism, art, and religion. At the
close of the twentieth century, it is obvious to most sensitive observers that
this convergence will require new ways of thinking about ourselves, our
world, and our culture. What is most obvious about the postmodern perspective is its challenge to the universalism and rationalism of the Enlightenment.
As Peter Hodgson has said, it is now clear that "thought and perception are
more radically conditioned by perspective, circumstances, and interests" than
we had previously supposed.[4]

In light of this broad intellectual ferment, it is hardly surprising that theological discourse has been undergoing some rather significant changes as well.
The philosophical wars between the pragmatists and the foundationalists have
spilled over into theological dialogue. Does our thought about God correspond to the reality of God, or do we speak of the truth about God in what

Sallie McFague has called "metaphorical" terms, or what Richard Rorty has called "ethnocentric" terms? In other words, is any language or human mental construct capable of describing the reality of God in terms not bound by time and culture? If not, what does it mean to claim that one's description of the reality of God is true in any universal sense?[5]

Equally important are the perspectives of new participants in the discourse on belief and practice in the Christian traditions. Many of these new voices are from countries outside Europe and North America, and they enter theological discussions informed not only by traditional Christianity but also deeply sensitive to the economic, social, and political realities of their particular contexts. They bring to the discussion of theology the insistence that social location in the broadest sense of that term is highly determinative in all interpretations of texts and events. These new voices are joined by other new voices who have been speaking from the margins of the Euro-American theological discussions, given the fact that there had been little audience for persons of their race or gender. Together they bring to the table of theological discussion a wide range of questions about theology and culture, questions that must be probed with new approaches to knowledge and in concert with academic conversation partners in the social sciences, anthropology, social history, literary criticism, and cultural criticism.

Significant changes have been occurring as well in the church constituencies from which are drawn the students and the financial support of most of the theological schools in the United States and Canada. From episcopal and other forms of ecclesiastical leadership to national denominational staffing to leadership in local congregations, minorities and women are increasingly visible and vocal in all aspects of institutional life. The World Council of Churches (WCC), supported by most of the so-called "old line" Protestant denominations in the United States and Canada, has been heavily influenced by "Third World" church leaders and theologians. As a result, the WCC has shifted much of its attention from doctrinal issues to the theological implications of major economic and political issues that complicate the relationships between the richer nations and the poorer nations. Specifically, the WCC has focused on political equality, both in terms of rights and participation; economic equality, at least in terms of access to basic necessities such as food, shelter, education, and health; and racial justice. In the Roman Catholic churches, recent papal encyclicals have reinforced the concern of the Church with economic justice and human rights. In the United States, the Roman Catholic bishops have repeatedly made clear their commitments to economic justice and peace, and their pastoral letter on economics became a significant contribution to the ongoing debate on economic justice in the United States. Their work was built partly on the groundbreaking work of the Latin American bishops who, in 1968 at a conference in Medellín, Colombia, made clear the Church's "preferential option for the poor," arguing theologically that God's action in history reflected God's interest in the plight of the poor and God's responding to the call of the poor for justice.

The combined impact of this wide-ranging change in our cultural situation became most evident at a national convocation of divinity school and seminary leaders called together by the ATS in 1984 to discuss emerging issues in theological education. Following on a series of regional forums in the early 1980s, the convocation was designed to initiate conversation on the future of theological education in light of the significant changes in the intellectual and cultural contexts of theological discussion. More than two hundred deans, presidents, and faculty members—both Catholic and Protestant, from all over the United States and Canada—met in small groups charged with identifying the most serious concerns pressing on the schools in the United States and Canada. Among the hundreds of concerns that surfaced during the three days of discussion, the one issue that dominated the discussion was that of "pluralism" in theological education. In retrospect, it was not difficult to see that "pluralism," as it was discussed at the conference, represented a cluster of concerns similar to those that had surfaced earlier in the discussions on globalization.

Moreover, there was considerable concern in the minds of many of the leaders present that the trends gathered under the rubric of "pluralism" might have high potential for conflict and fragmentation in the schools they represented. For example, pluralism, understood as the combination of the new gender diversity, age diversity, and ethnic diversity present in theological schools, tended to raise critical questions about the adequacy of traditional theological curricula for a changing student population and new constituencies.

Pluralism also referred to the emergence in theological studies of the various contextual approaches that seemed to challenge traditional approaches to theology and ethics. Particular attention was given to the work of liberation theologians and feminist theologians who joined in their insistence that theological thinking must begin with an analysis of historical, cultural, and economic contexts as the beginning point of theological reflection.

The concern about pluralism further reflected the concerns about the relationship of Christianity to other great living religious traditions. Large-scale migrations have placed actual congregations of believers from the great religious traditions in close proximity to each other. This has made the issue of religious pluralism both urgent and practical. Obviously, the position one takes on religious pluralism could shape one's views about revelation, incarnation, the authority of the scriptures, and the nature of the church. Beliefs about these matters in turn shape the practices of worship, education, evangelism, spiritual formation, and mission. In other words, what was seen to be at stake in the discussion of theology and religious pluralism was the nature and purpose of theological education.

From the discussions in the ATS, it has become clear that the call for globalization does not signify any attempt to move in the direction of any single approach to theological thinking or pedagogy in theological education. Quite the contrary, the discussions of globalization have tended to suggest that the changes being experienced in the churches and the theological schools indicate that a variety of approaches are necessary for the overall health and effectiveness of North American theological education. Still, globalization represents a common challenge that requires a significant response from all the theological schools in the Northern Hemisphere. As one participant in a recent joint ATS-WCC discussion put it, "For those of us in the South, theological education needs to be transformed by indigenization. For those of you in the North, theological education needs to be transformed by globalization." The central focus on globalization in the ATS, then, signifies a growing consensus among faculty and other leaders that a cluster of important challenges to traditional theological thinking should be given serious attention in all the theological schools of the United States and Canada.

CHALLENGES OF GLOBALIZATION

What are the challenges contained in the call for the globalization of theological education? I would mention the following three: (1) the contextualization of theological thinking; (2) the call for a change in Christian theological perspectives on other religions; and (3) the overcoming of anthropocentrism in theological thinking.

Contextualization of Theological Thinking

Globalization signifies, first of all, the contextualization of theological thinking: theological thinking about what it means to be a Christian in the world can no longer be framed in any sort of normative universal terms. Being a Christian in the world means living as a faithful Christian in a concrete world-historical situation of particular cultures, languages, and socio-economic conditions. Most of the voices urging the necessity for contextualization of theology have been those of individuals whose perspectives have been excluded from the table of conversation in theology until recently.

For example, in 1968 James Cone began to argue that one really cannot do theology in the context of the United States without careful attention to the pervasive presence of racism in American culture. The racism that one finds entrenched in the major institutions of the society and manifest in the attitudes of individuals in the society makes it necessary to begin the conversation about sin, repentance, suffering, and other significant themes of the Christian drama with an analysis of the way in which racism limits possibilities, creates estrangement, and causes suffering and death to fall disproportionately on relatively powerless minorities. What is more, the long-term effects of racism on the self-understanding of black Americans must be countered by a theological approach that will give them a new sense of their worth and dignity.[6] Black theology was the attempt to provide a theological perspective that would empower African Americans to affirm their own worth in spite of the continuing effects of racist ideology and oppression, while at the same time calling white Americans to repentance and efforts to change the cultural practices in which racism continues to flourish.

In a similar fashion, the Latin American theologian Gustavo Gutiérrez insisted that the analysis of economic oppression must be the beginning point for theology.[7] This is true because God acts in history in such a way as to bring liberation to the poor. Therefore, the encounter with God is possible only in the context of doing justice to the poor. To speak of redemption solely in terms of the spirit is no longer sufficient. To be sure, Christian theology must be a theology of hope, but that hope must be a concrete hope that God is on the side of the poor, that the suffering of the poor will be relieved by the action of God in history to overcome the ravages of generations of poverty and the human ills that always attend vast disparities in the distribution of economic goods. Such a theology will provide genuine hope for the poor as it calls the rich and powerful to repentance for their sins of domination and exploitation. Moreover, it is not primarily individual sin that is addressed in liberation theology. Reminiscent of Walter Rauschenbusch, liberation theology keeps its focus on the sin of oppressive structures and institutions that sustain patterns of dominance and exploitation over time. In other words, theological thinking about the action of God in history must address the concrete sociopolitical realities of the existence of the poor, if it is to break the hold of sin on our common historical existence and bring redemption to the lives of poor people everywhere.

Conversations between North American black theologians and liberation theologians from Latin America began to occur in the 1970s. Later these conversations expanded to include liberation theologians from other parts of the world, especially Asia and Africa, so that now an organized international conversation among theologians interested in the social and political context of all theological discourse is proceeding under the direction of the Ecumenical Association of Third World Theologians, a growing group of theologians committed to developing a body of literature that takes seriously the analysis of the structures and ideologies of oppression and domination no matter what their form or context.[8]

During the same period, feminist theologians in the United States insisted that, from their perspective, the persisting problem of patriarchy had to be addressed concretely by any theology that was to have redemptive significance for women. As Elizabeth Johnson has recently pointed out, the traditional ways of speaking about God "developed within a framework that does not prize the unique and equal humanity of women and bears the marks of partiality and dominance."[9] It is not enough to "feminize" a male God by describing God as relational, nurturing, and vulnerable (characteristics usually referred to as feminine). There is more at stake. So long as God is symbolized linguistically and artistically as male, women are excluded from the image of God, that venerable theological notion that forms the basis for the idea of equality in religious and political thought in the West. Moreover, such male-oriented theological symbolism does not acknowledge the experience of all faithful Christians, nor can it give an account of the full complexity of reality.[10]

It is in this context that the work represented in the first two volumes of *Reading from This Place* is best understood.[11] Drawing deeply both from the new wave of literary and cultural criticism[12] and the insights of feminist and liberation theologies, the new approaches to biblical interpretation represented in these two volumes call attention to several important matters. Of central importance is the insistence that the interpretation of a particular text is conditioned by the social location and historical experience of the interpreter. Therefore, investigations that make manifest what the interpreter brings to the text, the contemporary social and historical context of the reading of the text, and the common cultural backgrounds that shape the understanding of language and symbols for the hearers are of central importance to the new criticism. Thus, cultural analysis is as important, if not more important, than traditional historical criticism for the understanding of both the history of biblical interpretation and contemporary interpretations.[13]

Implied in this focus on cultural analysis is yet another important emphasis. The interpretation of a text, while requiring the work of scientific scholarship, must give an account of how the text might be heard by those communities to whom it is addressed. As Robert Schreiter has pointed out, the theology emerging from previously silent or ignored voices is engaging more than professional theologians. Much the same is true of the new biblical interpretation. For example, the theology that emerged from the "base communities" of Latin America involved a fresh reading of the Scriptures by a community of persons deeply involved in the search for guidance in faithful practice for their concrete situation. The texts took on a powerful prophetic "meaning" for them at their place and in their time.[14] Thus, their reading of a biblical text always led to reflection on what it meant to be a Christian in the world. In their model, then, the reading of a text is always one more movement in the ongoing process of theologizing by a faithful community seeking to hear the word of truth for them and to do what they are called to do.

In this sense, biblical texts, like all other literary constructions, take on a life of their own. The "meaning" of a text is never static or final. Rather it is a dynamic historical process. As Robert Neville has pointed out, there have always been significantly different theological traditions in Christianity because all traditions reflect the time and place of their birth. He states, "They are formulated to sustain the faith of their communities and to witness to particular 'mission fields.'"[15] What is new in the globalization discussion is the emergence of a strong demand for respect for theological offerings being made by new parties to the discussions, parties that have long been marginal to the Euro-American discussion. In fact, this has been the major focus of much of the discussion generated by the ATS.

Theological Perspectives on Other Religions

A second meaning of globalization in theological education, closely related to contextualization, is the call for a change in Christian theological perspectives on other religions. In the past, Christians have understood other major world religions primarily in one of two ways. On the one hand, other religions have been viewed by Christian theologians as pagan religions encountered during the missionary expansion of Christianity, and thus as religions to be overcome by conversion to the true religion of Christianity. On the other hand, other religions have at best been understood by Christian theologians as inferior religions that have some legitimacy in certain places and certain times but that are certainly not as advanced in their understanding of religiousness or faith as Christianity.

Over against these traditional postures toward other world religions, globalization means that Christians are capable of acknowledging that God is active in the world in other cultures than our own, that there is great value in the religions developed apart from the West. It means further that Christians are willing to hear what representatives of other religions have to say about the human condition and to be deeply affected by them. Globalization in this sense does not mean that Christians become less Christian at all. Christ remains decisive for the Christian story, but it is possible to have a genuinely Christian theology and yet not find it necessary to claim that Christians have a monopoly on religious truth. Globalization also implies that deep Christian convictions can be enriched by conversation with devout persons who come from other religious traditions.[16] In this sense, globalization is a movement from disdain and hostility toward other great world religions to a posture of respect and a strategy of engagement and dialogue.

A special case of the movement toward globalization is the call for a new understanding of Jewish-Christian relations. The reality of Judaism has always been a major problem in the development of Christian theology. Over time, the dominant attitude of Christians toward Jews has been an outright hostility that has created a history of religious persecution and forced conversions. That history culminated in the horrors of the Holocaust in Europe, an event that forms the persistent and enduring context of any serious theological reflection. That event in itself, according to Paul Van Buren, elevates the problem of Jewish-Christian relations to a position of fundamental importance in Christian theological discussions and dialogue. Specifically, the event of the Holocaust requires nothing less than a total reconstruction of Christian theology for the future. Until that reconstruction is undertaken, the future of Christian theology is highly problematic.[17] In this special case, then, not only is there a movement from disdain and hostility to respect but also a claim that a renewed understanding of the relationship between Christianity and Judaism, including a critique of the anti-Judaism of Christianity's most basic texts, is essential for the future integrity of Christian theology itself.

Overcoming Anthropocentrism in Theological Thinking

A third meaning of globalization is the overcoming of anthropocentrism in theological thinking. Anthropocentrism in general has been described by David Ehrenfeld as a certain kind of humanism characterized by the assumption that human intelligence is capable of rearranging the world of nature and society so that human life will prosper over time.[18] Theological anthropocentrism adds to this the belief that all of nature has been arranged by God in order to benefit humanity. It is there to provide the inexhaustible necessities of life and the raw material for human well-being. Thus, while God's action in creating the world of nature is important as a backdrop, the arena of human redemption is history. This belief, reinforced by the focus on historical redemption in the Hebrew scriptures and the incredible successes in the development of technology, led to a marriage of Christian messianism and the idea of progress that has dominated much of Western thought during the last two centuries.

This uneasy marriage, however, has been brought up short by the growing realization that the successes of technology have their price. The harnessing of nuclear power in weapons of destruction and the environmental crises together have made clear certain contrary realities and bred a certain uneasiness about the future that had not been characteristic of Western thought for several centuries. As a result, we have become deeply aware of the contingency of history, even the possibility of an end to human history by a nuclear war.[19] We have also come to see that we are totally dependent for life on the continuing health of our natural world and that our fate is conditioned by the possibilities and the increasingly visible limits of that world. In light of this new vision of the interdependence of life and the contingency of human history, what Sallie McFague has called a "new planetary agenda" is shaping theological reflection and human understanding in general. This new agenda

> involves everything and everyone. It involves everything because we now know that all things, all beings and processes on the planet, are interrelated, and that the well-being of each is connected to the well-being of the whole. The planetary agenda calls us to do something unprecedented—to think about "everything that is."[20]

History and nature are no longer separable in the drama of redemption, and the fate of the natural world is our fate as well. This new consciousness not only affects our understanding of human responsibility to God for the integrity of the natural world, but it also requires a new understanding of God's liberating work in all of natural life.[21] Obviously this new agenda brings to the table of theological discussion strong objections to any focus on globalization that pays attention only to social, political, and cultural change. In light of the fact that social and political analysis is so central to the globalization discussion, it is somewhat surprising that there is little mention of this aspect of the globalization of theology in the ATS literature. Its virtual absence from the globalization discussion is all the more surprising because it has been a major theme in recent theological discussions.

REACTIONS TO GLOBALIZATION

All of these movements toward globalization together have created a major challenge for the theological discussion in the churches and in the theological schools, and it is not surprising that a number of different responses have been generated from more traditional theologians.

On the one side, there are those, like Thomas Oden, who believe that the growing diversity in theological discussions is itself a major theological problem—the product of a bankrupt liberalism that has taken the project of toleration and inclusion to such extremes that no agreed-upon core of Christian theology remains.[22] What we have left, Oden argues, is a hopeless cacophony of voices professing subjective theological opinions having no foundation in or connection with the core traditions of Christian faith. Most practicing Christians, Oden believes, find this situation confusing and destructive of faith. Oden's proposal is to develop a "postmodern evangelical spirituality," a form of Christian practice grounded in the doctrinal consensus of the first five centuries of Christian history. Rejecting the methods of modern theological study, he has turned to selected evangelicals and to Eastern Orthodox communions— communities of faith that, in his view, reflect the early Christian ecumenical consensus on the Trinity, the authority of scripture, the bodily resurrection of Jesus Christ, and salvation only in Jesus Christ. Oden critiques a range of other postmodern proposals and roundly condemns the "exclusive-inclusiveness" of many postmodern theologians who have pioneered the work of globalization.[23]

In contrast, Peter Hodgson has described the combined forces of globalization as nothing less than a challenge to the entire Christian movement to continue "to speak meaningfully of God's presence and action in the world." He states,

> The presence of the transcendent God, who seems to be excluded from the modern one-dimensional, secular, closed world, may freshly appear in the liberation of the victims of history, or in the redemption of nature, or in the encounter of religions. The location of theology has shifted. Where is God? we ask. Look to the underside of history and the emancipatory struggles of oppressed peoples everywhere. Or look to the ecological quest for the wholeness and integrity of life. Or to the dialogical creation of common though shaky ground in the midst of cultural and religious differences.[24]

This sort of response to the new situation signaled by globalization is characteristic of many, perhaps most, of the theological faculties in the United States and Canada as well as the leadership of most of the mainline Protestant Christian denominations. Among these groups, it is widely agreed that it is no longer possible to do an adequate job of theological education without serious attention to all the major themes of globalization.

Yet, even though globalization does signal profound changes in our approach to knowledge and knowing, it is not at all clear that the discontinuities with the thinking of the past two centuries mean that we are suddenly at the point of denying all the methods and tenets of rational modernist thought. As Stephen Toulmin has pointed out in his essay on conceptual change, shifts in human understanding are not nearly so dramatic as Thomas Kuhn believed. There are, indeed, moments when discontinuities are far more obvious than continuities, but the process of change is more evolutionary than revolutionary.[25]

"Globalization," then, does indicate a significant conceptual change, but it does not deny much of the heritage of the modern period. Nor does the emphasis on globalization mean that the curricula of theological schools will, as Oden suggests they now do, ignore the study of past traditions. If anything, globalization will require more attention to past traditions as scholars attempt not only to transmit the traditions but also to understand them more fully within their social and historical contexts.

That the gospel is being spoken in new ways should come as no surprise to faithful Christians. The earliest traditions have taught us that the truth of God in Jesus Christ is spoken and heard in different ways at different times. If those words are to be efficacious, they must be heard in ways that can alter the experience of the hearers and open their eyes to authentic Christian practice *for them*. No single tradition will be adequate to the task of ministry in the next century, and it is not likely that common ground across theological divisions and denominational differences will be found for theological education or ministry. Still, it is urgent for the future of the church that the conversation about the future of theology and ministry in light of globalization continue to take place in seminaries and churches. It has been and will continue to be a painful conversation, but, in a spirit of hope and in spite of the sharpness of our differences, it can be carried on with grace and mutual respect.

NOTES

1. *Theological Education* 26 Supplement 1 (Spring 1990); 27 (Spring 1991); 29 (Spring 1993); 30 Supplement 1 (Autumn 1993); 30 Supplement 2 (Spring 1994). Mark Heim has provided a most helpful interpretive article in which he outlines the complexities and richness of the issues involved in the globalization discussions ("Mapping Globalization for Theological Education," *Theological Education* Supplement 1 [1990] 7-34).

2. John B. Cobb, Jr., "Revisioning Ministry for a Revisioned Church," unpublished lecture presented to a national conference on the future of ministry convened at Vanderbilt University in February, 1992. See also Peter C. Hodgson, who draws from Cobb in his excellent discussion of these matters (*Winds of the Spirit: A Constructive Christian Theology* [Louisville: Westminster/John Knox, 1994] 53-61).

3. Cobb, "Revisioning Ministry."

4. Hodgson, *Winds of the Spirit*, 56.

5. There is an interesting discussion of this problem of religious discourse in Richard J. Mouw and Sander Griffioen, *Pluralisms & Horizons* (Grand Rapids: William B. Eerdmans, 1993).

6. J. Cone, *Black Theology and Black Power* (New York: Seabury, 1969). Cone addressed these issues more fully and related his thought to the wider liberation discussion in his *God of the Oppressed* (New York: Seabury, 1975).

7. G. Gutiérrez, *A Theology of Liberation: History, Politics and Salvation* (15th Anniversary edition; Maryknoll: Orbis Books, 1973). First published in Spanish in 1971.

8. See Virginia Fabella and Sergio Torres, eds., *Doing Theology in a Divided World* (Maryknoll: Orbis Books, 1985), for a report on these conversations.

9. E. Johnson, *She Who Is: The Mystery of God in Feminist Theological Discourse* (New York: Crossroad, 1992) 15.

10. See my review essay, "Future Pastors, Future Church: The Seminary Quarrels," *The Christian Century* 112 (1995) 564-67, esp. 564-65.

11. See Fernando F. Segovia and Mary Ann Tolbert, eds., *Reading from This Place*. Volume 1: *Social Location and Biblical Interpretation in the United States* (Minneapolis: Fortress Press, 1995) and *Reading from This Place*. Volume 2: *Social Location and Biblical Interpretation in Global Perspective* (Minneapolis: Fortress Press, 1995).

12. For an introduction to literary theory, see Terry Eagleton, *Literary Theory* (Minneapolis: University of Minnesota, 1983). Jay Clayton's *The Pleasures of Babel: Contemporary American Literature and Theory* (Oxford and New York: Oxford University Press, 1993) is especially helpful in understanding the developments in literary criticism within the context of U.S. literary discussions.

13. For an overview of recent developments in the methodology of biblical interpretation, see Fernando F. Segovia, "'And They Began to Speak in Other Tongues': Competing Modes of Discourse in Contemporary Biblical Criticism," *Reading from This Place*, 1:1-32.

14. R. Schreiter, *Constructing Local Theologies* (Maryknoll: Orbis Books, 1985).

15. R. Neville, "Truth and Tradition," *Truth and Tradition: A Conversation about the Future of United Methodist Theological Education,* ed. Neal Fisher (Nashville: Abingdon Press, 1995) 37- 58.

16. For a full discussion of the theological issues raised by religious pluralism, see Alan Race, *Christians and Religious Pluralism* (London: SCM Press, 1983).

17. P. Van Buren, *A Theology of the Jewish-Christian Reality,* 3 vols. (San Francisco: Harper & Row, 1980-1988). See also John Pawlikowski, *Christ in the Light of the Christian Jewish Dialogue* (New York: Paulist Press, 1982); and Rosemary Radford Ruether, *Faith and Fratricide: The Theological Roots of Anti-Semitism* (New York: Seabury, 1974).

18. D. Ehrenfeld, *The Arrogance of Humanism* (Oxford and New York: Oxford University Press, 1978) 5-6.

19. For an analysis of the change in theological thinking brought about primarily by the loss of optimism in the West, see my article, "The Loss of Optimism as a Problem for Liberal Christian Faith," *Liberal Protestantism: Realities and Possibilities,* ed. Robert S. Michaelsen and Wade Clark Roof (New York: Pilgrim, 1986) 5-22.

20. S. McFague, *The Body of God: An Ecological Theology* (Minneapolis: Fortress Press, 1993) 8.

21. Charles Birch and John B. Cobb, Jr., *The Liberation of Life: From the Cell to the Community* (Cambridge: Cambridge University Press, 1981).

22. See further my review article, "Future Pastors, Future Church."

23. T. Oden, *Requiem: A Lament in Three Movements* (Nashville: Abingdon Press, 1995). Oden is by no means the sole representative of this point of view. He makes his own list of what he labels "Postmodern Paleo-orthodox Writers" who share his views. He also commends Asbury Seminary and Duke Divinity School as institutional strongholds of this view.

24. Hodgson, *Winds of the Spirit,* 65-66.

25. S. Toulmin, *Human Understanding* (Princeton: Princeton University Press, 1972) 98-117. The reference in Toulmin's discussion is to Thomas Kuhn, *The Structure of Scientific Revolutions* (Chicago: University of Chicago Press, 1970).

4

JESUS/THE NATIVE

Biblical Studies from a Postcolonial Perspective

Kwok Pui-lan

> Why are we so fascinated with "history" and with the "native" in modern times? What do we gain from our labor on these "endangered authenticities" which are presumed to be from a different time and a different place? What can be said about the juxtaposition of "us" (our discourse) and "them"? What kind of *surplus value* is created by this juxtaposition?　　　　—Rey Chow[1]

> New Testament survey books tell us that the first quest for the historical Jesus took place in the nineteenth century. But they do not specify that the quest took place in Europe and there were in fact two quests, not one: the quest for Jesus and the quest for land and people to conquer. Is it mere coincidence that the newest quest for the historical Jesus is taking place in the United States, when the U.S. is trying to create a Pax Americana?　　　　—Kwok Pui-lan[2]

Why are there so few racial and ethnic minority scholars in the field of biblical studies in the United States? African-American churches love the Bible, but there are only about twenty-five African-American scholars teaching the Bible in the country. The number of Asian and Asian-American scholars is fewer than ten, while the numbers for both Hispanic- and Native-American scholars are even smaller. What can this tell us about the training of biblical studies in general and about the perpetuation of eurocentrism in the discipline in particular?

The situation is such that for several years now the Committee on Underrepresented Racial and Ethnic Minority Persons in the Profession within the Society of Biblical Literature (SBL) has concerned itself with the training of the future generation of biblical scholars. Indeed, plans have been made for a series of ongoing recruitment conferences to introduce the discipline to college students as well as seminarians as a way of encouraging them to pursue a career in biblical studies. Moreover, within the context of the SBL Annual Meeting programs, African-American scholars have organized the African American Theology and Biblical Hermeneutics Group, while Asian and Asian-American scholars have formed the Asian and Asian-American Biblical

Studies Consultation, providing thereby an alternative space for the discussion of their own respective issues.

Still, one can point to many institutional barriers that serve to keep racial and ethnic minorities from entering the profession: the financial burden of a lengthy graduate program; the requirement of having to learn a variety of languages; the lack of role models and sympathetic mentors; the predominantly white and middle-class framework of most theological schools; the pressures of being one of a few minorities in a doctoral program; and the uncertainty of the job market after so many years of training. However, the major obstacle to attracting minorities to the profession, I would submit, has to do with the eurocentric assumptions, methodologies, pedagogical practices, ethos, hiring practices, and standards of excellence at work in the discipline.

In this article I begin by discussing the alienation that racial and ethnic students face in studying the Bible in seminaries and divinity schools in the United States, insofar as the study of the Bible has always been embedded in the larger cultural matrix and political ethos of the time. Then, with the quest for the historical Jesus as an example, a dominant concern of historical criticism, I proceed to elucidate the eurocentric assumptions at work in shaping the method of inquiry, defining the questions asked, and suppressing other pursuits as unscientific. From a postcolonial perspective, I argue that the study of Jesus in the nineteenth century was much influenced by the empire-building ethos of Europe and the projection of the "natives" in European consciousness. Indeed, under the rubric of objectivity and scientific inquiry, a kind of "epistemic violence," as described by Gayatri Chakravorty Spivak, was maintained.[3] Finally, I conclude by discussing how the "natives" can proceed to study the Bible in our postcolonial world. I should like to point out in this regard that I use the term "natives" in this study to refer to the eurocentric construction of the peoples conquered or colonized by Europe; as such, I recognize that aboriginal peoples may have other positive constructions of nativeness in their struggle for cultural survival and autonomy.[4]

As someone whose primary training is not in the field of biblical studies, I do not have firsthand experience regarding the process of socialization or certification operative within the discipline. In fact, we have very little public knowledge of the struggles, survival strategies, and coping mechanisms of minority students who have gone through the process, since few scholars are established enough and feel safe enough to make them known. However, as someone who has been interested in the study of the Bible for a long time, I enjoy the privilege of looking at the discipline from the outside and thus from a certain distance. It is my hope that the observations that follow prove to be of help to those who are already in the field as well as to those who would like to join its ranks.

IN OTHER WORLDS:
SETTING FOOT IN BIBLICAL STUDIES

John is a young African-American male from an urban church in San Francisco. His pastor is a dynamic community leader who has struggled for racial justice and has stood up for the oppressed. John was inspired by his powerful sermons and his feisty ways of bringing the Bible alive to address the issues of the day. He decided to go to seminary in order to become a minister and to serve his own people. In seminary he quickly found out that the approach of his teachers to the Bible was markedly different from that of his pastor. When he wanted to discuss how the Bible was used in his church, his teachers and classmates expressed little interest; they regarded the information as irrelevant, adding little of note to the biblical passage under consideration.[5]

Soon Young came to the United States from Korea when she was a child. She grew up in a Korean-American church in a suburb of New York. As a teenager growing up in a white neighborhood, she knew that the values taught by her Korean-American church were very different from those of the white society. Seeking to clarify her faith and identity, she enrolled in a divinity school on the East Coast. Through her white feminist teachers, she was exposed to feminist thought and feminist biblical hermeneutics. However, when she wanted to share her new perspectives with her church, her parents thought that she had been much too influenced by feminism, while her peers looked upon her as too "whitewashed."

The preceding stories of John and Soon Young illustrate the kind of frustration and alienation many minority students feel in their professional study of the Bible. Such issues, however, are seldom brought up for discussion in departmental meetings. Only when the Johns and Soon Youngs of this world do not do well in class—when they become a "problem" for discussion—does the faculty try to find ways to "help" them. It is always assumed that such students have problems in mastering the material in question; the possibility is never raised that the problem may lie with the syllabus, the pedagogy, or the assumptions regarding how the class should be taught. It is imperative, therefore, to examine further how and why such feelings of alienation occur.

The Other Tongues

A serious study of the Bible begins with wrestling with the original languages: Hebrew and Greek. Except for the very small percentage of minority students who have gone to private high schools and have enrolled in colleges with a strong and attractive liberal arts program, there exist few opportunities and little encouragement for minority students to study the classical languages. The languages of the Bible thus remain foreign tongues, imbued with much power, insofar as they are supposed to be the languages through which God spoke. A word of background in this regard proves illuminating.

Augustine and other church fathers favored the view that Hebrew was the original human language. Since Hebrew had a simpler grammar than Arabic, Greek, or Latin, scholars assumed that it was the most ancient language, the tongue of Adam. The divine origin of Hebrew was challenged at the beginning of the nineteenth century, when interest in Sanskrit supplanted interest in Hebrew. Scholars began criticizing Hebrew as primitive in structure and poor in abstraction as a result of their anti-Judaic bias.[6]

In contrast, Greek has always been hailed as the language of the literati and the language of the "master." Thus, for example, Henry Louis Gates recounts how the knowledge of Greek was used as a criterion with which to measure the humanity of blacks. During the anti-slavery movement in the 1830s, John C. Calhoun, the conservative senator from South Carolina, is reported to have said: "that if he could find a Negro who knew the Greek syntax, he would then believe that the Negro was a human being and should be treated as a man."[7] Gates remarks:

> The salient sign of the black person's humanity—indeed, the only sign for Calhoun—would be the mastering of the very essence of Western civilization, of the very foundation of the complex fiction upon which white Western culture had been constructed, which for John C. Calhoun turned out to have been Greek syntax.[8]

Such exaltation of the Greek language was also evident among eminent teachers and grammarians of Greek at the turn of the century. James Hope Moulton, whose *Grammar of New Testament Greek* was considered a standard reference work for generations of scholars, characterized Greek as "above all languages." It was the language spoken by a people, he declared, who in ancient time "attained the highest cultivation of mind and body that the world has ever seen."[9] As late as 1942, the influential biblical scholar William Foxwell Albright upheld the superiority of Greek culture in his understanding of the evolution of cultures. He wrote:

> But the gap between savage mentality and the mind of modern man is too great to be easily bridged by direct observation, and the attempt to fill the gap by studying the ideas of half-savage peoples of today is nearly always vitiated by the fact that these peoples have been strongly influenced by more highly developed civilizations, virtually all of which reflect a post-Hellenic stage of progress.... The only way in which we can bridge this gap satisfactorily is by following the evolution of the human mind in the Near East itself, where we can trace it from the earliest times through successive archaeological ages to the flowering of the Greek spirit.[10]

In the 1960s and 1970s, the debate on the origin of writing and the invention of the alphabet gained momentum. Scholars argued for the pre-eminent character of Greek, since it was the first language to have developed a full alphabet consisting of consonants and vowels, around 750 B.C.E. The alphabet system was seen to be instrumental in the spread of literacy and in the development of abstract thinking, philosophical systems, and early science.[11] Given the importance of Greek culture for the history of Western Europe, the exaltation of Greek simultaneously reinscribes the power of the language of the New Testament and the primacy of Western civilization.

The Other Location

The historical-critical method arose in Europe as a challenge to the dogmatic understanding of Scripture and the doctrinal authority of the Church. However, its usefulness for racial and ethnic minority churches is open to question. Thus, Renita Weems, an African-American biblical scholar, has pointed to the negative consequences of the historical-critical method, whereby the latter has served "to undermine marginalized reading communities by insisting that their questions and experiences are superfluous to Scripture and their interpretation illegitimate, because of their failure to remain objective."[12] In other words, a basically eurocentric reading method has been accepted as the standard and the norm for judging all other reading strategies.

This sense of alienation has led Brian Blount, an African-American New Testament scholar, to argue for a cultural and contextual interpretation of Scripture. Using sociolinguistic theories and a sociological model of liberation, Blount analyzes the cultural contexts of biblical interpretation in Nicaragua, in the Black Church, and in European academic settings. At the end, he explains why he undertook such a difficult task:

> The motivation of such an analytic move came from my observation that the black church and the black community it serves interprets biblical language in a demonstrably unique manner. I had two concerns. First, I was chagrined by the inability of traditional approaches to biblical interpretation to bring the text to life in the midst of my circumstances as a black Christian. Second, I was often stung by the criticism of black interpretations that, it was alleged, imposed a foreign ideology on the text. When I widened my perspective on this matter I found that the black church was not alone in the kind of interpretative independence it demonstrated. Other religious, ethnic, political, and social groups also interpreted the biblical texts in ways that were sensitive to their particular communal circumstances.[13]

If Blount experiences a kind of cognitive dissonance, the kind of frustration Soon Young feels is even more acute because of her multiple marginalization. First, an Asian reads the Bible from a situation of great alienation, as George Soares-Prabhu has noted:

> Unlike a Hindu reading of the Vedas, or a Buddhist reading of the Pali Canon, an Asian reading of the Bible is never a "natural" reading, taking place spontaneously within a living tradition. It always has to be a deliberate strategy, a forced and somewhat artificial exercise, a reading against the grain, a challenge to church orthodoxy or academic parochialism.[14]

Second, the experience of the ethnic church in which she grew up is not valued by the mainline churches and society. As the Korean-American New Testament scholar Chan-Hie Kim has stated, "Recent Christian immigrants have been heavily influenced by American Christianity in their theology and Christian practices. Yet the mother church looks upon these immigrant Christian congregations as if they were the illegitimate children."[15] Furthermore, in order to maintain a sense of cultural continuity in a strange land, many immigrant congregations transplant religious practices from home, some of which are patriarchal and hierarchical; as a result, there is not much room for an articulation of a feminist approach to biblical criticism. Third, if Soon Young is fortunate enough to have a female teacher in biblical studies, she is most likely to be a Caucasian. The issues of Asian-American women are seldom discussed in class, and Soon Young finds it difficult to appropriate the writings of Caucasian feminist scholars in her immigrant church. Although there are biblical reflections by Asian feminist scholars, Soon Young does not speak any Asian language and finds their context very different from hers. At the same time, there is but one Asian-American woman with an advanced degree in biblical studies. Consequently, the discussion on reading the Bible from an Asian-American perspective has just begun.

The Other Scholar

In the fields of theology and ethics, it has become more acceptable in recent times for a minority scholar to claim that she or he approaches a theological or ethical problem from a particular vantage point. The contextual nature of theological and ethical inquiry has been debated for a long time, especially after the emergence of feminist and liberationist paradigms. However, in the field of biblical studies, which still largely claims to be "value-neutral," a scholar's work becomes suspect when it bears the stamp of having been written from an African-American, Hispanic/Latino, Native, or Asian-American perspective.

In addition, many minority scholars have no choice but to teach in predominantly white schools. Many white students want to know the "standard" historical method in order to take the ordination examinations given by the mainline churches. They have little time or energy for engaging the minority teacher in his or her cutting edge of scholarship. In a field that is drastically changing shape, it is not easy to satisfy the needs of all students or to evaluate students from diverse backgrounds. As African-American New Testament scholar William H. Myers notes, "It is often difficult to separate method from a tradition of beliefs; hence, it is very difficult to affirm all students in their tradition while attempting to do major surgery on their method of interpretation."[16] At the same time, the course evaluations on the part of some grudging white students can have damaging effects on any process of hiring, tenure, and promotion involving minorities.

In a rare testimony of the predicament facing a minority biblical scholar, Fernando Segovia characterizes scholarship as a struggle because of the alien and *alienating* context in which minority scholars work: "A context where the contents and mode of their discourse are not acknowledged, much less accepted or respected, as an equal, as a different vision of reality."[17] Segovia

also refers to the glass ceiling that serves to limit the number of racial and ethnic minorities to only one or two from each group, and he points out how an
increase of minority scholars in an institution is interpreted as a decline in
quality. Moreover, he goes on to argue, collegial support of minority scholars
is not forthcoming: "We must remember that it is never proper for the happy,
thankful, and obedient native to begin to act in strange ways; in fact, we
should expect subtle as well as not so subtle evaluations as malcontents,
ungrateful, difficult, or problematic."[18] Given such a less than supportive
environment, minority scholars often have to work doubly hard to prove
themselves and to gain respect and acceptance.

IN OTHER EPISTEME: STUDYING JESUS/THE NATIVE

The alienating experiences of minority students and scholars in the field
prompt us to examine the underlying epistemological assumptions of the study
of the Bible in the modern period. The modernist project of the West unfolded
in the midst of the Enlightenment, the ascendancy of white supremacy, and the
process of colonial and territorial expansion. As Edward Said has demonstrated in his book *Culture and Imperialism*, the justification of empire-building undergirded Western cultural imagination in the nineteenth and early
twentieth centuries, influencing the high cultures of scholarship, novels, and
the arts.[19] Could the study of the Bible have remained immune?

Using the example of the quest for the historical Jesus, I would like to show
how the modern study of the Bible emerged simultaneously with bourgeois
culture and was influenced by the expansion of Europe. There were complex
social and cultural factors that called forth the scientific study of the life of
Jesus. The Enlightenment philosophers challenged church authority and the
supernatural nimbus surrounding the stories of virgin birth, miracles, and resurrection. The teachings of the church belonged to the old world and did not
fit with the emergence of modern science and the ideology of the rising bourgeoisie. As Albert Schweitzer notes:

> The historical investigation of the life of Jesus did not take its rise from
> purely historical interest; it turned to the Jesus of history as an ally in the
> struggle against the tyranny of dogma. Afterwards when it was freed
> from this πάθος it sought to present the historic Jesus in a form intelligi-
> ble in its own time.[20]

The debate concerning the historical Jesus took place in the mercantile and
bourgeois culture of the metropolitan centers of Europe. The scientific approach to the life of Jesus began with the work of Hermann Samuel Reimarus
(1694-1768), who lived in Hamburg, one of the oldest and most important
shipping and trading centers of Europe. "The pupils whom Reimarus was supposed to teach," explains Dieter Georgi, "were future merchants, industrial
producers, and owners of wharfs who would live in a world formed even more
by the bourgeoisie than before."[21] Joseph Ernest Renan (1823-1892), the most

important contributor from the French scene, was heavily influenced by the high cultures as well as the aesthetic feeling of nature and country life of French art. His influential volume, *La Vie de Jésus* (1863), marked an epoch not only for the Catholic world but also for the cultured world.[22] Georgi sums up the image of Jesus presented by Renan:

> Jesus was exemplary, a man of risk and challenge, calling others to risks. This fitted the bourgeoisie which was often self-critical to the point of masochism and which prided itself on its readiness to face competition and conflict, even under warlike conditions, whether in the market or in the hardships of what amounted to institutionalized civil wars in the exercises of bourgeois democracy.[23]

Another contributing factor to the debate on the historical Jesus, scarcely mentioned by scholars, was the ethos of empire-building and the expansion of Europe. Georgi notes the intense interest in Alexander the Great, the mythological empire-builder, in France and Germany during the eighteenth century: "This person who had been considered an exemplary divine man in Hellenistic-Roman culture began to fascinate the bourgeoisie in its final ascendancy."[24] Much influenced by Niccolò Machiavelli's *The Prince* (1513), Reimarus portrayed the messianic ideal of Jesus as that of a political ruler, the son of David. Having failed his political mission, Jesus' moral ethic of a radical commandment of love survived.[25] David Friedrich Strauss (1808-1874), another important figure in the debate, was an ardent supporter of a strong and united Germany under the hegemony of Prussia. He defended Germany's position in the Prusso-Austrian War and was much influenced by the theory of natural selection of Darwinism.[26] Renan went to Phoenicia and Syria under the auspices of Napoleon III.[27] A formidable figure in Phoenician archaeology, Semitic languages, and biblical exegesis, Renan was the one who introduced "Orientalism" into the study of philology.[28]

The quest for the historical Jesus was an obsession of the West. It first took place at a time when the power of Europe was at its zenith—the quest for Jesus went hand in hand with the quest for land and people to conquer. From a postcolonial perspective, we must plot the quest for the *authentic* Jesus against the search for knowledge of *authentic* "natives" for the purpose of control and domination. We will see that the two operated on the same episteme and were much related, because the increase of knowledge about the Mediterranean world came at the same time as the expansion of knowledge about the cultures the West had conquered. I will illustrate this point by discussing the quest for origins, the phenomenon of Orientalism in philology, and the eurocentric biases present in the study of comparative mythology.

Quest for Origins

The quest for the historical Jesus was a quest for the origins of Christianity. The search for Christian origins served several purposes: (1) It addressed the anxiety of the construction of modern identity in a rapidly changing Europe. By finding an Archimedean point in a primitive and primordial origin, it was hoped that a single common identity for Europe, or the Aryan race, could be forged.[29] (2) The Enlightenment understanding of history as linear and progressive and the evolutionary theory current at the time necessitated the creation of a myth of origins. (3) The consciousness of modernity created a binary opposite in the European imagination: the "primitive" or the "native." Since the "natives" were characterized by animistic, superstitious, and profane beliefs, the origin of Christianity had to be stripped of all mythology, miracle, and the supernatural. The search for Christian origins was not just a pure academic exercise but rather an integral part of the justification of the superiority of European culture.

In *A Myth of Innocence*, Burton Mack discusses how the myth of Christian origins, first presented in the Gospel of Mark, was used by scholars to judge and interpret all other cultures. The myth of Christian origins is based on the hypothesis that some imagined event of transformation was brought into the world by Christianity that accounted for the generation of a radically new perception, social formation, and religion. Such a Christian myth influenced the academic quest for the origins of human culture in general:

> During the nineteenth century developmental schemes were proposed that correlate nicely with the stages outlined in the Christian epic. . . . Applied to the reconstructions of the history of human culture, then, the developmental scheme regularly featured three phases: the primitive (read Old Testament), the religious (read Catholic Christianity from a Protestant point of view), and the rational (read the Protestant recovery of the originary revelation of God in creation and in Christ). This scheme was used to collect, classify, rank, and interpret the anthropological data that began to be amassed. . . . This is because the Christian gospel continues to function as the lens by which the world is viewed, ordered, and interpreted.[30]

Orientalism and Philology

The quest for the historical Jesus would not have been possible without certain corresponding developments in the field of philology. Thus, for example, while Reimarus was Professor of Oriental Languages at Hamburg, Renan, an Orientalist, was professor of Semitic Languages at the Collège de France. The interest in the study of non-European languages increased as the Western powers extended to different parts of the globe. New texts were brought back to London and Paris, and knowledge of these foreign tongues was seen as necessary for effective control and management. For example, the need to master Sanskrit arose when the British wanted to study ancient Indian laws. Power and knowledge joined hand in hand to further the goals of the empires.

As a discipline that emerged in the late eighteenth century, philology studied the origins of language and comparative grammar, and classified languages into families and groups. Philology opened a door for the comparison of

myths, cultures, and religions by relating linguistic structure to forms of
thought and features of civilization. Under the combined influence of racial
theory and comparative anatomy current at the time, philologists evaluated
the achievements of different languages and races. Said has pointed out that
the study of biblical languages was colored by the Orientalist biases of some
scholars. Compared to the living, organic, Indo-European languages, Semitic
Oriental languages were considered arrested in development, inorganic, ossi-
fied, and incapable of self-generation. Renan's study of the Semitic languages,
Said demonstrates, was full of racial prejudices and Eurocentric judgments.[31]
For example, Renan wrote:

> One sees that in all things the Semitic race appears to us to be an incom-
> plete race, by virtue of its simplicity. This race—if I dare use the anal-
> ogy—is to the Indo-European family what a pencil sketch is to painting;
> it lacks that variety, that amplitude, that abundance of life which is the
> condition of perfectibility.[32]

Just as the Orientalist was supposed to be able to rescue the Orient from
obscurity, strangeness, and alienation, so biblical scholars claimed to present
the life of Jesus with "scientific certainty" over against the authority of the
church. The past was *re-presented* in modern idiom: what was distant became
near; what was strange, familiar. Claiming to be objective and precise, scholars were able to tell "what actually happened" with an aura of facticity and
historicity. Combining the authority of a philologist, the sentiment of a novelist, and a taste for French culture, however, Renan's *La Vie de Jésus* was more
a cultural product of his time than a "factual" account of the life of Jesus.
According to Said, the book is

> a construction enabled by the historian's capacity for skillfully crafting a
> dead Oriental biography—and the paradox is immediately apparent—
> *as if it were* the truthful narrative of a natural life. Whatever Renan said
> had first passed through the philological laboratory; when it appeared in
> print woven through the text, there was in it the life-giving force of a
> contemporary cultural signature, which drew from modernity all its sci-
> entific power and all its uncritical self-approbation.[33]

Comparative Mythology

The quest for the historical Jesus emerged at the same time as heightened
interest in the study of myths from around the world and the founding of the
study of religion as a discipline. Earlier attempts to discover the historical
Jesus focused on separating the mythical from the historical in the gospel narratives. The need to present a historical account of early Christianity came as
a response to the emergence of historicism in the eighteenth century, the challenge of the scientific worldview, and the construction of the superiority of
Western culture. Christian Europe was taken to be rational, historical, and

scientific, while other cultures were labeled mythical, ahistorical, and un-scientific. The modernity of Europe was established with two reference points: the "natives" in the past and the "natives" in the present. The people in Palestine, from whom the Bible came, were considered "natives" of the past; the peoples colonized by the European powers in the nineteenth cen-tury were "natives" of the present. The former existed in European consciousness as forever frozen in the mythical past, denied a historical development; the latter were deemed to be steeped in the mythical present, with the past always impinging upon the present. Since mythical conscious-ness was cyclical, all "native" societies were considered as having progressed little over the millennia. Even if there might be developments of some sort, these societies would degenerate back to their pasts under the spell of the myth of "eternal return." Only Europe was able to break away from such a destiny because of its historical consciousness, which was linear and progressive.

It is within this larger framework of the search for European identity that the wider implications of the quest for the historical Jesus can be fully com-prehended. For example, Strauss explained that the myths about Jesus' life were formed because the "natives" of the past had uncultivated minds inca-pable of abstraction:

Imagine a young Church which reverences its founder all the more enthusiastically; the more unexpectedly and the more tragically his life course was ended; a Church impregnated with a mass of new ideas that were to recreate the world; a Church of Orientals, for the most part un-educated people, which consequently was able to adopt and express those ideas only in concrete ways of fantasy, as pictures and as stories, not in the abstract form of rational understanding of concepts; imagine such a Church and you are driven to conclude that under such circum-stances that which emerged had to emerge.[34]

After studying the works of Strauss, Renan, and other nineteenth-century authors on the historical Jesus, Schweitzer gave up his career as a theological professor to "save" the "natives" of his own time. Assuming the role of a "jungle doctor" in French Equatorial Africa (Gabon), he described the African "natives" in his autobiography: "In my intercourse with these primi-tive creatures I naturally came to put to myself the much debated question whether they were mere prisoners of tradition, or beings capable of really independent thought."[35] He maintained that only people of European descent had the will to progress, because of their affirmative attitude toward the world. Toward others he displayed a deep-seated ethnocentrism:

Among primitive and half-primitive peoples too, whose unformed view has not yet reached the problem of acceptance or rejection of the world, there is no will to progress. Their ideal is the simplest life with the least possible trouble.[36]

For these scholars, the myths of Jesus could be explained and the progress of Europe could be rationalized because of their construction of the "natives" of the past and the present.

IN OTHER WORDS:
HOW CAN THE "NATIVE" STUDY THE BIBLE?

The preceding analysis indicates that the historical-critical method, which claims to be neutral and objective, was embedded in the episteme of the nineteenth century and decisively influenced by the colonial and empire-building impulses of Europe. Given the fact that the historical method is still the reigning paradigm taught in most graduate schools in the United States and Europe, how can the "natives" use the "master's" tools without succumbing to their lure and power? I would suggest the following three strategies: parallel processing; beyond identification; and beyond noble savaging Jesus.

Beyond the Master's Framework: Parallel Processing

The historical method must be situated within the cultural space and political configurations of its own time. We must call into question its understanding of historical consciousness, historicity, and historiography from a postcolonial perspective. Since the "masters" would not go beyond their own episteme, we have to read their works within the larger framework of postcolonial criticism and other critical theories. For example, I would not be able to make the connection between the study of Jesus and the study of the "native" without reading Strauss, Renan, and Schweitzer alongside Said's *Orientalism*, Chow's *Writing Diaspora*, James Clifford's *The Predicament of Culture*,[37] and Eilberg-Schwartz's *The Savage in Judaism*.

I would like to name this strategy of reading "parallel processing," taking the cue from computers which are linked up to process vast amounts of data. Parallel processing entails expanding the database, making interfaces between different bodies of knowledge, generating new problem-solving areas, and storing data for future retrievals. The strategy requires not only that we teach all students—and especially the Johns and Soon Youngs of our world—the normative texts of the "master" in biblical studies, but also that we provide them with tools with which to critique such texts and reappropriate them in their own contexts. Since many professors of biblical studies were primarily trained in the historical method, without adequate knowledge of literary criticism, sociological criticism, and reader-response criticism—methods now flourishing in biblical studies—let alone postcolonial and critical theories, such teachers must undergo re-training and re-tooling in order to catch up with the times.

To demystify the framework of the "master," we cannot rely on the *internal* critiques of European scholars alone. Such critiques, though helpful, are not adequate because of their failure to see the West through the eyes of the "others." Thus, for example, Dieter Georgi's study of the interest in the life of Jesus provides invaluable information regarding the social contexts of the different paradigms in the history of interpreting Jesus. However, he has taken for granted that the context of biblical criticism was Europe, without questioning the ways in which "Europe" was constructed in relation to the rest of the world. Thus, he fails to derive implications from a global perspective. A second example involves Elisabeth Schüssler Fiorenza's critique of the newest quest for the historical Jesus, which exploded in the 1980s, during the Reagan-Bush era in the United States. From a feminist point of view, she insightfully criticizes the newest quest's restoration of historical positivism as corresponding to political conservatism and its emphasis on the "realia" of history as promoting scientific fundamentalism.[38] I would add, however, that the newest quest caught popular attention because of such ongoing issues in the country as the debate on the identity of American culture, the rising ethos of anti-immigration, and the postmodern and New Age search for new sages and gurus. The first quest took place when Europe, flexing its colonial muscle, encountered the world (the "natives") outside its borders; today, the United States, as the only superpower in the world, does not need to go out to seek the "natives," because the "natives" have come into its own borders. As middle-class, white America needs to redefine its identity and destiny, the search for the historical Jesus surfaces once again.

One of the most effective ways to debunk the authority of the "master's" framework is to see the Bible through multiple frameworks and lenses. The fact that there are alternative frames of reference serves to challenge the arbitrariness of assigning one interpretation as the normative one. People on the margins have shown that alternative readings are indeed possible and have offered such strategies as the following: materialist readings; postcolonial critiques; multifaith hermeneutics; and various shades of feminist and womanist criticism. Professors of biblical studies must learn to entertain diverse points of views and engage students in education for freedom. In *Teaching to Transgress*, bell hooks writes:

> Professors cannot empower students to embrace diversities of experience, standpoint, behavior, or style if our training has disempowered us, socialized us to cope effectively only with a single mode of interaction based on middle-class values.[39]

One of the most cherished values of the middle class is the unspoken liberal-humanistic assumption that human beings are all equal and the same. But the sad truth is that a small group of white people have always functioned as the spokespersons for all.

Beyond Identification: "Natives" in the Past/"Natives" in the Present

While it may be argued that contemporary European and American societies are drastically different from the agrarian culture of the biblical world, one should guard against the faulty assumption that the people of the Third World, the poor, and the marginalized have a priori privilege in interpreting the Bible. It is often tempting for contemporary "natives" to claim privileged status in understanding the "natives" of the past. From Africa, Temba L. J. Mafico has shown that similarities between African and Near Eastern cultures enabled him to add new dimensions to the interpretation of the appellation of the divine name Yahweh missed by Western scholars.[40] In Latin America, the belief in the "epistemological privilege" of the poor has given accent to the reading of the Bible by the poor and the marginalized. For example, Carlos Mesters has said repeatedly: "The common people are discovering things in the Bible that other readers don't find. . . . The common people are giving us a clearer picture of concepts that have been excessively spiritualized. . . . The common people are putting the Bible in its proper place. . . ."[41] In Asia, Hisako Kinukawa has pointed out that the Japanese society in which she lives has many parallels to first-century Palestine; she claims:

> As a woman, I can feel closer to the women in the Bible, since our expe-
> riences as women have so much in common with theirs. Such common
> experiences of shame/honor with boundaries of power, sexual status,
> and respect for others, in a group-oriented society of dyadic personali-
> ties, provide me with a powerful methodological device for studying the
> women and their experiences in Mark's Gospel.[42]

I have serious reservations in accepting all such arguments: (1) We should question the construction of the "native" (past and present) in the first place and not happily assume that we have privileged access to the Bible because of our "native" status. To do so would easily re-inscribe the unequal relation in the text and in our interpretation. (2) Our emphasis on the similarities between contemporary and biblical societies may overlook or downplay the differences. We should be cautious in using a few anthropological maxims, such as those proposed by Bruce Malina,[43] to characterize the multifaceted and multicultural character of the ancient Mediterranean world. (3) We should not commit the sin of Orientalism, which overlooks the historical development of Palestinian society and our own societies. (4) We should not assume that only the "common people," "the poor," or "the marginalized" are the authentic "natives" and that all others are inauthentic and thus unable to understand the Bible. There are many different kinds of "natives," some better educated than others; we have to avoid collapsing the "natives" into the "same." (5) By claiming that Western societies are fundamentally different from "native" societies (past and present), we continue to set North Atlantic cultures apart from the rest of the world and, in so doing, unwittingly re-inscribe the *we-they* dichotomy that has given such power to the white people.

Beyond Noble Savaging Jesus: Another Time, Another Space

Our refusal to be the "native" means that we will not occupy "the space of the past of which the white [people] will be the future."[44] This implies that we will look at the historical method with suspicion, because it is basically a modernist project. At the same time, we will not endorse postmodern interpretations, which are gaining momentum in biblical criticism, because they represent internal white critiques that fail to make connections with what is happening in the rest of the world.[45] The postmodern emphasis on deconstructing the subject, indeterminacy of language, and excess of meaning will not be helpful at all if it does not come to grips with the colonial impulse and the sense of white supremacy that make "modernity" possible in the first place.

Refusing to be the "native" also means that we will not interpret Jesus within a framework defined by European and Euro-American imagination that answers their crying social needs. I would call this strategy "Noble Savaging Jesus." In their encounter with the aboriginal peoples of the Americas, Europeans proceeded to call the latter "noble savages" and positioned them as the uncontaminated "other" of Europe. The intention was to provide a counterpoint with which to criticize the social ills and corruption of European societies. In the fantasy of scholars, Jesus becomes the "Noble Savage" par excellence. The contemporary images of Jesus as described by the newest quest—spirit-filled person; social prophet; healer; sage; movement-initiator; and peasant—still portray a Jesus that is foreign (to the West), yet tamable, because Jesus, though a "savage," is a noble one. The images of Jesus thus created are also meant to meet the crises of the time: social reformer; critic of the church; origin for the common identity of white Anglo-Saxon Protestants; and New Age guru.

Refusing to be the "native" also means that we will not enter the cultural space predetermined by others. The colonial subject, as Franz Fanon has pointed out, is always "overdetermined from without."[46] In addition, we will have to enter a different time-frame, a time-frame on the margins of both modernity and postmodernity. As Homi Bhabha has said:

> To reconstitute the discourse of cultural difference demands not simply a change of cultural contents and symbols; a replacement within the same time-frame of representation is never adequate. It requires a radical revision of the social temporality in which emergent histories may be written.[47]

This other time-frame allows us to speak of humanity through its differentiations—gender, race, class, ethnic groupings, sexual orientation, age, disabilities, and so on.[48] In this cultural space and time, nobody is a "native," and yet we are all "natives."

NOTES

1. R. Chow, *Writing Diaspora: Tactics of Intervention in Contemporary Cultural Studies* (Bloomington: Indiana University Press, 1993) 42; see 27-54 (Chap. 2: "Where Have All the Natives Gone?").

2. Kwok Pui-lan, "Discovering the Bible in the Non-Biblical World: The Journey Continues," *Journal of Asian and Asian American Theology* (forthcoming).

3. G. C. Spivak, "The Rani of Simur," *Europe and Its Others*, Vol. 1; ed. F. Barker et al. (Colchester: University of Essex Press, 1985) 131. Spivak describes how the imperialist project serves to keep the native subject muted.

4. On this point I am grateful to Laura E. Donaldson for her constructive criticism of an earlier draft of this study. She specifically mentioned that the refusal to be "native" according to its dominant eurocentric definition might suggest that the latter is the only construction of nativeness possible, a position which actually undermines the struggle of aboriginal peoples—American Indians, for example—to have their cultures and subjectivities taken seriously.

5. For a fuller analysis of the issues African-American students face, see W. H. Myers, "The Hermeneutical Dilemma of the African American Biblical Student," *Stony the Road We Trod: African American Biblical Interpretation,* ed. C. H. Felder (Minneapolis: Fortress Press, 1991) 40-56.

6. See M. Olender, *The Languages of Paradise: Race, Religion, and Philology in the Nineteenth Century* (Cambridge: Harvard University Press, 1992) 1-20; H. Eilberg-Schwartz, *The Savage in Judaism: An Anthropology of Israelite Religion and Ancient Judaism* (Bloomington: Indiana University Press, 1990) 72- 73.

7. A. Crummell, "The Attitude of the American Mind Toward the Negro Intellect," Occasional Papers, No. 3 (Washington, D.C.: The American Negro Academy, 1989), as quoted in H. L. Gates, Jr., "Authority, (White) Power, and the (Black) Critic: It's All Greek to Me," *The Nature and Context of Minority Discourse,* ed. A. R. JanMohamed and D. Lloyd (Oxford and New York: Oxford University Press, 1990) 74.

8. Gates, "Authority, (White) Power, and the (Black) Critic," 74.

9. J. H. Moulton, *An Introduction to the Study of New Testament Greek* (London: The Epworth Press, 1930) 1-2. For the grammar, see J. H. Moulton, *A Grammar of New Testament Greek* (Edinburgh: T. & T. Clark, 1908). Only the first volume, containing the prolegomena, was authored by Moulton.

10. W. F. Albright, *Archaeology and the Religion of Israel* (Baltimore: The Johns Hopkins University Press, 1942) 4.

11. J. Goody, *The Interface between the Written and the Oral* (Cambridge: Cambridge University Press, 1987) 60-77.

12. R. J. Weems, "Reading *Her Way* through the Struggle: African American Women and the Bible," *Stony the Road We Trod,* 66.

13. B. K. Blount, *Cultural Interpretation: Reorienting New Testament Criticism* (Minneapolis: Fortress Press, 1995) 176.

14. G. Soares-Prabhu, "Two Mission Commands: An Interpretation of Matthew 28:16-20 in the Light of a Buddhist Text," *Biblical Interpretation* 2 (1994) 270.

15. C. H. Kim, "Reading the Cornelius Story from an Asian Immigrant Perspective," *Reading from This Place.* Volume 1: *Social Location and Biblical Interpretation in the United States,* ed. F. F. Segovia and M. A. Tolbert (Minneapolis: Fortress Press, 1995) 172.

16. Myers, "The Hermeneutical Dilemma," 43.

17. F. F. Segovia, "Theological Education and Scholarship as Struggle: The Life of Racial/Ethnic Minorities in the Profession," *Journal of Hispanic/Latino Theology* 2 (1994) 12.

18. Ibid., 20.

19. E. W. Said, *Culture and Imperialism* (New York: Alfred A. Knopf, 1994).

20. A. Schweitzer, *The Quest of the Historical Jesus* (New York: Macmillan, 1968; orig. publ. 1906) 4.

21. D. Georgi, "The Interest in Life of Jesus Theology as a Paradigm for the Social History of Biblical Criticism," *Harvard Theological Review* 85 (1992) 75.

22. Schweitzer, *Quest of the Historical Jesus,* 181-82.

23. Georgi, "Interest in Life of Jesus Theology," 78.

24. Ibid., 75.

25. Ibid., 75-76.

26. Schweitzer, *Quest of the Historical Jesus*, 74-75.

27. Ibid., 180.

28. E. W. Said, *Orientalism* (New York: Vintage Books, 1994) 130-33.

29. On the search for a common identity, I benefit from a lecture by Elizabeth A. Castelli at Harvard Divinity School on December 13, 1995.

30. B. L. Mack, *A Myth of Innocence* (Minneapolis: Fortress Press, 1988) 369.

31. Said, *Orientalism*, 142; Olender, *The Languages of Paradise*, 51-81.

32. E. Renan, *Oeuvres complètes*, 8:156, as quoted in Said, *Orientalism*, 149.

33. Ibid., 146.

34. D. F. Strauss, *Das Leben Jesu kritisch bearbeitet*, as quoted in W. G. Kümmel, *The New Testament: The History of the Investigation of Its Problems* (Nashville: Abingdon Press, 1972) 122. It was George Eliot who translated the text of Strauss into English. For a discussion of how historical criticism influenced British literature, see E. S. Shaffer, *"Kubla Khan" and the Fall of Jerusalem: The Mythological School in Biblical Criticism and Secular Literature, 1770-1880* (Cambridge: Cambridge University Press, 1975).

35. A. Schweitzer, *Out of My Life and Thought: An Autobiography* (New York: Henry Holt and Co., 1949) 142.

36. Ibid., 151.

37. J. Clifford, *The Predicament of Culture* (Cambridge and London: Harvard University Press, 1988).

38. E. Schüssler Fiorenza, *Jesus: Miriam's Child: Sophia's Prophet* (New York: Continuum, 1994) 86-87.

39. b. hooks, *Teaching to Transgress: Education as the Practice of Freedom* (New York: Routledge, 1994) 187.

40. T. L. J. Mafico, "The Divine Name Yahweh Elohim from an African Perspective," *Reading from This Place*. Volume 2: *Social Location and Biblical Interpretation in Global Perspective*, ed. F. F. Segovia and M. A. Tolbert (Minneapolis: Fortress Press, 1995) 21-32.

41. C. Mesters, "The Use of the Bible in Christian Communities of the Common People," *The Bible and Liberation: Political and Social Hermeneutics* (Rev. ed.; ed. N. K. Gottwald and R. A. Horsley; Maryknoll: Orbis Books, 1993) 13-15.

42. H. Kinukawa, *Women and Jesus in Mark: A Japanese Feminist Perspective* (Maryknoll: Orbis Books, 1994) 16.

43. B. J. Malina, *The New Testament World: Insights from Cultural Anthropology* (Atlanta: John Knox Press, 1981).

44. Homi Bhabha (*The Location of Culture* [New York: Routledge, 1994] 237-238) notes that Franz Fanon rejected the "belatedness" of the black man: "the black man refuses to occupy the past of which the white man is the future." The natives are considered backward, underdeveloped, and without a future, whereas the white people are deemed as controlling the present and masterminding the future.

45. I recognize that postcolonial theorists such as G. C. Spivak and H. K. Bhabha have built on the work of postmodern theories. The relationship between postcolonial and postmodern criticism needs to be further debated and clarified. See the insightful discussion in L. E. Donaldson, *Decolonizing Feminisms: Race, Gender, and Empire Building* (Chapel Hill: University of North Carolina Press, 1992).

46. F. Fanon, *Black Skin, White Masks* (London: Pluto, 1986) 116.

47. Bhabha, *The Location of Culture*, 171.

48. Ibid., 238.

5

FOUR FACES OF THEOLOGY

Four Johannine Conversations

Jean-Pierre Ruiz

What makes someone a theologian? Someone recently set me to thinking about that question by asking it just like that. As I continued to ponder it in the process that now yields these reflections, I came to recognize that the words which first came to mind, my initial answer to the question, were inadequate, sorely inadequate. I mistakenly addressed the question in academic terms, strictly academic terms. What makes a professional theologian? A doctorate, I answered overquickly. The degree means qualification *by* the academy, *in* the academy, and *for* the academy. Is that it? Is that really all? I think not.[1] Granted, I was answering the question in the context of theological education, postgraduate theological education in a university setting, but that context does not excuse either the haste or the inadequacy of the reply.

For one thing, that reply would exclude lots of people, and excluding is something that elites (and not just academic elites) often do frighteningly well. If the possession of an earned doctorate were said to be the sole standard for admission to the community of competent, qualified theologians, that would exclude the many generations of *doctores* who lived the quest for the Mystery of faith prior to the foundation of the first universities and theological seminaries.[2] We would be excluding the whole cloud of witnesses, women and men, lettered and unlettered, past and present, on whose relentless Spirit-driven quest for Truth our own houses of wisdom are founded. If theology can be

From June 11 to 14, 1995, the Academy of Catholic Hispanic Theologians of the United States (ACHTUS) and the Black Catholic Theological Symposium (BCTS) held their first joint meeting in Douglaston, NY. During the working sessions of this meeting, the forty participants engaged in discussion focused on four key areas of mutual concern: theological method; culture as a source for theology; history as a source for theology; and mujerista/womanist theologies. The present essay was originally delivered during that meeting as the ACHTUS presidential address, and it appears here substantially as it was presented on that occasion, including particular references to the situation of Hispanic-American and African-American theologians.

described as *fides quaerens intellectum*, then every believer is at least potentially a theologian. Matthew's Jesus wisely warns, "You are not to be called rabbi, for you have one teacher (*didaskalos*), and you are all students (*adelphoi*)" (Matt 23:8).

I cannot presume to tell you either what theology is or who you are as theologians, nor can I tell you how to practice the craft of theology. The descriptive task is beyond my ability and beyond the scope of these reflections; the second task, prescriptive in nature, would inappropriately fence in your horizons and restrict your vision. It remains trendy enough to speak in terms of social location, emphasizing the particular rather than the general, the local rather than the universal, my village rather than someone else's empire. Yet we should not mistake that circumspect modesty for a merely indifferent postmodern relativism, for a lukewarm noncommittal stance, or, worse yet, for a retreat behind the walls of the familiar so as not to be challenged by encounters with the unknown. It is instead a matter of dealing with otherness by respectfully allowing the other to remain different from the self, even when both the self and the other energetically engage in the risky business of mutual self-disclosure. For the theologian, the refusal to domesticate the other is a matter of reverence towards the Mystery in which the other participates. While the heat of some theological conversations is generated by the friction of pride against pride, vigorous conversation can likewise be moved by the desire to learn from the other and by the humble admission of our interdependence. Such conversations ultimately hope to generate not heat, but warmth and light.[3]

I want to speak of figures who model the challenge of theology for me. In doing so I will be speaking from and on the basis of my training in biblical studies, in a deliberate instance of "reading from this place," as a Hispanic American addressing an audience that includes Hispanic-American and African-American practitioners of various theological disciplines.[4] In what follows it will be my intention to paint with broad strokes and impressionistically. Retreating to the classical jargon of my discipline for just a moment, let me suggest that in what follows the tension between *exe*gesis and *eise*gesis, between what comes out of the text and what goes into the text, will be configured so as to allow the sort of productive dialogue with the biblical text from which new meanings can emerge. Let me also suggest that while what follows in these pages has midrashic overtones, I am reluctant to legitimate it by borrowing either the name or the particular genius of that rich tradition of biblical interpretation.[5]

I am acutely conscious of how important it is for specialists in biblical studies to pursue conversations with practitioners of other theological disciplines, a pursuit which presumes a reaffirmation of the theological character of biblical studies.[6] Therefore, the reflections that follow include a serious effort to engage in the sort of actualization recommended by the 1993 instruction of the Pontifical Biblical Commission on "The Interpretation of the Bible in the Church."[7]

In the Mishnaic tractate *'Aboth*, the sages urge the student of Torah to seek out a study partner (*'Aboth* 1:6), for the give-and-take of human intersubjectivity disposes the partners to attune the ears of their souls to the presence in their midst of the self-disclosing God of the covenant, the God who chooses to inscribe Torah on the hearts of people. Said Rabbi Hananiah ben Teradion, "When two are sitting, and words of Torah do pass between them—the Presence is with them" (*'Aboth* 3:2). Likewise, Matthew's Jesus instructs his disciples, "Where two or three are gathered in my name, I am there among them" (Matt 18:20). With that in mind, I would like to propose four study partners for us, four biblical models with whom we will enter into dialogue about four facets of the theological enterprise we share, four partners with whom we will continue the sacred give-and-take to which we commit ourselves as theologians.

Our four study partners are John the Baptist, the Samaritan Woman, Mary Magdalene, and John of the Apocalypse. Each of them has something to contribute to the dialogue. Thus, we will converse with John the Baptist on the theologian as prophet, with the Samaritan woman on the theologian as disciple, with Mary Magdalene on the theologian as evangelist, and with John of the Apocalypse on the theologian as visionary. I will not stack the deck too far in advance by specifying just what I mean by prophet, disciple, evangelist, or visionary, nor will I pretend that these are the terms which our biblical study partners might have claimed for themselves. Yet I would venture to suggest that our conversation with these four biblical study partners demonstrates that our *teologías de conjunto* (joint theologies) have depth—a vertical, historical dimension that complements their horizontal extension.[8]

That accounts for the "Four Faces" in the title of this essay. It has nothing directly to do with the four living creatures of the prophet Ezekiel's inaugural vision of the divine Presence, although that coincidence is felicitous, given my own interest in that perplexing prophetic personality. Indirectly, though, theologians long to see with their own eyes "the appearance of the likeness of the glory of the Lord" (Ezek 1:28), that vision beyond describing of which Ezekiel wrote in words at once modest and extravagant. As for the second portion of the title, "Johannine Conversations," it has to do with the very broadly Johannine connections that link each of the four study partners I have chosen.

One of the four, the Samaritan Woman, appears only in the Fourth Gospel. While another of the four, Mary Magdalene, appears in the Synoptic gospels, it is mainly her presence in John 20 that will concern me. As for John the Baptist, who leaves traces not only in the gospels but also in Josephus (*Antiquities* 18.5.2 §116-119), his name and his presence in the Fourth Gospel converge so as to allow us to identify our conversation with him as Johannine. Our fourth study partner, the seer of the Apocalypse, identifies himself by name as John. Because he writes in the name of the risen Jesus to the churches of the seven cities of Asia, among them Ephesus, readers of the Revelation have explored the affinities between that book and the Johannine school.[9] Probing a bit further beneath the surface of these broadly Johannine associations of each of our four study partners, I have chosen to cast these reflections as Johannine conversations because of the dynamics of the dialogues between Jesus and his conversation partners in the Fourth Gospel. With Nicodemus, with the Samaritan Woman, and with others besides, the Johannine Jesus engages in revelatory dialogues that invite them to draw closer and closer to the Light.

JOHN THE BAPTIST: THE THEOLOGIAN AS PROPHET

At least two interrelated factors contribute to a recent resurgence of interest in the figure of John the Baptist. The first is the ongoing "third quest for the historical Jesus," from which research into the historical John the Baptist, "John the Baptist in his own right," has developed as an outgrowth.[10] A second factor is the ongoing and increasingly lively research into the social world of Second Temple Judaism, broadly speaking, and of early Christianity. A number of concerns find shelter under that umbrella. Attention to the mysteries of the Dead Sea Scrolls leads to curiosity as to the possible connection between John the Baptist and the community that underlies the Scrolls.[11] In Johannine studies, attention to the history of the community within which the Fourth Gospel and the Johannine epistles took shape has led to consideration of the relationship between disciples of John the Baptist and disciples of Jesus.[12] Other studies have sought to understand how the person and the preaching of John the Baptist are to be situated within the complex sociohistorical context of first-century Palestine.[13]

All four of the canonical gospels describe John the Baptist against the backdrop of Isa 40:3, "A voice cries out: 'In the wilderness prepare the way of the Lord, make straight in the desert a highway for our God.'" The gospels modify this text of Second Isaiah so as to situate the voice itself in the wilderness: "The voice of one crying out in the wilderness: 'Prepare the way of the Lord, make his paths straight'" (Mark 1:3; Cf. Matt 3:3; Luke 3:4; John 1:23).[14] All four gospels identify the text as Isaian, while the Fourth Gospel sets the citation on the Baptist's own lips as his answer to the question posed by priests and Levites sent from Jerusalem, "What do you say about yourself?" Luke extends the citation beyond Isa 40:3 to include vv. 4-5: "Every valley shall be filled, and every mountain and hill shall be made low, and the crooked shall be made straight, and the rough ways made smooth; and all flesh shall see the salvation of God" (Luke 3:5-6).

The use of Isa 40:3 as a lens through which the sectarians of the Dead Sea Scrolls identified themselves,[15] through which the New Testament located John the Baptist, and through which John the Baptist may even have situated himself, suggests that there is something more to the wilderness than mere geography. I am not taking sides with Willi Marxsen's disembodying remark about Mark 1:4, "The desert is not a geographical place,"[16] heeding instead Meier's call for attention to "the facile opposition still met in Gospel studies between geographical facts and theological symbolism."[17] Meier urges,

> We must realize that the geographical realities called the Judean desert and the Jordan River were suffused with religious meaning for the real inhabitants of Palestine centuries before the Baptist, the evangelists,

or redaction critics were attracted by the OT's heritage of "salvation geography."[18]

Deserts and wildernesses are made, not found: they are social constructs, defined in opposition to population centers, in opposition to places more hospitable to human habitation. Settlement in the wilderness is perceived as eccentric in the etymological sense: it is marginal, beyond the boundaries, stretching the limits of human resourcefulness. Settlements in the wilderness arouse curiosity by virtue of their isolation: why would anyone choose to live under such precarious conditions? Ongoing academic and popular fascination with the ruins at Qumran are a case in point. Thus, the placement of John the Baptist in modified Deutero-Isaian terms as a voice in the wilderness is a powerful statement about his marginal position and his prophetic identity.

It is one thing to choose to dwell in the wilderness, and quite another to be forced into the desert. John the Baptist chose to exercise his prophetic vocation from that location, standing at the margins so as to call forth *metanoia* (repentance) from individuals and to call for the transformation of the entire people. From his place in the Judean wilderness, John the Baptist attracted attention from the sincere, the curious, the suspicious, and the hostile alike, from those who came to immerse themselves in his words and in the waters of the Jordan, and from those who failed to recognize their thirst for conversion. According to Mark 1:5-6: "People from the whole Judean countryside and all the people of Jerusalem were going out to him, and were baptized by him in the river Jordan, confessing their sins." Tax collectors, soldiers, and even Jesus himself found their way to the wilderness to encounter John (Luke 3:10-14; Mark 1:9). Those at the center vacillated between surprise and suspicion, wondering whether John was Elijah redivivus, God's eschatological agent heralding the final transformation. Emissaries were sent from the center of power to figure out who John was and where he stood, and he answered by withdrawing further and further from their expectations:

> This is the testimony given by John when the Jews sent priests and Levites from Jerusalem to ask him, "Who are you?" He confessed and did not deny it but confessed, "I am not the Messiah." And they asked him, "What then? Are you Elijah?" He said, "I am not." "Are you the prophet?" He answered, "No." Then they said to him, "Who are you? Let us have an answer for those who sent us. What do you say about yourself?" (John 1:19-22)

John finally answered by aligning his person, his place, and his message with Isa 40:3. Ultimately, the challenge John posed from the margins became intolerable for those mighty ones accustomed to being at the center. When his call for change threatened to alter the dynamics of power, to overturn a status quo from the exploitation of which some prospered, first they incarcerated that prophet whose message could neither be contained nor confined, imprisoning the body whose voice could not be brought under human control. Then they silenced that voice in the wilderness, putting John to death. That was by no means an unexpected end for prophets, as Jesus laments: "Jerusalem, Jerusalem, the city that kills the prophets and stones those who are sent to it!" (Matt 23:37; Luke 13:34). The center cannot easily abide the perspective from the margins, the voices of those who speak from the wilderness.

In choosing to dwell in the wilderness, the prophet must guard against using it as a refuge, as Elijah sought to flee in the wilderness from the wrath of Ahab and Jezebel (1 Kgs 19). The prophet cannot afford to employ the wilderness as a hiding place, for there is no hiding either from the challenge of prophetic activity or from its consequences. God pursues Elijah, insisting, "Get up and eat, otherwise the journey will be too long for you" (1 Kgs 19:7). God provides the prophet with food and drink, but that gift of nourishment is given for the sake of the road ahead, the road that eventually leads Elijah to ascend in the whirlwind (2 Kgs 2). John the Baptist, Elijah redivivus, announces the transformation of the wilderness itself into a highway for the Mighty One.

Otto Betz offers two anecdotes that bear witness to the abiding appeal of John the Baptist, testifying that the death of the messenger could not kill the message, indeed that Elijah returns again and again. Betz writes:

> More than twenty years ago, when I was teaching at the University of Chicago, one of my black students said to me, "I want to be like John: a voice in the desert, crying for the outcasts, unmasking the hypocrites, showing sinners the way to righteousness!" A year later the wave of student revolts had reached my own university at Tübingen, where I had returned. I recall a good Christian student who suddenly declared: "Please, not Jesus! John the Baptist is my man!" And he gave up his theological studies.[19]

Hoping that our own encounter with John the Baptist will strengthen our own commitment to theological study, what might we learn about the theologian as prophet by our conversation with John the Baptist? Here, as with the three conversations yet to come, I want to focus on how our conversation with these study partners might shape our own theological discourse. Let me suggest that our encounter with John the Baptist reminds us that our words alone are insufficient, that being a "voice in the wilderness" is more than a matter of speech.

In conversation with John the Baptist about the theologian-as-prophet, we recognize that Hispanic-American and African-American theologians know the wilderness altogether too well. The hyphens themselves symbolize marginalizations imposed, not chosen, an ambivalent condition of being *arrojados*, thrown, into the complexity of the Diaspora.[20] For those in such wildernesses, the prophetic challenge emerges from the Deutero-Isaian text by which John the Baptist's mission is identified:

> Make straight in the desert a highway for our God. Every valley shall be filled up, and every mountain and hill be made low; the uneven ground

shall become level, and the rough places a plain. Then the glory of the
Lord shall be revealed, and all people shall see it together, for the mouth
of the Lord has spoken. (Isa 40:3b-5)

As voices announcing new Exodus and new Creation, Hispanic-American and
African-American theologians-as-prophets face a challenge that is more than a
matter of charting the wilderness, of mapping it so as to subdue it. On the contrary, the real challenge is to participate in the transformation of the wilderness
and to understand our journeys through that desert towards the fulfillment of
the promise.[21] Likewise we are not given the luxury of becoming too comfort-
able in the wilderness, or of using it as a refuge from danger, a hiding place
from the consequences of prophetic engagement with others. We cannot flee:
our God finds us there to nourish us for the road ahead.

THE SAMARITAN WOMAN: THE THEOLOGIAN AS DISCIPLE

There is something more than a little disturbing about the anonymity of Jesus'
dialogue partner in John 4, the woman at Jacob's well in Sychar, who is identified not by name but as a Samaritan. While understanding her as a representative figure—or as a character whose literary presence serves to tell the tale of
the Johannine community's postpaschal incorporation of Samaritan converts—helps to explain her literary function in the Fourth Gospel, neither
explanation completely lifts the veil of her anonymity.[22] She is not alone
among key characters in the Fourth Gospel to remain unnamed: both the
mother of Jesus and the beloved disciple are identified in terms of their privileged relationships with Jesus rather than by name. As for Jesus' dialogue partner in John 4, she is identified by gender and by ethnicity.

By choosing her as a study partner, I hope to learn something about the theologian as disciple, learning about that facet of the theological enterprise from
what she says and what is said of her in John 4.[23] The decision to converse
with her about the theologian as disciple emerges mainly from John 4:27. As
the male disciples of Jesus returned from their shopping trip in the village, we
learn that "They were astonished that he was speaking with a woman, but no
one said, 'What do you want?' or 'Why are you speaking with her?'"
Uncomprehending, the male disciples refused to resolve their astonishment by
asking the obvious questions either of Jesus or of his interlocutor. Not so the
Samaritan Woman: from the beginning of the encounter, she engaged her
interlocutor in probing religious and even theological questions.[24] In the end,
she went to the village from which the male disciples had just returned. She
went not to buy, not to acquire or to receive anything from the villagers, but to
share with them the self-disclosure that resulted from her encounter with
Jesus. She went to invite them to a similar encounter: "Come and see a man
who told me everything I have ever done!" (John 4:29).

Unlike Nicodemus' nighttime encounter with Jesus, the encounter at the
well takes place at noon, when there can be no hiding from the bright light of
Truth. The woman's words to Jesus start by recognizing the complex border

crossing taking place at Jacob's well: "How is it that you, a Jew, ask a drink of me, a woman of Samaria?" The narrator hastens to explain, "Jews do not share things in common with Samaritans" (John 4:9).[25] Identified by her ethnicity, the Samaritan Woman stands her ground and confronts Jesus with difference: "Our ancestors worshiped on this mountain, but you say that the place where people must worship is in Jerusalem" (John 4:19-20).[26]

What might we learn about the theologian as disciple by conversing with the Samaritan Woman? The contrast sharply drawn between her attitude and the silent confusion of the male disciples reminds us that authentic discipleship is not a task for the timid, that there is no hiding from the hard questions. The challenge of discipleship involves close attention not only to the answers with which the Teacher satisfies our thirst for Truth, but also to the sources from which the questions themselves well up. The Samaritan Woman's honesty about the conflict between Gerizim and Jerusalem teaches us not to suppress tension, difference, or disagreement. The Samaritan Woman also gives voice to the hopes of her people: "I know that Messiah is coming . . . ," she declares, "When he comes, he will proclaim all things to us" (John 4:25).

In conversation with the Samaritan Woman about the theologian as disciple, we come to recognize that African-American and Hispanic-American theologians are challenged to stand with our peoples, with a deep and nuanced knowledge of their histories, their experiences, and their aspirations. In a sense, we are disciples *of* and disciples *with* our peoples, for they are teachers to us and fellow learners alongside us. The Samaritan Woman's example cautions us against making the arrogant and fraudulent claim that we can speak definitively either for or on behalf of our peoples, for to claim ownership of their voice amounts to robbery. Because, as disciples, we are invited to ask questions of our teachers, we learn from the Samaritan Woman that we should neither deny hard questions their space nor settle for easy answers that fail to quench more than momentary thirst.

Recognizing Jesus' interlocutor at Jacob's well as a Samaritan keeps this study partner at a safe distance as a remote other, for time and place separate us from Samaritans past or present. Recognizing our study partner as a woman brings her closer, brings her into range as a proximate and therefore potentially challenging other. To begin with, in John 4:27 the male disciples are not disturbed that Jesus is engaged in conversation with a Samaritan. It is Jesus' engagement in conversation with a woman that disturbs them.[27] Over the course of the centuries, the reactions of many others who have come upon the dialogue between the woman of Samaria and Jesus have been even more dangerous than the silent astonishment of the male disciples on the scene. Many (mostly male) interpreters have misconstrued the Johannine reappropriation of the already dangerous Hebrew prophetic metaphor of Israel's religious infidelity as female sexual infidelity, misreading John 4:18 in literal terms so as to deny the personal integrity of the woman of Samaria by accusing her of sexual immorality. One recent male commentator speculates, "this woman must have had a series of divorces and now lived with a man without marriage," and this commentator likewise rejects any symbolic reading of John 4:18 vehemently: "This exegesis is not to be countenanced ... the Evangelist does not allegorize in this manner."[28] Such vehemence is sad and deadly. By conversing with the woman of Samaria about the theologian as disciple, African-American and Hispanic-American theologians are warned that there are deadly ways of reading sacred texts, ways of wounding and maiming with words meant to bring life.

MARY MAGDALENE: THE THEOLOGIAN AS EVANGELIZER

The gospels tell us precious little about Mary Magdalene.[29] Reference to her during the course of Jesus' public ministry is limited to a passing mention among those who followed Jesus as "he went on through cities and villages, proclaiming and bringing the good news of the reign of God" (Luke 8:1). Her name is listed among the women "who had been cured of evil spirits and infirmities ... who provided for him [Jesus] out of their resources," and she is specifically identified as someone "from whom seven demons had gone out" (Luke 8:2-3). Luke tells us that these women who journeyed with Jesus from Galilee to Jerusalem, Mary Magdalene among them, were present at his crucifixion and burial and that they came to the tomb and found it empty on the first day of the week (Luke 23:49-24:12).

The Fourth Gospel focuses on the figure of Mary Magdalene at the empty tomb. She alone ventured outside the city, going to the tomb early on the morning of the first day of the week. She alone discovered it empty and ran to report that distressing discovery to Simon Peter and the beloved disciple. She alone witnessed the angelophany, and it was Mary Magdalene who first declared, "I have seen the Lord" (John 20:18). Yet believing did not have to do with seeing: she did not recognize Jesus as he stood there. Mistaking him for the gardener, she continued her quest for her Lord by asking him the whereabouts of the body. She did not find what she was looking for or what she could reasonably have expected: there was no corpse in the tomb. Yet hearing was believing: as she heard Jesus speak her name, she recognized her Teacher. Then, like the Samaritan Woman earlier in the Fourth Gospel, Mary Magdalene could not but speak the good news she experienced.

Mary Magdalene went to the tomb to mourn, but there was no body in the unsealed tomb, no corpse over which to shed lavish tears, no corruptible remains of a life handed over to death, nothing to give silent testimony to the incarnation of God's Word. Yet that tomb was empty because it was unneeded, for there were no shrouded remains, no body embalmed to stave off the consequences of mortality. This tomb was no place for mourning, because the Word-made-flesh had put death to death, because no stone could bar the door from which the Risen One emerged, leaving the trappings of death behind. Fittingly enough, the Living Word spoke to Mary Magdalene, calling her by name. It was fitting too that she heard the Word and recognized him as the Lord. How fitting then, that the Risen Word instructed her to bring the word of his exaltation to others.

After hearing the Word call her by name, after recognizing his voice (Cf.

John 10:3), Mary Magdalene was called upon to speak, to bear witness to the resurrection. What she said is telling, for she did not begin by announcing that Jesus had been raised from the dead, but by declaring, "I have seen the Lord." That was not the sort of wishful imagining that emerges from grief, but the testimony of an encounter with the one who had answered the query of would-be disciples, "Rabbi, where are you staying?" with the invitation, "Come and see" (John 1:38-39), of an encounter with the one who addressed Thomas, "Have you believed because you have seen me? Blessed are those who have not seen and yet have come to believe" (John 20:29). Mary Magdalene could dare to speak of the resurrection because she had come to the tomb, because she knew death and grief, loss and mourning. It was through her tears and then through her words that others who had not seen would be invited to believe.

What of the impact of Mary's message? How was it received? Strangely, the Fourth Gospel gives us no indication at all. However, in Mark 16:10, part of the longer ending, we learn that "when they heard that he was alive and had been seen by her, they would not believe it." In Luke 24:11, when the group of women disciples reported their discovery and the angelic proclamation to the apostles, "It seemed to them an idle tale, and they did not believe them."

In conversation with Mary Magdalene about the theologian as evangelizer, African-American and Hispanic-American theologians learn that we are called to mourn with our peoples, called to weep with them over the many ways in which death casts its pallid shadow over their lives, in which violence in its countless destructive forms robs life from individuals and communities and even entire peoples. Even as we are called to mourn, and precisely because we are called to mourn, we are also called to stand together against death, to claim and to proclaim the power of the resurrection. Mary Magdalene invites us to recognize that the Risen One calls us by name, calls us to life, calls us to share in the ascent that takes him beyond death's wrappings into communion with the Living One. Likewise Mary Magdalene warns us that while others may not listen when we speak, and may even resist the word we bring, that cannot prevent us from continuing to speak. That cannot keep us from declaring that the tomb is empty because death itself has been robbed of its power over life. The message is clear: life wins, death loses.

JOHN OF THE APOCALYPSE:
THE THEOLOGIAN AS VISIONARY

Addressing himself to the churches of the seven cities of the Roman province of Asia during the reign of the emperor Domitian (81-96 C.E.), a Christian prophet writes,

> I, John, your brother who share with you in Jesus the affliction and the sovereignty and the patient endurance, was on the island called Patmos because of the word of God and the testimony of Jesus. I was in the spirit

on the Lord's day, and I heard behind me a loud voice like a trumpet saying, "Write in a book what you see and send it to the seven churches."
(Rev 1:9-11a)

As early as Tertullian (*De Praescript. Haer.* 36), John's presence on Patmos
"because of the word of God and the testimony of Jesus" was explained as the
result of a sentence of *relegatio in insulam*, banishment to an island by the
Roman authorities, as a result of his Christian convictions.[30] Yet that is not
what John tells his audience, and more recent reconsideration of the situation
of the churches in Roman Asia during the late first century C.E. yields no evidence either of active persecution of Christians or of the use of Patmos as a
place of banishment.[31]

What John does tell his audience at the beginning of the Revelation's inaugural vision (Rev 1:9-20) is significant enough, especially for our purposes.
Writing at a geographical distance from his original audience and at a historical distance from subsequent audiences, the seer of the Apocalypse begins to
address them by mapping the common ground between them. Eschewing the
apocalyptic convention of pseudonymity, his first revelation to the seven
churches is a disclosure of his own name, John, followed by a threefold specification of the solidarity he claims as their brother.

John shares with the members of the churches the eschatological affliction
(*thlipsis* is not to be narrowly construed as persecution) and the reign
(*basileia*), as well as the patient endurance (*hypomonē*), that enables believers
in Jesus to draw hope amid the tension of the negative and positive dynamics
of life in an urgent age. After naming the threefold bond that links him with
those who receive his words, John identifies the place from which he writes.
On one level, this specification is geographical, Patmos. On another level, it is
theological and christological, insofar as he is on Patmos "because of the
Word of God and the testimony of/to Jesus" (Rev 1:9).[32] We are left to wonder
what this twofold specification means until later in the book. In Rev 19:10 we
learn with John, through the words of an interpreting angel, that "the testimony of/to Jesus is the spirit of prophecy." To hold the testimony of/to Jesus is
potentially perilous: in Rev 6:9 we hear the outcry of those who were slaughtered on account of the Word of God and the testimony they had given. The
church at Pergamum was already painfully aware of these perils: in Rev 2:9
the risen Jesus speaks to that church of "Antipas my witness, my faithful one,
who was killed among you."

John completes the introduction to his inaugural vision with two further
specifications: "I was in the spirit on the Lord's day" (Rev 1:10). That ecstasy,
deliberately framed in terms drawn from Israel's prophets (e.g., Ezek 3:12),
took him beyond the boundaries of ordinary human consciousness.[33] The tem-
poral indicator "on the Lord's Day" specifies the liminality of John's visionary
experience as a betwixt-and-between condition mediated by ritual, specifically
by Christian worship.[34] With blessings pronounced on the lector and on the
listeners in Rev 1:3, it becomes clear that John granted access to his visionary
narrative by the Apocalypse's original audiences in and through their worship.

The liturgy of the seven churches was the sacred space and time within which they were to confront both the particular admonitions of the messages to the seven churches (Rev 2:1-3:22) and the disclosure of the mystery of God (Rev 10:7) that was offered in the seven-sealed scroll entrusted to the Lamb (Rev 4:1-22:21).

In conversation with John on Patmos about the theologian as visionary, Hispanic-American and African-American theologians are called to write what they see, just as they see it. John saw clearly the irreconcilable conflict between Babylon and Jerusalem. John recognized the conflict of cultures and challenged his audience to take sides, to refuse to melt into the melting pot, and to stand fast against compromise no matter the consequences.[35] From John we learn that we are held accountable for what we say and what we write. That accountability is not limited to the intersecting circles of church, academy, and public, for what we say and write has cosmic implications. As John was commanded to ingest the little scroll and to prophesy about many peoples and nations and languages and kings (Rev 10:8-11), theologians are to live the words they pronounce.

From John who wrote in the spirit on the Lord's day and who invoked blessings on the lector and congregation who received his book, we learn that if liturgy is a metaphor for life, it is hardly surprising that there should be real dissonance between vehicle and tenor, or that the vehicle (liturgy) itself reflects the tensions present in the tenor (life).

From John we learn that the genuine visionary sees differently, deeply committed to understanding matters that are infinitely more complex than they seem, confident in God, the Revealer of mysteries to the prophets. With John we hear the loud outcry of those "who had been slaughtered for the word of God and the testimony they had given" as they plead "How long, O Lord?" (see Rev 6:9). That lament is no faint and distant echo in our ears: it is present in the cries of those who continue to be martyred for their honest testimony to God's word and will. With John we also share the vision of a new creation: new heavens, a new earth, a new Jerusalem. There "death will be no more; mourning and crying and pain will be no more" (Rev 21:4).

CONCLUSION: HOPE AND WATER

Allow me to conclude by beginning to sketch the composite challenge that emerges from the four Johannine conversations in which we have just engaged. As a prophet like John the Baptist, theologians inhabit the wilderness. As disciples like the Samaritan Woman, theologians go to the well. As evangelists like Mary Magdalene, theologians go to the tomb. As visionaries like John of the Apocalypse, theologians go to their own Patmos, drawn there "because of the word of God and the testimony of/to Jesus." Let me say a word about each of these spaces, about what might bring theologians there, and about what theologians might find when they arrive there.

As a wilderness dweller, the theologian-as-prophet ventures outside the walls, not to flee from the city, but to address the city and its inhabitants from that vantage. Caught in the Johannine dilemma of being *in* the world but not *of* the world (John 15:19; 17:11), theologians are called upon to venture into uncharted territory. Unlike the missionaries who accompanied the *conquistadores*, who wielded the cross as a weapon subtler than lance or sword, it is not the work of the theologian to dominate. Like John the Baptizer, the theologian is called to be Elijah, the eschatological forerunner, announcing the imminence of divine action.

As a disciple like the Samaritan Woman, the theologian is drawn to the well from which life-giving water is drawn, there to encounter the one who "will proclaim all things to us" (John 4:25). Bringing the jar of self and people to the ancestral well, the theologian drinks deeply by listening closely, then invites others to quench their thirst, to taste the living water.

As an evangelizer like Mary Magdalene, the theologian is drawn to the tomb. Yet the tombs to which theologians are called today are not empty. They are the graves, marked and unmarked, of all the world's victims, the resting place of those who were given no peace in life, and of those whose sleep in death is troubled by the ongoing violence of the world they left behind. There is no room for naïve or innocent optimism for those who stand by such graves as these. Even so, while standing at the tomb, theologians are called to be bearers of the gospel, of a gospel that subverts this world's power. Theologians, and indeed all believers, are to speak the gospel of a God who raises the dead to life, calling each by name.

As a visionary like John of the Apocalypse, the theologian is drawn to Patmos, to speak and write of what was and what is and what is to come. Sharing "the affliction and the sovereignty and the patient endurance" with those who receive their testimony—standing with them even when distant—theologians are called upon to be faithful without compromise and true to church and academy and world. Like John of the Apocalypse, theologians are invited to dispose themselves to being in the Spirit on the Lord's Day.

For the prophet, the disciple, the evangelizer, and the visionary, hope flows freely as water, cleansing water that nourishes hope and life. That is good news for those who sit in exile beside the arid waters of Babylon longing for Zion. John baptized with water. The Samaritan Woman drank of living water, and from it received strength and courage to invite others to see and hear and drink. Mary Magdalene saw death denied victory in the blood and water pouring forth from the wounded side of Jesus. John of the Apocalypse, separated by water from the churches to which he was bound by "the affliction and the sovereignty and the patient endurance," saw from Patmos the stream of life-giving water that flows from the throne of God and the Lamb to heal the nations. To the victor goes the promise of life-giving water that springs from the well of Truth and Life itself, the Bread of Life that feeds our people for the journey through the wilderness to the fulfillment of the promise.

NOTES

1. In the introductory overview of theology he offers, J. J. Mueller includes academic credentials in his "profile of a theologian," but hardly restricts the profile to that criterion (*What Is Theology?* [Zacchaeus Studies: Theology; Collegeville: Liturgical Press, 1991] 93-94). Indeed the profile is growing increasingly complex and diverse. See the autobiographical presentation by James Cone in his 1994 Bellarmine Lecture at St. Louis University, "The Vocation of a Theologian," *Theology Digest* 41 (1994) 303-13; as well as W. H. Myers, "The Hermeneutical Dilemma of the African American Biblical Student," *Stony the Road We Trod: African American Biblical Interpretation,* ed. Cain Hope Felder (Minneapolis: Fortress Press, 1991) 40-56. See also the Congregation for the Doctrine of the Faith's *Instruction on the Ecclesial Vocation of the Theologian* (Vatican City: Libreria Editrice Vaticana, 1990), which situates the theologian's activity within the ecclesial context from the Roman Catholic standpoint. On globalization both as theme and as pressing challenge for the practice of theology and for the theological training of ministers, see *The Globalization of Theological Education,* ed. A. F. Evans, et al. (Maryknoll: Orbis Books, 1993).

2. The first universities were founded in Europe around the year 1200. Jaroslav Pelikan has ventured to suggest that the most important action of the Council of Trent, several centuries later, may well have been "the legislation of its twenty-third session of July 1563, bearing the title 'Forma erigendi seminarium clericorum'," which decreed the establishment of diocesan seminaries for the training of the clergy (*The Idea of the University: A Reexamination* [New Haven and London: Yale University Press, 1992] 107-108). See John Van Engen, "Catholic Higher Education: Historic Past or Distinctive Future?" *The Challenge and Promise of a Catholic University,* ed. T. M. Hesburgh (Notre Dame: University of Notre Dame Press, 1994) 353-69.

3. On the hermeneutics of conversation, influenced by the work of David Tracy, see J.-P. Ruiz, "Contexts in Conversation: First World and Third World Readings of Job," *Journal of Hispanic/Latino Theology* 2 (1995) 8-11.

4. In addition to the essays in the earlier volumes of this project, *Reading from This Place,* see J. E. Massey, "Reading the Bible as African Americans" and F. F. Segovia, "Reading the Bible as Hispanic Americans," *The New Interpreter's Bible,* ed. Leander Keck et al. (Nashville: Abingdon, 1994) 1:154-60 and 1:167-73, respectively.

5. On midrash, see the convenient treatment and bibliography provided in G. G. Porton, "Midrash," *Anchor Bible Dictionary,* ed. D. N. Freedman (New York: Doubleday, 1992) 4:818-22.

6. One of the fringe benefits of the resurgence of Jesus research has been a renewal of interest in the conversation between biblical scholarship (New Testament scholarship in particular) and systematic theology. See, for example, Francis Schüssler Fiorenza, "The Jesus of Piety and the Historical Jesus," *CTSA Proceedings* 49 (1994) 90-99.

7. *Origins* 23:29 (January 6, 1994) 520-21.

8. See Roberto S. Goizueta, "Rediscovering Praxis: The Significance of U.S. Hispanic Experience for Theological Method," *We Are a People! Initiatives in Hispanic American Theology,* ed. R. S. Goizueta (Minneapolis: Fortress Press, 1992) 51-77.

9. Elisabeth Schüssler Fiorenza, "The Quest for the Johannine School: The Book of Revelation and the Fourth Gospel," *The Book of Revelation: Justice and Judgment* (Philadelphia: Fortress Press, 1985) 85-113.

10. John P. Meier, *A Marginal Jew: Rethinking the Historical Jesus.* Volume 2: *Mentor, Message, and Miracles* (Anchor Bible Reference Library; New York: Doubleday, 1994) 1-2.

11. See, e.g., Otto Betz, "Was John the Baptist an Essene?" and James C. Vanderkam, "The Dead Sea Scrolls and Christianity," *Understanding the Dead Sea Scrolls,* ed. Hershel Shanks (New York: Random House, 1992) 205-214 and 181-204, respectively.

12. Raymond E. Brown, *The Community of the Beloved Disciple* (New York: Paulist Press, 1979) esp. 69-71.

13. See, e.g., Paul W. Hollenbach, "Social Aspects of John the Baptizer's Preaching in the Context of Palestinian Judaism," *Aufstieg und Niedergang der römischen Welt* II/19.1 (1979) 850-75; R. L. Webb, *John the Baptizer and Prophet: A Socio-Historical Study,* Journal for the Study of the New Testament—Supplement Series 62 (Sheffield: JSOT Press, 1991).

14. Meier, *Mentor, Message, and Miracles*, 87-88.

15. See, e.g., 1QS 8:13-14: "... in compliance with these arrangements they are to be segregated from within the dwelling of the men of sin to walk to the desert in order to open there His path. As it is written: 'in the desert, prepare the way of ****, straighten in the steppe a roadway for our God.'" The translation is from Florentino García Martínez, *The Dead Sea Scrolls Translated: The Qumran Texts in English,* trans. Wilfred G. E. Watson (Leiden: E. J. Brill, 1994) 12.

16. W. Marxsen, *Der Evangelist Markus* (Göttingen: Vandenhoeck & Ruprecht, 1959) 22, as quoted by Meier (*Mentor, Message and Miracles*, 46).

17. Ibid., 45-46.

18. Ibid., 46.

19. Betz, "Was John the Baptist an Essene?" 208.

20. See Fernando F. Segovia, "Toward a Hermeneutics of the Diaspora: A Hermeneutics of Otherness and Engagement," *Reading from This Place*. Volume 1: *Social Location and Biblical Interpretation in the United States,* ed. Fernando F. Segovia and Mary Ann Tolbert (Minneapolis: Fortress Press, 1995) 60-61. On "life in the hyphen," see I. Stavans, *The Hispanic Condition: Reflections on Culture and Identity in America* (New York: Harper Collins, 1995) 7-30.

21. On the strengths and weaknesses of the reappropriation of the Exodus metaphor, see J.-P. Ruiz, "New Ways of Reading the Bible in the Cultural Settings of the Third World," *The Bible as Cultural Heritage,* ed. Wim Beuken and Seán Freyne, *Concilium* 1995/1 (London: SCM; Maryknoll: Orbis Books, 1995) 75-76.

22. On the Samaritan Woman as a representative figure, see Raymond F. Collins, "Representative Figures," *These Things Have Been Written: Studies on the Fourth Gospel* (Grand Rapids: William B. Eerdmans, 1990) 16-19. On the information John 4 provides about the origins of Johannine Christianity, see Brown, *Community of the Beloved Disciple*, 35-40.

23. On discipleship in John's Gospel, see Fernando F. Segovia, "'Peace I Leave with You; My Peace I Give You': Discipleship in the Fourth Gospel," *Discipleship in the New Testament,* ed. Fernando F. Segovia (Philadelphia: Fortress Press, 1985) 76-102. On the Samaritan Woman as disciple and apostle, see Sandra M. Schneiders, *The Revelatory Text: Interpreting the New Testament as Sacred Scripture* (San Francisco: Harper Collins, 1991) 180-99; also Mary Margaret Pazdan, "Nicodemus and the Samaritan Woman: Contrasting Models of Discipleship," *Biblical Theology Bulletin* 17 (1987) 145-48.

24. Schneiders, *The Revelatory Text*, 189.

25. On the narrator's explanation of the Samaritan Woman's question, see Charles H. Talbert, *Reading John: A Literary and Theological Commentary on the Fourth Gospel and the Johannine Epistles* (New York: Crossroad, 1992) 112-13. See also Stephen D. Moore, "Are There Impurities in the Living Water that the Johannine Jesus Dispenses? Deconstruction, Feminism, and the Samaritan Woman," *Biblical Interpretation* 1 (1993) 207-227; and Jerome H. Neyrey, "What's Wrong with This Picture? John 4, Cultural Stereotypes of Women, and Public and Private Space," *Biblical Theology Bulletin* 24 (1994) 77-91.

26. For a convenient presentation of Samaritan history, literature, beliefs, and practices, together with a current bibliography, see R. T. Anderson, "Samaritans," *Anchor Bible Dictionary* 5:940-47.

27. Schneiders writes, "The brief episode of the return of the disciples, looked at from a feminist perspective, reveals the all-too-familiar uneasiness of men when one of their number takes a woman too seriously, especially in the area of the men's primary concern" (*The Revelatory Text*, 195).

28. George R. Beasley-Murray, *John,* Word Biblical Commentary 36 (Waco: Word, 1987) 61.

29. On the figure of Mary Magdalene in the gospels and beyond, see S. Haskins, *Mary Magdalen: Myth and Metaphor* (New York: Harcourt Brace, 1993). On Mary Magdalene as resurrection witness, see G. O'Collins and D. Kendall, "Mary Magdalene as Major Witness to Jesus' Resurrection," *Theological Studies* 48 (1987) 631-46.

30. For example, G. B. Caird, *A Commentary on the Revelation of St. John the Divine* (Harper's NT Commentaries; New York: Harper & Row, 1966) 21-22.

31. See L. Thompson, *The Book of Revelation: Apocalypse and Empire* (New York: Oxford University Press, 1990) 95-115. On the other hand, J. Roloff continues to insist, despite the lack of evidence for Patmos as a place of banishment, "that John was exiled to Patmos by the authorities in Ephesus as a promoter of official unrest on the basis of his strong view against the cult of the Caesar" (*Revelation,* Continental Commentary [Minneapolis: Fortress, 1993] 32). Nowhere does the Apocalypse give indication of such a sentence.

32. On the expression *martyria Iēsou,* see J.-P. Ruiz, *Ezekiel in the Apocalypse: The Transformation of Prophetic Language in Revelation 16, 17-19, 10,* European University Studies 23, 376 (Frankfurt am Main: Peter Lang, 1989) 514-16.

33. See Charles H. Giblin, *The Book of Revelation: The Open Book of Prophecy,* Good News Studies 34 (Collegeville: Liturgical Press, 1991) 68; R. L. Jeske, "Spirit and Community in the Johannine Apocalypse," *New Testament Studies* 31 (1985) 452-66.

34. See J.-P. Ruiz, "Betwixt and Between on the Lord's Day: Liturgy and the Apocalypse," *1992 Society of Biblical Literature Seminar Papers,* ed. Eugene H. Lovering, Jr. (Atlanta: Scholars Press, 1992) 664.

35. See Elisabeth Schüssler Fiorenza, *Revelation: Vision of a Just World,* Proclamation Commentaries (Minneapolis: Fortress Press, 1991) esp. 129-39.

Part II

SOCIAL LOCATION
AND BIBLICAL PEDAGOGY
IN THE UNITED STATES

6

CROSSING THE LINE

*Three Scenes of Divine-Human Engagement
in the Hebrew Bible*

Francisco García-Treto

> *This is my home
> this thin edge of
> barbwire.*
> Gloria Anzaldúa
> *Borderlands/La Frontera: The New Mestiza*

In his programmatic article in the first volume of this project, Fernando Segovia delineates a hermeneutical stance which he styles "a hermeneutics of the diaspora," a Hispanic-American hermeneutics of otherness and engagement, whose fundamental purpose is to read the biblical text as an other—not to be overwhelmed or overridden, but acknowledged, respected, and engaged in its very otherness.[1] I would argue that the sort of reading Segovia envisions can only begin by paying close attention to scenes of engagement *within the biblical text itself*, scenes in which God—the Bible's ultimate Other—is engaged by a human character. "Engagement," I would argue, is the proper way to refer to what is happening in biblical scenes in which God, rather than remain a monologic "voice from above," is a character in dialogue, addressed in (re)turn by a human actor, and as such open to criticism and even to change of mind. Rather than being hard-edged and impenetrable, as indeed much traditional hermeneutics—not to say dogmatics—has assumed it to be, God's discourse is permeable to human discourse: lines are crossed, borders become meeting places where humans "talk back" and, most importantly, God's announced agendas can be changed in response to a human voice.

Three scenes in particular stand out for me in the Hebrew Bible as "borderline" moments in which human characters engage God in dialogue about one of the latter's just-announced decisions or commands, questioning its wisdom or its justice, and forcing God to reconsider, to make concessions, or to modify his command. Let me say at the outset that Job, who may at first glance seem to be the first case to consider, proves on closer examination not to fit the criterion just mentioned. The three scenes, then, are those played between God and, respectively, Cain in Gen 4:9–16, Abraham in Gen 18:22–23, and Ezekiel in Ezek 4:9–15.

God's human interlocutors in these three scenes share and represent a characteristic which I find most appealing: they are all, in one way or another, and for a variety of reasons, exiles. The narratives present these characters as driven by a promise or by a curse; fleeing from captivity or herded into it; "on the way," settled neither in what is "no longer" nor in what remains "not yet," neither in the old world nor in the new, however inescapably they remain tied to both. It should of course be clear to the reader by now that my personal life situation, like that of many other Cuban–Americans of my generation,[2] and like the lives of many other contemporary hyphenated Americans, is one ruled by the personal experience of exile.

Borrowing a term coined by the Cuban sociologist Rubén Rumbaut, the Cuban-American poet and critic Gustavo Pérez Firmat dubs his (my) generation of Cuban exiles who "belong to an intermediate immigrant generation whose members spent their childhood or adolescence abroad but grew into adults in America," the "one-and-a-half" generation, those whose existence his most recent book describes as "living on the hyphen."[3] It is this generation, Pérez Firmat maintains, that has been mostly responsible for shaping Cuban-American culture, "for their intercultural placement makes them more likely to undertake the negotiations and compromises that produce ethnic culture. Life on the hyphen can be anyone's prerogative, but it is the one-and-a-halfer's destiny."[4] Pérez Firmat does not ignore the galling disadvantages of the marginality that that destiny involves, nor the reality of the ache of exile (he refers, poetically, to it as the "Carolina blues"), but nonetheless emphasizes the unique advantages which the exile's condition can confer:

> While one-and-a-halfers may never feel entirely at ease in either one, they are capable of availing themselves of the resources—linguistic, artistic, commercial—that both cultures have to offer. In some ways they are both first and second generation. Unlike their older and younger cohorts, they may actually be able to choose cultural habitats. . . . One-and-a-halfers are translation artists. Tradition bound but translation bent, they are sufficiently immersed in each culture to give both ends of the hyphen their due.[5]

Segovia speaks precisely of the advantages which a recognized and embraced *otherness*—to use his term—yields to those of us who are working to establish a liberating Hispanic-American hermeneutical voice, first among which is the basic perception that all worlds, nature itself, are constructions, and all laws, nature's laws among them, conventions.[6] Exiles have this perception forced upon them, since what is customary in one society may be illegal in another; in other words, the hierarchy of values is different in different cultures, and the concrete forms of expression given to those values may be radically different across the border. The "one-and-a-halfer's" sense of bicultural-ism (again, to use Segovia's term) engenders a constant arbitration in which every value, every fiat, every truth expressed by one culture is compared to, questioned by, and given a new spin by those of the other. This bicultural arbi-tration is what Pérez Firmat calls "translation," when he says that "one-and-a-halfers are translation artists . . . tradition bound but translation bent."

Informed by this point of view, the hermeneutical process becomes dialogic, a negotiation with the text, rather than a passive reception of "what the text says." When we remember that the writers and redactors of the Hebrew Bible were themselves products of a culture massively influenced by exile, we can understand the special appropriateness of the hermeneutical stance of a con-temporary "one-and-a-halfer" for interpreting the texts they penned and the characters they depicted.

CAIN: THE RIGHTS OF OUTCASTS

My punishment is greater than I can bear! Today you have driven me away from the soil, and I shall be hidden from your face; I shall be a fugi-tive and a wanderer on the earth, and anyone who meets me may kill me. (NRSV, Gen 4:13, 14)

The first of God's interlocutors is perhaps the most unlikely one: Cain, the first murderer, on the point of being banished from the land that drank the blood of his brother, is sentenced by Yahweh to perpetual exile. The narrative leaves no doubt as to Cain's guilt. In fact, Yahweh had even warned him before-hand of the likelihood of an escalation of his angry disappointment at the rejec-tion of his sacrifice. Everett Fox's translation captures accurately the tone of the warning: "Why are you so enraged? Why has your face fallen? . . . if you do not intend good, at the entrance is sin, a crouching-demon, toward you his lust. . . ." (Gen 4:6–7).[7] But while making no attempt to exonerate Cain from the guilt of the premeditated murder of his brother Abel, what the biblical nar-rative does not do is to demonize Cain into an alien "other," in the way that much traditional interpretation, particularly Christian interpretation, has.

Augustine, following a line of interpretation already marked out by Philo, did much to set a dualistic pattern in this story, which dominated Christian readings of Cain, and of course of Abel, for centuries to come. In Book XV of the *City of God*, Augustine in fact traces the origins of his two cities to the primeval brothers:

Now Cain was the first son born to those two parents of mankind, and he belonged to the city of man; the latter son, Abel, belonged to the City of God. . . . When those two cities started on their course through the succession of birth and death, the first to be born was a citizen of this world, and later appeared one who was a pilgrim and stranger in the world, belonging as he did to the City of God.[8]

In a recent study of the literary history of the theme, Ricardo J. Quinones credits Philo, and following him, Augustine, for the revolutionary and long influential reading of Cain and Abel that transformed "the biblical brothers ... into universal, rival, and contending principles."[9] Cain is of course demonized and made monstrous, while Abel, the blameless pilgrim and innocent victim, becomes a type of Christ and a model for Christians. Jerome, Augustine's contemporary, follows the lead of the Septuagint and (mis)reads Cain's complaint as a confession of guilt: "My iniquity is too great to deserve forgiveness" (maior est iniquitas mea quam ut veniam merear [Vulgate, v. 13]), thus setting the tone for centuries of Western interpretation in which Cain, whether the misbegotten spawn of Satan that he became in much medieval exegesis or the Byronic rebel of romanticism, is a type of the unforgiven, demonic, and irreconcilable Other.[10]

Contemporary exegesis allows, indeed can be said to require,[11] a different reading, represented for example in the NRSV's "My punishment is greater than I can bear!" or Fox's "My punishment is too great to be borne!" (v. 13). Cain's complaint, simply put, is that Yahweh has placed upon him—guilty though he is of fratricide—too extreme a punishment, a sentence that would place him outside the bounds of lawful human existence, that condemns him to the "solitary, poor, nasty, brutish and short" life of the Hobbesian state of nature. Cain fears that, banished ("cursed") from the land that drank his brother's blood, he will also disappear from Yahweh's presence ("and from your face must I conceal myself" [Fox, v. 14]) and fall therefore outside the only guarantee he knows—precisely because he is its first transgressor—of the sanctity of human life. But to be an "outlaw" is to be beyond appeal to any law, beyond the protection of any law; it is to be "fair game" for anyone's aggression: "I shall be a fugitive and a wanderer on the earth, and anyone who meets me may kill me" (NRSV, v. 14).

When God sentences him to radical and inexorable exclusion, a sentence which, left to stand unmodified, would turn him into the archetypal demonized "Other," Cain's protest appeals to bonds which even Yahweh is forced to recognize. In effect, the ground for Cain's complaint is precisely that the bonds of common humanity, and of humankind with God, are not broken; in fact, they cannot be broken, not even for the guilty. Westermann is surely right when he recognizes in this verse the compressed, but nevertheless complete, outline of an "I-lament" or "individual lament," a frequent form among the Psalms,[12] proleptically issuing from the lips of Cain.

Cain appeals, and God responds to his appeal (v. 15) in a literary form in which the tones of the temple liturgy resonate, however faintly: he may be banished, but he is not "excommunicated," at least not from Yahweh, whose response has the startled tone of sudden recognition: "Not so!" (NRSV, v. 15). Yahweh then proceeds to institute blood-revenge as a primitive and problem-fraught, to be sure, but nonetheless positive guarantee of protection for human life. The mark that God puts on Cain is clearly not meant to designate him forever as a murderer, but to signify the abiding divine protection which even the so-called "Godforsaken," the "fugitives and wanderers upon the earth," the often alienated and demonized Others, indelibly bear. In a profoundly ambiguous ending to the story, the biblical account gives Cain a future which is both banishment and journey, both forced exile and migration, "in the land of Nod, east of Eden." There, the fratricide becomes the founder of a city and the father of a line that originates the arts, crafts, and economic pursuits of civilization, and *pace* Augustine and his followers, nothing in the Genesis account allows for a negative reading of those accomplishments.

"Cain and Abel in a single soul," says Octavio Paz, masterfully characterizing the *mestizos* of seventeenth-century Mexico.[13] For reasons which I will explore further in this paper, that characterization is eminently applicable to Hispanic-American culture, a culture fundamentally defined by what has been variously designated as *mestizaje*, or *mulatez*, or *mezcolanza*. Suffice it to say that to be conscious of the history that formed us is to understand its truth. My reading of Cain's encounter with Yahweh stems from that consciousness: I live "east of Eden, in the Land of Nod." The angry god who requires Abel's blood from his brother's hand is also the god who hears the plea of Cain and backs away from demonizing him, allowing him to go into exile bearing not only his guilt but also the redemptive possibility of a future and a hope.

ABRAHAM: JUSTICE, ABOVE ALL

> Heaven forbid for you to do a thing like this, to deal death to the innocent along with the guilty, that it should come about: like the innocent, like the guilty, Heaven forbid for you! The judge of all the earth—will he not do what is just? (Fox, Gen 18:25)

When considered against the relatively small range of biblical passages in which human beings dare to "talk back" and engage God in a discussion about a divine decision just announced, Gen 18:22–33, Abraham's questioning of Yahweh concerning the justice of the latter's announced intention to destroy Sodom, stands alone in its audacity. Chapter 18 begins (vv. 1–16) with the theophanic visit of the "three men" to Abraham's camp by the oaks of Mamre. There, having accepted the patriarch's legendary hospitality, they announce the imminent fulfillment of the long-delayed promise concerning the birth of Sarah's son. It seems somewhat incongruous, then, to delay the narrative with the digression which the dialogue between Yahweh and Abraham (vv. 19–33) concerning the fate of Sodom represents. For the author of this passage—in all likelihood post-exilic[14]—the question of whether God himself, "the judge of all the earth," can be said to act with even-handed fairness toward all peoples is important enough to warrant the insertion of this "factitious (constructed) narrative,"[15] or better, "midrash,"[16] as a "theological critique"[17] in which Abraham dares to raise the question with Yahweh himself. For a consciousness formed by exile—acquainted with the vagaries of political power and their potential for devastation and uprooting of what had seemed fixed and immutable—no theological question is more pressing than that of the ultimate justice, or one might say, the absolute sense, of it all: "The judge of all the earth—will he not do what is just?"

Before Abraham initiates the dialogue in v. 23, the account begins in monologue: the internal monologue in which Yahweh "thinks out loud"[18] about his intention to *communicate* to Abraham what at that point he considers an unquestionable *fait accompli*, that is, his decision to destroy Sodom for its wickedness. Yahweh is prepared to externalize his monologue, to let Abraham hear his intentions, as Fox renders v. 17: "Now YHWH had said to himself: Shall I cover up from Abraham what I am about to do?" The reason for the divine urge to disclosure is, in part, to create and perpetuate a relationship in which Abraham's descendants will, at second and third hand ("in order that he may charge his sons and his household after him"), continue to assent to Yahweh's mandates as the definition of justice ("they shall keep the way of YHWH, to do what is right and just" [Fox, v. 19]). Abraham is apparently intended to be a spectator, warned beforehand of what Yahweh is about to do so that he will be properly awed by the manifestation of Yahweh's power that the destruction of Sodom will represent.

Robert Alter[19] has shown the cardinal importance of this scene for the unfolding plot of the Genesis narrative: the promises made and reiterated to Abraham are here, for the first time, made conditional upon the maintenance of justice, or in Alter's words: "survival and propagation . . . depend on the creation of a just society." That is to say, a new dimension is added to the divine/human relationship, and it is one mediated by a concept of universal justice, a standard which, as this amazing text insists, must apply to divine as well as to human action. To quote Alter again: "Abraham, aghast at the possibility that the righteous might be wiped out with the wicked, tosses back the very phrase God has just used about human ethical obligations: 'Will the judge of all the earth not do justice?'"[20] Abraham reaches out for the only guarantee that—exile and sojourner that he is—he trusts as a safeguard of his own existence: a standard of justice without privilege or prejudice, which obligates even Yahweh to assure even the wicked men of Sodom a fair shake.

Among recent interpreters, Walter Brueggemann has perhaps most clearly emphasized the radical innovation which this text represents. We have already referred to his denomination of the text as a "theological critique," and what is important to note about that critique is that, as Brueggemann puts it, "It is as though Abraham is Yahweh's theological teacher and raises a question that is quite new for him,"[21] that is, the question of whether a "closed" system—to use Brueggemann's term—monologically defined and with no room for the flexibility of grace, serves well enough as a definition of justice. Once we realize the enormity of the fact that this text suggests instead, a dialogic engagement in which Abraham in fact gets Yahweh to concede and to modify his stance by agreeing to commute (admittedly wicked) Sodom's sentence for the sake of even ten (hypothetical) innocent inhabitants, the relevance of the text becomes very clear.

It is somewhat beside the point to observe, on the one hand, that the sentence on Sodom and Gomorrah was in the end carried out, with Lot and his daughters the only survivors, and on the other, that the frankly patriarchal flavor of the text leaves at least this contemporary reader wondering whether the women and children of the city, whom the text does not name as participants in the abominable behavior[22] of the men of Sodom, should not have been counted as innocent and granted immunity. What the daring of Abraham accomplishes is, in fact, to open the dialogical space, to engage the voice of Yahweh in such a way that those questions become proper and possible thereafter. Brueggemann, again: "Most remarkably in this text, the faithfulness of Abraham consists in boldly pressing God to be more compassionate. . . . It is clear to both Abraham and to Yahweh (in that order) that God is not a tyrant but really God. And from that flows good news."[23] The good news, I must insist, is not simply that in this story God becomes more compassionate as a result of Abraham's critical intervention, though that is true. From the point of view of an outsider, of an exile and a sojourner, the really good news is that the human/divine dialogue concerning what is just always remains open, including and inclusive of the points of view and interests of ever-increasing circles of sojourners; that it never freezes into purely monologic discourse.

It is clear on the other hand that in the Bible itself, not to speak of its interpreters from the earliest moment on, the opposite point of view is abundantly present. The other archetypical narrative of the destruction of a city, the destruction of Jericho in Joshua 6, for example, is totally devoid of the kind of reflection on the justice of the fate of its inhabitants that the midrashist introduces in Gen 18:19-32. The Bible itself does not hold a single point of view. If the poet of Nahum chauvinistically gloats over the destruction of Nineveh, the author of Jonah sensitively raises the question of God's care for the Ninevites. If Ezra 9 and 10 promote a sort of "ethnic cleansing" by repudiation of the foreign wives which men of Israel had married, along with their children, the author of Ruth paints a powerful portrait of the strong and faithful Moabite wife of Boaz the Bethlehemite, fated to become an ancestress of King David himself. The text of the Hebrew Bible is the record of a long and impassioned conversation about these crucial matters. If that conversation does at times tend to narrow into a closed monologue, there have always been voices from the edge, on the margins, at the border, who, like Abraham, ask the questions that dialogize and open it again to new insights.

EZEKIEL: MIXTURE, WITH DIGNITY

Ah Lord GOD! I have never defiled myself; from my youth up until now I have never eaten what died of itself or was torn by animals, nor has carrion flesh come into my mouth. (NRSV, Ezek 4:14)

Coming at the end of a disturbing scene in which Yahweh compels the exiled prophet to engage in a constellation of bizarre behaviors, making him a human symbol of the raw dreadfulness of Babylonian exile, a sort of living warning against psychological denial of the reality of their existence, the last divine command—that the prophet bake his bread on a fire fed by human dung—goes too far even for the overawed and compliant prophet. There is a line that he will not cross and across which he will not be pushed, even by God. To recapitulate: Yahweh orders the exiled prophet to shut himself up within his Babylonian house (3:24), semiparalyzed and speechless (3:26). There he is to create a graphic portrayal of the siege of Jerusalem on a clay brick (4:1-3) and lie on his bed for a symbolic number of days, "prophesying" against the city (4:4-8).

What follows in 4:9-15 is perhaps the most enigmatic of these bizarre actions. The prophet is to take a mixture of grains and legumes ("wheat and barley, beans and lentils, millet and spelt" [NRSV, v. 9]), put them in one vessel, presumably make them into a dough, and bake his daily bread from the mixture. Much has been made, particularly by commentators of an older generation, of this act as a supposed violation of the prohibition of *kil'ayim* (mixtures), derived from the ban on planting the fields with mixtures of seed stated in Deut 22:9 and Lev 19:19.[24] The assumption that Ezekiel felt obliged to concoct a mixture that was in itself abominable is, as Walther Zimmerli shows, not tenable. As he says, not "even in the Mishnah tractate *Kil'ayim*, where we might expect it, do we find that the prohibition . . . was related to the mixing of different kinds of cereal in foods."[25] His conclusion, then, is that the "compulsory admixture" of all sorts of scraps is allusive of the kind of eking out of scarce food which is to be the fate of Jerusalem under siege. The *Harper Collins Study Bible*,[26] following this interpretation, says in a note to v. 9 that the mixture "probably symbolizes that no one grain or legume is found in sufficient quantity to allow the preparation of something to eat." While there is undeniable truth to this line of interpretation—Ezekiel is symbolizing, for his fellow exiles in Babylonia, the dire circumstances of their compatriots in Jerusalem—we cannot forget that symbols can be polyvalent and simultaneously convey more than one meaning.

While Ezekiel's mixture is clearly permissible (if exceptional) as food, interpreters have missed the hint inherent in the fact that all the edible grains and legumes it contains are also seeds. The Mishnah speaks very precisely about the ambiguous status of "*kil'ayim* of seeds" in *Kil'ayim* VIII.1. In immediate contrast with "*kil'ayim* of the vineyard," which may neither be sown, nor allowed to grow, nor used in any way, but is to be destroyed by fire, "it is forbidden to sow Diverse Kinds [*kil'ayim*] of seeds or to suffer them to grow, *but they are permitted as food*."[27] The mixture straddles the border between the permitted and the forbidden: it is one thing or the other according to circumstance and use, and therefore it is both. The borderline is traced in this case by the tenet of ancient Israel's priestly religion that Mary Douglas clearly stated: "Holiness means keeping distinct the categories of creation."[28] On the other side of that purist line is the simple practical impossibility of keeping arbitrarily determined categories distinct. Mixture, hybridization, cross-pollination, miscegenation, and the like, inevitably present in the world of nature, are moreover apparently essential in the world of culture, and, in spite of dogmatic attempts at denial, ancient Israel's culture was as much a product of intermixture as any other. Ezekiel's *kil'ayim* bread is a powerful symbol, as multiple in meanings as in ingredients. At one level, it symbolizes the plight of besieged Jerusalem, of course. But the symbol also speaks to the situation of the exiles from Jerusalem, who like Ezekiel cannot escape the necessity of eating their bread and making their living in a foreign land, and the land of their captors at that, in osmotic contact with their cultures and religions.

The culture and the religion of exilic and postexilic Judaism were shaped by the emergence of what Daniel L. Smith has called "the religion of the land-less," a religious strategy aimed at group survival under the conditions of exile, in which a system which equates purity and separation is put at the core of Jewish identity. In a fashion similar to the adaptive behaviors of other, modern, dominated minorities, says Smith,

> [Exilic] Israel conduct[ed] the creative rituals of survival and resistance reflected in the carefully elaborated laws of the "pure" and "impure," and especially in the concern about the transfer of impurity through contact with the impure. . . . The most creative response to Exile by the priestly writer . . . was . . . the elaboration of these laws to emphasize transfer of pollution and the association of holiness with separation.[29]

These "social boundaries erected as a mechanism for survival during the Exile led to conflicts after the return to Palestine,"[30] to be sure, and, as I have mentioned above, there is abundant evidence to be found in the biblical corpus of the presence of differing points of view among its authors: some separatist and purist, some inclusivist critics of that attitude.

Yahweh's next command, that the prophet deliberately defile the bread he was to eat by baking it on a fire fed by human excrement (v. 12), can in my opinion be understood best as an expression of the purist attitude's bias. Ezekiel is, after all, about to eat the *kil'ayim* bread of exile in an "unclean" land, simultaneously proclaiming the ritual defilement of Jerusalem by the very Babylonians among whom he lived. Why not then literally internalize the defilement to complete the symbol? The prophet's protest at the thought makes it clear that to follow the command would in fact constitute a horrible distortion, in which he would take upon himself, accept, and internalize the negative valuation given to displacement and to mixture by the separatist concept of "holiness." While there can be no doubt that Ezekiel is rooted theoretically in that concept, he is also a human being, living out his life as an exile, and it is his human dignity that speaks out, challenging God (as well as himself) from across the too-exclusively drawn borderline: "Ah Lord GOD! I have never defiled myself; from my youth up until now I have never eaten what died of itself or was torn by animals, nor has carrion flesh come into my mouth." Thus challenged by an unexpected outburst of human self-respect (the Spanish term *pundonor* is even better for this), Yahweh retreats, almost apologetically, and instead of the ritually defiling human excrement, allows the prophet to use cattle dung, a common household fuel in ancient Mesopotamia, for his fire. A comic and small victory, perhaps, but a victory nevertheless for the dignity of the human individual.

Ezekiel's predicament resonates strongly in the situation of the *mestizo*, a figure of central importance for the Hispanic-American experience. As Octavio Paz put it, the *mestizo* in colonial Mexico was,

> the victim of ambiguity . . . he was neither criollo nor Indian. Rejected by both groups, the mestizo had no place either in the social structure or in the moral order. In the light of traditional moral systems—the Spanish, based on honor, and the Indian, based on the sacredness of family—the mestizo was the living image of illegitimacy.[31]

That description has validity beyond Mexico and, *mutatis mutandis* (the most important change being to include the African peoples who became important components of Caribbean societies, for example), applies also throughout Ibero-America's history. However, *mestizos* (as well as *mulatos*) became, in spite of being defined as pariahs by their societies, the true children, the true novelty of New Spain and of Ibero-America.[32]

The recent emphasis that Hispanic-American theologians have placed on *mestizaje*,[33] *mulatez*, or *mezcolanza* as terms that define the Hispanic/Latino human condition, and that, specifically, give us a standpoint from which to read the Bible, is a celebration of the power that overcame oppression derived from ideological dreams of ethnic and cultural "purity," to create the vital, mixed, polyphonic, and multiflavored culture that nurtured us. We who now live as exiles can be very conscious of what we contribute, as well as of what we assimilate, in our new situation. In the symbol of Ezekiel's bread, made up from scraps and odds and ends of many kinds of foodstuffs, I recognize my culture and my roots. And I admire Ezekiel for standing up, even to the voice he recognized as God's, for the dignity of his humanity, even under the condition of *mezcolanza* that was his exile, or that in fact is mine.

CONCLUDING COMMENTS

> Dialogism is the characteristic epistemological mode of a world dominated by heteroglossia. Everything means, is understood, as a part of a greater whole—there is a constant interaction between meanings, all of which have the potential of conditioning others. . . . One may, like a primitive tribe that knows only its own limits, be deluded into thinking there is one language, or one may, as grammarians, certain political figures and normative framers of "literary languages" do, seek in a sophisticated way to achieve a unitary language. In both cases the unitariness is relative to the overpowering force of heteroglossia, and thus dialogism.[34]

To the tribes of grammarians, politicians, and literary nabobs, we may add the one to which many a biblical interpreter owes allegiance, for whom the Bible is a world closed within its own restricted limits, a monoglot domain where only one voice is heard. In speaking for a very different approach, I have sought to show that the biblical text itself is the record of the interactions of many voices, and specifically, of instances where the divine part does not go unchallenged by a human counterpart. The human/divine relationship is not defined univocally then, but in dialogue or, to return to Segovia's term, in engagement. Cain the criminal can still successfully claim a basic right to a life and a future, as he successfully resists a sentence of utter outlawry that would have dismissed and demonized him. Abraham the just can insist that even Yahweh must submit to an absolute standard of justice which demands that, even in Sodom, the innocent not be punished along with the wicked. Ezekiel the dispossessed finds, even in a situation of exile that threatens his very definition of identity, that he can make Yahweh hear the claim of his irreducible dignity. For exiles and sojourners, for people who know what it is to be put in the role of the demonized or marginalized other, these are words of power.

NOTES

1. F. F. Segovia, "Toward a Hermeneutics of the Diaspora: A Hermeneutics of Otherness and Engagement," *Reading from This Place.* Volume I: *Social Location and Biblical Interpretation in the United States,* ed. Fernando F. Segovia and Mary Ann Tolbert (Minneapolis: Fortress Press, 1995) 59.

2. Among the other authors involved in this project, the following fit this description as well: Justo González; Ada María Isasi-Díaz; and Fernando Segovia.

3. G. Pérez Firmat, *Life on the Hyphen: The Cuban-American Way* (Austin: University of Texas Press, 1994) 4.

4. Ibid.

5. Ibid., 5.

6. Segovia, "Toward a Hermeneutics," 66-67.

7. E. Fox, *In the Beginning: A New English Rendition of the Book of Genesis* (New York: Schocken Books, 1983).

8. Augustine, *Concerning the City of God, against the Pagans,* trans. Henry Bettenson, ed. David Knowles (Harmondsworth: Penguin Books, 1972) 596.

9. R. J. Quinones, *The Changes of Cain: Violence and the Lost Brother in Cain and Abel Literature* (Princeton: Princeton University Press, 1991) 23.

10. That tradition continues even in some modern versions; see, e.g., Luis Alonso Schökel's *Nueva Biblia Española,* which renders it as follows: "Mi culpa es grave y me angustia."

11. See the discussion in Claus Westermann, *Genesis 1-11: A Commentary,* trans. John J. Scullion, S.J. (Minneapolis: Augsburg Publishing House, 1984) 309.

12. "The defense is articulated in a lament. It can be recognized as a real lament in that it contains, even if only by way of hint, all three elements of the lament (God-lament, I-lament, enemy-lament . . .)" (ibid.).

13. O. Paz, *Sor Juana or, The Traps of Faith* (Cambridge: The Belknap Press of Harvard University, 1988) 32-33. The phrase came to my attention first in Quinones' work (*The Changes of Cain,* 243).

14. For a discussion of the argument for this date, see Claus Westermann, *Genesis 12-36: A Commentary*, trans. John J. Scullion, S.J. (Minneapolis: Augsburg Publishing House, 1985) 286-87.

15. Ibid., 286.

16. See Joseph Blenkinsopp, "Abraham and the Righteous of Sodom," *The Journal of Jewish Studies* 33 (1982) 119-132; and "The Judge of All the Earth: Theodicy in the Midrash on Genesis 18:22—33," *The Journal of Jewish Studies* 41 (1990) 1-12.

17. See Walter Brueggemann, *Genesis*, volume I of *Interpretation: A Bible Commentary for Teaching and Preaching* (Atlanta: John Knox Press, 1982) 167–176.

18. Fox, *In the Beginning*, 67.

19. R. Alter, "Sodom as Nexus: The Web of Design in Biblical Narrative," *The Book and the Text: The Bible and Literary Theory*, ed. Regina Schwartz (Oxford: Basil Blackwell, 1990) 146-160.

20. Ibid., 150.

21. Brueggemann, *Genesis*, 169.

22. According to ancient Jewish tradition, the sin of Sodom was arrogant mistreatment of strangers and of the poor—they are, in this respect, the very antithesis of Abraham. See, for example, the enlightening and amusing compilation of *midrashim* on this subject in Hayim Nahman Bialik and Yehoshua Hana Ravnitzki, eds., *The Book of Legends: Sefer Ha–Aggadah* (New York: Schocken Books, 1992) 36-37 (numbers 30-35).

23. Brueggemann, *Genesis*, 176.

24. For a discussion of this passage, including other critical views, see Walther Zimmerli, *Ezekiel 1: A Commentary on the Book of the Prophet Ezekiel, Chapters 1—24* (Philadelphia: Fortress Press, 1979) 168-70.

25. Ibid., 169.

26. *The HarperCollins Study Bible: New Revised Standard Version*, ed. Wayne Meeks (New York: HarperCollins Publishers, 1993).

27. Herbert Danby, trans., *The Mishnah* (Oxford: Oxford University Press, 1933) 37. (Italics mine.)

28. M. Douglas, "The Abominations of Leviticus," *Purity and Danger* (New York: Frederick A. Praeger, 1966) 53; see also 41-57.

29. D. L. Smith, *The Religion of the Landless: The Social Context of the Babylonian Exile* (Bloomington, IN: Meyer Stone Books, 1989) 149.

30. Ibid., 197.

31. Paz, *Sor Juana*, 32.

32. Ibid., 33.

33. See, e.g., Virgilio Elizondo, *Galilean Journey: The Mexican-American Promise* (Maryknoll: Orbis Books, 1983); and *The Future is Mestizo: Life Where Cultures Meet* (Bloomington, IN: Meyer Stone Books, 1988).

34. Michael Holquist, "Glossary," *The Dialogic Imagination: Four Essays by M. M. Bakhtin*, ed. M. Holquist (Austin: The University of Texas Press, 1981) 426.

7

READING FROM
AN INDIGENOUS PLACE

Mark Lewis Taylor

"Who will open Tibet, or claim the last acre of the Amazon, the hills of central India, the jungles of Borneo, the steppes of Siberia—the merchant or the missionary? When the war is over, let us take the Sword of the Spirit and march."
—William Cameron Townsend, 1942. Founder, Wycliffe Bible Translators.

March, indeed, he did. In league with American corporate power, above all with associates of the powerful Rockefeller family, "Cam" Townsend worked alongside the Central Intelligence Agency of the United States and many a local dictator in order to plunge the "Sword of the Spirit" deep into the lands and cultures of indigenous peoples. All the while, like all too many missionaries before him, Townsend carried the Bible to "Bibleless tribes" and so gave crucial cultural support to the devastation of indigenous people being ground under by military and economic empire.

Before World War II, Guatemala, with a population of about 60 percent indigenous peoples, was one of those countries featuring many "Bibleless tribes," and it had already become one scene of Townsend's efforts. After the war, in the 1980s, his associates at the Summer Institute of Linguistics would even be serving there as translators of indigenous languages for local powers aiming to wipe out indigenous peoples who resisted the conditions of their impoverishment.[1] In that same Guatemala of the 1980s, a Mayan grandmother bequeathed to her son her own invented Spanish term for understanding how the powerful descendants of Europe and the United States continue to destroy her indigenous people. The term was *desencarnación*. It is not a standing Spanish word, and in English it would probably best be translated as "disincarnation." The ideas are a "de-fleshing," a disembodiment, an emptying out of life-force.

Her son still embraces the term as a way to understand the five hundred years of indigenous peoples' suffering at the hands of Euro-American powers. Moreover, from within the social location of the Mayans in contemporary Guatemala, the term takes on a particularly potent, even grisly, relevance. The term there refers not only to a generalized life-draining system of economic austerity measures, which Guatemala's indigenous and poor have now suffered since the mid-1980s at the insistence of a U.S.-based International Monetary Fund in Washington, D.C. The term also refers to the many acts of torture and death—many by napalm, bayonet, and interrogation technique—that more than five hundred indigenous villages experienced at the hands of the Guatemalan army in the early 1980s, often with substantial amounts of aid from the U.S. military or allies.

The near-ritual dismemberment of the mother of Mayan Nobel Peace Prize winner, Rigoberta Menchú Tum, was quite literally an act of *desencarnación*, as her rape and torture bore witness. This was at once the pain of the Menchú family, of Guatemala's Mayan peoples, and of many indigenous in "the Americas."[2] The flesh and blood of indigenous peoples have often existed for Euro-American cultures as only a life-substance to be harnessed for their own uses or else to be routinely spilled, sliced up, and slowly drained off by Euro-American pressures.

Can there be an interpretive use of the Bible, this infamous "Sword of the Spirit," which can actually restore, instead of destroy, the flesh and blood of indigenous people? That is the question of this essay.

INDIGENOUS STRUGGLE: THE CONTINUING VIOLATION

As I write this essay, reminders of the life-destroying ways of imperialist power, especially as suffered by indigenous peoples, are close at hand. Thus, for example, the oft-conservative U.S. congressman from my state of New Jersey, Robert Torricelli, has angered his Republican colleagues by revealing the "dirty secret" of the CIA: the U.S. government's long support of the Guatemalan security forces in their onslaught against Mayan peoples. Guatemalan elites served on U.S. payrolls while doing their worst against thousands of indigenous and working peoples.[3]

Moreover, even as I write, the structural antipathy of U.S.-based transnational banks and corporations toward indigenous peoples has surfaced in a January 1995 memorandum of the Chase Manhattan Bank, prepared by Professor Riordan Roett of Johns Hopkins University. For the sake of investment security in Mexico, and especially for U.S. investors, Roett prescribed a "medicine" for restoring the health of investors that again threatened the flesh and blood of indigenous peoples. He ascribed Mexico's inability to secure the confidence of investors to the indigenous peasant rebels known as the Zapatistas (the EZLN) and active in the state of Chiapas:[4]

> While Chiapas, in our opinion, does not pose a fundamental threat to Mexican political stability, it is perceived to be so by many in the investment community. *The government will need to eliminate the Zapatistas* to demonstrate their effective control of the national territory and of security policy.[5]

Within two weeks of this memo, and extending throughout February of 1995, 60,000 Mexican troops, again U.S.-supplied, moved into indigenous territory in Chiapas, not only forcing EZLN rebels deep into the Lacondon jungle but also intentionally terrorizing more than 20,000 villagers, who were also forced to take refuge in the jungles, where they struggled with malnutrition and exposure and many died. Admittedly, one bank memo does not mobilize a whole Mexican army, but it is a signal of the way Euroamerican corporate investment culture has been, and still is, ready to sacrifice Indian peoples to its lust for money. Here again, indigenous flesh and blood is at risk—not by temporality, the passing of time that brings death and suffering to us all, but by abusive power that forces many poor to "die before their time."[6]

Desencarnación, then, is a complex force depending upon a web of power relations, involving our banks, armies, governments, and the ways we organize cultural practices within the reach of those powers. None of us, especially in U.S. cultures, are pure. We are all implicated in one way or another in the travail of indigenous peoples. Even descendants of indigenous groups can be part of an ethos of their own domination. This complexity means that we can write no simple "victimist" history with easily identifiable victims and oppressors. Nevertheless—and I emphasize the "nevertheless"—there are identifiable sufferers, identifiable callous bystanders, and equally identifiable perpetrating agents and forces. There is a difference, for example, between U.S. cavalries with heartless lieutenant-generals and village women and children disemboweled by them. One should remember in this regard the slaughter by the U.S. military at Sand Creek in Colorado.

Similarly, there is a difference, which complexity does not dissolve, between a Riordan Roett whose academic discourse is disseminated by Chase Manhattan and an academic activist like Jorge Santiago who sits in Mexican jails during the Mexican army's sweep in Chiapas because of his work for indigenous peoples' right to live with dignity. Only a self-indulgent "postmodernism," or an effete will-not-to-know, could use complexity and critique of "victimist" thinking as ways to gloss the essential difference between perpetrators of violence and those whose flesh and blood are sacrificed. Ethnocritic Arnold Krupat has put it eloquently:

One may grant that not all Euroamericans were rapacious, genocidal monsters, and that not all Indians were, in the purest and most absolute sense, their hapless, innocent victims: nonetheless, it seems to me beyond question that—all things considered—the indigenous peoples of this continent, along with African Americans, women, and many other groups, have overwhelmingly been more sinned against than sinning. If this is so, to construct one's discourse on such a premise is not necessarily to engage in the revisionist allegory of victimism. Some people *have* been hurt by others and if that is not the only and the most interesting thing to say, it most certainly remains something that still, today, can probably not be said too often.[7]

The conferences at Vanderbilt, which situated biblical hermeneutics in the context of critique and counter-critique between old and new voices on the global scene, surfaces new awareness of the legacy of pain sown by centuries of Western expansionism and domination. This paper works in the purview of that awareness. I presuppose a group of scholars who move beyond immobilizing guilt. I eschew any pure righteous indignation and sense of duty on behalf of others. It is simply in all of our interests not to compromise with anything less than a hermeneutics that works to restore flesh and blood on an earth whose death may be foreshadowed by the *desencarnación* ruthlessly imposed on earth's indigenous peoples.[8]

THE BIBLE, FLESH-AND-BLOOD READERS, AND A THESIS

Those who see biblical interpretation as only a textual matter, using historical and literary methods of textual discipline, will be puzzled by the consideration of such political and cultural issues as those that arise across the pages of articles in these volumes of *Reading from This Place*.

One way of describing the present state of biblical hermeneutics is to say that Bible scholars today are finding it necessary, as perhaps never before, to consider biblical meaning and truth in relation to the vicissitudes of flesh-and-blood interpreters. In this section, I will summarize the major moves that have delivered us to this point and then offer a thesis that I will develop in the rest of this essay.

Biblical criticism, especially where developing in conversation with a wide array of university disciplines, has moved into and beyond (though never completely out of) three modes of focusing biblical interpretation. Each mode privileges a distinctive dimension of our process of interpreting the Bible. In order to describe these modes of focusing, I shall draw from some distinctions occurring in Paul Ricoeur's discussions of the location of meaning in texts. How might we envision the "meaning of a text" when we go looking for it as interpreters?

1. One option is to say the meaning is "*in* the text." The relevant dimension which is here explored by readers is predominantly intratextual, i.e., pertinent to the text's literary form. Within this option I would include the sophisticated literary critic who carefully studies the narrative texts, those who in untrained ways read it "literally" and "simply," and even those who just let the Bible leaves fall open to reveal some meaning for the moment. For all the real differences between these readers, what they have in common is a focus on the textual dimension. Here we give attention (whether disciplined, habitual, or haphazard) to the book. That is where the meaning is. Similarly, arguments for the truth of such meanings (if one wants to go after that ever elusive notion, "truth") will focus on getting precise and rigorous about what is "in the text." The reader may thus be advised to read the text more carefully; to check its setting in the book, in the canon, in that type of literature; to pay close attention to linguistic forms, structure, emplotment.

2. A second option entails a move *"behind* the text" in order to get at the biblical meaning. Signs, themes, and narrative in the texts are important, but more crucial here is a move beneath or "behind" the text to the historical milieu from which it came. To understand the meaning of the spatial designation of "behind," one may envision a present-day reader standing in front of the Bible with the text's historical, past environs lying on the other side of the text from the reader. The text is located in a historical period that has the past as its major horizon. The text might be viewed as a kind of product of that historical past, which can be explained by reference to actors, authors' experiences and intentions, and sometimes cultural movements in that world behind the text.

Much of what has been called "historical criticism" made the move behind the text to an author's intention ("What was Paul really trying to get at when writing his epistle with the city of Corinth in mind?"). It should be pointed out, however, that the move behind the text can also include cultural and sociological analyses of institutions and practices deemed to exist in a text's historical milieu. The basic point is that whether taking a personal-historical route to study a Paul or a Mark (authors with certain intentions) or a cultural-historical route to examine dynamics like Pharisaism, the Herodian elite, Christian anti-Jewish sentiments, or Roman imperialism, the meaning of the text as well as claims to truth are quickened around an analysis of the dynamic interplay in the milieu behind the texts.

Both of these first two options usually shared a commitment to a hegemony of objective method, a method that searched for, sifted, and debated evidence pertaining to textual and literary theses and structures (*"in* the texts") or historical and cultural events (*"behind* the texts").

3. Within each of these options—and under the pressure of diverse currents such as twentieth-century hermeneutics (in the mode of Friedrich Schleiermacher, Wilhelm Dilthey, and Hans-Georg Gadamer), linguistic philosophy (in the mode of Ludwig Wittgenstein), neo-pragmatist writings (Hilary Putnam and Richard Rorty), and ideology critique and studies of the politics of interpretation[9]—another dimension was brought to the fore. We may term it, following Ricoeur again, a dimension *"in front of* the texts."

When one highlights this dimension of the interpretive process, then other complexities are brought to light. Each of these involve dynamics of interaction going on "between" the texts and their present-day readers. This area in-between is made up of several dynamics which I will only briefly highlight here:

a. First, several aspects of a text's language have enabled students of language to speak of texts "generating" or "producing" meanings. Because of the richness of certain textual forms of language (especially in their narrative, symbolic, or metaphorical forms), worlds of meaning seem to "move out from" texts toward readers, make a claim upon them, catch them up in a world of meaning. Language in texts "leans forward," if you will, toward readers' worlds. The oft-quoted sutra metaphor, "Poetry is a finger pointing to the moon," is, for example, a construction so provocative that it has a certain vitality, enabling new meaning to surge out toward readers. This position can be maintained without a full-blown notion of inspiration. It is not so much that the text as "letter" is here indwelt by an external spirit, as that metaphorical language, as in this sutra, has this creative, insurgent power. Through such a linguistic vitality, meaning surges forth from texts onto a middle ground, in front of the text, between texts and readers.

b. A second dynamic, often discussed in the world between text and reader, is "tradition"—the stream of many interpretations of a text that "carries" the text into the world of present-day readers. Here, the text's language is not primarily emphasized as surging toward readers; rather, the text and its language flow into readers' worlds through the surging stream of tradition(s). Those who focus on tradition often insist that even highly critical readers of a text stand in tradition. To criticize the tradition presumes some engagement with the text, and this "engagement" suggests an influence of tradition upon the interpreter. The complexities and debates here are many, but my point is that the exploration of tradition is another way of focusing and discussing the world in front of the text, or between text and reader.

c. The hermeneutical world "in front of" the text reaches its creative complexity, however, when one turns attention to the contribution of present-day readers. Here is where the notion of "social location" is most dramatically relevant. Readers who interpret are not just discrete individuals, singular thinkers carefully following exegetical methods. They are, more profoundly, persons interacting with others in distinctive social environments. They dream, spin cultural patterns, hold political convictions, struggle, exploit, and are exploited.

The more detailed we become in analyzing readers in front of the text, the more it is clear that these socially located readers carry many different kinds of interest into interaction with meanings from the text. Indeed, now, with an awareness of how active readers can be when interpreting texts, the stress falls on the many ways that interest-laden readers "construct" meanings of texts.[10] In fact, those meanings often thought to be generated by the text's linguistic or narrative content may be—if not entirely, at least in part—living creations brought into being by present-day readers. In order to connote maximum concreteness and complexity to these kinds of readers, Ricoeur referred to them as "flesh-and-blood readers."[11]

When this point is reached, hermeneutics (perhaps even biblical hermeneutics) becomes something more akin to what Fernando Segovia calls "cultural studies." The social location of readers of texts has become so important a dimension of interpretation that the cultures and social locations of the readers themselves become subject matter for hermeneutics. Segovia summarizes this kind of "cultural studies" as the application of cultural criticism not just to texts but to readers' worlds. This is an application that Segovia sees as emergent since the 1970s and which now constitutes an acute challenge for biblical criticism:

This new development posits ... a very different construct, the flesh-and-blood reader: always positioned and interested; socially and histor-ically conditioned and unable to transcend such conditions—to attain a sort of asocial and ahistorical nirvana—not only with respect to socio-economic class but also with regard to the many other factors that make up human identity.[12]

It is precisely through readers exposed and understood in these ways that the issues of power and position inevitably flow into hermeneutics. With such readers on hand, what they *do* and *how* they read become crucial to the mean-ings brought forth from the texts. Because interpretations are constructs of socially located flesh-and-blood readers, culture and politics belong at the cen-ters of inquiry into the meanings of texts. Moreover, if these readers know anything of the colonizers' uses of the Bible, the ways that merchants and mis-sionaries wielded the "Sword of the Spirit" against the very lives of indigenous peoples, then readers' interpretations will entail judgments about the value and use of that book. Whether the Bible is seen as defensible from charges that it is damaging to indigenous health or confirmed as indictable and thus expendable—all this assessment goes on in the strife between flesh-and-blood readers in front of the text.

As one reader who is aware of the Bible's role in colonizing power, I now offer a thesis. It is a thesis that proposes a distinctive reading strategy—a cul-tural-political criticism for biblical reading, which, when further developed, I also term an "indigenist criticism." The thesis is as follows: (a) The worth of reading the Bible and the desirability of embracing or enacting its perspectives, depends upon (b) its being situated among readers who pursue a multi-vocal/global criticism, (c) in a way that privileges the voices and needs of indigenous peoples and their lands. It must remain beyond the scope of this essay to offer new readings of the Bible. My main concern is to identify the kind of community of criticism within which such new readings might be pos-sible in the future.

TOWARD AN INDIGENIST CRITICISM

Let us look, in turn, at each of the key phrases of the proposed thesis. The commentary that follows sketches what I take as the main lines of an "indi-genist criticism."[13]

The Worth of Reading and Embracing the Bible

The thesis presupposes that the Bible is not necessarily and in itself worth read-ing, or its perspectives in themselves worth embracing. The Bible will seem to many of the faithful unquestionable, important to read, and worth embracing and enacting. I am here presuming, however, readers who know the Bible's complicity in culturally reinforcing the decimation of indigenous peoples.

Within that frame of reference, biblical worth can at best be a hard-won conviction, especially if biblical worth means that the book might make some contribution to a practice of life and freedom for indigenous peoples.

Most claims that the Bible is valuable, then, presume that, unless certain conditions are present, pertaining to the way the Bible is used, it easily functions abusively. So, is "the good book" good? Well, it depends. It depends on certain conditions being met. Most readers and devotees intuitively affirm the fact of this dependence, if only by their insistence that the Bible be "rightly interpreted," i.e., read and used in a context wherein certain conditions are held to apply. Conditions for right interpretation may include a "faithful attitude," the reverent heeding of some Spirit, perhaps the presence of a company of other committed Christian readers, or maybe the employment of disciplined standards of professional exegesis. Whatever the case, certain presumed conditions are intrinsic to any claim that the Bible is worth reading and affirming.

The first phrase of the thesis, then, constitutes a declaration born of suspicion and past historical and cultural abuse. The "only" suggests the radical conditionedness of our using this book in our times. The first phrase, we might say, is a "dependent clause"—dependent, that is, on certain conditions being met. The remaining two phrases of my thesis specify what I consider to be two necessary conditions if any post-imperialist readings of the Bible are to become possible.

A Multi-vocal/global Criticism

This first condition specifies a certain kind of hermeneutical site which takes seriously the presence of socially located readers. This site is one that is multi-vocal/global. Why it is that I append the designation "global" will become clearer below. Let me stay for now with the notion of multi-vocality.

In the present era of academic "culture wars," such notions as multi-vocal, like "multi-ethnic" or "multi-cultural," can connote either a crude practice of balkanizing identity politics (trying to have one or a few representatives of many groups) or a haphazard celebration of a thousand blooming flowers. In contrast to both, I envision an embrace of multi-vocality that features a certain *discipline* that we can even identify as a mode of criticism. Multi-vocality, as a key trait of the world of socially located readers, involves attending to two critical tasks.

1. The first task is the foregrounding of one's own complex voice and position. A socially located reader, however, is not simply a singular ego who reads. There is always a play of voices in a reading individual. Developmentally, there may be the voice of the mother, other-parents, care-givers. As a socialized being, a reader is already multi-vocal within himself or herself. This is true, I think, for all readers, but even more for culturally liminal readers, bi-cultural readers, who have, through displacement or travel, experienced the voices of different cultures within themselves. Moreover, when any reader (already multi-vocal) speaks and interacts through language and action with other read-

ers in his or her present, as socially located beings do, then new voices become part of the repertoire of any given reader's voice. The reader is part of a reading community, wherein many voices are heard. Multi-vocality as a key trait of a socially located reader, then, involves attending to this complexity.

Segovia signals the critical process here when he writes of interpreters "fully foregrounding themselves as flesh-and-blood readers variously situated and engaged in their respective social locations."[14] This process of full foregrounding of oneself is no quick and easy task, especially if one really explores the interaction between a complex personal journey and the cultural dynamics of conditioning. No easy label-making can produce such foregrounding.

This first task of multi-vocality, then, is a discipline that is always exploring the voice of oneself that is foregrounded. Antonio Gramsci termed this "critical self-inventory."[15] It is "hermeneutical self-implicature" as Calvin Schrag still more verbosely puts it.[16] Whatever the term, the task demands nothing less than a process of continuing experiment and studied awareness. Ask an artist or writer how easy it is to find one's "voice" (or one's voices?). Not to do this is to risk having one's voice taken over (usurped and co-opted) by others. Not to have found one's voice is often to lack one's place in conversation. Not knowing our own particular voice-in-place is also to risk usurping and speaking "for" others. Both dangers (depending on who the speakers are)—of being usurped and being usurper—rise to meet us, if we are not about the disciplines of foregrounding our voices, from our places—speaking "in our own tongues," as Segovia put it.[17]

2. A second critical task of multi-vocality is that of dialogically engaging the voices of others who are encounterable within communal interchange. This, too, is a difficult set of tasks, involving the disciplines and risks of listening, the courage to speak and to engage others in return. It involves learning languages, cultural styles, navigating and resisting the power-plays, the power-politics, and the complex wars of opposition that usually attend the social locations of readers. Hearing others—in the many and varied contexts of the United States, for example—will involve crossing diverse cultural and subcultural boundaries and hearing diverse subordinated peoples: the voices of beaten and silenced women, of impoverished sufferers of economic exploitation, of the silent disabled people, and of the targets of white supremacism. Multi-vocality, as disseminated along these and other modes of power and difference, calls forth a maddening array of disciplines for critical engagement.

Both tasks of multi-vocality are crucial to creating a criticism and a postcolonial kind of normativity. This would be a criticism that nurtures manifold voices, in contrast to the imperialist pretension to not only project one cultural voice, but to do so as carrier of the one "civilized" or "universal" perspective. The disciplined tasks of multi-vocality—finding and foregrounding one's own voice *and* critically engaging others' voices—are a way to build *breadth* into reflection and into interpretation.

It is by now a truism, in the perspective of recent hermeneutics, that "foundations," "bases," and "archimedean points" are not free from social-cultural construction. Whether reflection and interpretation are persuasive, capable of marshalling a sense of "truth," depends less on the solidity or singularity of a base and more on the breadth of the differences in the conversation through which foundations or bases are worked out. What Charles Peirce said about persuasive reasoning might be identified as the hallmark of multi-vocality as a disciplined criticism. This criticism does "not form a chain which is no stronger than its weakest link, but a cable whose fibers may be ever so slender, provided they are sufficiently numerous and intimately connected."[18]

Readers who work on sites of multi-vocal criticism, then, pursuing the disciplines sketched above, forge the "strength" of their positions (i.e. their "normativity" or "persuasiveness") in such a way as this. Numerous voices, seeking intimate and precise connection—this kind of breadth is the fruit of multi-vocal criticism. As such, it offers what is most crucial to persuasive, "strong" interpretations: breadth and diversity. It is this seeking of strength in interpretation by cultivating breadth that continuously drives multi-vocal criticism toward "global" horizons. Hence, now I can attend to the "global" as implicit in the multi-vocal.

This movement of multi-vocality toward the global is neither a grasp for the homogeneous One, nor a drive to command a panoptic vision that surveys totality. By the "global" intending within multi-vocal criticism, I mean the continual, unceasing penchant to widen the horizons of one's dialogue. In Segovia's language, the inquirer "looks for a truly global interaction."[19] This penchant keeps one asking ever broadening questions. Is the dialogue, in fact, broad? In what sense? Is the dialogue remaining broad? Are the horizons of its breadth changing? Are accepted views of difference in need of challenge? Which subordinated voices are still silent, not included? A criticism that is "multi-vocal/global" seeks dialogue with difference in a milieu that continually includes/seeks/asks for the most distant, widely arrayed, and challenging "others." Moreover, these horizons—ideally always honored and always sought—are themselves changing. These are not set horizons. The horizons of "broad" multi-vocal criticism are always receding and re-emerging. Multi-vocality is thus kept dynamic and insurgent.

How different Euroamerican hermeneutics would have appeared if it had sought multi-vocal/global discipline as its mode of testing interpretations! Instead, this hermeneutics sought to pose as the one expanding voice. When did merchant and missionary let Taino or Cakchiquel voices be heard? When and where did European speakers and planners allow Aztec or Inca to speak forth their agendas? How different things might have been if Euroamerican leaders had not only known their own voice as diverse, particular, and finite, but also then honored the voices of Renape, Powhattan, and Osage!

The "spirit" of multi-vocal/global criticism does not allow the biblical text to appear as a singular, sharp, penetrating "sword," as Cam Townsend would have it. Amid multi-vocality, text may still have shape, but what kind? Maybe text, now, awaits transformation to something more like wind or water. Something fluid, always, as for the Sioux medicine man, Horse, to which missing things need to be added.[20] It is to such a multi-vocal criticism that the biblical text as Euroamerican "sword" must now submit. What text becomes then, this must be a later subject. But to multi-vocal/global criticism I will entrust the Bible. Its criticism constitutes the first condition on which depends any worth of biblical reading and practice.

Reading from an Indigenous Place

The thesis asserts, however, an embrace of not only multi-vocal/global criticism and its play of differences. It also insists upon a privileging of certain voices—those of indigenous peoples and their lands. This particular privilege is a second condition I propose as a necessary feature among the flesh-and-blood readers who would interpret the Bible.

Again, the possibility of the Bible's retrieval within a legacy of imperialist destruction of indigenous peoples has become radically questionable. Above all, the notion of a people chosen by God to possess the land and its peoples has been used repeatedly to sanction forced removal and genocide of indigenous peoples. One thinks not only of the religious justification of Afrikaner "State Theology" in South Africa but also of the sacral "manifest destiny" applied by Euroamericans against the original inhabitants of America, the new "promised land." Biblical story-lines and abusive biblical interpretations have not led to the flourishing of indigenous peoples.[21]

If we here speak now of "privileging" indigenous voices, this is not simply some reactive oppositionalism, a mere giving glory to what before was denigrated. Corrections, reversal of past abusive history, even reparations—all these must be considered. But "the place" of indigenous voices is one worth privileging, I argue, because of its importance for orienting the criticism that *any* of us undertake and because, also, that privilege is crucial to creating the practices we must exhibit if our *entire* planet is to remain inhabitable. Redressing the needs of Indian peoples, then, is not simply to acknowledge and offer the justice long denied them. It is that, and perhaps that first of all. But it is also to assure for criticism an inclusive hermeneutical vision and to begin a practice crucial for all peoples and creatures of the planet.

The fundamental question I seek to answer in this final section is this: what is it about the indigenous place that, when privileged, does not just create a new tyranny by a new ethnic group but instead nurtures radical and fruitful inclusion? An answer lies in noting three traits intrinsic to indigenous place. A crucial reminder is in order, however. None of the discussion of "privilege" which I offer below should conceal the fact that, as voices in the context of multi-vocal/global criticism, indigenous peoples speak "in their own tongues" and are different and particular in their forms and interests. All the interpretive strategies that cultivate a valuation of difference are, therefore, necessary in order to hear and assess critically the claims and visions of indigenous peoples—as Osage, Renape, Apache, Mescalero Apache, Cherokee, variously acculturated Cherokee, and so on. In the multi-vocal setting, any indigenous speakers are at once speakers of their own tongues, of several tongues among the many indigenous tongues, and of several tongues among the many tongues and voices of the world's indigenous and non-indigenous peoples. The indigenous voice is far from homogeneous.

I explore here, however, what may seem a curious phenomenon: exploring the unique differences of and within indigenous peoples' voices exposes the greater comprehensiveness of those voices for reading and criticism. Reading from an indigenous place facilitates a more global, radically inclusive vision for criticism and practice. And so I take up now the three ways in which indigenous voices can be seen as "privileged":

1. The indigenous place is, first of all, *a subaltern place*. It is not only a place where speakers from the multi-vocal scene of conversation experience otherness (the "altern"), it is also a place where the shock and interruption of subordinated others (the subaltern) are encountered. Indigenous peoples and their speech have not been annihilated, but their tongues and their lives continue to be marked by oppression.

I need not here recount the legacy of that violation, that *desencarnación*, as I discussed it above. Whether looking at the impact of Spanish cultures on Mesoamerican and South American peoples, whether confronting European and U.S. cultures' decimation of North American indigenous peoples, whether meditating again on U.S. domination of all "the Americas" and its continuing destruction of indigenous place(s)—all these exercises only dramatize the pain of individual Amerindians and that of whole communities.

Here I point out the interpretive valence of that subaltern or oppressed legacy. What is the meaning of privileging indigenous place, the indigenous social location? We may begin to derive a response from previous discussions of "the hermeneutical privilege of the oppressed."[22] We can acknowledge this privilege not in the ludicrous sense that interpretation from the spaces of oppressed peoples should be immune from criticism and suspicion. No, the "privilege" lies rather in the special kind of hermeneutical vantage point of oppressed peoples, the unique contributions they make to the scene of multi-vocal/global dialogue.

The key is to recall that the oppressed are often the voices excluded from criticism and conversation. This is still a challenge, in fact, in university settings where "multicultural" values are sought. The oppressed are the ones often "put out of hearing," the ones put at a distance from established scenes of conversation, where decisions are made, power is centralized, cultural values are ratified and celebrated. In criticism and hermeneutics, therefore, to read from an oppressed place is to read from "a distant place"—far from the center, at the horizons of discourse, at the edge.

The tendency of oppressed voices to be at the distant horizon of discourse and criticism, for all its injustice, is a productive, hermeneutical feature. Recall my earlier argument to the effect that, in a world marked by multi-vocality, "strong interpretations" depend upon cultivating "breadth," a penchant for seeking out positions and voices on the distant horizons, the most silenced ones (sometimes these silenced ones are physically near, as feminist and womanist writers have emphasized about the silenced ones who inhabit professionals' families). The seeking of these set at a distance from established centers is precisely what is needed for breadth and hence strong interpretations. The oppressed voice, thus, is not only one among many voices. It is also a voice that has a special power in nurturing the need of multi-vocal criticism for going global by orienting criticism to the ever-changing horizons of discourse where dwell the voices made distant. To the extent that the indigenous place participates in such oppressed space, the space of the subaltern (the subordinated others), then it shares also in the kind of hermeneutical privilege that characterizes that space.

We can note other ways to describe the standpoint of oppressed peoples as "privileged." The acute suffering born by oppressed peoples steeps oppressed interpreters in what Hans-Georg Gadamer has termed "experiences of negativity."[23] Extreme experiences of negativity grant to the social locations of oppressed peoples a quality of not simply being "other" but of rupturing established orders that organize groups in relation to centers and peripheries, the "same" and the "other." Emmanuel Levinas also writes of the particular power of the poor, the "destitute other," to rupture the received order of things.[24] Because of the negativity of indigenous peoples' experiences, their alternity is a subalternity that ruptures the received order and has often therefore a greater capacity for fresh and new insight on the whole. Again, if multi-vocal criticism, as *multi-* vocal, means playing out fully and radically the differences at work in criticism, then it is crucial to expose ourselves to the otherness of oppressed peoples' experiences of negativity. Or, if we the interpreters ourselves are indigenous, which I am not, then it is crucial to foreground one's indigenous standpoint with its rupturing and insightful potential.

We can also discuss the ways multi-vocality is itself uniquely built into the oppressed voice. Here, too, is another kind of testimony to the privilege of oppressed peoples' standpoints. The interpretive voices of oppressed peoples tend to be intensely multi-vocal within themselves. Many empirical, cultural studies have confirmed that subordinated peoples often develop a bicultural or bilingual (sometimes tricultural and trilingual) capacity in speech and vision.[25] This is born out of the demands of struggle under conditions of long-term subordination. Subordinated peoples, for survival, usually have to learn not only their own subordinated culture's life-ways but also those of the subordinating culture. Speakers and interpreters from dominator cultures tend to know less about the cultures they dominate and control than the controlled ones know about the dominator cultures.

The position of greatest power in a given context, therefore, is not necessarily the position from which the most comprehensive and complex knowledge of the whole is available about that context. Quite to the contrary, the richer and more diverse layers of vision are more usually resident in the bi- and tri-vocality and vision internalized in oppressed peoples' lives. "Indigenous place," especially, is privileged with this multi-layered and complex space. This multi-layered complexity has only intensified in recent years. Indigenous peoples have neither been assimilated nor have they died out. Stefano Varese argues that a new sociology is needed to grapple with the complex space and standpoints they inhabit. No longer simply the rural villagers that anthropologists traditionally studied, they are now also "transnationalized, urban, proletarian, border-crossing, bilingual and trilingual, professional."[26]

2. The indigenous place which we have just now described as one of subalternity, or oppression, is also a privileged one as *a place where the voices of the dead proliferate.*

In the United States, Uncle Sam was, as Chickasaw novelist and poet, Linda Hogan, writes, "a cold uncle with a mean soul and a cruel spirit."[27] According to some of the more cautious estimates of Native American population at the time of the emergence of the U.S. "Founding Fathers" in 1796, somewhere between 1.5 and 1.8 million Indians still lived within the continental United States.[28] During the first century of the country's existence, the probability is thus that "the U.S. destroyed 80 to 85 percent of 'its' Indians." Even if many deaths of Indians, both before and after the rise of the U.S. government, were due to disease, this was not simply a matter of "natural disaster" or a mere inevitable spin-off from cultural "encounter" and "discovery." The entire contact and encounter between Europeans and Indigenous took place within a colonialist intention and paradigm. In addition, disease was more than once intentionally spread among the Indians or stimulated by policies of forced relocation and destruction of village infrastructure. Even today, the Mexican military has pulled up latrine works and destroyed Indian villages in Chiapas, leaving almost every lake, river, and stream infected with deadly cholera.

The U.S. government never acted to halt such disease among the Indians; in fact, its actions by military and para-military militia groups only took disaster to more horrific depths.

> A bare sampling of some of the worst must include the 1854 massacre of perhaps 150 Lakotas at Blue River (Nebraska), the 1863 Bear River (Idaho) Massacre of some 500 Western Shoshones, the 1864 Sand Creek (Colorado) Massacre of as many as 250 Cheyennes and Arapahoes, the 1868 massacre of another 300 Cheyennes at the Washita River (Oklahoma), the 1875 massacre of about 75 Cheyennes along the Sappa Creek (Kansas), the 1878 massacre of still another 100 Cheyennes at Camp Robinson (Nebraska) and the 1890 massacre of more than 300 Lakotas at Wounded Knee (South Dakota).[29]

These are all impersonal numbers. A Colorado rancher, who was forced out of bed to ride with U.S. Colonel Chivington's soldiers against 600 Cheyennes and Arapahoes camped at Sand Creek with over 400 of their women and children, gives a more personal account:

> The warriors put the squaws and children together, and surrounded them to protect them. I saw five squaws under a bank for shelter. When the troops came up to them they ran out and showed their persons to let the soldiers know they were squaws and begged for mercy, but the sol-

diers shot them all. . . . There seemed to be indiscriminate slaughter of men, women, and children. There were some thirty or forty squaws collected in a hole for protection; they sent out a little girl about six years old with a white flag on a stick; she had not proceeded but a few steps when she was shot and killed. All the squaws in that hole were afterwards killed, and four or five bucks outside.

Lieutenant James Connor surveyed the same scene on the following day:

In going over the battleground the next day I did not see a body of man, woman, or child but was scalped, and in many instances their bodies were mutilated in the most horrible manner—men, women and children's privates cut out, etc. I heard one man say that he had cut out a woman's private parts and had them for exhibition on a stick; . . . I also heard of numerous instances in which men had cut out the private parts of females and stretched them over the saddle-bows and wore them over their hats while riding in the ranks.[30]

I wish one could say these were rare and exceptionable atrocities. Unfortunately, not. They were widespread and crucial for the enactment of what the powerful thought was essential for American "manifest destiny," and part of what makes America what it is. In spite of the living vitality of the Indians today, as a non-annihilated people, to read from their place is to read from a place of the dead.

What can this mean hermeneutically, "to read from a place of the dead"? Does one even want to derive "hermeneutical insight" about reading, of *any* kind, from such horror? If reading goes on in communities of flesh-and-blood readers, rooted in the histories of ancestors, what does the decimation of many Indian bodies mean now? Can we ever read a text—the Bible or any other text—without hearing the voices of the dead? I am not pressing for some hermeneutical "guilt-consciousness." The histories of indigenous travail do not merely seek to create guilty consciences. Guilt should be there for white Americans, should be heeded, grieved, and borne. I am more interested, however, in a reading and a practice that face the horror and do not run from the voices of the indigenous dead.

If we academics traffic in discourse called "hermeneutics," chances are that notions like "voices of the dead" seem superstitious, alien intrusions into sophisticated inquiry. But one should think again. Have we not said that, in significant ways, interpreters always belong to their pasts and to their traditions?[31] Then, one should recall that our pasts are not simply abstract historical forces but very concrete and embodied ways of belonging culturally. Our ancestors' cultural ways of living *and* their ways of dying shape the present worlds we inhabit. Does this not mean that how they lived and died—perhaps who killed them and who they killed, and the relations of power entailed in the killing and being killed—sets the tone and timbre of our contemporary living-space? Given the extent of a cultural way of life that was based on what

M. Annette Jaimes has called a "killing process"[32] waged against North American indigenous peoples (in addition to the killing process intrinsic to the uprooting and the enslavement of Africa's indigenous people brought to the United States), would we not today have to be completely numb or extraordinarily tone deaf not to hear some voices crying, some voices of the dead, of the unjustly slaughtered?

We contemporary critics often know what it means to lose parents, loved ones, and friends to death, and thus know well what it means to still hear their voices, to think and live from their points of view. I am not really, here, suggesting something so new. Is it really too much to ask—too "superstitious" to expect—flesh-and-blood critical readers to listen to the voices of the indigenous dead? Or will we go on and not listen, thereby keeping the grand "family secret" of these dead who sully our nation's claims to greatness.

Such a listening to these dead, I suggest, is not only possible, but it is also a way to experience the privileged standpoint of the indigenous place. Hearing and "including" those voices intensify the "breadth" of the reading community—a breadth that I argued above is central to strong interpretation. Multi-vocal criticism that really "tends to the global" must tend to the dead, those slain before their time, those whose exclusion took the form of being ripped from their communities and lands—from life itself. Receding and re-emerging, the voices of the dead might constitute the horizons of a reading community as very few others can. Linda Hogan reminds us that the North American Indians tend to be "the shadow people living almost invisible on the fringes. . . ."[33]

Reading from an indigenous place means listening to, learning from, speaking with, these ones from the shadows—and this will often also entail a working for their exodus from the debilitation that comes from being consigned to those shadows. A practical struggle for indigenous liberation is thus intrinsic to, and necessary for, multi-vocal criticism. When conversing with "shadows," we may begin to see, as Hogan also suggests, that the white worlds are but "wisps of smoke stealing by and around their [the Indians'] own more solid world."[34] To refuse to "hear the voices of the dead" or of the lives of the shadow peoples is to stand outside of life's full historical and present complexity. It is to stand outside of life, and this "standing-above" is the really problematic "superstition" (the standing, -stare, which is super-, above and disengaged).

The indigenous place is a privileged place of reading, then, because in U.S. cultural criticism especially it is a space with a site of criticism broadened even toward that horizon from which the dead might speak.

3. In conclusion, there is a final sense in which reading critically from "the indigenous place" is a privileged way of reading. Not only does it give the breadth and strength accruing to the site of the oppressed, or the added intensification of breadth that globally intends even the dead's voices. The "indigenous place," especially, if within it we hear and learn from the voices of the indigenous dead, is privileged also because it is *a place where land is intended*—where landedness of interpreters becomes an issue and where also the impact of interpretations upon land are assessed.

The focus here on land is not simply implied by a stereotypical embrace of the "nearness to nature" of Native American traditions, so central to notions of the "Noble Savage" that extend from eighteenth-century travelogues to late twentieth-century Disney movies like "Pocahontas." The evidence does warrant our observing, however, that cosmologies throughout *Abya Yala* do highlight, take as essential, the earth and land in ways that the arriving European cultural members did not.[35] The *continents* that are home, *Abya Yala*, are fruitful, fructifying *earth*. This is signaled by the very construction of indigenous voices of the dead and of their peoples' experiences of forced removal. In fact, terms like "experiencing death" and "forced removal" are too abstract, i.e., they are descriptions of suffering that fail to note that the pain involved is more complex by reason of the separation from earth and the nature systems. The Chickasaw novelist, Linda Hogan, again well describes the whole circuit of pain, when she deftly portrays forced removal for education in white men's schools as negative because it "lifted them up, screaming, *from the ground.* . . ."[36] To hear the indigenous voice, dead or dying, is to hear not just a lament of a human person or a culture but also the travail of being separated from the earth. In this way, land and earth are implicated in critical reading strategies that take seriously the voice of the dead.

There is an even more direct manner, however, in which land makes its way into the hearing, speaking, and interpreting that are central to critical communities of reading. The voices heard in the indigenous place are not just voices of those separated from earth, torn away from it. The earth *itself* is treated as having desires, voice, and also rage. Hogan writes of a voice inside people that is a voice of rage—"the rage of mother earth." This rage, like earth's desires generally, is not avoidable by humanity. Earth and its peoples can be violated, but the terrain and nature, earth, will remain greater. As Hogan writes, "the earth had a mind of its own . . . the wills and whims of men were empty desires, were nothing pitted up against the desires of earth."[37]

Listening to the land's voice of rage and desire interjects another powerful, often unconsidered, voice and standpoint into the critical community of readers. To talk about the crucial concept of "flesh-and-blood readers" without addressing the issues of land and earth which nurture flesh and blood would be to continue the problematic anthropocentrism of European cosmologies. A full reading from an indigenous place means hearing also the voice(s) that reside in and resound from the material matrix from which flesh-and-blood readers emerge and to which they return. Mayans, and many other native traditions as well, remind us of this by their beliefs to the effect that corn grown from earth's soils is also the flesh of the human. As a result, corn, in various ways, takes on sacral meaning.[38]

This insight—which might be explored further as an ethnographic, cosmological, or religious topic—is here important because of its pertinence to critical reading and hermeneutics. To pursue criticism in dialogue (multi-vocal/ global) with flesh-and-blood readers who are engaged *as landed*, i.e., with a sense of relatedness to land and of what that means for our relation to each other, is a "privileged" kind of criticism, because both the particularity of voices and the articulation of the global sense are intensified. Reading from an indigenous place, aware of the dimension of the landedness of readers, is to cultivate a stronger sense of local place, *and*, through that locatedness, it is also to find one's place on a larger field of vision, ultimately to be on the way, through dialogue, "from place to place" in a larger cosmic whole. "Better" criticism and interpretation, we might say, is achieved by privileging the indigenous place upon which land and earth's voices come to expression and are heard. Multi-vocal/global criticism is not simply a matter of dialogue with many flesh-and-blood readers, representing many diverse social locations. It is that, but most important it is doing this with a sense of the land-and-earth matrix within which interpretive practice occurs.

With this insight the emphasis on "social location" crystalizes around the notion of locale, of location. We are reminded that place cannot be reduced, in indigenist criticism, to voice. Locale orients and embraces flesh-and-blood.

CONCLUDING COMMENTS

In conclusion, I should like to entertain a final query. If multi-vocal/global criticism and then also reading from the rich and privileged indigenous place are the conditions for affirming the value and worth of the Bible, what does all that suggest about specific biblical texts and the message(s) of the Bible for indigenous peoples? I believe it premature to answer such questions. The Christian liberationist in me would like to come forth with messages that are liberating to counteract the imperialist biblical hermeneutics that have reinforced so much *desencarnación*. We will not be able to derive such readings, or know that they are possible, until there exist sustained reading communities that are multi-vocal/global and that exhibit reading strategies that assure the presence of indigenous interpreters and their radically inclusive voices.

I am not holding out for a perfect community of strategic readers, a pure practice of multi-vocality and privileging of indigenous place. I am suggesting, however, that communities are needed which embrace as disciplinary ideals the dialogical practices of multi-vocal/global criticism and privileged indigenous standpoints. Until such critical communities of landed, flesh-and-blood readers begin to come forth, any rehabilitation of biblical meaning for indigenous peoples is premature. First, it is necessary to have the new reading communities. In those communities, the Bible, once "the sword" of imperial spirit, will have to find its new possibilites amid many other spirits that its Christian bearers often spurned. Maybe one finds a foretaste of conversation in new communities of criticism in the Sioux medicine man's talk with his people about the Bible:

> "First, I have to tell you about the book they call the Bible. It is a holy book for the European people, like those who live in the towns. It carries visions, commandments, and songs. I've added what I think is missing from its pages."
>
> One of the younger women interrupted him. "Why can't you just speak it?"

"They don't believe anything is true unless they see it in writing."
Then he explained to the many listeners, "You know all this. It's very simple. That's why it took me so long to write it."

He began reading, "Honor father sky and mother earth. Look after everything. Life resides in all things, even the motionless stones. Take care of the insects for they have their place, and the plants and trees for they feed the people. Everything on earth, every creature and plant wants to live without pain, so do them no harm. Treat all people in creation with respect; all is sacred, especially the bats.

"Live gently with the land. We are one with the land. We are part of everything in our world, part of the roundness and cycles of life. The world does not belong to us. We belong to the world. And all life is sacred."[39]

NOTES

1. G. Colby and C. Detton, *Thy Will Be Done—The Conquest of the Amazon: Nelson Rockefeller and Evangelism in the Age of Oil* (New York: Harper Collins, 1995) 809-810.

2. See P. Richard's constructive use of *Abya Yala* for the worlds of the Americas, in "The Hermeneutics of Liberation: A Hermeneutics of the Spirit," in *Reading from This Place*. Volume 2: *Social Location and Biblical Interpretation in the Global Scene*, ed. Fernando F. Segovia and Mary Ann Tolbert (Minneapolis: Fortress Press, 1995) 263–80.

3. A. Nairn, "CIA Death Squad," *The Nation* 17 April, 1995: 511-13.

4. Chiapas is the southernmost Mexican state, in which indigenous turbulence has been most pronounced and focused since the Zapatistas announced their opposition to NAFTA by attacking the town halls of major municipalities in the state. For a close analysis of these developments, see J. Ross, *Rebellion from the Roots: A Peasant Uprising in Chiapas* (Boston: Common Courage Press, 1995).

5. R. Roett, "Mexico-Political Update," Chase Manhattan's Emerging Markets Group Memo, 13 Jan. 1995. The full memo is available on PeaceNet, and full discussion and background about the memorandum is available in *The Nation* 6 March 1995: 306-11.

6. G. Gutiérrez, *Las Casas: In Search of the Poor of Jesus Christ* (Maryknoll: Orbis Books, 1993) 4.

7. A. Krupat, *Ethnocriticism: Ethnography, History, Literature* (Berkeley: University of California Press, 1992) 21.

8. On indigenous peoples' visions of the fate of the earth and one group's teachings about this, see A. Ereira, *The Elder Brothers* (New York: Alfred A. Knopf, 1990).

9. W. J. T. McNeill, *The Politics of Interpretation* (Chicago: The University of Chicago Press, 1982).

10. On meaning as "constructed," see P. Ricoeur, *Hermeneutics and the Human Sciences* (Cambridge: Harvard University Press, 1981) 174-175.

11. P. Ricoeur, *Time and Narrative,* trans. Kathleen McLaughlin and David Pellauer (Chicago and London: The University of Chicago Press, 1988) 3:171.

12. F. F. Segovia, "'And They Began to Speak in Other Tongues': Competing Modes of Discourse in Contemporary Modes of Biblical Criticism," in *Reading from This Place*. Volume 1: *Social Location and Biblical Interpretation in the United States,* ed. F. F. Segovia and M. A. Tolbert (Minneapolis: Fortress Press, 1995) 29.

13. On the notion of "indigenism" and "indigenist," see W. Churchill, *Struggle for the*

Land: Indigenous Resistance to Genocide, Ecocide and Expropriation in Contemporary North America (Monroe, MN: Common Courage Press, 1993) 403-451.

14. Segovia, "'And They Began to Speak in Other Tongues,'" 31.

15. See C. West, *The Ethical Dimensions of Marxist Thought* (New York: Monthly Review Press, 1991) xv-xvi.

16. C. O. Schrag, *Communicative Praxis and the Space of Subjectivity* (Bloomington: University of Indiana Press, 1986).

17. Segovia, "'And They Began to Speak in Other Tongues.'"

18. C. S. Peirce, *The Collected Papers,* ed. Charles Hartshorne and Paul Weiss (Cambridge: Harvard University Press, 1931-1935) 5:264.

19. Segovia, "'And They Began to Speak in Other Tongues,'" 31.

20. L. Hogan, *Mean Spirit* (New York: Ivy Books, 1990) 341.

21. G. E. Tinker, *Missionary Conquest: The Gospel and Native American Cultural Genocide* (Minneapolis: Fortress Press, 1993).

22. In this section I summarize points made in a number of essays and books about this "hermeneutical privilege" as well as arguments in several of my previous works. For sources and arguments, see M. K. Taylor, *Remembering Esperanza: A Cultural-Political Theology for North American Praxis* (Maryknoll: Orbis Books, 1990) 60-66; and "Celebrating Difference, Resisting Domination: The Need for Synchronic Strategies in Theological Education," in *Shifting Boundaries: Contextual Approaches to the Structure of Theological Education,* ed. E. Farley and B. Wheeler (Louisville: Westminster/John Knox Press, 1991) 259-93.

23. H.-G. Gadamer, *Truth and Method,* 2nd ed. (New York: Continuum, 1984) 353-54.

24. E. Levinas, *Totality and Infinity: An Essay on Exteriority,* trans. A. Lingis (Pittsburgh: Duquesne University Press, 1969) 24-25.

25. J. E. Perlman, *The Myth of Marginality: Urban Poverty and Politics in Rio de Janeiro* (Berkeley: University of California Press, 1976); S. Ardener, ed., *Perceiving Woman* (London: J. M. Dent and Sons, 1975) 1-17; and bell hooks, *Feminist Theory: From Margin to Center* (Boston: South End Press, 1984).

26. S. Varese, "Think Locally, Act Globally," in *Report on the Americas: The First Nations, 1492-1992* (North American Council on Latin America) 25:3 (December 1991): 16.

27. Hogan, *Mean Spirit,* 221.

28. M. A. Jaimes, ed., *The State of Native America: Genocide, Colonization, and Resistance* (Boston: South End Press, 1992) 37.

29. Ibid., 34.

30. D. Brown, *Bury My Heart at Wounded Knee: An Indian History of the American West* (New York: Henry Holt and Co., 1970) 89 and 90.

31. Gadamer, *Truth and Method,* 262-63.

32. Jaimes, *The State of Native America,* 7.

33. Hogan, *Mean Spirit,* 81.

34. Ibid., 340.

35. K. Sale, *The Conquest of Paradise: Christopher Columbus and the Columbian Legacy* (New York: A Plume Book, 1990) 74-90.

36. Hogan, *Mean Spirit,* 36 (emphasis added).

37. Ibid., 186.

38. A. R. Sandstrom, *Corn Is Our Blood: Culture and Ethnic Identity in a Contemporary Aztec Indian Village* (Norman, OK: University of Oklahoma Press, 1991).

39. Hogan, *Mean Spirit,* 361-62.

8

PEDAGOGICAL DISCOURSE AND PRACTICES IN CULTURAL STUDIES

Toward a Contextual Biblical Pedagogy

Fernando F. Segovia

I have argued that with the ongoing fundamental shift in the complexion and exercise of biblical criticism, a shift encompassing more or less the final quarter of the twentieth century and resulting in four competing paradigms or umbrella models of interpretation, a number of crucial questions regarding the discipline have been thrown wide open for discussion and now call for explicit and sustained attention. One such question concerns the critic's vision regarding the handing on of the discipline in this day and age.

I have already undertaken, by way of prelude to the present study, a process of critical reflection regarding this question of pedagogy.[1] I have, in effect, already examined the pedagogical discourses and practices at work in the first three paradigms of historical, literary, and cultural criticism. I have further examined a number of recent voices, all within the ambit of the fourth paradigm of cultural studies, that have called for a thorough reconception and reorientation of such discourses and practices, in the light of the increasing diversity of interpretive approaches and, above all, the expanding globalization of practitioners at work in the discipline. In the present study, therefore, I should like to pursue in a more sustained and systematic way the question of pedagogical discourse and practices within the context of the cultural studies paradigm.

To be sure, as in the case of the other paradigms, the proposed task is not without difficulties. By way of contrast, however, it should be noted that this umbrella model, unlike the other three, poses no problem whatever with regard to pedagogy. In fact, as the analysis of the recent voices for change shows, the model has consistently turned to and addressed the question of pedagogical discourse and practices, often as a point of departure. In so doing, it has followed recent developments in theological studies,[2] cultural studies,[3] and pedagogical studies.[4] The difficulties in question are thus of a different sort altogether, and two come readily to mind.

First, there is the question of consolidation. This is a model that is still in the process of formation and maturation: the precious benefit of hindsight is simply lacking—twenty-five years in the case of literary criticism and cultural criticism, and close to a century and a half in the case of historical criticism. Needless to say, dealing with any phenomenon in the making is not only more daring but also more tentative. Second, there is the question of diversity. Cultural studies, as I have argued, is a child of mixed parentage: on the one hand, the heir of methodological and theoretical diversity; on the other, the scion of sociocultural and demographic diversity. As such, the rise of cultural studies is directly related, on the one side, to the ever-expanding options and choices in method and theory facing the critic in the discipline. On the other side, it is directly related as well to the ever-increasing presence of outsiders (Western women; non-Western critics and theologians; non-Western minorities residing in the West) in a discipline that has been, from its inception, thoroughly male, clerical, and Western. This is a model, therefore, that is global in scope: critiques and proposals issue forth not only from within the heart of the West, but also from every quarter of the world where Western imperialism and colonialism brought the religion of Christianity (or, more accurately, the religions of Christianity) as an essential component of its ideological apparatus. Again, dealing with any phenomenon of global dimensions can prove downright intimidating if not entirely overwhelming.

At the same time, such difficulties are by no means forbidding. In fact, they can be made to serve as marvelous opportunities for creative and innovative work on the part of the critic, now forced to deal at one and the same time with the task of deploying a new umbrella model of interpretation and the responsibility of so doing by way of engagement with the many voices of the global "others." I would add, moreover, that I come to this question, once again, neither as a complete stranger nor as a participant observer, but as a cognizant and interested insider—as someone who has arrived at cultural studies by means of a professional pilgrimage through the other three paradigms, and thus through the thicket of the methodological and theoretical jungle, and as someone who is a member of a non-Western ethnic minority group at the heart of the West, and hence a child of the colonized among the colonizers.

In what follows I shall proceed in two stages. First, I shall comment, within the context of my own conception of cultural studies as a paradigm, on the various diagnoses and remedies advanced by the recent calls for new directions in teaching and education within the discipline. My aim is to compare my own diagnosis of and corresponding prescription for change in the discipline with those offered by these other voices. Needless to say, the spirit at work in such an exercise is, once again, especially given my own fundamental agreement with the tenor and direction of such calls, not one of scorched-earth tactics but rather one of critical dialogue. Then, in the light of this discussion, I shall go on to advance a pedagogical proposal of my own that is in keeping with my overall project of intercultural criticism.

CULTURAL STUDIES: DIAGNOSES AND PRESCRIPTIONS

I should like to begin by recalling, as I did in the case of the other paradigms, a number of preliminary observations advanced in my earlier description of the pedagogical model envisioned by the fourth paradigm of cultural studies.[5] First, given the diversity in methodological strategies and theoretical orientations, the model moves beyond any demand for a common methodological and theoretical apparatus on the part of readers who wish to become critics. Second, given its emphasis on the contextualized and perspectival nature of all readers, including critics, the model no longer regards the latter as in any way hermeneutically privileged and intrinsically superior to all other readers. Third, further in keeping with this principle that all reading and interpretation is contextualized and perspectival, the model calls for all would-be critics, indeed for all readers, not to learn how to efface themselves, in itself an impossible task, but, on the contrary, to learn how to read themselves and their readings. In the end, I argued, this is a model that calls for an abandonment of the long-established practice of learned impartation and passive reception in favor of a self-conscious, highly critical, and global dialogue involving unceasing and ever-shifting processes of impartation and reception. For such a model the ideal is no longer that of the voice of reason, rising arduously but triumphantly above the endless vagaries of everyday life, but that of multiple voices, multicentered and multilingual.

It is precisely such voices, like the ones highlighted for analysis in my earlier study, that have begun to call for basic changes in pedagogical discourse and practices within the discipline. These are calls, once again, with which I find myself in fundamental agreement, sharing with them a similar view of the discipline, both by way of diagnosis and prescription. At the same time, I would register some differences with respect to certain concrete aspects of such proposals, not so much in terms of their perception of the present state of affairs but rather in terms of the prescribed remedies for change. In what follows, therefore, I should like to pursue, by way of critical dialogue, such similarities and differences, following the four points highlighted in my earlier summary of these positions:[6]

1. I argued that all such voices offered a remarkably similar diagnosis of the discipline: a view of biblical criticism as profoundly Western, while pretending to scientific objectivity and distance. This is an evaluation with which I would heartily agree. Indeed, I have argued throughout that, from the beginning until quite recently, the discipline has had a male, clerical, *and* Western orientation. As such, I would further agree, biblical criticism has confined the task of interpretation to antiquity; has concentrated, within an empiricist view of both text and world, on the original meaning of the text; has insisted on particular approaches to the text and even particular understandings of the text, with a definite penchant for questions of a religious nature; and has viewed instruction as universal and undifferentiated, with enormous emphasis on the passive learning of information.

2. I pointed out that such a state of affairs was deemed to have deleterious consequences for all outsiders to the West: such individuals and groups find themselves in a foreign world altogether. This is an assessment with which I would heartily concur as well. In fact, I have argued throughout that ethnic and racial minorities both inside and outside the West find the discipline to be both an alien and an alienating world. Thus, I would further agree, such individuals find their own traditions of interpretation excluded from consideration as unscientific, their own questions and concerns ignored as irrelevant, and their own selves regarded as biased and hence expected to conform to the traditions, concerns, and leadership of the dominant and normative position, if they are to become scientific, universal, and impartial.

3. With regard to the remedies offered for change, I would make a distinction between principle and specific proposals. Thus, I find myself in complete agreement with the basic principle at work: the need to take into account the lives and contexts of "the other." In effect, I have argued consistently for what amounts to a variation of this principle: the need to take real readers into consideration—the contextualized and perspectival character of all flesh-and-blood readers. I also find myself in agreement with a number of the actual remedies proposed: a different approach to the question of textual meaning, with a focus on both texts and interpreters; an emphasis on readers from around the globe, now in the process of gaining a voice for the first time; a commitment to postmodernism and its view of reality as fractured—especially in terms of class, ethnicity, and race; recourse to a broad range of methods and theories; a view of the texts as both religious and social.

However, I would point to some discrepancies as well:

• I would much prefer to talk in terms of going beyond the canon rather than broadening the canon itself. I would be in favor, therefore, of surveying the whole panorama or spectrum of expression at any period of time, past or present.

• I would eschew any type of formulation that would imply or suggest, no matter how lightly or unintentionally, the presence of a pre-existing, independent, or stable meaning in the text, the mind of the author, or the world of the text—formulations along the lines of the meaning back-then, letting the text speak, being true to the past, or achieving a fuller meaning of the text.

• I would go beyond recourse to a broad range of methods and theories to an emphasis on metatheory, on the origins and developments of the different methods and theories as well as on the relationships between and among such methods and theories.

4. With regard to the goals and hopes undergirding such remedies for change, I would again make a distinction between principle and concrete proposals. To begin with, I find myself in total agreement with the principle invoked: the need for the discipline to become less Western, more inclusive, and more global. In point of fact, I have argued consistently that the influx of outsiders

into the discipline has radically changed its character for the better and that such developments will continue, inexorably, in the future. I further find myself in agreement with some of the goals and hopes expressed: an awareness of Christianity as a global religion, presently undergoing a profound shift in numbers and vitality away from the West and toward the Two-Thirds World; dialogue among the different groups and cultures, now approaching the texts from such diverse locations and points of view; the vision of liberation.

At the same time, I would express the following reservations:

- I would not share any view of the Bible that would regard it, no matter how unintentionally, as non-ideological and thus as an ideal corrective for a fragmented reality, whether expressed along the lines of the Bible as a depository for the principles of human dignity, justice, and peace or as a magna carta for the liberation of all men and women.

- I would not favor the prospect of having the different groups and peoples engage in a recontextualization of the images and stories of the Bible into their own contexts.

With all such preliminary observations and comparisons in mind, I should like to advance at this point, within the context of my own previous delineations of intercultural criticism as a reading strategy,[7] a constructive proposal for the teaching of the discipline in the face of a new century.

CULTURAL STUDIES AND PEDAGOGY: A PROPOSAL

The proposal has two basic frameworks or driving forces at its core, both derived from central components of intercultural criticism. First, it is a proposal that takes diversity to heart—diversity in texts, diversity in readings, and diversity in readers. In so doing, it follows closely my description of the path of recent biblical criticism as a movement of liberation: from hegemony of approach and practitioners, to diversity in approaches, to diversity in practitioners. The proposal sets out to incorporate such diversity into the discipline at every step of the way. Second, it is a proposal that takes the reality of empire, of imperialism and colonialism, as an omnipresent, inescapable, and overwhelming reality in the world—the world of antiquity, the world of the Near East or of the Mediterranean Basin; the world of modernity, the world of Western hegemony and expansionism; and the world of today, of postmodernism and postliberalism, the world of postcolonialism on the part of the Two-Thirds World and of neocolonialism on the part of the West. As such, it follows closely my description of the course of recent biblical criticism as a movement of decolonization: away from its Western moorings, toward an exercise of truly global dimensions. The proposal seeks to integrate this imperial/colonial dimension into the discipline at every step of the way—at the level of texts, readings of texts, and readers of texts.

The structural selection and deployment of these two driving forces or basic frameworks should be seen as by no means fortuituous but rather as deliberately reflecting specific, distinctive, and formative developments of a sociocultural and sociopolitical character at the turn of the century. That is to say, both liberation and decolonization, while certainly no strangers to the world of the nineteenth century—indeed, one should never forget in this regard the primordial and remarkable example of the Haitian Revolution (1790–1804)[8]—and the early part of the twentieth, emerged as distinctive global battle cries in the later course of the century. I would only add that, while the element of diversity is pursued in full in what follows, that of imperialism/colonialism is introduced by way of anticipation, as a sign of things to come.[9]

Some further observations are in order. First, the proposal advances a modus operandi, a pedagogical agenda or program, that is still very much bipolar in nature and hence very much in process as well: on the one hand, to be sure, the proposal does reflect actual practices and guiding principles in my own present exercise of the profession; on the other hand, I would readily acknowledge, the proposal also reflects certain goals and ideals that still remain not only out of reach but also out of focus at this point. Second, the proposal represents an exercise in cultural studies: a self-conscious construction that takes as its point of departure the context of postmodernism and postliberalism and that has as its point of destination a postcolonial pedagogy within the academic context of religious and theological studies. Third, the proposal is made from the perspective of a Christian theologian and critic, a lay person from the Roman Catholic tradition.[10]

Diversity in Texts

Scope of Diversity. With regard to the ancient texts themselves, I would argue that diversity should be actively pursued at three different levels: (1) diversity of texts; (2) diversity within texts; and (3) diversity within cultures. To be sure, all three elements have been pursued by practitioners of the discipline in the past, beginning with historical criticism itself, where the various critical impulses outlined below (metacanonical analysis of texts; focus on tensions within texts; and comparative studies of the history-of-religions variety) may be found at one time or another. The proposal gathers these various impulses together, in sustained and systematic fashion, as a first step in its programmatic pedagogical agenda.

1. By diversity of texts I have in mind a deliberate move away from any exclusively or highly canonical approach to the discipline, whereby the focus of inquiry is placed, solely or primarily, on a study of the "New Testament" or the "Old Testament," that is, on those texts collectively known, acknowledged, and revered as "Scripture" or "Word of God." The proposed collapse of the canonical boundary gives way to a study of ancient Judaism or early Christianity,[11] as the case may be, in terms of the entire literary production of the period in question, with "canonical" texts set indistinguishably alongside "extracanonical" texts. As a result, each religious tradition is analyzed in its entirety, that is to say, in the light of all surviving voices from any particular

period or angle of study. Thereby, no particular voice or group of voices is privileged a priori. Rather, emphasis is placed instead on the din of texts and authors as such, the cacophony of voices in the ancient agora or forum, coming from every direction and going every which way—voices drawing away from or intersecting one another, ignoring or engaging each other, supporting or clashing with one another.

The aim behind this metacanonical approach is not to move beyond the obviously theological element of canon in search of a more "objective" standpoint, for such an approach is in the end as theological as any canonical approach. The aim, rather, corresponds to a fundamental pedagogical imperative: the need to survey the totality of what was produced at any one time within either tradition—the spectrum of expression—with a corresponding emphasis on variety, interaction, relationships, contrasts, struggles. The aim, therefore, is not to highlight the canonical, what became authoritative and normative, but rather to jump into the thick of the discussion—to listen to its manifold voices, note the ceaseless give-and-take, observe the inevitable power plays—always with the realization in mind that what has survived must represent but a minimal part of the discussion at any one time.

2. By diversity within texts I mean not only the possibility that a text may contain within itself actual remnants of an earlier text (an earlier draft of itself or a different document altogether), as traditionally entertained by historical criticism in its quest for pre-existing sources, but also that such other elements as dissenting voices, suppressed voices, or contradictory voices may be found within it as well. Thus, even when a text is judged to constitute a literary unity, a unified and coherent whole, ruling out thereby the presence of any disparate or conflicting literary layers, the possibility still has to be considered that such a text: (1) achieves a unity that is, given the juxtaposition of irreconcilable voices, forced, illusory, and evanescent—voices that the "whole" simply cannot keep together; (2) preserves within itself, no matter how faintly, echoes or hints of different or discordant voices—suppressed voices now largely bypassed and present only as telling silences in the text; or (3) undertakes a direct repudiation of other voices—dissenting voices with which it finds itself in fundamental disagreement, if not outright struggle. In this view, therefore, a text may in itself embody a number of different texts whose voices also form part of and contribute to the overall din at work. A second pedagogical imperative is very much at work here as well: the need to bring all such voices to the fore.

3. By diversity within culture I have in mind the placement of all such texts, canonical and extracanonical alike, within the overall sociocultural framework of the period under consideration. In other words, the analysis of the full literary production of early Christianity or ancient Judaism is further undertaken in terms of the wider literary production, religious or otherwise, surviving from the period or angle of study in question, with the former texts as a subset of the latter. Thus, just as the first example of diversity in texts described above involved the breakdown of any canonical division, so does

this final example represent a similar breakdown of any religious division, whether formulated along the lines of Jews/Gentiles or Christians/pagans.

The intention, once again, is not to leave behind the obviously theological element of a socioreligious tradition in quest of a more "neutral" vantage point, for again no such vantage point is to be had. The proposed approach is as theological as any confessional approach. The intention, rather, corresponds to a third pedagogical imperative: the need to survey the totality of what was produced at any one time, the panorama of expression, whether in terms of religious texts from other traditions or texts of a different orientation altogether. The end result, of course, is a far greater din of texts and authors, a much louder cacophony of voices in the ancient agora or forum, within which the voices of either tradition, in themselves highly pluriform, constitute but one element or dimension of the overall din.

Concluding Comments. What such an approach entails by way of pedagogical practice is—taking my own field of study, early Christianity, as an example— a reading of the extant texts without reference to canonical status, as sundry expressions of early Christian life and thought; a reading of such texts as potential metaphorical palimpsests, possibly bearing within themselves sediments of other texts, whether by way of pre-existing sources, contradictory positions, revealing silences, or open polemics; and a reading of such texts against the larger sociocultural background of the Mediterranean Basin. The goal would be as wide a presentation as possible of the din of voices emerging out of the early Christian experience, by way of open and hidden texts, within the much larger din of voices to be found in the area of the Circum-Mediterranean.

Diversity in Texts and Intercultural Criticism. In my exposition of intercultural criticism, in itself grounded in a hermeneutics of otherness and engagement, I argued for a consideration of the ancient texts as *others* (with italics signifying a positive sense of otherness—a self-defined and affirming otherness) rather than "others" (with quotation marks signifying a negative sense of otherness— an imposed and denigrating otherness)—as realities from a very different social and historical context that are to be acknowledged, respected, and engaged rather than overridden and overwhelmed. I went on to argue, therefore, for a three-fold approach to the reading and interpretation of these texts, with a first movement involving a view of the texts as literary or artistic products, rhetorical or strategic products, and cultural or ideological products.

In other words, a text is to be seen as constructing, from a particular perspective and underlying social location, a multilayered or multifaceted reality— a poetic reality by way of its artistic architecture and texture; a rhetorical reality given the strategic concerns and aims behind such a poetic reality; and an ideological reality on account of both the view of the world and of life in that world conveyed by means of such a poetic and rhetorical reality. This approach calls in turn for a combination of formalist, practical, and cultural methods in order to interpret texts and dis-cover their reality as *others*.

A number of comments are in order regarding the relationship between the first pedagogical goal of diversity in texts and this first interpretive movement of texts as constructs:

1. For the pedagogical agenda, it is the din of authors and texts that is important; for the interpretive project, it is that reality constructed and advanced by texts that is important. As such, reality is seen as neither common nor universal but as a multitude of realities constructed by the different texts, all perspectival and contextualized in nature. It is this fluid, polyvalent, polyglot view of reality that ultimately informs and guides the pedagogical focus on the cacophony of voices in the ancient agora or forum. Each voice, whether canonical or non-canonical, is regarded as a poetic, strategic, and ideological product.

2. From the perspective of the interpretive project, the possibility is granted that the reality constructed by any one text may be diffuse rather than concordant, due to the presence of pre-existing, dissident, suppressed, or contradictory texts within it. Such texts would be seen as poetic, rhetorical, and ideological products of their own—even if presently filtered through the reality of the primary text within which they are contained, and thus available only as "others." From the perspective of the pedagogical agenda, such diffuseness in texts would add to the overall din of authors and texts at work at any one time.

3. For the pedagogical agenda, such a cacophony of voices would be situated within the far more extensive din of texts and authors present in the broader sociocultural context. For the interpretive project, such a comprehensive sociocultural context would be seen in terms of a far more numerous multitude of realities created by its texts—an overall reality in which the texts of early Christianity or ancient Judaism would interact in ever so many ways with the texts of the Near East or the Mediterranean Basin.

4. Finally, I have argued that the goal behind this first movement of intercultural criticism lies not in antiquarian interest, even if that were theoretically possible, but rather in critical engagement with the texts—in dialogue and struggle in the light of one's own reality and experience. Similarly, I would argue that the goal of this first pedagogical emphasis on diversity in texts is not simply to jump into the thick of the discussion, marveling at its complexity and following its endless paths, but rather to take an active and critical part within it, thus adding one's own voice to that overall din of a very different time and a very different culture.

Imperial-Colonial Framework. For this first pedagogical goal of diversity in texts, I would argue further for an analysis of the texts of ancient Judaism and early Christianity that takes seriously into consideration their broader sociocultural contexts in the Near East and the Mediterranean Basin, respectively, in the light of an omnipresent, inescapable, and overwhelming sociopolitical reality— the reality of empire, of imperialism and colonialism, as variously constituted and exercised during the long period in question. Some preliminary observations regarding this phenomenon of empire are in order.[12]

First, the reality of empire should be seen as a structural reality that is largely defined and practiced in terms of a primary binomial: on the one hand, a political, economic, and cultural *center*—more often than not symbolized by a city; on the other hand, any number of *margins* politically, economically, and culturally subordinated to the center. This grounding binomial entails and engenders, in turn, any number of secondary or subordinate binomials: civilized/uncivilized, advanced/primitive, cultured/barbarian, progressive/backward, developed/undeveloped/underdeveloped. Second, such a structural reality, despite the many and profound similarities in common, should not be seen as uniform in every imperial context across time and culture—say, for example, from the world of Assyria and Babylon, to the world of Greece and Rome, to the world of Europe and the United States—but as differentiated in constitution and deployment, though again with many and profound similarities in common. Third, this reality, I would argue, is of such reach and such power that it inevitably affects and colors, directly or indirectly, the entire artistic production of center and margins, of dominant and subaltern, including their respective literary productions.

From the point of view of ancient Judaism and its literature, it is necessary to speak not just of one empire but of a succession of empires involving, depending on the locality of the center in question, the Near East as well as the Mediterranean Basin—Assyria, Babylon, Persia, Greece, Rome. From the point of view of early Christianity and its literature, it is obviously the massive presence and might of the Roman Empire, master and lord of the entire Circum-Mediterranean, with its thoroughly accurate if enormously arrogant classification of the Mediterranean Sea as *mare nostrum*.

A number of key questions come to the fore as a result: How do the margins look at the "world"—a world dominated by the reality of empire—and fashion life in such a world? What images and representations of the other-world arise from either side? How is history conceived and constructed by both sides? How is "the other" regarded and represented? What conceptions of oppression and justice are to be found?

Diversity in Readings

Scope of Diversity. With respect to the readings of ancient texts, I would argue for diversity to be actively pursued, once again, at three different levels: (1) diversity of reading traditions; (2) diversity of disciplinary paradigms; and (3) diversity within paradigms. It is only in recent times, with the breakdown of the stranglehold of traditional historical criticism on biblical criticism and the emergence of alternative critical approaches in the discipline, that such considerations have begun to make their way into the discipline. The present proposal places such critical impulses at center stage, in sustained and systematic fashion, as a second step in its programmatic pedagogical agenda.

1. By diversity of reading traditions I refer to the existence of a variety of long-standing and overarching ways of interpretation: the academic or scholarly;

the theological or churchly; the religious or devotional; the cultural or popular. To be sure, this first level of analysis does impinge upon the category of diversity in readers to follow, insofar as it begins to deal with the socioeducational and socioreligious identities of real readers. Nevertheless, quite aside from the fact that these categories are in themselves interrelated and porous, I include such a concern at this point in the discussion, under the category of diversity in readings, because of what I regard as a fundamental pedagogical imperative: the need to conceive of the discipline as discipline—that is, as an academic field of study, with its own area of inquiry and research and its own base in institutions of higher learning of whatever kind—and thus to look upon its academic or scholarly way of reading these ancient texts as one among several such modes.

To do so, it is necessary to distinguish the academic type of reading from the other traditions of reading—the theological or churchly, the religious or devotional, the cultural or popular. This can be readily accomplished by describing the different ways of reading available within each tradition. First, with regard to the churchly or institutional mode of reading, one must deal with the following spectrum of approaches: the dogmatic or traditionalist;[13] the fundamentalist or literalist;[14] the denominational or ecclesiastical;[15] and the liberationist or sociopolitical.[16] Second, with respect to the devotional or spiritual mode of reading, one needs to examine the many actual and enduring practices of reading observed in daily life: from the cover-to-cover, sequential reading of the text; to the flipping-of-pages, at-random reading for the message of the day or the moment; to the recurring, ad hoc reading of specific texts for edification at specific moments or occasions—to name but a few.[17] Third, with regard to the popular or intertextual mode of reading, one should look at the broad appropriation and deployment of biblical motifs, scenes, situations, and themes in such diverse fields as literature, film, art, music, and so forth.[18]

It has been my experience over many years of teaching that the vast majority of students who take up biblical criticism for the first time do so out of specific and cherished institutional, spiritual, and/or intertextual modes of reading. As such, it is essential to begin with a critical analysis of the different traditions of reading—their origins, contours, and claims—in order to allow students not only to bring to the surface and come to terms with their own already established mode(s) of reading but also to realize what the academic study of these texts implies and entails and how such reading contrasts with their own traditional and beloved practices.

2. By diversity of disciplinary paradigms I point to the fact that the academic or scholarly mode of reading is by no means monolingual. Thus, once such a mode of reading has been properly differentiated from the other major reading traditions, it is necessary to analyze its own origins, contours, and claims as well. This can be readily done in terms of the different paradigms or umbrella models of interpretation developed within the discipline, in the past as well as in the present. Three specific elements make such a task less daunting than it would otherwise seem: (1) the discipline as discipline is not that old, tracing its

origins—as in the case of so many other disciplines—to the intellectual ferment that marked the aftermath of the French Revolution in the early nineteenth century;[19] (2) for a very long period of time, indeed close to a century and a half, the discipline remained under the tight control of one such paradigm, historical criticism;[20] (3) all major paradigms in question can still be found at work, to one degree or another, in the discipline today.

Given my sustained analysis of these paradigms—historical criticism, literary criticism, cultural criticism, cultural studies—in the course of this project, I would only emphasize at this point a second pedagogical imperative: the need for an expansive and informed perspective regarding the grounding, tenor, and import—the presuppositions, language, and ramifications—of all such paradigms. Its aims would be as follows: to construct a comprehensive interpretive spectrum; to be able to situate within such a spectrum the different types of readings in question, including one's own; to be capable of establishing a sound critical dialogue with such ways of reading. In other words, the time is now past, irrevocably, when the discipline could be transmitted uniformly, when one paradigm could be conveyed as the sole paradigm of interpretation, often without any awareness regarding its own character as a paradigm, and when all students could be given essentially the same training in the academic reading of these texts. This means, of course, that scholarly training today must involve, from the first, a degree of sophistication in metatheory, that is, in the principles underlying the various paradigms as well as in the relationships among the paradigms themselves.

To be sure, such a task proves, more often than not, highly disconcerting to the student, whether coming to biblical criticism for the first time or having been previously taught within the confines of a single paradigm (invariably historical criticism). In effect, the student now faces, from quite early on, a series of difficult challenges: an unfamiliar array of critical approaches to a text, each with its own distinctive mode of discourse; modes of discourse whose technical terminology and conceptual apparatus require familiarity with other disciplines; and the growing realization that, sooner or later, a personal choice and rationale for such a choice are inevitable. Nevertheless, despite all such difficulties, there is no other way out of this quandary, since to opt for training within any one paradigm first often leads to the privileging of such an umbrella model and a corresponding view of other umbrella models as superfluous, if not altogether deficient. It should go without saying as well that, under such circumstances, mastery of all paradigms is simply out of the question, for no individual—no matter how gifted, learned, or devoted—can possibly assimilate the range of materials in question. The aim behind such training, therefore, cannot be full control but rather informed awareness, a sort of working sophistication sufficient to follow and interact with a number of particular lines of argumentation, to engage in border-crossings, so to speak.

3. By diversity within paradigms I refer to the fact that no paradigm or umbrella model of interpretation, despite the presence of a distinctive mode of discourse, is monolingual. Consequently, once the various paradigms at work

in the discipline have been properly identified and described, it becomes necessary to examine in turn the variety of methods and theories, reading strategies and theoretical orientations, that make up each paradigm and account for its characteristic mode of discourse. This means, of course, that one must examine each paradigm in terms of its own origins, contours, and claims.[21]

Again, since in the course of this project I have had occasion to analyze the different paradigms in terms of their respective constitutive components, I limit myself at this point to a third pedagogical imperative, actually an extension of the second one mentioned above: the need for an expansive and informed perspective regarding the grounding, tenor, and import— the presuppositions, language, and ramifications—of the major lines of interpretation to be found within each paradigm. The basic aims behind such a proposed expertise remain the same: to delineate a series of concrete interpretive spectrums; to be able to situate within each spectrum the different types of reading in question, including one's own, should one choose to write in that vein; and to be capable of establishing a sound critical conversation with such readings.

Even when historical criticism functioned as the sole paradigm in the field, it was still necessary to become acquainted with its different lines of interpretation, from textual criticism to composition criticism. The situation has now changed drastically in two respects. On the one hand, with the proliferation in paradigms has come a corresponding multiplicity in constitutive components. On the other hand, such multiplicity within historical criticism always remained much closer, from both a linguistic and a conceptual point of view, than it ever does within the new paradigms. In other words, the differences in technical terminology and conceptual apparatus among the various lines of interpretation within each of the recent paradigms prove far sharper to master and bridge than the differences within historical criticism itself. This means, of course, that scholarly training today must involve not only a measure of sophistication in metatheory at the level of paradigms but also at the level of their respective components, in the principles underlying the various interpretive models and the relationships among the models themselves.

Such a task, of course, proves even more disconcerting to the student, now faced as well with a broad variety of methods and theories within any one paradigm: an array of different though related approaches to a text, each with its own particular mode of discourse; modes of discourse that demand familiarity with a number of specific movements both inside and outside the field; the further realization that beyond a choice of umbrella model lies a choice of working interpretive model as well. Again, there is simply no way out of this situation. At the same time, it should be clear as well that even mastery of a paradigm is out of the question, that the most one can aim for is a sort of informed awareness, a working sophistication, that enables one to follow and interact with a variety of interpretive models, to engage in border-crossings.

Concluding Comments. I argued in the previous section that the goal behind the pedagogical emphasis on diversity in texts was to unfold as broadly as possible the din of texts and authors, the cacophony of voices in the ancient agora or forum, present in either ancient Judaism or early Christianity within the much larger din of texts and authors surviving from either the Near East or the Mediterranean Basin. The added emphasis on diversity in readings represents a significant extension of this goal. What such an approach entails by way of pedagogical practice is a reading of the extant texts—canonical or non-canonical, open or hidden—in terms of the many readings and interpretations—the panorama of expression—produced by different reading traditions, different paradigms within the academic tradition, and different methods and theories within each scholarly paradigm. The result is a deafening din of texts and authors, a more extensive as well as more pronounced cacophony of voices in the modern marketplace or *mercado*, as the ancient texts become refracted into endless readings and interpretation within the tradition of the West.

Diversity in Readings and Intercultural Criticism. Again, given its call for a consideration of the ancient texts as *others*—as realities from a very different social and historical context that are to be acknowledged, respected, and engaged, rather than overridden and overwhelmed—intercultural criticism calls in turn for a three-fold approach to the reading and interpretation of these texts. The third movement within such an approach involves a view of all readings as literary or artistic products, rhetorical or strategic products, and cultural or ideological products. To begin with, for intercultural criticism, textual meaning is the result of interaction between texts and readers—socially and historically conditioned texts and socially and historically conditioned readers. As such, a text is always regarded as a "text"—as read and interpreted in a certain way by a certain reader or group of readers within a certain context (time and place). Consequently, each "text" or reading is also seen as constructing, from a particular perspective and social location, a multilayered or multifaceted reality—an artistic reality, with a poetics of its own; a strategic reality, with a rhetorics of its own; and a cultural reality, with an ideology of its own.

Again, therefore, intercultural criticism calls for a similar combination of formalist, practical, and cultural methods in the analysis of "texts." The goal of such analysis is two-fold: first, to help in dis-covering the reality of texts as *others*, given one's own reading of the text and production of a "text"; second, to assist in dis-covering the reality of these "texts" as *others* in their own right—as realities from different social and historical contexts than one's own. In other words, in foregrounding readings of the texts as it does, intercultural criticism seeks to prevent any overriding or overwhelming of texts by readers and to place any one reading or interpretation—any one "text," including one's own—within a full spectrum of expression.

Some observations are in order regarding the relationship between the second pedagogical goal of diversity in readings and this second interpretive movement of readings as constructs:

1. For the pedagogical agenda, it is the deafening din of "texts"—of readings and interpretations, in terms of major and overarching reading traditions, par-

adigms within the academic type of reading, and methods and theories within the various scholarly paradigms—that is important. For the interpretive project, it is that reality constructed and advanced by each and every "text" or reading that proves important. In effect, there is no meaning of the text out there, stable and extractable, preceding, guiding, and sanctioning interpretation; instead, what one finds is a multitude of "texts," of readings of the same text, all perspectival and contextualized in nature. It is such a fluid, polyvalent, polyglot view of meaning and text that ultimately informs and guides the pedagogical focus on the cacophony of voices in the modern marketplace or *mercado*. Each "text" is looked upon as a poetic, strategic, and cultural product.

2. Given the fact that for the interpretive project there is no final or definitive text or meaning as such, the unfolding of the din of readings and interpretations with regard to any one text as part of the pedagogical agenda is not intended to produce or aim for a final and definitive reading and interpretation of such a text, but rather to drive home the spectrum of opinion resulting from the choice of reading glasses available with which to approach the text, both outside and inside biblical criticism, that is to say, the academic or scholarly reading tradition. The point is to see in each reading of a text not only a "text," a version of that text and a rendition of its meaning, but also a text of its own, a product in its own right.

3. Finally, the goal behind this second movement of intercultural criticism is not intellectual curiosity per se but critical engagement with "texts"—in dialogue and struggle in the light of one's reality and experience. Likewise, the goal of this second pedagogical emphasis on diversity in readings is not to become a mere spectator of the discussion, witnessing its goings-on and taking pleasure in its many twists and turns, but to fashion a "text" of one's own by taking an active and critical role within the discussion—to offer a version of the text and, in so doing, produce yet another "text" within the overall din of many different times and different cultures.

Imperial-Colonial Framework. For this second pedagogical goal of diversity in readings, I would argue as well for an analysis of the readings and interpretations of the texts of Jewish and Christian antiquity that takes seriously into account their broader sociocultural context in the West, whether by way of Europe or North America, in the light of the same omnipresent, inescapable, and overwhelming sociopolitical reality that surrounded the production of the texts of ancient Judaism and early Christianity—the reality of empire, of imperialism and colonialism, now with regard to the Western imperial tradition of the last five hundred years. Some preliminary remarks are again in order.

First the imperial tradition of the West may be approached in terms of three different phases and periods:[22] (1) early imperialism, with reference to the beginning, mercantile phase of European imperialism—from the fifteenth century through the nineteenth century, from the monarchical states of Portugal and Spain to the early modern states of England, France, and the Netherlands, among others; (2) high imperialism, involving monopoly capitalism with its integration of industrial and finance capital in the major capitalist nation-states—from the end of the nineteenth century through the middle of the twentieth century, with England as prime example; and (3) late imperialism, with reference to both the end of formal colonialism and the continued impact and power of imperial culture in the world—from mid-century to the present, with the United States as its prime example.

Second, this tradition of Western empire-building was accompanied by a very prominent socioreligious dimension as well. Thus, the Western missionary movement may be divided into two major waves and periods, represented by the highly symbolic dates of 1492 and 1792.[23] The first date stands, of course, for the first European landfall in the "New World." This first stage of the missions (1492–1792) is primarily Catholic in orientation, involves the massive evangelization of the Americas, and finds itself near exhaustion by the end of the eighteenth century. The second date, not as well-known, recalls two different though related events: (1) with regard to Asia (India), the publication of William Carey's *Enquiry into the obligation of Christians to use means for the propagation of the Gospel among the heathens* and concomitant formation of his missionary society; (2) with regard to Africa (Sierra Leone), the establishment of the first church in tropical Africa in modern times (interestingly enough, by people of African birth or descent from North America). This second stage (1792–present) is at first primarily Protestant in nature, concerns the massive evangelization of Africa, Asia, and remaining areas of the Americas, and remains quite vigorous today. Over the last five centuries, therefore, the different phases of European imperialism and colonialism brought with them, wherever they turned, their respective religious beliefs and practices, whether Catholic or Protestant.

Third, a comparison of this two-fold division of the missionary movement of the West with the previous three-fold division of Western imperialism proves instructive: on the one hand, the first missionary wave of the fifteenth through the eighteenth centuries coincides with the first imperialist phase—the mercantile stage of early imperialism; on the other hand, the second missionary wave of the nineteenth and twentieth centuries coincides with the transition from the first to the second imperialist phase in the nineteenth century and its full bloom at the end of the nineteenth century and the beginning of the twentieth—the monopoly capitalist stage of high imperialism.

As such, the structural binomial reality of empire should be seen as involving a strong socioreligious component as well. The political, economic, and cultural center also functions as a religious center; that is to say, the practices and beliefs of the center are invariably grounded on, sanctioned, and accompanied by a set of religious beliefs and practices. Consequently, the primary binomial of center and margins entails and engenders a further binomial in this sphere as well: believers/unbelievers-pagans, which in turn gives rise to a number of other secondary and subordinate binomials, such as godly/ungodly (worshippers of the true God/worshippers of false gods) and religious/idolatrous-superstitious. As a result, the margins politically, economically, and culturally subordinated to the center must be brought into religious submission as well: their religious beliefs must be corrected and uplifted; their gods attacked and destroyed; their practices ridiculed and replaced.

Finally, such a reality, I would argue once again, further colors and affects, directly or indirectly, the entire artistic production of both center and margins, the dominant and the subaltern, including their respective literary productions.

From the point of view of biblical criticism, therefore, it is clear that the academic study of the texts of ancient Judaism and early Christianity, given the formation and consolidation of the discipline in the course of the nineteenth century, parallels the second major wave of the Western missionary movement as well as the transition period to the second, high phase of Western imperialism and colonialism: first, as Europe turns to Africa and Asia, in a renewed and frantic scramble for territories and possessions; second, as the United States turns West and beyond, with its eyes increasingly set on the islands of the Caribbean, the heart of Mexico, and territories in the Pacific.

How do such readings and interpretations, coming from the metropolitan centers of the West as they do, address and present such issues in the ancient texts as empire and margins, oppression and justice; the world and life in the world as well as the other-world and its inhabitants; history and "the other," mission and conversion, followers and outsiders; salvation, election, and holiness?

Diversity in Readers

Scope of Diversity. With regard to the readers of ancient texts, I would argue that diversity should be pursued at two different levels: (1) diversity of intratextual readers; and (2) diversity of extra-textual readers. While the former consideration goes hand in hand with the emergence of alternative critical approaches in the discipline, the latter comes to the fore with the recent and ever-increasing influx of outsiders into the discipline. In effect, with the emergence of literary criticism and, above all, of reader-response criticism within literary criticism, one begins to find formal interest in the reader constructs employed in the analysis of the ancient texts. Similarly, with the influx of outsiders, one begins to find formal interest as well in flesh-and-blood readers and on how the social location of such readers affects and influences their analysis of ancient texts.

Early stirrings in this direction can be detected in both feminist and liberation hermeneutics. On the one hand, the discourse of feminism arises within the West (Western women), brings the element of gender to critical consciousness, and is then simultaneously deconstructed and expanded through the irruption of non-Western women as well as ethnic/racial minority women in the West.[24] On the other hand, the discourse of liberation arises in Latin America, raises the element of social class (the poor and the oppressed) to critical consciousness, and is then simultaneously deconstructed and expanded through the intervention of African and Asian theologians, women theologians of all three continents, and diasporic theologians in the West.[25] In both cases real readers begin to raise their own voices as flesh-and-blood readers and become increasingly differentiated in the process. By the early 1990s, as the recent calls for change indicate, the discussion reaches a crucial and sophisticated stage. The proposal places such critical concerns, in sustained and systematic fashion, at a climactic position, as a third and final step in its programmatic pedagogical agenda.

1. By diversity of intra-textual readers, I understand readers "in the text," that is, the variety of reader-constructs developed and employed by flesh-and-blood readers for the reading and interpretation of texts, including the texts of Jewish and Christian antiquity. I have in mind such categories as implied reader, intended reader, naïve reader, seasoned reader, and so on. This first level of analysis might be said to belong more properly within the previous category of diversity in readings, insofar as it deals with the different reader-constructs presupposed and activated by the various reading strategies adopted vis-à-vis the text. In other words, as interest and sophistication in reading strategies and theoretical orientations increases, so does interest and sophistication in the development and employment of reader-constructs. However, quite aside once again from the highly interrelated and porous nature of these categories, I have included it at this point, under the category of diversity in readers, because of what I take to be a first pedagogical imperative: the need to be aware of the different reading "masks" or "personas" adopted by flesh-and-blood readers, including oneself, with regard to the texts.

Elsewhere I have characterized this distinction between intra-textual readers and extra-textual readers in terms of a universal-reader/real-reader axis.[26] Within such an axis, intra-textual readers represent variations of a universal-reader construct, with the following characteristics in common: uncontextualized or without location, and hence neither historically situated nor culturally conditioned; perceptors and describers of reality; objective and value-free.

Such variations may be further classified in terms of three different analytical perspectives: the process of reading; the knowledge of the reader; and the experience of reading. First, the process of reading yields a firsttime-reader/multiple-reader axis, depending on the degree of acquaintance with the text accorded to the reader: while the former construct possesses no previous familiarity whatsoever with the text, the latter has had extensive dealings with it. Second, with knowledge of the reader comes a historical-reader/textual-reader axis, depending on the sort of information relied upon by the reader: the former construct would read the text as if living in the same time and culture as those of the text, availing itself of all sorts of information external to the text, while the latter would read the text as if it were its implied reader, relying solely on the information provided by the text itself. Finally, the experience of reading yields a naïve-reader/informed-reader axis, depending on the information granted the reader with regard to the subject matter of the text: while the former construct approaches the text with innocence, the latter does so with sophistication.

2. By diversity in extra-textual readers, I understand readers "outside the text," that is, the variety of flesh-and-blood readers who set out, for whatever

reason, to read and interpret texts, including the ancient texts of ancient Judaism and early Christianity. While a focus on the flesh-and-blood readers themselves has not formed part of the discipline, I place such a consideration at this climactic position in the proposal because of what I regard as a second pedagogical imperative: the need to realize that behind all readings and interpretations of ancient texts, behind all reading "personas" or "masks" used to read such texts, stand real readers.

Within the universal-reader/real-reader axis, extra-textual readers represent variations of the real-reader construct, with the following characteristics in common: thoroughly contextualized and located, and thus historically situated and culturally conditioned; constructors of "reality"; subjective and value-oriented. Such variations may be further classified according to two different analytical points of view: the identity of the reader and the reaction of the reader. First, with the question of the reader's identity emerges an individual-reader/social-reader axis, depending on whether the reader is approached as an individual subject or as a social subject, a member of distinct social groupings or communities: while the former construct emphasizes psychological location and the psychological issues of the individual in question, the latter emphasizes social location and the social issues of the grouping(s) or communities in question.

To be sure, both constructs admit of many variations. In the case of the individual-reader construct, such variations are theoretically countless, though limited in practice by the number of options available regarding psychological or psychoanalytic models to be used. In the case of the social-reader construct, such variations are numerous, depending on which dimension(s) of social identity is (are) highlighted (e.g., sociocultural, sociobiological [including gender and race], sociopolitical, socioreligious, socioeconomic, socioeducational, sociolinguistic, and so forth). Second, the question of the reader's reaction yields a compliant-reader/resistant-reader reaction, depending on the basic posture adopted by the reader vis-à-vis the perceived claims of the text as an ideological construct: while the former construct willingly submits without question or reserve to such claims, the latter has nothing to do with them and may even actively oppose them.

Concluding Comments. I argued in the previous section that the goal behind the pedagogical emphasis on diversity in readings—in itself an extension of the goal informing and guiding the pedagogical emphasis on diversity in texts—was to display as fully as possible what I referred to as the deafening din of texts and authors, the more extensive and more pronounced cacophony of voices in the modern marketplace, resulting from the refraction of ancient texts into the endless readings and interpretations within the tradition of the West. This concluding emphasis on diversity in readers represents a further and substantial extension of such a goal.

What this approach entails by way of pedagogical practice is a reading of the flesh-and-blood readers who stand behind the reading and interpretations of the ancient texts (canonical or non-canonical, open or hidden) and hence behind the production of the many readings and interpretations of such texts (by way of different reading traditions, different paradigms within the academic tradition of reading, and different methods and theories within the scholarly paradigms themselves). Such a reading calls for attention to the various sorts of reading "masks" or "personas" (the intra-textual readers) employed, implicitly or explicitly, by flesh-and-blood readers as well as to the flesh-and-blood readers themselves (the extra-textual readers), both as individual subjects and as social subjects.

Such a reading further involves, given present developments in the discipline, paying close attention to the new flesh-and-blood readers at work within the discipline for the first time in its history—female practitioners, both Western and non-Western; non-Western practitioners, both male and female, both at home and in the diaspora. The result is an incredible din of texts and authors, an even more extensive, indeed global, and more pronounced, indeed multilingual and multicentered, cacophony of voices in the contemporary marketplace or *mercado*, as all sorts of readers everywhere, now increasingly outside the West, go on refracting the texts of ancient Judaism and early Christianity into countless readings and interpretations within their own respective contexts and traditions.

Diversity in Readers and Intercultural Criticism. Once again, in keeping with its call for a consideration of the ancient texts as *others*—as realities from a very different social and historical context, not to be overridden or overwhelmed but rather acknowledged, respected, and engaged—intercultural criticism also calls for a three-fold approach to the reading and interpretation of these texts. The third and final movement within such an approach involves a view of all readers as literary or artistic products, rhetorical or strategic products, and cultural or ideological products.

First of all, it should be recalled that for intercultural criticism all "texts," all readings and interpretations of the ancient texts, are the result of interaction between socially and historically conditioned texts *and* socially and historically conditioned readers. In the end, therefore, there is as much of the reader as of the text, if not more, in any "text." From this theoretical perspective, it proves necessary to examine not just the many readings and interpretations of the ancient texts, but also the readers behind such "texts" as well. As such, an analysis of flesh-and-blood readers becomes imperative, as one seeks to understand and explain how and why real readers, both as individual and social subjects, reach and produce certain readings and interpretations of these texts. In the process, the flesh-and-blood readers come to be looked upon as "texts" themselves—constantly engaged as they are, whether implicitly or explicitly, in a process of "self"-construction. Consequently, real readers are approached in the same way as both the ancient texts and the readings and interpretations of such texts, that is, as constructing, from a particular social location and perspective, a multilayered or multifaceted reality—an artistic reality, with a poetics of the "self"; a strategic reality, with a rhetoric of the "self"; and a cultural reality, with an ideology of the "self."

Once again, therefore, intercultural criticism deems a similar combination of formalist, practical, and cultural methods as essential for its analysis of readers. The goal behind such analysis is two-fold: First, to be of further help in establishing or dis-covering the reality of both texts and "texts" as *others*, given the emphasis placed on the otherness of the real readers who proceed to read such texts and produce such "texts." In other words, by highlighting the otherness of the flesh-and-blood readers, their provenance from very different social and historical contexts, the otherness of both their readings of texts and of the ancient texts themselves is further reinforced as well. Second, to move beyond an analysis of readers in terms of their own readings of texts (their intra-textual reader-constructs) to an analysis on the basis of their own readings of them-"selves" (as extra-textual constructs), thus bringing attention to bear on the complex relationship that exists between their construction of their own "selves" and their corresponding readings and interpretations of ancient texts. By foregrounding the real readers in this way, intercultural criticism seeks to prevent, once again, any overriding or overwhelming of texts by readers, including oneself, and to explore the relationship between how readers read themselves and how they read the ancient texts.

A number of comments are in order regarding the relationship between the third pedagogical goal of diversity in readers and this third interpretive movement of readers as constructs:

1. For the pedagogical agenda, it is the incredible din of readers—both by way of readers in the text and readers outside the text—that proves important. For the interpretive project, it is that reality constructed and advanced by each reader that is regarded as important, again both in terms of the intra-textual reader-construct adopted and the shape of the extra-textual "self" assumed. In other words, there is no universal or objective reader out there, engaged in scientific and value-free interpretation, abstracted from all the social and historical circumstances of this world; on the contrary, what one finds is a host of flesh-and-blood readers, socially conditioned and historically situated, who construct their own "selves" in any number of ways, who approach the ancient texts from within such constructions, all perspectival and contextualized in nature, and who develop a variety of intra-textual readers in so doing. It is such a fluid, polyvalent, polyglot view of the reader that ultimately informs and guides the pedagogical focus on the cacophony of voices in the contemporary marketplace or *mercado*. Each reader is looked upon, therefore, as a poetic, strategic, and cultural product.

2. Since for the interpretive project there exists no ultimate and definitive reader-construct as such, given the fact that all such constructs are contextualized and perspectival, the displaying of the din of the readers as part of the pedagogical agenda is not for the purpose of producing or aiming toward such a final construct but of emphasizing the fact that all readers are "textual" constructions and that out of such constructions they proceed to approach the ancient texts and produce the readings and interpretations of such texts that they do. The point is that behind any reading or interpretation

of a text stands not only a version of that text, a "text," but also a flesh-and-blood reader.

3. The goal behind this third movement of intercultural criticism is not intellectual curiosity per se but critical engagement with other readers—in dialogue and struggle in the light of one's own reality and experience, one's own construction of one-"self" as reader. Similarly, the goal of this third pedagogical emphasis on diversity in readers is not simply to stand in awe of the many and varied flesh-and-blood readers engaged in the discussion but to produce as a flesh-and-blood reader oneself a reading and interpretation of the ancient text, to be aware of the relationship between such a "text" and one's own construction of one-"self," and to introduce thereby one more reader, both individual and social, into the overall discussion.

Imperial-Colonial Framework. For this third pedagogical goal of diversity in readers, I would argue once more for an analysis of the readers of the texts of ancient Judaism and early Christianity. This analysis must take seriously into consideration their broader sociocultural contexts in the global sphere, whether in the West or outside the West, in the light of the same omnipresent, inescapable, and overwhelming sociopolitical reality that engulfed the texts of Jewish and Christian antiquity as well as the readings and interpretations of such texts in the West. This analysis must also take into consideration the reality of empire, of imperialism and colonialism, now in terms of not only the Western imperial tradition of the last five centuries but also the reaction against such a tradition from outside the West within the context of the postcolonial yet neocolonial world of the last half-century. Some preliminary observations are once again in order.

First, despite what I have described as its omnipresent, inescapable, and overwhelming character, the structural binomial reality of imperialism and colonialism is never imposed or accepted in an atmosphere of absolute and undisturbed passivity. Always in the wake of the fundamental binomial of center/margins and ultimately deconstructing it as well, in principle if not in praxis, lies the inverted binomial of resistance/fear. I say "inverted" because this is the one binomial opposition where the margins actually take the initiative, while the center is forced into a reactive position.

In effect, there is always—sooner or later, major or minor, explicit or implicit—resistance to the center on the part of the politically, economically, culturally, and religiously subordinated margins, even when such resistance brings about, as it inevitably does, further measures of control on the part of the center, designed to instill fear into the hearts and minds of the margins. Such measures, to be sure, only serve to contribute to a further deconstruction of the binomial reality, as the civilized, advanced, cultured, progressive, developed, and believing center turns increasingly to measures of an uncivilized, primitive, barbarian, backward, undeveloped, and unbelieving order against the marginal groups. At some point, such resistance on the part of the margins may come to a climax, and this climax may involve in turn a variety of grada-tions: open challenge and defiance; widespread rebellion and anomie; actual overthrow and reorientation.

Second, I would argue that such resistance is precisely what has occurred in the discipline in the last quarter of the century, as more and more outsiders have joined its ranks. Such outsiders can be classified according to two group-ings: women from the West; men and women from outside the West as well as from ethnic and racial minorities in the West. In both cases, a similar pattern of resistance can be observed: early stirrings in the 1970s—what could be called a situation of open challenge and defiance; maturation and solidifica-tion through the 1980s—a clear situation of widespread rebellion and anomie; sharpened sophistication in the 1990s—what could be compared to a situa-tion of actual overthrow and reorientation.

Third, it should not go unobserved that such disciplinary changes take place not long after the commencement of the third major phase of Western imperialism and colonialism, marked by the end of formal colonialism, with wars of independence and the loss of colonies everywhere—the age of the postcolonial, and the continued impact of imperial culture everywhere—the age of the neocolonial. More specifically, such developments, one should recall, come soon after the crisis experienced by the West, both in Europe and North America, during the late 1960s and the early 1970s. Quite clearly, the upheaval in the world at large ultimately affects the discipline as well.

Finally, such a reality, I would argue yet again, does affect and color as well, directly or indirectly, the entire artistic production of center and margins, dominant and subaltern, including their respective literary productions.

From the point of view of biblical critics, then, it now becomes necessary to distinguish between two general groupings: on the one hand, those readers associated with the long imperial tradition of the West, from the period of imperialism proper to the present phase of neocolonialism within late imperi-alism—still the vast majority of critics; on the other hand, those associated with the colonies of the Western empires, what has come to be known as the Two-Thirds World, now raising their voices for the first time during the present phase of postcolonialism within late imperialism—a growing minority of critics.

How do traditional (male) critics, from the metropolitan centers of the West, stand—and construct them-"selves"—with regard to the relationship between empire and margins, the West and the rest, Christendom and out-siders; mission and conversion, oppression and justice, history and the other; salvation, election, and holiness; the this-world and life in the world as well as the other-world? What is the position of Western women in this regard, in their role as previous outsiders from the West itself? How do men and women from outside the West as well as from ethnic and racial minorities in the West respond to such issues?

CONCLUDING REFLECTIONS

I should like to bring this discussion to a close with some reflections on various implications and ramifications of the proposal for the discipline:

1. It should be evident that the proposal itself is of a theoretical rather than practical sort; that is to say, it deals with pedagogical discourse and practices in general, in the abstract, rather than with concrete strategies for teaching the various courses of the curriculum. As such, the proposal calls for a considerable amount of creative work on the part of the professor in the academy—regardless of the level of instruction involved, whether graduate or professional or undergraduate/ tertiary—regarding the translation of such general visions and directives into specific curricular visions and course designs.

   Thus, each and every course—from the basic introduction to sociohistorical context and subject matter, to the general introduction to a particular body of works, to the concentrated analysis of a particular writing, to the specialized seminar on a specific theme or problem or tradition—calls for a different application of the basic pedagogical principles and imperatives invoked. Similarly, the curriculum itself calls for the development of an overall personal vision to guide and inform not only those courses for which one is directly responsible but also the curriculum as a whole—its sense of unity and coherence, of sequence and teleology. In the end, the goal is not to develop a structuralist type of grid—a series of steps to be followed in proper sequence, with the instructor ultimately in control of the process. The goal, rather, is to provide a working framework: a set of general contours or parameters within which the various principles and imperatives in question can be applied in any variety of ways, innovative ways, with the instructor aiming throughout for freedom of space and freedom of imagination.

2. Mention of the academy serves as a reminder that the proposed pedagogical agenda has dealt primarily with the academic or scholarly tradition of reading and thus with the discipline of biblical criticism, with its base in institutions of higher learning, of whatever kind, means, and orientation. In this regard the academic reader or critic should always keep in mind that such a way of approaching the texts of ancient Judaism and Christianity is but one of several modes of reading, and a relatively recent one at that. This awareness should immediately bring to the fore as well a number of related issues and concerns:

   a. While biblical criticism has openly and consistently looked down upon alternative modes of reading as subjective and deficient, it in turn has been accused, both traditionally and in recent times, as decidedly rationalistic, elitist, and removed from the life of the church and the concerns of the world. In many respects such corresponding evaluations are the result of a failure on the part of all modes of reading, including biblical criticism itself, to see and understand themselves as *modes* of reading, socially and historically conditioned as well as perspectival in nature. Such self-awareness on the part of all modes of reading is not only salutary but also imperative in this day and age.

b. Academic readers must come to terms with the fact that they are highly privileged individuals, not so much from a socioeconomic perspective—although the economic social location of such readers, especially in the West, should by no means be downplayed—but certainly from a socioeducational point of view, insofar as they have attained a degree of educational expertise and sophistication that ranks them far beyond most other readers of these texts. Such privilege, moreover, is not without responsibilities. Thus, for example, it is incumbent upon critics to analyze the other traditions of reading with as much zeal, seriousness, and thoroughness as they have used to examine the ancient texts as well as the traditions of interpretation within the discipline. Indeed, academic reading is better equipped, in principle, than the other traditions of reading to carry out such a task, given precisely the intellectual sophistication and expertise it has acquired in the academy. However, the spirit behind such analysis should be one of critical dialogue, with a vision of how the different modes of reading relate to and impact upon one another, both historically and in the present. In other words, the role of criticism in this regard should be not only to teach but also to learn.

c. Biblical critics should never forget, given the admittedly elite nature of their training, teaching, and writing, that the audience they reach is a very limited one indeed, more often than not consisting of other fellow members of the academy. In other words, their influence and power is thoroughly circumscribed. Quite aside from a much-needed spirit of humility, such considerations should drive home the point that, while necessarily elite in nature, their mode of reading need not and should not be elitist, turning a cold shoulder to all other traditions of reading. In other words, critics need to wrestle with certain questions that have up to now been largely bypassed in the discipline: what is the proper role of the academic reader of these texts with regard to such other traditions of reading? to the academy? to the church? to society at large? Instead of living a life of leisure in an imagined past, critics must come to terms with the present, not only with the ramifications of their own reconstructions of the past for the present but also with the fact that it is in the present that they construct them-"selves" and the past.

d. Finally, in the light of their own highly circumscribed audience and influence, academic readers should come to terms with how they have tended to treat one another in the past: the frantic quest for academic renown and glory; the insatiable drive to provide the ultimate and definitive interpretation of any one text or even of antiquity itself; the untoward exaltation of one's self and one's work; the demolition and humiliation of others and their work; the desire for control of and devotion on the part of students, sometimes to the point of abuse and harassment; the subtle and sometimes not-so-subtle disdain for those who never had the means or ability to pursue higher studies of any kind. Surely, the times call for a different type of critical dialogue, with an emphasis on both "critical" and "dialogue."

3. It would be quite foolish to think, even for a moment, that the adoption of the proposed pedagogical agenda will be a largely painless exercise; quite to the contrary, its incorporation into the curriculum will inevitably face serious difficulties, both from within and from without. I shall mention but a few:

a. The question of metacanonical diversity is a hard one for many individuals and institutions to contemplate. There is so much invested in the canon, in "Scripture" or "the Word of God"—whether socially or ecclesiastically, ideologically or theologically—that any attempt to set the canon as an indistinguishable or non-distinctive element within the wider scope of ancient Judaism and early Christianity, let alone within the more expansive scope of their broader sociocultural contexts, will often meet with enormous resistance if not theological odium. I would recall in this regard that the aim behind such a pedagogical move is quite sound, ecclesiastically as well as socially, ideologically as well as theologically: to set forth and engage as fully as possible, in the past as well as in the present, the whole panorama of expression—to let all voices speak and to engage in critical dialogue with all voices. In other words, if one tends to look askance at canons today, why should one not do so with regard to canons of antiquity?

b. There is also the problem of the sheer volume of subject matter involved, not only at the level of texts but also at the level of readings and readers of such texts. I would only point out that what is important here is the principle, even if the praxis is perforce limited: to establish the din of voices and to be aware that such a din is always at work.

c. Along the same lines, there is the problem of metatheory as well, the enormous range of methodological apparatuses and theoretical orientations present in the discipline today. I would emphasize again that it is the principle that is important above all, even if mastery of such various discourses and practices is beyond any one's grasp: to be aware of the din of voices and to establish, as much as possible, a working familiarity with such voices, in order to be able to understand and engage them.

d. The question of regarding all texts, readings, and readers as literary, rhetorical, and ideological products and constructions, highly contextualized and perspectival, represents a bitter pill for many to swallow, especially with regard to the last element. So much has been invested in the ideal of the objective reader—as well as in committed readers of various kinds—that to throw wide open the question of social location and perspective vis-à-vis readers is to shatter any number of sacred and beloved mythologies. I would respond in this regard that the proposal involves, no more and no less, than to do unto readers of the ancient texts what they themselves have not hesitated to do unto the texts themselves.

In the end, of course, as the history of any one discipline readily shows, it is good to keep in mind that any new proposal more often than not calls forth opposition from the powers that be. I would argue that such opposition is actually to be welcomed, even if oftentimes its tone is much to be regretted, insofar as it may serve as an opportunity for further reflection, correction, and development.

4. Academic readers should never, even for a moment, forget that they are social subjects and belong to any number of social groupings. In addition to the intellectual traditions and currents to which they subscribe as members of the academy, they should be conscious of their own inescapable relationship to the other theological disciplines, to religious communities, and to society at large.

First, critics should not see themselves as mere suppliers of raw data for the rest of the theological disciplines but as theologians or religious thinkers in their own right: their religious or theological visions (or lack thereof) are at work in the way they approach the data, reconstruct the past (its textual remains and physical remains), and expound it to the contemporary world.

Second, critics should not see themselves simply as members of the academic community but also as members, faithful or estranged, of religious communities: such affiliations—faint or strong, favorable or hostile—not only find their way into their search for and representations of antiquity, but also call for critical responses vis-à-vis the communities themselves, whether by way of sympathetic commitment or radical critique. In other words, membership in academic communities should be no excuse for abstention from contemporary issues and disputes in the socioreligious or theological sphere, although obviously the degree of involvement will differ from reader to reader, issue to issue, situation to situation.

Third, critics should not see themselves, much as they might like to be, as citizens of times long past and cultures far removed. They are very much citizens of their own times and cultures and should see themselves as such: the way they read and interpret ancient texts as well as the way they read and construct them-"selves" not only reflects their social location and perspective, but also has ramifications for such contexts and agendas. Criticism involves taking positions, implicitly or explicitly, at all times: the past provides neither shelter nor escape from the present. Critics should, therefore, be constantly aware of both the presuppositions and the ramifications of their critical practices and discourses. Indeed, I would add, critics should be aware of their own location and stance in a world that is still under the shadow of empire—a postcolonial world, almost free of empire in the Two-Thirds World, yet a neocolonial world, in continuing subjection to Western imperial culture.

A final word would seem utterly unnecessary yet remains imperative. It would be most ironic for a proposal that has insisted so much on diversity and empire to present itself in any way as the one and only way for the future. I would only reiterate that this is a personal proposal, ultimately rooted in my own project of intercultural criticism and grounded in a postmodernist and postliberal, postcolonial and neocolonial, view of the world—the world at the turn of the century.

NOTES

1. See the Introduction to this volume, "Pedagogical Discourse and Practices in Contemporary Biblical Criticism," 1–28 above.

2. See, e.g., C. Foster, ed., *Ethnicity in the Education of the Church* (Nashville: Scarritt Press, 1987); W. A. Lesher and R. J. Schreiter, eds., *Fundamental Issues in Globalization*, special issue of *Theological Education*, Vol. 26, Supplement 1, Spring 1990; B. G. Wheeler and E. Farley, *Shifting Boundaries: Contextual Approaches to the Structure of Theological Education* (Louisville: Westminster/John Knox Press, 1991); A. Frazer Evans, R. A. Evans, and D. A. Roozen, eds., *The Globalization of Theological Education* (Maryknoll: Orbis Books, 1993); D. S. Schuller, ed., *Globalization: Tracing the Journey, Charting the Course*, special issue of *Theological Education*, Vol. 30, Supplement 1, Autumn 1993.

3. See, e.g., S. Aronowitz and H. A. Giroux, *Postmodern Education: Politics, Culture, and Social Criticism* (Minneapolis and Oxford: University of Minnesota Press, 1991); G. Graff, *Beyond the Culture Wars: How Teaching the Conflicts Can Revitalize American Education* (New York and London: W. W. Norton, 1992); D. J. Gless and B. Herrnstein Smith, *The Politics of Liberal Education* (Durham and London: Duke University Press, 1992); C. McCarthy and W. Crichlow, *Race, Identity, and Representation in Education* (New York and London: Routledge, 1993); bell hooks, *Teaching to Transgress: Education as the Practice of Freedom* (New York and London: Routledge, 1994).

4. See, e.g., D. Schoem et al., eds., *Multicultural Teaching in the University* (New York: Praeger Publishers, 1993); B. P. Bowser, T. Jones, and G. Auletta Young, eds., *Toward the Multicultural University* (New York: Praeger Publishers, 1995); D. A. Harris, ed., *Multiculturalism from the Margins: Non-Dominant Voices on Difference and Diversity* (New York: Bergin & Garvey, 1995); B. Kanpol and P. McLaren, eds., *Critical Multiculturalism: Uncommon Voices in a Common Struggle* (New York: Bergin & Garvey, 1995); R. Ng, P. Staton, and J. Scane, eds., *Anti-Racism, Feminism, and Critical Approaches to Education* (New York: Bergin & Garvey, 1995); B. W. Thompson and S. Tyagi, eds., *Beyond a Dream Preferred: Multicultural Education and the Politics of Excellence* (Minneapolis: University of Minnesota Press, 1995).

5. See F. F. Segovia, "Cultural Criticism and Contemporary Biblical Criticism: Ideological Criticism as Mode of Discourse," in *Reading from This Place*. Volume 2: *Social Location and Biblical Interpretation in Global Perspective*, ed. F. F. Segovia and M. A. Tolbert (Minneapolis: Fortress Press, 1995), 1–17, esp. 15.

6. For my assessment of the discipline, see, in addition to the various studies already published as part of this project of *Reading from This Place*, my "Racial and Ethnic Minorities in Biblical Studies," in *Ethnicity and the Bible*. Biblical Interpretation Series 19, ed. M. G. Brett (Leiden-New York-Köln: E. J. Brill, 1996), 469–92.

7. See F. F. Segovia, "Toward Intercultural Criticism: A Reading Strategy from the Diaspora," in *Reading from This Place*, 2:303-30; see also, "Toward a Hermeneutics of the Diaspora: A Hermeneutics of Otherness and Engagement," in *Reading from This Place*. Volume 1: *Social Location and Biblical Interpretation in the United States*, ed. F. F. Segovia and M. A. Tolbert (Minneapolis: Fortress Press, 1995), 57–73.

8. A story often silenced not only by historians of the period but also by subsequent historians as well. See M.-R. Trouillot (*Silencing the Past: Power and the Production of History* [Boston: Beacon Press, 1995]), who sees Haiti as the first modern state of the Third World, subject to all the trials and tribulations of postcolonial nation-building, and understands such silencing along the lines of the denial of the Holocaust in Europe and the debate over the Alamo in the United States.

9. See F. F. Segovia, "Biblical Criticism and Postcolonial Studies: Toward a Postcolonial Optic," in *The Bible and Post-Colonial Criticism*. The Bible and Post-

Colonialism 1; ed. R. S. Sugirtharajah (Sheffield: Sheffield Academic Press, forthcoming, 1998).

10. First of all, as a "Christian" theologian and critic, I remain quite aware that the Christian Bible contains not only the Christian Scriptures but also the Hebrew Scriptures and thus the scriptures of another religious tradition, an independent and living tradition. Such a situation, needless to say, calls for special sensitivity as well as circumscribed claims: my proposal emerges out of a Christian context. Second, as a "Catholic" theologian and critic, I am also quite aware of the fact that for me, historically or experientially, the Bible does not represent the sort of semantic and symbolic world that it does for the Protestant tradition in general. Such a situation calls for openness and sensitivity on all sides: my proposal emerges out of a Catholic context. Third, as a "lay" theologian and critic in the Catholic tradition, I am quite aware as well that I am in no way an official representative for the institutional and hierarchical Church. Such a situation, much to my liking, involves rootedness as well as independence: my proposal emerges from the ranks of the educated lay people.

11. The issue of nomenclature is problematic for anyone writing out of the Christian tradition, not so much from the point of view of Christianity but from the point of view of Judaism (see n. 10 above). With regard to Christianity, such appellations as "early Christianity," "texts of early Christianity," and "texts of Christian antiquity" are intended to refer, first and foremost, to the literary production of the first two centuries of the Christian movement, although such a designation could be readily expanded to include the pre-Constantinian period as a whole and even beyond. With regard to Judaism, the question is how to avoid supersessionism in these matters, difficult as that is, given both the inclusion of the Hebrew Scriptures as part of the Christian Bible and the view of Judaism as pointing to Christianity and central to the foundational documents of the latter. Avoiding supersessionism thus means, on the one hand, moving beyond a historical classification of Judaism in terms of its relationship to Christianity and, on the other, taking into consideration the long history of Judaism itself, not only as preceding Christianity by an enormous period of time but also as an ongoing living tradition alongside its entire history. In the end, I have settled for the use of the terms "ancient Judaism," "the texts of ancient Judaism," and "texts of Jewish antiquity" to refer to its literary production through the Second Jewish-Roman War (132–135 C.E.).

12. For good, concise introductions to the phenomenon of imperialism and colonialism in general, see E. Said, "Yeats and Decolonization," *Nationalism, Colonialism, and Literature,* ed. S. Deane (Minneapolis: University of Minnesota Press, 1990), 69–95; E. Said, "Overlapping Territories," in *Culture and Imperialism* (New York: Alfred A. Knopf, 1993), esp. pp. 3–61; S. Deane, "Imperialism and Nationalism," in *Critical Terms for Literary Study,* ed. F. L. Lentricchia and T. McLaughlin, 2nd enl. ed. (Chicago: University of Chicago Press, 1994), 354–68.

13. I have in mind the historical ways of interpreting the Bible with the church and theology in mind: from the patristic, to the medieval, to the Reformation and Counter Reformation, to the nineteenth century and the rise of modernism. See, e.g., R. M. Grant and D. Tracy, *A Short History of the Interpretation of the Bible,* 2nd ed., rev. and enl. (Minneapolis: Fortress Press, 1984).

14. See, e.g., J. Barr, "The Problem of Fundamentalism Today," in *The Scope and Authority of the Bible* (Philadelphia: Westminster Press, 1980), 65–90; N. Ammerman, "North American Protestant Fundamentalism," in *Fundamentalisms Observed,* ed. M. Marty and R. S. Appleby (Chicago: The University of Chicago Press, 1991), 1–65; G. M. Marsden, *Understanding Fundamentalism and Evangelicalism* (Grand Rapids: William B. Eerdmans, 1991).

15. I have in mind the different ways of interpreting the Bible with the church and theology in mind from the modernist period—that is to say, alongside the academic read-

ing—through contemporary times. See, e.g., Pontifical Biblical Commission, "The Interpretation of the Bible in the Church," *Origins* 23:29 (January 6, 1994): 498–524; C. E. Braaten and R. W. Jenson, eds., *Reclaiming the Bible for the Church* (Grand Rapids and Cambridge: William B. Eerdmans, 1995).

16. See, e.g., C. Boff, "Hermeneutics: Constitution of Theological Pertinency," in *Theology and Praxis. Epistemological Foundations* (Maryknoll: Orbis Books, 1987), 132-53; C. Rowland and M. Corner, *Liberating Exegesis. The Challenge of Liberation Theology to Biblical Studies* (Louisville: Westminster/John Knox Press, 1989).

17. See, e.g., C. McDannell, "The Bible in the Victorian Home," in *Material Christianity: Religion and Popular Culture in America* (New Haven-London: Yale University Press, 1995), 67–102.

18. One should note in this regard the launching of a new journal by Sheffield Academic Press, *Biblicon*, with Alice Bach as general editor, to serve as a forum for the analysis of the cultural appropriation of the Bible as well as for cross-cultural debates on the popular use of the Bible.

19. On this point, see J. Appleby, L. Hunt, and M. Jacob, Part I: "Intellectual Absolutisms," in *Telling the Truth about History* (New York-London: W. W. Norton & Co., 1994), esp. 15–125; P. Novick, Part I: "Objectivity Enthroned," in *That Noble Dream. The "Objectivity Question" and the American Historical Profession* (Cambridge: Cambridge University Press, 1988), esp. 21–108.

20. See R. A. Harrisville and W. Sundberg, eds., *The Bible in Modern Culture: Theology and Historical Critical Method from Spinoza to Käsemann* (Grand Rapids: William B. Eerdmans, 1995).

21. Recent times have witnessed the appearance of a new genre of scholarly literature in biblical criticism, in which the variety of methods and theories, both within paradigms and across paradigms, is addressed by means of critical introductions on the part of a corresponding variety of scholars. See, e.g., S. L. McKenzie and S. R. Haynes, eds., *To Each Its Own Meaning: An Introduction to Biblical Criticisms and Their Application* (Louisville: Westminster/John Knox Press, 1993); F. Watson, ed., *The Open Text: New Directions for Biblical Studies?* (London: SCM Press Ltd., 1993); E. V. McKnight and E. Struthers Malbon, eds., *The New Literary Criticism and the New Testament* (Valley Forge: Trinity Press International, 1994); J. B. Green, ed., *Hearing the New Testament* (Grand Rapids: William B. Eerdmans, 1995); The Bible and Culture Collective, *The Postmodernist Bible*; P. F. Esler, ed., *Modelling Early Christianity: Social-Scientific Studies of the New Testament in Its Context* (London-New York: Routledge, 1995). This valuable genre will be significantly expanded and transformed with the launching of a new major series by Sheffield Academic Press, Crossways: Reading Strategies in Current Scholarship, which will consist of more than twenty-five volumes, each devoted to a specific method and assigned to an individual author. Clearly, the generic progenitor of and model for all such endeavors, present and to come, was the splendid series entitled Guides to Biblical Scholarship of Fortress Press, still ongoing.

22. I find myself in agreement with the caution offered for postcolonial studies in general by Michael Sprinker ("Introduction," in *Late Imperial Culture*, ed. R. de la Campa, E. Ann Kaplan, and M. Sprinker [London-New York: Verso, 1996], 1–10), who insists on the need to offer and follow a historical periodization of the different types of imperialism at work in the West over this period of five centuries.

23. I follow here the thesis of Andrew Walls ("Christianity in the Non-Western World: A Study in the Serial Nature of Christian Expansion," *Studies in World Christianity* 1 [1995]: 1–25).

24. On this, see the excellent essay: "Feminist and Womanist Criticism," *The Postmodernist Bible*, 225-71.

25. On this, see "Ideological Criticism," *The Postmodernist Bible*, 272–308.

26. See F. F. Segovia, "Reading Readers of the Fourth Gospel and Their Readings: An Exercise in Intercultural Criticism," in *"What Is John?": Readers and Readings of the Fourth Gospel*, ed. F. F. Segovia (Atlanta: Scholars Press, 1996), 240–42. I would emphasize that the nomenclature used for this axis as well as for all those to follow, although seemingly binomial in character, characterizes the opposite poles of the axes and thus presupposes a full spectrum of opinion between such poles.

9

A NEW TEACHING WITH AUTHORITY

A Re-evaluation of the Authority of the Bible

Mary Ann Tolbert

At the middle of the twentieth century, Rudolf Bultmann, drawing upon the work of Wilhelm Dilthey, argued very convincingly that the Bible deserved no "special hermeneutics" designed for reading and interpreting it alone; it should, instead, he asserted, be treated exactly as one would treat any other ancient text.[1] Whether persuaded by—or even aware of—Bultmann's views or not, most biblical scholarship of the last fifty years has followed his lead. Methods and approaches drawn from other disciplines, like history, literature, sociology, and anthropology, and regularly applied to other ancient texts, dominate the current study of the Bible in the United States and Europe. Even many of the self-consciously indigenous liberation theologies of the third world owe a considerable debt to major European intellectual theories like Marxism or to other traditions of textual analysis prominent in their own cultural settings. In the modern scholarly world, Bultmann's proscription against isolating the interpretation of the Bible from all other intellectual systems or insisting on a special method of reading suitable only for it has certainly won the day.

Moreover, because modern scholarship forms and informs those who teach the Bible in colleges, universities, and seminaries, this "general hermeneutics" approach to the Bible has deeply influenced pedagogical practices. Even in most confessional educational settings, explicating the Bible as literature and history accompanies whatever more devotional or spiritual perspectives are employed in teaching it. The character of the Bible as a collection of ancient texts from different cultures and different historical periods, and the importance of understanding the Bible using the methods of interpretation applicable to other similar texts, seem to be widely supported conventions of study and teaching in most colleges, universities, and seminaries in this country.

However, if one looks at the way many modern Christians and major church groups or denominations often employ the Bible in public debates, especially those debates over social and ethical issues, one generally finds a different set of reading conventions being employed, a set of conventions profoundly molded by claims for the Bible's normative or authoritative status. Moreover, this authoritative manner of reading the Bible insists on distinguishing it from all other ancient texts as a work inspired in one way or another by a Divine Author.[2] Thus, it is a unique text, so it is claimed, and the way it is to be read must be similarly unique. In other words, the Bible requires precisely the "special hermeneutics" that Bultmann argued so elegantly against in his essay. Bultmann's essay, "Das Problem der Hermeneutik," was itself, of course, an attempt to counter the special reading practices proposed by Karl Barth in his dogmatic approach to the Bible.[3] Almost fifty years after his article and regardless of the pedagogical and research practices of most biblical scholars before and since it was written, the bifurcation, which Bultmann faced at mid-century, between the "general hermeneutics" approach to the Bible advanced by scholarship and the "special hermeneutics" taught by many ecclesiastical bodies continues to reign supreme.

In this essay, I want to explore not the reading conventions of biblical scholarship, but instead the dynamics and results of reading the Bible as many in church communities are encouraged to hear it, as a "teaching with authority." What happens to biblical texts when they are circumscribed by a discourse of authority? What are some of the elements of the "special hermeneutics" still so prevalent in dogmatic considerations of the Bible, and what effects have they had on the way the Bible has been taught to and used by many within the churches, especially in public debates on social issues? I must confess that part of the impetus for this reflection comes from my increasing frustration over the apparent inability of biblical scholarship to influence current popular understandings of Christianity and from my perplexity at what laity and pastors, who have been educated in the historical, literary, and sociological milieu of the biblical world and biblical literature, do or do not do when they leave their college or seminary classrooms and enter their church communions. There appear to be (at least) two separate discourses about the Bible present in American society, the historical and literary discourse of scholarship and the authoritative discourse of the churches. This is not to say that some important denominations and individual church groups are not profoundly influenced in their understanding of the Bible by the past several centuries of biblical scholarship, nor is it to say that there are no biblical scholars who participate both personally and professionally in promoting discourses of authority and normativity. My claim is only that the dominant form of hermeneutics used by most biblical scholars in research and teaching, as witnessed, for example, by professional journals, papers delivered at international, national, and regional Society of Biblical Literature meetings, and discussions on the practices of teaching, is markedly different from the dominant form of hermeneutics found in most ecclesiastical bodies. And, whatever else it may rest upon, this difference certainly has to do with claims of authority and normativity.

In pursuing this reflection, I will look first at the history of doctrines concerning the authority of the Bible; then I will review briefly some of the effects of authoritative readings on public debates over social and ethical issues, and from that review begin to sketch the conventions of reading the Bible which this "special hermeneutics" requires. Finally, I will suggest an alternative view of the function of the Bible in the church, which attempts to bridge the present bifurcation between the scholarly and ecclesiastical patterns of reading.

THE DEVELOPMENT OF DOCTRINES
OF BIBLICAL AUTHORITY

Although the texts of the Christian canon have demonstrated the rhetorical power of their narrative worlds on generations of believers, and they have certainly had profound formational impact on the evolution of Christian piety and discourse from the early centuries of the Common Era, the development of doctrines concerning the authority of the Bible, which in some sense fix or legalize the rhetorical and formational importance of the Bible,[4] are of more recent origin. For the most part their production evolved after the Reformation period when the doctrine of *sola scriptura* came to the forefront of Christian, especially Protestant Christian, debate. Moreover, not only were such doctrines relatively late bloomers, coming mostly from the seventeenth and eighteenth centuries, they were also contrived in very problematic ways. A number of scholars in recent years, most notably James Barr in several publications,[5] have pointed to difficulties in the formulations and uses of Protestant doctrines of biblical authority. The foremost problem, stated in its baldest form, is that orthodox Protestant doctrines of taking the Bible as the ultimate authority in all doctrinal matters cannot *itself be verified from the Bible*. The "biblical world," that historical period in which God's revelation occurred as witnessed by the biblical writings, *antedates* those writings themselves. The Word of God did not come to Isaiah as a document to be interpreted, and although Jesus and Paul, the major characters in the "New Testament period" had, unlike Moses and Isaiah, a scriptural tradition to use, the freedom with which they altered it, repudiated it, or interpreted it is striking.[6] Indeed, James Dunn, in arguing for an evangelical perspective on the authority of the Bible based on "the New Testament attitude to, and use of, scripture" must deny "that Christians today can necessarily treat the scriptures . . . with the same sovereign freedom exercised by Jesus and Paul,"[7] thus leaving evangelicals in the contradictory position of both appealing to the New Testament as norm and at the same time denying the current applicability of what is found there. The problem, seen in relation to the specific issue of canon, can also be found in chapter I of the seventeenth-century Westminster Confession, the document upon which the Reformed tradition continues to base its doctrine of scriptural authority: The Confession states that only the sixty-six books of the (Protestant) canon compose scripture as inspired by God and therefore provide the sole basis of all doctrinal formulation; yet, *no* passage in any of those sixty-six books provides a list of which texts are inspired, or which are not, nor is there a numerical limit to that group.[8] Evidence for the canon of scripture and its precise limits can only be found *outside* the canon!

In addition to this major doctrinal difficulty of being unable to ground the authority of scripture in scripture itself, most formulations of the doctrine of biblical authority evince obvious inconsistencies by tending to see some elements of scripture as more authoritative than others. The "canon within a canon" pattern is quite ancient and could, in fact, claim as scriptural warrant the story of Jesus' declaration of the two great commandments, love of God and love of neighbor, as the essence of all the law and the prophets (Matt. 22:36-40). Luther's view of Christian salvation as "by grace through faith" had the effect of elevating the writings of Paul and dooming the Epistle of James, among others, to ridicule or oblivion. One might then suppose that the point of developing a doctrine of biblical authority was to underline major themes within biblical material as essential to Christian faith today. However, James Barr has argued quite persuasively that the main reason was precisely the contrary: traditional Protestant orthodoxy needed the authority of an inspired canon, not to emphasize dominant biblical patterns, but rather to elevate as essential theological beliefs "elements which had comparatively slight and even marginal representation within the biblical material: the virgin birth, predestination, the inspiration of scripture."[9] Consequently, the *doctrine of biblical authority* supplies ecclesiastical bodies with power to proclaim as normative Christian belief, not love of God and love of neighbor, but those peripheral and "thinly evidenced" (by one, two, or three separate proof texts) issues like the inspiration of scripture, the legality of slavery, or the sinfulness of homosexuality. Moreover, because these elements are often so rarely addressed within the canon as a whole, both changing social values within the broader, contemporary society and dissenting interpretations by other Christian groups can sometimes erase or deny formerly "essential" biblical teachings (e.g., "slaves obey your masters" or the definition of predestination). Thus, the *doctrine of biblical authority* has generally functioned to assure not the continuing importance of widely attested or programmatic themes in scripture, but rather the divine inspiration of the tenuous and the marginal. Indeed, from just a superficial overview of Christian history since the Reformation, the invocation of the tenet of biblical authority has been remarkably negative; that is, it has been employed most often to *exclude* certain groups or people,[10] to *pass judgment* on various disapproved activities,[11] and to *justify* morally or historically debatable positions.[12] I am *not* saying that the Bible has been primarily negative in its influence over the centuries, for that assertion would be easily challenged by the lives of many good-hearted Christians, working for peace, liberation, justice, and human salvation, who have drawn much of their inspiration from the Bible. Nor am I arguing that attempts to formulate the place of the Bible theologically in relation to the Christian life have always arisen from necessarily exclusivistic aims,[13] although that might well sometimes have been the case. It is not the Bible itself but the overt, often institutionally based appeal to an already formulated *doctrine of biblical authority* that displays this generally negative, exclusivistic pattern. It is this use of biblical authority by various ecclesiastical bodies, especially in contemporary situations, that requires serious investigation.

THE USE OF BIBLICAL AUTHORITY IN THE SOCIAL ARENA

While it is certainly true that many saintly and influential people as diverse as

Mother Teresa, Albert Schweitzer, and Dr. Martin Luther King, Jr., have found inspiration for liberation, justice, and mercy in the pages of the Bible, its institutional, authoritative use in some of the most important social and ethical conflicts in recent American history has often pitted the Bible against those struggling for equality and human dignity. A few examples will suffice to illustrate this disturbing point.

William Lloyd Garrison, one of the founders and most important figures in the abolitionist movement of the 1830s and 40s became convinced of the abomination of slavery out of his connection with the Great Revival movements of the nineteenth century. Garrison and his followers found in the Bible, from cover to cover, a total repudiation of the practice of slavery. In the early 1830s, Garrison clearly believed that the spirit of the Bible "spoke with such unequivocal authority against slave owning that no sincere Christian, whether minister or lay person, could fail to be persuaded."[14] But fail they did. Instead of embracing this liberative reading of the spirit of the Bible, white ministers and lay Christians in both the South and the North contested Garrison's interpretations of scripture by pointing to the many instances in both the Hebrew Bible and New Testament where slave holding was simply taken as a fact of life. And more than that, did not Paul (or his followers) on several occasions actually instruct slaves to obey their masters? Whether or not slavery violated the "spirit" of the Bible, it most certainly did *not* violate many elements of its "letter." Consequently, by 1837, Garrison was so disgusted by this "Christian" response to the moral suasion of abolitionism that he renounced the validity of scripture, the authority of ministers, and deemed all organized religion as "pernicious" and "malevolent."[15] A movement that started as a response to the moral vision of revivalism and the Bible ended up attacking the Bible and organized Christianity in general as its arch enemy in the quest for human freedom. In the slavery debates, the weight of biblical authority was clearly on the side of systems of oppression.

Much the same experience, I believe, has faced women of all races in both the earlier suffrage movement and the more recent feminist movement in this country. Without question many Christian women, and I would count myself among them, recognize their formation in the biblical tradition as one of the prime roots of their social activism. From the prophets' calls for justice and liberation to Jesus' welcoming of women and men to follow him and become part of the family of God, Jewish and Christian feminists have found inspiration, hope, and courage in the texts of the Bible. Yet, like the earlier abolitionists, they have also found there the warrants for much of their second-class treatment in Western society. Conservative church leaders and many others, not especially interested in Christianity but very concerned to preserve their own privileges, quote the Bible's many injunctions against the full enfranchisement of women: women should keep silent in the church, women should not be allowed to teach men, women are the possessions of their fathers and husbands, women are sexually promiscuous, women are responsible for the Fall of humanity, etc. And did not Paul (or his followers) on several occasions actually instruct women to obey their husbands, since their husbands were their heads as Christ was the head of the church? Although there are some positive descriptions of individual women in the Bible (Deborah, Hulda, Junica, Priscilla, etc.), the preponderance of biblical material in both the Hebrew Bible and the New Testament presents women in subordinate, passive, victimized, or less-than-fully-human roles. Thus, the Bible serves to naturalize and authorize the misogynous estimation of all women as victims, servants, or seductresses—ones whose control by others is always appropriate.

In both the public debates over slavery and those over the secondary standing of women, the Bible actually provides abundant material to justify the continuation of systems of exploitation and abuse. Even the detestable use by the Nazis of the New Testament invective against the Pharisees to defend their monstrous policy of Jewish extermination rests on a frighteningly ample biblical base. However, in the current debate over homosexuality, the Bible has very little to say at all—though you certainly would not know it from listening to many church leaders, both fundamentalist and mainline. In this case especially, the use of claims to biblical authority for supporting textually tenuous positions is manifestly apparent. At the most generous estimate, the entire Bible contains only nine brief references to homoeroticism, six in the Hebrew Bible and three in the New Testament, occupying in all less than twelve verses of text. And even those numbers are misleading, since four of the references in the Hebrew Bible (Deut. 23:17, I Kings 14:24, I Kings 22:46, II Kings 23:7) may actually simply be prohibitions against prostitution by men and women[16] and two of the references in the New Testament (1 Cor. 6:9-11 and 1 Tim. 1:10) are based on interpretations of Greek words whose exact meanings are actually unknown or unclear.[17] This leaves only the two references in the Holiness Code of Leviticus (18:19-23 and 20:10-16) and Paul's one assertion in Romans as to what he thinks is "natural" and "unnatural" (the only citation in the Bible that even mentions female homoeroticism, if that is indeed what it is about[18]) as the sole biblical witnesses for a modern Christian rejection of homosexuality. Jesus in the gospels says absolutely nothing about the subject, and indeed if you define homosexuality as people of the same gender living together, loving and caring for each other in a primary relationship, Jesus' relationship to his male disciples, as it is depicted in all four of the canonical gospels, would clearly fit the definition. After all, most of the people Jesus is said to love in the Bible are other men. However we understand the portrayal of Jesus' own intimate preferences, his teachings about divorce, for example, are much less ambiguous, more heavily attested, and much clearer than anything the New Testament has to say about homoeroticism. Yet, most Protestant denominations which will not ordain openly homosexual people, supposedly because of biblical authority, are quite willing to ordain divorced people. It is the appalling hypocrisy of such use of biblical authority that makes the current church debates over homosexuality so invidious and so infuriating.

In the cases of all three of these recent social movements for human liberation, the repressive role of the Bible in public discussions of who, in a democratic society, should have inalienable rights and who should not, is remarkable and gives ample evidence of the easy complicity of the Bible with systems of exploitation, exclusion, and death. This complicity, I want to argue, cannot be dismissed as solely the result of deliberate and selective misinterpretations of biblical texts. Most repressive interpretations, though certainly not all, are instead generally defensible readings of what the text says and indeed what it probably said to its ancient audiences. I think Paul did believe that slaves should be faithful to their owners and that wives should be subordinate to their husbands. He also probably thought relations between women or between men were "unnatural," though his understanding of what was "natural" in sexual relations was likely quite different from contemporary views, since sexual relations in antiquity were constructed primarily in terms of social status rather than gender.[19] The pressing question is not whether *Paul* believed these things, but whether or not *we* do. Are slavery, the subordination of women, or the "natural" sexuality of dominance and submission what Christians in a democratic society of the late twentieth century ought to believe and want to preach to others?

The Bible, of course, does not come from a democratic society of the late twentieth century. It was formed in the profoundly hierarchical and patriarchal cultures of the ancient Hebrews and the early Christians, and much of the negative role of the Bible in contemporary public debates arises precisely from this formation. The Bible, like any other book, is saturated by the social, cultural, political, and religious understandings of the peoples who produced it. They lived in a strictly hierarchical world order with the king, the high priest, or the emperor at the top of a pyramid of power; in the early Roman period when the texts of the New Testament were written, the family was to be a microcosm of the empire, with the *pater familias*, the father, at the top, and his wives, children, and slaves in ordered sequence beneath him. Every page of the Bible is shaped by similar social and cultural conventions. However, unlike all other books so shaped, in the modern ecclesiastical world this ancient Bible often participates in an institutional discourse of authority and control, is viewed as normative by some Christians, and is revered as an icon by many others. One result of granting transcendent, authoritative status to this text is that we are also granting normative status to the hierarchical, patriarchal worldview of the first millennium B.C.E. and the first centuries C.E., since the regulations and stories of the Bible cannot be abstracted from the languages, cultural views, and social practices of their contexts of production. But if we no longer have kings or emperors, should we insist on keeping slaves or subordinating women? Do the legitimate fears of a marginal tribal society for its survival, which influenced its many prohibitions about wasting "the seed," really provide any rationale whatsoever, in our seriously overpopulated world, for modern discrimination against homosexuals?

Moreover, the authoritative use of the hierarchical, patriarchal organization of the biblical world has not only promoted the negative role of the Bible in public social debates, it has also had, I would argue, detrimental effects on the structures of contemporary Christian communities. While it is certainly true that all social affiliations involve relations of power, hierarchy organizes these generally fluid power relations vertically in such a way that those few at the top dispose a disproportionate amount of power in relation to the much larger groups below them. In addition, I understand the word "patriarchal," a word that has been rightly criticized recently by some feminists, to refer to those social structures that freeze power relations and ascribe them rigidly to set groups within the culture, reserving the most powerful positions for the most economically privileged males of the dominant race or ethnic group. Many modern Christian communities use the hierarchical, patriarchal structures of the biblical world as models for structuring their own fellowships. In my view such modeling is extremely dangerous, for it fosters, among other things, the increasing and lamentable chasm between clergy and laity, church boards and the people they serve. And worse still, it advances the pervasive and demoralizing attitude of regarding laity as passive, perpetual children sunk in theological and spiritual inertia who need to be superintended, often very patronizingly, by spiritually superior clergy. Furthermore, because of the permanent, disproportionate power placed in the hands of clergy, they are elevated to a spiritual pedestal that virtually assures their inability to be honest about their own lives with their congregations or, all too often, even with themselves. Nor are their continually infantile parishioners, always subject to the judgment and reprimand accorded children, in any better shape. Along with theologian Rebecca Chopp,[20] I would assert that one of the most disturbing aspects of contemporary Christian life is that churches today are not places in which people are free to speak the truth about their own lives.

All of these communal and social difficulties I have just illustrated—and many I have not—accompany the invocation of the doctrine of biblical authority. By looking closely at these examples and others, we can begin to uncover some of the conventions presupposed by the "special hermeneutics" adopted for reading the Bible as authoritative or normative.

THE "SPECIAL HERMENEUTICS" OF BIBLICAL AUTHORITY

We have already observed that appeals to the doctrine of biblical authority tend to be mounted only in situations of a conflict of viewpoints, usually to exclude what some powerful members of a religious community take to be threatening beliefs by those both within and outside the community. It is important to notice that issues upon which most of the community or denomination agree, whether approved within the biblical text or—most revealingly—disapproved within the text (e.g., divorce, usury), are never discussed under the rubric of biblical authority. Moreover, perspectives championed in the Bible, which many modern Christian communities reject as inappropriate (e.g., polygamy, slavery, specific hair lengths for men and women, communal ownership of property), are also rarely the subject of discussions of biblical authority. In the case of these latter concerns especially, the historical conditionedness of the biblical text is often raised as a reason for ignoring embarrassing biblical mandates; in other words, with texts deemed to be out of step with modern ethical and theological sensibilities, employing the "general hermeneutics" approach of biblical scholarship is perfectly acceptable. Thus, the "special hermeneutics" of biblical authority or normativity is not the constant practice of any ecclesiastical community,[21] but rather a practice employed only in certain selected moments of division and debate. When biblical authority is invoked, it profoundly affects the way in which the Bible is read and understood. This "special hermeneutics" has at least four major practices that distinguish it sharply from the general way in which other ancient texts are read: First, it is ahistorical; second, it idealizes and normativizes antique society; third, it isolates texts from their contexts; and finally, it insists on one correct reading of the text. Let us look in more detail at each of these practices.

The Historical Versus the Transcendent Text

To claim that a text written almost two to three thousand years ago has authority over the lives and actions of people in the present, or further, to claim that it establishes norms which all people in all cultures at all times in all circumstances should obey, one must assume that the text itself in some very real sense transcends history. If its words and views are timeless, applicable to all occasions, then it must not in any way be limited or even conditioned by its own historical society, its own cultural period, or its own individual context of production. It is truly and radically *a*historical. Even the works of Plato and Aristotle, works which have had an immense influence on the development of Western philosophy and science, are not viewed in such an ethereal light. While some of their positions may be respected and even adopted as insightful, it is always with the full awareness of their historical and cultural limitations. In other words, one can *argue* with the viewpoints of Plato and Aristotle or Cicero and Virgil; one can analyze and critique their assertions; one can assess their value for living in a radically different historical context. Arguing with, analyzing, critiquing, and assessing the ancient mandates of the Bible are not permitted in the "special hermeneutics" of biblical authority. Instead, the biblical text—or a selected portion of it—is raised to the level of transcendence of its Divine Author, omniscient and omni-relevant.[22]

    While such a claim assures the authority of every element of the text, it also necessitates a selective blindness to those texts that modern sensibilities eschew,[23] as we noted above. In addition, it requires considerable interpretative creativity to find guidance in scripture for those issues undreamt of in the ancient Mediterranean world (e.g., cloning, atomic weapons, space travel, television, *in vitro* fertilization, etc.) or considerable interpretative latitude to fit ancient perspectives to modern constructs (e.g., ancient views on money and commerce to modern venture capitalism, ancient practices of kingship to modern presidential and parliamentary democracies, ancient understandings of homoeroticism to modern homosexuality, ancient ideas about begging to modern concerns with homelessness and welfare, etc.). Indeed, the very need for such creativity and latitude itself tends to undercut seriously the claim for the transcendence of the text. In dealing with contemporary concerns, the Bible all too often seems thoroughly historically constrained. The covert, if not overt, recognition of that constraint is one reason the "special hermeneutics" of authority is rarely ever the sole hermeneutical position adopted by an ecclesiastical body, even though logically it should be the only option, if, indeed, the Bible is the normative, transcendent text it is claimed to be.

The Worldview of Modernity Versus the Worldview of Antiquity

Ironically, the denial of the historical conditionedness of biblical material claimed as normative or authoritative actually serves to leave in place the pervasive shaping of biblical material by its ancient cultural and social worldview. In assuming the direct applicability of the text to any contemporary context, one is required to ignore the specific ancient Mediterranean cultural views that underpin the text's meaning and function. While obvious issues like monetary systems, political structures, and social customs are often easy to recognize and sometimes neutralize by compensation,[24] far more influential and pervasive cultural ideologies are sometimes much less noticeable and almost impossible to neutralize. For instance, Paul's rejection of homoeroticism in Romans 1:26 is profoundly dependent on the pervasive Jewish and gentile view in the first century C.E. of the inferiority of women. What makes relations between men and between women "unnatural" is the requirement that a man, who is "naturally" dominant, be submissive *like a woman*, or that a woman, who is "naturally" submissive, be dominant *like a man*. It is the underlying cultural imperative that men are dominant and superior while women are submissive and inferior—and never the twain shall meet—that stands as the foundation to Paul's views.[25] Applying Paul's words on homoeroticism directly to the present carries along with it this undergirding belief in female inferiority because one position is dependent upon the other.[26]

The importation of the hierarchical and patriarchal worldview of Mediterranean antiquity into the present as a normative ideal has had many destructive effects on the church and on society, as we illustrated earlier. Though some people prosper under this ideology—mainly the most powerful men in the dominant racial or ethnic group—and, thus, considerable pressure is always at work to keep it in place, most people are reduced to some inferior or subservient status. Besides the advantage it bestows on an elite minority by privileging them, it is hard to understand why the worldview of a certain historical period in antiquity should become the norm for all time. I suppose it could be argued theologically that since Jesus entered history at a certain particular moment, that particular culture and society must hold some distinctive status for Christians. However, I would want to point out that the society and culture into which he was born was also the society and culture that crucified him and persecuted many of his earliest followers. Indeed, the Jesus of the canonical gospels expends much of his ministry on breaking down the social, religious, and status boundaries which permitted some to claim power and superiority over all others in that historical period. The sad irony is that by idealizing the worldview of the Bible, we establish as a modern norm that very world the Jesus of the gospels challenged to the point that it responded by murdering him.

Finally, reading biblical passages as authoritative and normative for present situations has the tendency to distort the present in order to make it "fit" the biblical injunction. The present situation must often be mythologized, purposely misconstrued, or greatly simplified to bring out its supposed parallels with the biblical text being used. For example, the complex biological, theological, and ethical issues surrounding the development of a fetus from conception to birth must be utterly simplified in order for anti-abortionists to claim the biblical authority of "You shall not kill" (Exodus 20:13) as applicable to the decision of a mother to abort at the earliest stages of pregnancy. The ambiguity of the actual situation must be denied for the sake of biblical authority. Or, the mythology of women as nurturing, retiring, and passive beings must be imposed over the contemporary reality of women as able leaders in politics, business, education, and other important areas of public life in order for the biblical mandate against women having authority over men (1 Timothy 2:12) to be used to justify the denial of women's ordination. Because the normative assertion must always be that of the Bible, the present actual situation has at best secondary status. Indeed, in some cases the normative authority granted to the Bible is used to judge lived experience as evil and rebellious or just misguided—thus, women who want to be ordained are labeled prideful sinners or mistaken children rather than appreciated as passionate believers who have heard a spiritual call from God. Consequently, the "special hermeneutics" of authority can re-interpret negatively events people themselves experience as spiritually compelling or life-giving. At the very least, it often shields or prevents us from seeing and dealing with the full reality of our present condition.

Contextual Reading Versus Strings of Quotations

"Proof-texting" is a reading strategy which Christians who appeal to biblical authority are often accused of practicing. In its most extreme and caricatured form, it is a practice of interpreting tiny fragments of scripture in complete isolation from—and sometimes in opposition to—their context. By pulling a few words or a verse completely out of any biblical context and placing them in some other context altogether, the Bible can literally be made to prove anything at all.[27] Although this radical level of proof-texting is the image that often stands behind the condemnation of the practice, to be fair it is relatively rare in most Christian communities, except for the extreme fundamentalist fringe. However, proof-texting in the more general sense of using only small portions of scripture out of the context of their overall narrative or poetic frameworks, is a regular feature of the "special hermeneutics" of biblical authority and constitutes a way of reading quite different from the ways in which other texts are read.

The dynamics of reading have been at the center of much research in the humanities over the past twenty-five years or so.[28] While conventions of reading vary from culture to culture and from historical period to historical period, reading in the present is generally understood as a sequential process of making meaning. In the terms used by Hans-Georg Gadamer, the "horizon" of the reader must merge with the "horizon" of the text[29] for communication to occur, and the horizon of the text is built up in the sequential process of reading. Moreover, such horizons are always fluid, always changing as the reading process continues, with the fullest comprehension of the text's horizon coming only at its end, since each new event or episode may alter the way one views the whole. For example, if one were only to look at the characterization of the twelve male disciples in the Gospel of Mark in its first three chapters, one would view them as totally positive characters, called by Jesus and specially designated to be with him. However, as one reads on, that totally positive evaluation begins to erode as the twelve continue to disbelieve and misunderstand Jesus' words and actions until in the end they are the ones who flee from him, betray him to his enemies, and deny their association with him. By the end of the gospel, one's evaluation of the twelve is very different from what it was after only three chapters; one's understanding of the text's horizon has, in fact, changed dramatically. Even in other genres of literature besides narrative, the cumulative effect of the whole process deeply affects one's understanding of the importance and value of each individual element.[30] It is for this reason that literary critics insist on the importance of the *context* of every word, phrase, and text for its interpretation.

The "special hermeneutics" of biblical authority interrupts and distorts this contextual process of meaning making. Because every word of scripture is authoritative in itself and because the formation and use of biblical authority has so elevated the importance of "thinly evidenced" material, the conventional practice of taking only a portion of a text as its full meaning is the common practice of reading the Bible as authoritative. While the more responsible forms of this practice may well consider the immediate surrounding material, they rarely, if ever, consider the overarching work as a whole. This truncated form of reading is unique to the Bible and could perhaps be seen as the radicalization and formalization of the long tradition of lectionary reading. However, lectionary readings generally place small portions of biblical text—usually, though not always, complete episodes, poems, parables, oracles, etc.—into the context of worship, often with some homiletic reflection on them, while the "special hermeneutics" of biblical authority tends instead to associate small portions of text—often only a verse or two taken out of an episode or other formal unit—with other small portions of scripture taken from different locations altogether. For example, in arguing that women should not be ordained, those using biblical authority might point to the gospels to show that Jesus did not designate any women among his special twelve disciples, to 1 Timothy to confirm that women should not have authority over men, and to Genesis 2-3 to indicate that woman is created from man as his "helpmate"; or, in asserting that gay men and lesbians are practicing a sinful "lifestyle," they might point to the Holiness Code in Leviticus 18-20 for the "abomination of male with male," Paul's comment in Romans 1:26 for the sin of "unnatural" relations, and to Genesis 1-3 for confirmation of male and female relations as the created norm. This pasting together or stringing together of references is one of the most common conventions of the special hermeneutics of biblical authority.

The overarching context of each element in these strings of texts is usually ignored or only minimally acknowledged; in fact, the elements in each string actually function as the interpretative context for each other. In other words, in this special reading strategy, Leviticus 18-20 becomes the primary context for understanding Romans 1:26 and *vice versa*, or 1 Timothy 2:12 becomes the context for Jesus' action of calling disciples in the gospels and *vice versa*.[31] Because contexts are so important in how one understands the meaning of a text, this procedure of creating strings of texts tends to be self-fulfilling; that is, the texts reaffirm the beliefs guiding the process that selected them in the first place. Indeed, it could be argued that this practice of stringing together disparate quotations is actually a process of creating an altogether new text.

The justification for this odd process of reading comes again from the affirmation that God is the Author of scripture. While that affirmation for most Christians does not entail a word-for-word dictation process, it does mean that all of scripture is in some sense the product of the Divine Mind and Will. One then only needs to proclaim that the Divine Mind must be of one piece to proclaim that material scattered in many different locations in scripture and used for many different purposes carries a basically consistent set of meanings. A similar argument stood as the foundation of another ancient form of reading the Bible, harmonization. Since the Bible was believed to be the definitive revelation of the Eternal and Unchanging God, whatever was found in one place could be used to complement different material found in another place. As Barr illustrates, "Though it was possible to write a Gospel which did not mention the Virgin Birth, the mention of it, where it *was* mentioned, was allowed to complement the non-mention of it elsewhere."[32] Varying reports of the same event were understood to supplement each other rather than contradict or undercut each other. Hence, biblical material could be added all together to form a harmonized reading of the whole.[33] While their justification rests on a similar foundation, the "special hermeneutics" of authority differs from harmonization in that it makes no attempt to discern the meaning of the "whole." Indeed, as we have just argued, it fragments the holistic horizon of a text or of scripture in order to recontextualize small portions of scripture into authoritative strings of text.

Multiple Meanings Versus a Correct, Single Meaning

In Gadamer's version of the process of reading, meaning occurs when the horizon of the reader merges with the horizon of the text. This way of understanding reading emphasizes the importance of the reader in the process. While an author creates a text according to the conventions of his/her own language group and culture, the meaning of that text is construed by readers according to the conventions of their language group and culture. A similar point is made in recent cultural theory: for a communicative event to occur, the production or encoding of a discursive form must result in its translation or decoding.[34] The recipient of a discourse, whether a reader, hearer, or viewer must decode the message for any transmission of meaning to have taken place. This dependence on readers for the construal of meaning points to one of the reasons for the existence of multiple interpretations of the same text. Different readers merge their own different horizons, their different life experiences, with that of the text, inevitably resulting in different construals of meaning. In addition, as cultural theorists point out, the practices of encoding and decoding "do not constitute an 'immediate identity'" because they are rarely "perfectly symmetrical."[35] Thus, since readers also develop the horizon of the text as they read or decode it, the lack of symmetry between the encoding and decoding of a discursive form becomes yet another source of multiple meanings. The cultural, social, and linguistic codes used by the producer of the text can be quite distant from those of its recipient. Readers attribute meaning to the text as they sequentially develop its horizon on the basis of conventional cultural strategies of reading that they have been taught, cultural strategies which themselves change over different historical periods and in different social sub-groups within any historical period. Consequently, reading itself, as expressed in the language of semiotics, "is a process of making meaning, a process of sign production where the reader actively attributes significance to signifiers on the basis of previously learned cultural codes."[36] From the merging of their own horizons to their construction of the text's horizon, readers at the very least must be considered co-creators of the meaning of any text, and some reader-response critics and deconstructionists would go considerably further by arguing that no text exists until a reader construes its meaning.

The history of the interpretation of the Bible provides ample proof of the influential role of the reader or community of readers in the construction of the text's meaning. Looking at the history of interpretation of the Bible from the early church to the present and observing the many different ways the same texts have been understood—allegorically, typologically, literally, symbolically, historically[37]—it is difficult to avoid the conclusion that even biblical meaning in some very significant ways is, and always has been, reader-dependent. Such a conclusion seems eminently reasonable from the standpoint of the "general hermeneutics" of contemporary biblical scholarship because all texts are capable of being construed in multiple ways; the Bible is just one more vivid instance of this general rule.

For the "special hermeneutics" of authority, however, the suggestion that the Bible may legitimately mean different things to different people is impossible to accept. It challenges the whole basis of using the Bible as a clear source of authoritative mandates and norms. Moreover, it raises a serious point overlooked in most arguments about biblical authority: whatever one may believe about the divine authorship of the Bible, throughout history it is very human readers who have been construing the meanings of those texts. Unless the Divine Author also controls the reading of the text, the very medium chosen for the message, that of language with its inherent indeterminacy and ambiguity, undercuts the singularity and directness of the communication. Doctrinal discussions of biblical authority usually try to address this issue by pointing out that the reading of scripture must be done prayerfully and with the help of the Holy Spirit. The concept of some divine assistance in discernment of meaning is very ancient, witness the *Paraklētos* of the Gospel of John or the "Master Within" of Augustine. However, the problem is not erased by such measures because they do not explain the multiple meanings present throughout the history of interpreting the Bible. Evidently, even with the help of the Holy Spirit, multiple meanings of scripture abound. How is this issue to be adjudicated for the "special hermeneutics" of biblical authority?

Among those for whom the Bible is authoritative or normative, it is important to argue that only one meaning can be the correct one and all of the others must be mistaken.[38] But which one is correct? And by what criteria is that correctness to be determined? Historical observation demonstrates that the "correctness" of a reading is generally determined by the leaders of the dominant group or sub-group in any cultural period according to their own current intellectual and religious criteria and all other readings are rejected as wrong.[39] However, those criteria themselves change over time. For example, in the twelfth century allegorical readings were deemed to be correct, intended by God, the way the Bible was meant to be read, but by the twentieth century under the dominance of the historical paradigm, allegorical readings are judged as wrong, as instances of the terrible sin of eisegesis. Or, in the nineteenth century slavery was taken to be blessed by biblical mandate, but in the late twentieth century it is currently assigned to those texts to be read only from a "general hermeneutics" perspective.

If it is the case that readers co-create the meanings of the texts they interpret, then claiming biblical authority as the justification for a certain view or belief serves to disguise the role of the reader or community of readers in crafting that viewpoint. As feminists have argued for years, there are no neutral interpretations. All readings are interested; that is, they are shaped by the advocacies and beliefs of readers, but this general rule becomes something much more dangerous in the "special hermeneutics" of authority. In that case, readers construct readings of the Bible according to their *own* perspectives and conventional practices and then endow those readings with transcendent and eternal authority over the lives of others—hiding from others, and sometimes even from themselves, the degree of personal interest shaping their readings.[40] Thus, the "special hermeneutics" of authority opens the way for individuals or groups to proclaim their own experiences of life, their own particular beliefs, and their own notions of moral and ethical norms to be the will of the Eternal and Unchanging God, whose authoritative word they are proclaiming for all others to obey. Under the "special hermeneutics" of authority, the Bible becomes a powerful weapon in the hands of some to force their will and beliefs on others. The destructive results of such a perversion of scriptural influence can be found spread across the pages of history, as we saw earlier. How might these difficulties in the church's use of the Bible be avoided? How might the Bible in the church become a blessing on creation rather than a weapon of aggression?

THE BIBLE AS THE INSPIRED WORD OF GOD

Is it possible to so reformulate the function of the Bible in ecclesiastical endeavors as to retain its valuable vision of liberation, justice, peace, and mercy but remove its public role as legitimater in discourses of abusive authority, power, and control? How could the Bible and the communities it validates be reconstituted for justice, love, and respect for difference in our present time and historical context? While the "general hermeneutics" of biblical scholarship offers some advantages and is, indeed, used by most Christians and most ecclesiastical bodies at certain moments, it really does not have a way of respecting the sacredness or the faith attachment many Christians feel in the Bible. This lack may be one of the major reasons that studies of the Bible by scholars often seem irrelevant, or even sometimes offensive, to some Christians. In treating the Bible as they would any other ancient text, scholars, as scholars, can only describe from the outside the spiritual connection many believers experience in reading the text itself. Any reformulation of the function of the Bible must account for this important experience of believers.

My vision for reconstituting the present situation begins with a firm rejection of any doctrine of biblical authority. When the Bible is set in the context of discourses of authority and normativity, its interpretations take on the socially oppressive and destructive characteristics I have been discussing. The "special hermeneutics" of authority is much too destructive and potentially devious a practice of reading to be ethically embraced by any ecclesiastical body, in my view. If the Bible is not to be doctrinally authoritative or normative for Christian life today, what role can it have? I believe it might be understood as primarily *inspirational*, both inspired in its writing and inspiring in its reading, which is after all the way Jesus and the earliest Christians seem to have viewed scripture in the first place. Scripture is able to inspire, literally to "breathe in," the hope, religious joy, and vision of its ancient authors and audiences. It does not dictate what our current views, hopes, or visions should be but instead allows us to witness the successes and failures of those before us in the struggle to be faithful doers of the will of God. Their courage in their particular historical contexts can inspire us to be courageous in our own historical situations. But their social, cultural, and theological limitations need not be adopted in the present world as God's eternal command, as they now often are. Understanding the Bible as the inspirational, rather than authoritative, center of Christian fellowship requires contemporary Christians, much like the earliest Christians, to take full responsibility for their own theological and ethical decisions. Interpretations of the Bible can no longer be used as a warrant or proof-text to disguise the human drives to power and control of its readers. Like Paul and the Corinthians, modern Christians will have to define and argue for their own theological positions in open encounter with those whose theological positions are quite different, without hiding behind the Bible as guarantee that one is right and the other is wrong.

For such debates to occur, one momentous change in contemporary Christian communities must take place: laity must become theologically liter-

ate. I believe the theological and spiritual inertia that haunts many congregations and parishes must end, if Christianity is to have any viable future in the
next millennium. Clergy need to become spiritual interpreters and theological
educators who are committed to cultivating the theological and spiritual
maturity of their parishioners. While there is still a division between a student
and a teacher, the purpose of good education is to close that gap by eventually
bringing the student to the teacher's level of knowledge; this is far different
from the perpetual theological chasm that now generally yawns between pastors and their congregations. What I envision is no less than the democratiza-
tion of the church. While such a horizontal re-ordering of power relations
would not make church life easier, it would make it more vital, more honest,
and more capable of responding to the real world of twentieth-century society.

Furthermore, when I look at the Bible for inspiration for living in this real
world of remarkable diversity, I find the portrayal of Jesus' vision of the kingdom, particularly as it is presented in the Gospels of Mark and Luke, central to
my thinking. Jesus' actions of healing the sick, feeding the poor, eating with
the oppressed and socially outcast, defying traditional regulations of purity
and piety to help those in pain or in need regardless of their gender or their
religious or ethnic affiliation embodied a love of people in all their differences.
Such views challenged the social and religious conventions of Jesus' own historical period. They stand as metaphors for a revelation of God's kingdom as
the rejection of human traditions of exclusivity and the reconstruction of
human creation as it was intended to be: fully heterogeneous yet inclusive,
with dignity and respect for everyone.

Because scripture functions as inspiration, not as a transcendent, authoritative model, I am also free to name and reject the manner in which some of these
metaphors, taken normatively, have been used to demean those who are ill or
blind or paralyzed. Because the gospels often symbolize the kingdom by Jesus'
healings, illness itself or disability have sometimes been evaluated as signs of
God's punishment or as barriers to full membership in Christianity or even to
full humanity itself, the very opposite of the inclusivity, dignity, and respect the
kingdom inspires. Consequently, even the gospel writers' own metaphors for
the radical inclusivity of the kingdom are partial and flawed, as indeed were the
attempts of the earliest Christians to embody that revelation. Nevertheless,
they did try, and especially in the early Christian mission, the radical potential
of Jesus' revelation of the kingdom inspired the free extension of God's
promises to include gentiles, the non-Jewish "nations," many of whom had historically been the oppressors of the Jewish people. Although Paul himself was
more limited in his vision than some early Christians who conceived of a fully
inclusive society without slavery, the oppression of women, or the ownership of
children, Paul clearly rejected the views of other Christians, who were only
willing to extend the kingdom of God to gentiles who became like themselves
by adopting circumcision and Jewish food regulations.

Clearly, for early Christian missionaries like Paul the open incorporation of
believers of all races, ethnicities, and religious backgrounds into full and equal
partnership in the traditional contract of God to Abraham and the Jewish peo-

ple was an act of outrageous inclusivity. As radical as it was in its own historical milieu, the gentile mission was still only a partial embodiment of the renewal of creation called for by Jesus' revelation of the kingdom, but it can inspire us to further radical incorporations—incorporations that extend equal participation to people of both genders and all nations and races, ethnicities, sexual orientations, classes, physical abilities, and cultural and religious traditions.

This is my vision for reforming Christian communities. But my vision is just that, *my vision*. It is not a prescription or a blueprint, and it is restricted by the historical and social limitations of my own specific perspective. Of course, everybody's vision is just that. The Bible itself is composed of similar visions of many diverse people from different cultures and different historical periods, and our readings of the Bible are our ways of bringing our own visions into conversation with theirs. However, even when we can affirm that the Bible overflows with stories of love and justice, that has not prevented it from being employed by discourses of authority to justify exclusion, persecution, suffering, and even death for those deemed as outsiders to the current "normative" vision, whatever it might be. We must stop teaching and learning this "special hermeneutics" of authority, because while reading the Bible can be a spiritual, imaginative, and inspirational activity, it also must be an *ethical* activity, and those readings we should enact in our lives and our communities, I believe, are those which make of the Bible a blessing, and not a curse, on God's good creation.

NOTES

1. Bultmann, "Das Problem der Hermeneutik," *Glauben und Verstehen* (Tübingen: J.C.B. Mohr [Paul Siebeck], 1961) II: 231-32.

2. Actually, many ancient authors believed that the texts they wrote were inspired by divine guidance. Hesiod, for example, in his *Theogony*, begins by praising the Muses, through whose inspiration he is writing his work on the gods. This rather common claim for divine inspiration in ancient texts is usually ignored in claiming special status for the inspiration of the Bible.

3. Ibid., pp. 233-35.

4. These three possible forms of textual authority I am suggesting bear a very rough correspondence to the three forms of social authority posited by Max Weber: charismatic (narrative/rhetorical), traditional (formational), and rational (doctrinal). For a discussion of Weber's views on authority, see S. Lukes, "Power and Authority," in *A History of Sociological Analysis*, ed. T. Bottomore and R. Nisbet (New York: Basic Books, 1978) pp. 663-65. See Sandra Schneiders, *The Revelatory Text: Interpreting the New Testament as Sacred Scripture* (San Francisco: HarperSanFrancisco, 1991) for another take on the issue of biblical authority. Although Schneiders retains the term "authority" for the role of the Bible, I believe that in her view the type of "authority" scripture should have is more "formational" than "doctrinal."

5. See, e.g., his *The Scope and Authority of the Bible* (Philadelphia: Westminster Press, 1980) and *Holy Scripture: Canon, Authority, Criticism* (Oxford: Clarendon Press, 1983); see also, L. William Countryman, *Biblical Authority Or Biblical Tyranny? Scripture and the Christian Pilgrimage* (Philadelphia: Fortress Press, 1981); Donald K. McKim, ed., *The Authoritative Word: Essays on the Nature of Scripture* (Grand Rapids: William B. Eerdmans, 1983); and James D.G. Dunn, *The Living Word* (Philadelphia: Fortress Press, 1987).

6. Barr, *Holy Scripture*, pp. 12-19. As Barr notes, "The authority attached to the Old Testament within the New did not mean that New Testament Christianity took pre-existing scripture as its dominant and controlling ideological base. . . . The undoubted authority of the Old Testament as Word of God does not alter the fact that for the New Testament it is no longer the unique starting point: its positions may be criticized, may be modified, and it is no longer an absolute. Its authority is relative to the supreme authority of Jesus Christ" (pp. 18-19).

7. Dunn, *The Living Word*, p. 127.

8. See the discussion of the canon in Barr, *Holy Scripture*, pp. 23-28.

9. Ibid., p. 39. It is worth remembering that these doctrines were being proposed during the same period when the reason-based discourses of modern science and modern historiography were becoming influential, both of which, in the minds of many church leaders, threatened the foundations of certain respected church dogmas. Some of these dogmas could be shored up by insisting on the authority of every element—even minimal elements—of scripture.

10. E.g., although their aim was to correct church abuses and give individual Christians greater freedom in determining their own practice of religion, by making the authority of the Bible supreme over all other traditions, the Protestant Reformers exercised one of the greatest exclusions in Christian history which resulted in the division of Western Christianity. Moreover, the tendency to use biblical interpretations to create boundaries between "us" and "them" continues in the proliferation of Protestant denominations. Within present ecclesiastical organizations, biblical warrants may be claimed to exclude women from ordination or positions of power in the church structures, to exclude homosexuals from ordination, to forbid divorce or re-marriage, etc.

11. E.g., the prohibition movement earlier in this century, especially in the form of the Woman's Christian Temperance League, posited a biblical mandate for prohibiting the use of alcohol; anti-abortionists cite the commandment against killing as legitimating their fight for the unborn; etc. This use of biblical authority to authorize national political agenda makes the issue of the appeal to the authority of the Bible one of concern to all citizens and not just Christians or Protestant Christians.

12. E.g., historically problematic claims for creationism and the repudiation of evolutionary theory in favor of the literal existence of the Garden of Eden or the Great Flood of Noah all stem from attribution of authority to the Bible. Again, especially at the state level, these claims are often politically mounted to affect the curricula of public school systems or the selection of textbooks.

13. Theological formulations concerning the authority of the Bible have generally been attempts to understand the place of the Bible in the context of revelation, faith, and the workings of the Holy Spirit, and they can be found in the Christian tradition as far back as Origen and Augustine. For example, the Westminster Confession of Faith, drawn up in the seventeenth century and still the basis of many evangelical Christians' doctrine of biblical authority, argued that only through the work of the Holy Spirit in the heart of each person could that person come to understand the Bible as the Word of God, and it was a Word that contained all things necessary to human salvation and faith. For a brief discussion of various understandings of the place of the Bible in Christian tradition, see J.B. Rogers, "The Church Doctrine of Biblical Authority," in *The Authoritative Word: Essays on the Nature of Scripture*, ed. Donald K. McKim (Grand Rapids: William B. Eerdmans, 1983), pp. 197-224. See also, David Kelsey, *The Uses of Scripture in Recent Theology* (Philadelphia: Fortress Press, 1975).

14. James Brewer Stewart, "Abolitionists, the Bible, and the Challenge of Slavery," in E. Sandeen, ed., *The Bible and Social Reform* (Philadelphia: Fortress Press; Chico, CA: Scholars Press, 1982), pp. 38-39.

15. Ibid., p. 44.

16. Whether the practice of cultic prostitution was an actual practice of religions surrounding Israel or instead an Israelite polemic against its enemies has become a major point of debate surrounding these verses; see, e.g., Ken Stone, "The Hermeneutics of Abomination: On Gay Men, Canaanites, and Biblical Interpretation" *Biblical Theology Bulletin* 27 (Summer 1997): 36-41.

17. See the extensive lexigraphical study of the Greek in John Boswell, *Christianity, Social Tolerance, and Homosexuality* (Chicago: University of Chicago Press, 1980), pp. 335-353, and more recently the thorough discussion in Dale Martin, "*Arsenokoitês* and *Malakos*: Meanings and Consequences," in *Biblical Ethics & Homosexuality: Listening to Scripture*, ed. Robert L. Brawley (Louisville, KY: Westminster John Knox Press, 1996) pp. 117-136.

18. For other possible meanings, see, e.g., James Miller, "The Practices of Romans 1:26: Homosexual or Heterosexual?" *Novum Testamentum* 37 (1995): 1-11.

19. For the ancients, sexuality was defined as dominance and submission; thus only relations between socially dominant individuals, mostly free adult males, and socially submissive individuals, which could be either women or slaves or youth, were considered "natural." For a full discussion of the construction of sexuality in antiquity as well as through history, see the fine study by Thomas Laqueur, *Making Sex: Body and Gender from the Greeks to Freud* (Cambridge, MA: Harvard University Press, 1990). For a thorough analysis of the importance of Paul's cultural and social world for his views on women and homoeroticism, see Bernadette J. Brooten, *Love Between Women: Early Christian Responses to Female Homoeroticism* (Chicago: University of Chicago Press, 1996), especially pp. 215-302.

20. Comment made during the Cole Lectures, Vanderbilt University Divinity School, February 8-9, 1994.

21. I would argue that this is true even of fundamentalist groups whose view of biblical authority has been heightened mightily into a claim for biblical "inerrancy." Many fundamentalist leaders are able to select which rules are relevant to today and which are not through the use of "dispensationalism," a view that divides history into a set number of dispensations. Interestingly—and arguably heretically—the present dispensation in which we now live began *after* the death of Jesus and so only the material in the Bible referring to "our dispensation" is actually relevant to today's world, making the words of Jesus in the gospels of much *less* concern than the letters of Paul or the Pastoral Epistles. For more information on fundamentalists' techniques of reading the Bible, see, e.g., Kathleen Boone, *For the Bible Tells Them So: The Discourse of Protestant Fundamentalism* (Albany: State University of New York Press, 1989) and James Barr, *Fundamentalism*, 2d ed. (London: SCM Press, 1981).

22. See, e.g., Chapter I, Section iv of the Westminster Confession, which asserts that God is the sole Author of all of scripture.

23. This need for selective blindness is not a new problem. Origen, in calling for allegorical interpretation of scripture, argued that the literal meaning of biblical passages could not be supported in those many cases in which the passage was "unworthy of God."

24. For example, by substituting in one's reading the amount of an average contemporary day's wage for the text's use of "denarius."

25. See the careful delineation of this argument in Brooten, *Love Between Women*, pp. 215-266.

26. See Brooten's telling critique of the work of Richard Hays, who wants to hold onto Paul's rejection of homoeroticism as normative while ignoring the denigration of women on which it is based. Ibid., p. 245.

27. I learned this lesson very early in life. When I was a pre-teen, a friend of mine from church told me that the Bible proved women could smoke. When I expressed disbelief that the Bible had anything to say about smoking, my friend pointed to Genesis 24:64,

which in the King James Version we were using, said, speaking of Rebekah, "she alighted the camel."

28. Some representative theorists would be, e.g., Wolfgang Iser, *The Act of Reading: A Theory of Aesthetic Response* (Baltimore: Johns Hopkins University Press, 1978); Mikhail Bakhtin, *The Dialogic Imagination: Four Essays*, ed. Michael Holquist, trans. Caryl Emerson and Michael Holquist (Austin, TX: University of Texas Press, 1981); Frank Lentricchia, *Criticism and Social Change* (Chicago: University of Chicago Press, 1983); and Hans-Georg Gadamer, *Truth and Method* (New York: Crossroad, 1982). For a discussion of the variety of reader-response criticisms, see Susan Suleiman and I. Crosman, eds., *The Reader in the Text: Essays on Audience and Interpretation* (Princeton: Princeton University Press, 1980); Jane Tompkins, ed., *Reader-Response Criticism: From Formalism to Post-Structuralism* (Baltimore and London: Johns Hopkins University Press, 1980); and Jonathan Culler, *On Deconstruction: Theory and Criticism After Structuralism* (Ithaca: Cornell University Press, 1982).

29. *Truth and Method*, pp. 340-341. "Horizon," a term that Gadamer takes from Husserl, refers to that ". . . which constitutes the unity of the flow of experience . . ." (p. 217).

30. In the most common genre in the New Testament, the letter, this cumulative effect is often now studied in terms of ancient rhetoric, the conventional forms of arrangement and argumentation taught and practiced throughout the Greco-Roman period.

31. It is especially revealing to notice how the same text placed in a different string takes on a very different function. For example, when the creation story in Genesis 2-3 is associated with a string of quotations on the second-class status of women, the Genesis material is read to show that women come second in creation and are only valued as helpers to men. When, on the other hand, the same story is put into the homosexuality string of Romans 1:26 and Leviticus 18-20, the text becomes a proof of the importance of the creation of two different sexes who are intended to become one. In the latter case, the inferiority of women is elided or denied in the oneness that only two different sexes can achieve. The context provided by the other quotations in the string makes all the difference in how the passage projects the supposed normal status of women: are they inferior to men or are they one with men?

32. Barr, *Holy Scripture*, p. 3.

33. The hermeneutical practices of biblical inerrantists give an extreme twist to ancient harmonization. Since the Bible is believed to be inerrant historically as well as in every other way, events that are told in several even slightly different versions are proclaimed to have happened more than once historically. For instance, since the trial of Jesus before Pilate is related in three rather different accounts, those of Mark/Matthew, Luke, and John, some inerrantists claim that Jesus was actually, historically tried three times by the Romans. Although this rather bizarre practice does explain the differences between the accounts, it still makes the individual gospel writers out to be poor or very misleading authors, since each one tells of only *one* trial before Pilate, not the "historical" *three*.

34. Stuart Hall, "Encoding, decoding," in *The Cultural Studies Reader*, ed. Simon During (London and New York: Routledge, 1993): 91-92.

35. Ibid., p. 93.

36. J. A. Radway, *Reading the Romance: Women, Patriarchy, and Popular Literature* (Chapel Hill and London: University of North Carolina Press, 1984) p. 7.

37. See, e.g., Robert Grant and David Tracy, *A Short History of the Interpretation of the Bible*, 2nd ed. (Minneapolis: Fortress Press, 1984). For a fascinating recent popular compendium of the variety of readings, often conflicting readings, found in appeals to biblical authority, see Jim Hill and Rand Cheadle, *The Bible Tells Me So: Uses and Abuses of Holy Scripture* (New York: Anchor Books/Doubleday, 1996).

38. This view has infected biblical scholarship in the past as well, probably arising

from its early formation in historical positivism; see the discussion in Mary A. Tolbert, "When Resistance Becomes Repression: Mark 13:9-27 and the Poetics of Location," in Fernando Segovia and Mary A. Tolbert, eds., *Reading from This Place* Volume 2: *Social Location and Biblical Interpretation in Global Perspective* (Minneapolis: Fortress Press, 1995) pp. 339-46.

39. See Hayden White's discussion of the importance of noting who has the authority in any situation to determine, not only the meaning of a text, but even what questions are proper to put to a text, in "Conventional Conflicts," *The New Literary History* 13 (1981): 145-60.

40. A excellent example of this problem occurred recently in a class of mine. A male African-American pastor turned in a paper on the household code in Colossians 3:18-4:6 in which he argued that the command to slaves to obey their masters was part of the ancient history of the text and in no way applicable to the present. However, he went on to argue that the command to wives to obey their husbands was still an authoritative norm for today because it was supported in the creation story in Genesis 2-3 where women are created to be the helper of their husbands. Thus, this student ignored the possible strings of texts that have been used to support the God-givenness of slavery but constructed a string that would show the continued applicability of the dictate about the subordination of women. In talking with the student, it became clear to me that he was essentially oblivious to the fact that his interpretation served to negate a biblical mandate that would (and has) hurt him but to preserve a mandate in the same text that privileged him above women. The degree to which his own personal interests shaped his reading of which portion of scripture was authoritative and which was not was obvious to everyone else in the class but not to him—nor, one fears, his congregation.

10

A MEETING OF WORLDS

African Americans and the Bible

Vincent L. Wimbush

The African American embrace of the Bible is a strange historical phenomenon. Forced in the first place into a strange New World, a world in which a document, the Bible, was prominently, even iconically, featured, one would think Africans, a people known in general to be steeped in oral traditions, should not have embraced or found comfort in the Bible or in a "religion of the Book." Nevertheless, in a fascinating and complex way, such a phenomenon developed rather quickly—and perdures for an astonishingly large segment of African Americans.

But why? Why did this happen? And how did this happen? How *could* this happen? These as well as other related questions and issues are to be problematized, if not fully answered, in this essay. They are questions and issues that need to be addressed if an adequate understanding, appreciation, and critique of the richness and complexities of African American religious traditions and consciousness are to be realized. Moreover, they are questions and issues that can—taking the African American religious tradition as exemplum of a particular complex culture within which are to be found particular historical moments, social locations, and orientations—throw light on important aspects of the broader phenomenon involving the formation and maintenance of religious self-understandings (religious conversion and traditioning), especially as focus is placed upon the phenomenology—as well as political functions and effects—of the "Holy Book" (or "scripture"). I also see such an investigation, however preliminary and sketchy, as a contribution to hermeneutics, insofar as it strengthens the argument for a repositioning (decentering!) of the text in the interpretive agenda.

AFRICAN AMERICAN ENGAGEMENT OF THE BIBLE

From the beginning of their forced presence in the New World that eventually became the United States, Africans, as is their custom, consistently fell back upon religious myth, language, and ritual in shaping and defining their world

against the world, that is, in finding affirmation and strength.[1] For some—
especially in isolated places in North America (e.g., Gullahs off the coast of
Georgia and South Carolina) and in the more syncretistic culture of the
Caribbean—the conditions were such that the African traditions they knew
could to some extent still be embraced. For most, however, the continuous exercise of the traditions known was either not permitted or deliberately frustrated.

In all situations in the New World, but especially within those situations
that were the most physically, spiritually, and psychically oppressive and con-
straining, Africans did that for which Africans have been well known—they
adapted. Although at first warily and under duress and oppressive conditions,
they embraced and then manipulated the religious rhetorics and traditions of
European Christianity until such traditions became their own and began to
reflect their views about themselves as well as the world to which they had
been brought. The major turning points in the history of the Africans' engagement of religion in North America—especially within, but not limited to, certain Protestant camps—reflect the significant and complex role of religion in
the development of Africans in America.

From the beginning of their experience in the New World, upon hearing the
powerful narratives of the Bible and moving hymns, some Africans responded
to the preachings of white evangelists and exhorters representing respectable
and not-so-respectable religion. Many more responded (en masse) to the
exhortation of already "converted" Black evangelists and exhorters: they
joined local white churches and helped to build historic churches and large
denominational groups; they founded their own separate local churches and
denominational groups in protest against racism and in advancement of racial
solidarity; they later founded splinter groups—"cults" and "sects"—in protest
against both ("mainline") African American social and religious apostasy and
respectability and white American racism. More recently, some have been
attracted to Black and white fundamentalist communities and institutions.

These different religious responses or turns among African Americans
require more careful sorting out and detailed accounting. No one response represents the sensibilities and orientations of all African Americans. And it is clear
that any comprehensive explanation and schema will certainly need to address
the issue of the functions of the Bible in any of the above or other responses that
might be delineated. Because the Bible has figured so prominently in the history
of (especially) Protestant-dominant American culture and religious self-defini-
tions,[2] and because the great majority of African Americans have historically
been formed in a culture of evangelical Protestantism, it must be given serious
consideration in any effort to understand, address, and influence the thinking
and orientations of a still large segment of African Americans.

In the founding, growth, and rise to world power of the United States, the
Bible has functioned as something of an icon[3]—at first providing the fledgling
nation with a basis for its ideological and principled stance against British
rule; subsequently providing justification for its brutalities against natives and
its enslavement of Africans, its expansionist policies, and its longlived traditions and policies of racism, racial brutality, and apartheid.[4] Ironically, it was

precisely because these and other hallmarks of the making of America were articulated through and justified by readings of the Bible that African Americans embraced the Bible, recognizing in it a source of social, religious, and political power. Although viewed at first as a rather strange source or locus of power by peoples steeped in rich oral cultures,[5] the Bible quickly came to be embraced as a powerfully arresting and expansive language world—full of poignant, memorable stories, breathtaking visions, pithy sayings and riddles, haunting prophecies; full of the adventures of heroes and heroines, of the pathetic travails and great triumphs of a rootless people, of a savior figure who is mistreated and abused but who ultimately overcomes.

During the times leading up to and immediately following the Civil War, the Bible came to function as an ideological and rhetorical weapon on an ideological and rhetorical playing field. Different regions of the country, different religious and cultural groups, different racial and ethnic groups, and different social classes turned to the Bible both to articulate and justify their views on slavery, the great controversial topic of the times. African Americans-turned-evangelical Christians saw in the period just after the second Great Awakening (early nineteenth century) the opportunity to enter the rhetorical, ideological playing field. They sang, preached, exhorted, prayed, joked, and debated issues in biblical terms and categories.

In eighteenth- and especially nineteenth-century evangelical culture, individuals were to an extent free to discern the will of God for their lives, inasmuch as it could be discerned in the Bible. On the part of Africans, engagement of the Bible was primarily oral and therefore somewhat fluid, reflecting not only their origins but also the conscription placed upon them. Since the letters of the Bible could not be engaged by very many African Americans throughout the eighteenth and nineteenth centuries,[6] a strict literalism did not characterize their engagement of the Bible. This situation led to the laying of the foundations for a rich tradition of a culture-specific reading of the Bible. There was, after all, little that white evangelical Christians could do to check the hermeneutical exercises of the Africans-turned-Christians. The Book had been opened and read and heard. And the Africans knew themselves to be free to mine the Book for those stories and oracles that spoke to their situation. They knew they were free—in accordance with African sensibilities that did not hold the letters or texts to be sacrosanct—to manipulate the biblical stories in ways that would guarantee their continuing relevance and poignancy.

Such hermeneutical freedom and playfulness was psychologically and ideologically felt. But it was not the same as passivity, as many have argued, even if the expressions or transcripts of that freedom were somewhat veiled or hidden.[7] It was a freedom involving the release of the collective cultural imagination in the engagement of the Bible, which was translated into psychic affirmation and power—the power to imagine the other, something other than the given of slavery and disenfranchisement. It was the power of a "cognitive minority" to imagine a different future situation that was better than, if not always altogether a reversal of, the status quo. Although rarely recognized for what it is and might effect, such freedom and power endures among a significant segment of African Americans.

AFRICAN AMERICAN ENGAGEMENT OF THE BIBLE ON THEIR OWN TERMS

This sketchy and summary history of the engagement of African Americans with the Bible only begins to raise some of the serious remaining historical-interpretive questions. The most important of these, I would argue, is the question about how African Americans made that first significant step toward the engagement of the Bible *on their own terms*. So the question is not so much or simply *when* and *where* and *what sociohistorical conditions*—the usual historical and ethical- theological questions—under which an enslaved people, a people cut off from roots and homeland, turned to the religions and the Holy Book of their enslavers. It is not so much the simple historical question about *how*, insofar as this question has to do with the social, economic, and political conditions in which the engagement occurred. It is, rather, a larger phenomenological question about *how*—going beyond the biblical evangelical exhortations and sentiments of the whites, beyond their stated and unstated and histrionically demonstrated bibliolatry—how it could happen that a people steeped in rich oral traditions could find in the Bible a language and image world, some comfort, hope and joy, a source of power, a reference point for meaning, self-definition, and fulfillment. How did *this* happen? How *could* this happen?

These last questions are especially significant and poignant, as Sam Gill argues, given a number of comparative situations in which peoples of "nonliterate" (as opposed to "preliterate")[8] or oral traditions are more often than not forced to engage the literary traditions and cultural ways of the dominant others. The difficulty of making the psychical and psychological transference from oral to literate tradition is captured within many different stories related about Native Americans and their encounter with whites and their world. None is more dramatic, legendary, and to the point than the one about Frank Hamilton Cushing, an ethnologist for the Smithsonian, assigned in 1879 to study the Zuni people of New Mexico:

> Cushing was a frail man with unusual dedication. While the research party he was with made an encampment near the village of Zuni, Cushing soon found even this short distance from the Zuni a barrier to his goals. He moved uninvited into the home of the governor of Zuni where he would stay for the remainder of the study, a period expected to be two months. He was so fascinated with the Zuni, that he embarked upon the effort to become Zuni so that he might understand them fully. His stay stretched to four and a half years and then he left only because his devotion to the Zuni threatened to prevent the illegal acquisition of Zuni lands by relatives of a U.S. congressman. After a period of adjustment, the Zuni accepted Cushing and attempted to make him Zuni. He

was initiated into a priesthood and given the high office of War Chief, a position that being held by this white man, had obvious advantages to the Zuni ... Cushing became fluent in Zuni language. He was initiated into religious societies. He lived like and claimed to think like a Zuni. ...[9]

However, from the perspective of the Zuni, there were important differences. One of the most important of these was recalled in a song performed for Cushing upon the occasion of his initiation into the priesthood of the Bow Society:

> Once they made a White man into a priest of the Bow
> he was out there with other Bow Priests
> he had black stripes on his body
> the others said their prayers from their hearts
> but he read his from a piece of paper.[10]

The poignancy of the text of this song is made clear by the fact that the translation for the Zuni term for written page is "that which is striped." Cushing was seen, therefore, as "a walking page of writing," fully dependent upon books for knowledge and power, in contrast to the Zuni openness to and dependence upon the spirit. The latter was assumed to be far superior to the former, as the dualistic truth-claim of a member of the British Columbian Carrier tribe makes clear:

> The white man writes everything down in a book so that it might not be forgotten; but our ancestors married the animals, learned their ways, and passed on the knowledge from one generation to another.[11]

The same sensibilities are in evidence in African culture. Contrasting the Africans' strong oral traditions with the literacy and dependency upon writing of other peoples, a contemporary West African historian-poet has written with pride and conviction about the difference between European (so it is assumed) and African culture on the basis of openness to the greater world of spirit:

> Other peoples use writing to record the past, but this invention has killed the faculty of memory among them. They do not feel the past anymore, for writing lacks the warmth of the human voice. With them everybody thinks he knows, whereas learning should be a secret. The prophets did not write and their words have been all the more vivid as a result. What paltry learning is that which is congealed in dumb books![12]

There are numerous other expressions, including stories and anecdotes, that make the nonetheless serious point that the sensibilities of oral, nonliterate cultures and the sensibilities of literate cultures are quite different, if not antagonistic.[13] From the beginning of the making of what has become the United States, both oral and literate cultures were placed alongside each other. These two cultures and corresponding orientations and sensibilities were for the most part, although not completely, divided along racial-ethnic lines—those of European descent on the one hand; Africans and Native Americans on the other.

The *folk* culture of the Europeans was certainly oral.[14] To be sure, the enslaved Africans were by background steeped in oral traditions. In the context of the New World, both poor whites and their folk culture as well as Africans and Native Americans were considered marginal and inferior. The Africans, especially, were defined as "the other," as the inferior and powerless; this was part of the whites' justification for their enslavement of the Africans and massacre of the Native Americans. One of the most powerful indices of the Africans' radical otherness and powerlessness in the minds of whites was their inability to read and write, to communicate with the whites in the language of the whites. That this was a logical and historical impossibility, given the whites' enslavement and disenfranchisement of Africans, as well as a dramatic example of cultural myopia and hegemony, was not addressed. The fact was that inability to come to speech in the way of cultured white society, to read and to write, represented inferiority and powerlessness among whites, in that tiny minority that nonetheless represented powerful "polite society." Such inability in turn came to be seen as justification for the continued oppression and exploitation of Africans and others.[15]

ACCOUNTING FOR SUCH ENGAGEMENT

Given the predominant orality of African culture, the evidence for antagonism between the sensibilities and orientations of oral and literate cultures, and the initial legal, social, and religiously sanctioned proscription against African engagement of letters that affected the great majority of Africans, the step toward the positive, even aggressive, African American engagement of letters in general—and the Bible in particular—was enormously complex and of course not without political, religious, and cultural ramifications. It is a fact that such engagement took place, and in aggressive and creative ways—that is, eventually on African Americans' own terms. An accounting of this engagement, specifically, of the initial steps or phases in this engagement, must be offered in connection with an accounting of both the politics of reading and writing in early America and the phenomenology of reading and writing on the individual and collective psyche.

As regards the politics of reading and writing, it has already been mentioned above that reading and writing in early America was for the most part a class-specific capacity and privilege. It was for this very reason, therefore, that many Africans in this strange and new context willingly, aggressively, often furtively, sometimes at the risk of severe punishment and death, engaged letters, including but not limited to the Bible. It was a matter of wanting power, or access to power. This motive was not different from, certainly not antithetical to, the religious impulse; it was an intricate part of it.

Because it was assumed in Protestant America to represent social, economic, political, and religious power, or access to such power, the desire to read and write could hardly be divorced in anyone's mind from the religious quest. The point that Oswald Spengler made about writing, that it ". . . implies a complete change in the relation of man's [sic] waking consciousness, in that it liberates it from the tyranny of the present . . . ," is applied generally to human beings encountering the challenge of transition to the world of letters.[16]

The introduction of reading and writing into a culture brings with it enormous changes.[17] With specific reference to ancient Greece, but with cultures worldwide in mind, Jack Goody and Ian Watt argue that the ramifications of such an introduction are many and radical:

> The writing down of the main elements in the cultural tradition . . . brought about an awareness of two things: of the past as different from the present; and of the inherent inconsistencies in the picture of life as it was inherited by the individual from the cultural tradition in its recorded form. These two effects . . . have continued and multiplied themselves ever since. . . .[18]

Many African slaves in the New World seemed eager early on to learn to read and write in the language of those who had enslaved them. Janet Cornelius notes a number of different reasons for such eagerness: survival—negotiating day to day challenges and experiences in the dominant white world of literacy; reinforcement of self-worth—attaining the power that reading opened up to relate to oneself and others on a different plane of consciousness; and attainment of a liberating religious consciousness—creation of an affirming religious language and religious world that was the impetus for the founding of separate religious institutions.[19]

Cornelius, however, does not go far enough in problematizing the matter of the engagement of the letters that were the Bible. The Africans' early engagement of the Bible was aggressive and passionate, creative and playful, not merely utilitarian or strategic, certainly far beyond or different from what the actual socio-economic situation seemed to warrant. Even in situations where it is clear that literacy in general for the sake of negotiating the white world was not so important, the Bible nevertheless was important. How do we account for this phenomenon? How do we explain how a people proverbially referred to as oral, "preliterate," came to adore and invest so much in the book that is the Bible?

AFRICAN AMERICANS AND THE BIBLE:
A MEETING OF WORLDS

I want to suggest that the sustained and passionate African American engagement of the Bible can best be explained by positing a meeting of "worlds," of similar ways of viewing the world and the self in the word. In effect, the Bible contained dramatic stories of underdogs surviving and conquering, of slaves and homeless, of wandering peoples and their exploits, of a Savior figure who is humiliated and oppressed but conquers, of followers of such a figure who are marginal and stigmatized—a book with such stories had enormous appeal. So much of the Bible was written from the perspective of—thus, in solidarity with—the humiliated and oppressed that it was not at all surprising that African slaves would readily identify with it, even come to see it as their own.

The sources for the earliest African American "reading" of the Bible suggest that in the stories of the Bible African Americans recognized not only descriptions of worldly (social, economic, political) situations that appeared similar to their own, but also similar critical attitudes toward such situations and toward the "world" (the dominant, oppressive forces). The perception of the similarity between the situation and attitude of heroic figures of the Bible and the situation and attitude of the African in the New World is a better explanation for the initial impetus behind the African American "dance" and play with the Bible than any other explanation so far advanced. In essence, the argument is that there was in the African American embracing of the Bible a meeting of worlds—the world of the oppressed African in the New World and the world of the oppressed in biblical stories. Little that white slaveholders said or did— whether by way of encouragement toward a conservative, status quo "reading" of the Bible, active discouragement of the more radical identification of African slaves with the humiliated of the Bible, or total discouragement from reading of any type—prevented the African encounter with the Bible.

Just as it must now be recognized that the African slaves did not so much "convert" to "Christianity" but rather converted Christianity to themselves, so it must be recognized (as a particular reflection of this larger phenomemon and springboard for further research) that the Bible was more than just a simple deleterious socializing (Christianizing) agent. As is the case with most symbols, the Bible as language world is complex: it can "mean" different things to different peoples in different situations. Thus, it came to mean something quite different among Black peoples in the United States. This different meaning, it is important to stress, concerns more than just a different understanding about certain books of or passages within the Bible or a particular hermeneutic in and of itself; it has to do with a consistently different worldview and ethos that the Bible is assumed to reveal and with which African Americans identify.

That a hermeneutical stance or theory is implicit in this identification and engagement is clear enough, but no explication of the hermeneutical implications in question will capture all that is implied in the claims about the African American relationship to the Bible. Ultimately, only something approaching a fusion of "worlds" can explain the phenomenon of the African American engagement with the Bible. "Fusion" here suggests a shared stance from which all things that matter are viewed. Critical here are the meaning of "stance" and agreement about the "things that matter." With all of their shortcomings and the questions they raise, Clifford Geertz's notions about "ethos" and "worldview" probably best describe what I intend in referring to "stance" and "things that matter most."

The Bible was transformed by African Americans into a language world into which they could enter freely and in any manner they desired—a language world with(in) which they were able to manipulate received (or forced) tradition and construct an affirming culture; come to speech about themselves; raise a critical voice about their world and the world that scorned them; define themselves as those who, much like the biblical characters, are "hard pressed" but nevertheless destined for release and victory. Thus, in the world they must, like the protagonist individuals and communities of the Bible, persevere when under siege and, when possible, wage battle against foes. This was the existential stance or point of view from which African Americans developed their culturalist engagement of the Bible.

CONCLUDING COMMENTS

This essay represents only an attempt to raise the question about the usefulness of considering the identification of "worlds"—the similarity in social location between biblical characters and African slaves—as the psychic and phenomenological impetus for the original African-initiated play with the Bible. It is, I think, a useful springboard for further studies, not only in the origins, construction, and development of African American religious consciousness, but also in the cultural reception of sacred texts.

It is also a challenge to the tendency in most contemporary biblical interpretation to still begin with and retain focus upon the text (or historical event or person) as opposed to (contemporary) society. The African American history of engagement with the Bible points to the methodological complexity and fecundity present, not only in reading worlds as texts and texts as worlds, but also in exploring how the different worlds presented in texts and in a society interact. The focus upon African Americans almost forces the issue of the appropriateness, if not the need, for a shift in the focus of interpretation from text to society. As much as any one people could be so considered, African Americans represent a modern-day "biblical formation."[20] To study them is to study the Bible and its effects. To study the Bible in the modern-day United States is to study what such a people have done with the Bible; what they have said about themselves, their world, and others through the Bible; what they have done in light of and because of—and sometimes in spite of—the Bible, with its profound and dramatic mix of good and bad effects.

In such notions there are, to put it mildly, enormous curricular implications for religious and theological studies. The place to begin in historical-interpretive studies, I would argue, is with the decentering of the text and a focus upon social formations in their scripturalizing[21] features.

NOTES

1. N. Q. King, *African Cosmos: An Introduction to Religion in Africa* (Belmont, CA: Wadsworth Publishing Company, 1986) 112-13.

2. See N. O. Hatch and M. A. Noll, eds., *The Bible in America: Essays in Cultural History* (New York: Oxford University Press, 1982); and A. S. Phy, ed., *The Bible and Popular Culture in America* (Philadelphia: Fortress Press; Chico, CA: Scholars Press, 1985).

3. M. Marty, *Religion and Republic: The American Circumstance* (Boston: Beacon Press, 1987) chap. 7.

4. For the early period, see D. G. Mathews, *Religion in the Old South* (Chicago: University of Chicago Press, 1977) chap. 4.

5. See S. D. Gill, "Nonliterate Traditions and Holy Books: Toward a New Model," *Holy Books in Comparative Perspective,* ed. Rodney Taylor and W. Denny (Columbia, SC: University of South Carolina Press, 1985) 226-27.

6. See J. D. Cornelius, *"When I Can Read My Title Clear": Literacy, Slavery, and Religion in the Antebellum South* (Columbia, SC: University of South Carolina Press, 1991) chap. 4.

7. See J. C. Scott (*Domination and the Arts of Resistance* [New Haven: Yale University Press, 1990] chaps. 1, 8) for a crosscultural discussion of the concept of "hidden transcript" as a strategic reason and weapon among the humiliated.

8. Gill, "Nonliterate Traditions and Holy Books," 224-25.

9. Ibid., 225.

10. Ibid.

11. Ibid., 226.

12. Ibid., 228.

13. See Harold W. Turner, *Religious Innovations in Africa* (Boston: G. K. Hall, 1979) chap. 23.

14. R. Isaac, "Books and Social Authority of Learning: The Case of Mid-Eighteenth Century Virginia," *Printing and Society in America,* ed. W. L. Joyce, D. D. Hall, R. D. Brown, et al. (Worcester, MA: American Antiquarian Society, 1983) 230.

15. Ibid., 230-31.

16. J. Goody and I. Watt, "The Consequences of Literacy," *Literacy in Traditional Societies,* ed. J. Goody (Cambridge: Cambridge University Press, 1968) 53.

17. See Walter J. Ong, *Orality and Literacy: The Technologizing of the World* (London and New York: Methuen, 1982) chap. 4.

18. Goody and Watt, "The Consequences of Literacy," 56.

19. Cornelius, *"When I Can Read My Title Clear,"* 2-3.

20. This expression comes from T. H. Smith, *Conjuring Culture: Biblical Formations of Black America* (New York: Oxford University Press, 1994).

21. See W. C. Smith (*What Is Scripture? A Comparative Approach* [Minneapolis: Fortress Press, 1993]) for elaboration upon the concept and for providing provocative challenges for biblical scholarship.

Part III

SOCIAL LOCATION
AND BIBLICAL PEDAGOGY
IN GLOBAL PERSPECTIVE

II

A READING OF THE STORY OF THE TOWER OF BABEL FROM THE PERSPECTIVE OF NON-IDENTITY

Genesis 11:1-9 in the Context of Its Production

J. Severino Croatto

It is still customary to use the Bible as a deposit of "holy" words. In catechesis and theology as well as in liturgy and preaching, people tend to use isolated texts, words taken out of their literary contexts and interpreted according to the Christian tradition. In this study I argue for a different approach to and use of the Bible altogether, an approach that, in turn, bears immediate ramifications for the way in which biblical studies are conducted. Using the story of the Tower of Babel as an example, I shall engage in an exegetical and hermeneutical exercise that not only takes the *whole* text into account, both with regard to itself (Gen 11:1-9) and its literary context in Genesis and the Pentateuch, but also carries out a sociopolitical analysis of the text through an examination of its original context of production.[1] I turn to the episode of the Tower of Babel in particular, because I see it as one of the most highly distorted by traditional readings. Somehow, therefore, it is imperative to start anew and, in so doing, to recover a powerful message of hope and trust in the God who walks with the oppressed.

INTRODUCTION

This strange story from the Book of Genesis has always aroused a great deal of interest, as the history of exegesis, the history of art, and the history of literature clearly attest. In our own day, however, this narrative has been resurrected

---

This is a translation by Fernando F. Segovia of the Spanish original, "El relato de la Torre de Babel, leído desde la no-identidad (Génesis 11:1-9 en el contexto de su producción)."

in a much more fruitful way, through new rereadings from the point of view of situations of oppression, especially cultural oppression. Such rereadings point to the fact that the use of this story in theology, in catechesis, as well as in Christian reflection in general must undergo a radical change.

Three stages in the history of the interpretation of this passage can be readily distinguished:

• To begin with, over the centuries the text has been and indeed continues to be explained as an etiology for the multiplicity of peoples and languages in the world. This type of reading can be found even in the most recent scientific commentaries. Such multiplicity, moreover, is generally presented in terms of "punishment," contrary to what is said in Genesis 10.

• More recently, there have been efforts within the Third World to invert the way in which this story has been read, with diversity of peoples and languages in the world now seen as a blessing for the oppressed. From this point of view, unity of language constitutes the essential instrument for domination wielded by any imperial project.

• Further, the concentration of all humanity into a political and economic center (the city) is seen as yet another indispensable element of imperial praxis. Cultural reality, however, presupposes diversity—whether ethnic, linguistic, or semiotic. The history of the European colonization of the new lands is replete with stories pointing to the suppression of regional or local languages as well as the abrogation of the natural boundaries of the different ethnic groups in favor of borders imposed by the dominant nations. From this perspective, the Tower of Babel story emerges as a demand for the freedom of cultures, in their twofold ethnic and linguistic dimensions.

I am of the opinion, however, that it is possible to go beyond such an interpretation of the story and to recover its original meaning within its own context of production, which is none other than that of the Judeans in exile. Let me begin with a negative formulation of this proposed meaning: (1) Gen 11:1-9 has nothing to do with the multiplication of languages; (2) Gen 11:1-9 has nothing to do as well with the creation of the different peoples of the world. These two negations imply, to be sure, a number of corresponding affirmations, which the analysis of the text will make known in due time. Indeed, what the text has to say is of enormous kerygmatic significance. Something taxative is being proposed by means of a divine action against a project of imperial domination. It will be seen as well that the story advances, with enormous irony, a foundation myth in opposition to the Mesopotamian tradition regarding the founding of Babylon.

For the exiles, as well as for all those who find themselves oppressed by any empire, this text is bound to produce a profound emotional impact, which in turn will give rise to the hope for a radical change in history. With these introductory comments behind us, I proceed to an analysis of the text.

OVERVIEW OF THE TEXT

From a narrative point of view, the episode that has come to be known by the title of "The Tower of Babel" forms part of the fourth period of the history of the world, that of the sons of Noah (Gen 10:1-11:9), the first block of which contains a "genealogical" register of its various divisions (10:1-32). This register describes, emphatically (vv. 5, 20, 31-32), the separation of the sons of Noah into clans and languages on the one hand, and peoples and lands on the other. Many are the questions that arise out of this rather brief passage. The text itself proceeds as follows:[2]

> (11:1) The whole earth had but one tongue and one language. (11:2) It so happened that, as they migrated from the east, they came upon a plain in the land of Šin'ar, and there they settled. (11:3) Then, they said to one another, "Come, let us build bricks and bake them at the fire." They used the bricks for stones and the pitch for mortar. (11:4) Then, they said, "Come, let us build ourselves a city and a tower with its top in the heavens, and let us make thus a name for ourselves, so that we do not disperse over the face of the whole earth." (11:5) Yahweh came down to see the city and the tower that human beings had built. (11:6) Yahweh said, "Look, one people and one tongue for all, and this is but the beginning of their doings! Now, it will be impossible to prevent them from doing whatever they wish to do!" (11:7) "Come, let us go down and there confuse their tongue, in such a way that no one can understand what the other is saying." (11:8) And from there Yahweh dispersed them over the face of the whole earth. And they ceased building the city. (11:9) Therefore, he called it "Babel," because it was there that Yahweh confused the language of all the earth and from there that Yahweh dispersed them over the face of the whole earth.

Brief as it is, this text has been carefully put together, making use especially of stylistic, phonetic, and lexical features to highlight certain ideas. Nothing is wasted. In my own translation above I have attempted to reproduce the original as closely as possible. Quite aside from the question of whether one finds in the text two traditions that have been superimposed, or different readings of an original text, the repetitions should be seen not as reflecting a dearth of literary artistry but rather as making possible the existing play of language.

Such a brief text readily lends itself to an exercise in successive readings, each focusing on a different structural or literary element of the text. For example, one can point to the recurrence of the lexeme "there" (*šam*), which clearly represents a play of words with the substantive "name" (*šem*), essential for the reconstruction of the original meaning. The particle *šam* (there) is not purely literary in character—indeed, it could have been omitted in a number of places—but produces, in combination with *šem* (name), a resounding meaning-effect: in that place where the city is being built, there is a quest for fame and renown, but the only thing that shall endure is its name, which means "confusion." Likewise, one can point to the opposition between unity and diversity, focused on the motif of language. A contrast is highlighted thereby between two projects (no dispersion/dispersion) and the role played by language in each case. The confusion of language is opposed to concentration and unification. Further, vv. 1 and 9 underline the motif of language, which in itself forms part of a literary inclusion grounded in the lexeme "earth." The same sort of connections could be shown with regard to a number of other terms, as I shall do in part in the detailed analysis to follow. In the end, such a close reading of the text in terms of superimposed layers makes it possible to grasp both its literary framework and the depth of "what is said."

From another point of view, also literary but on the narrative level, one can discern as well the transformation performed on the initial "status of the subject." The action of the narrative begins with v. 2, as if in accord with the action of the human beings themselves. As I shall argue below, vv. 1 and 2 should be read together, despite the fact that they constitute separate units of possibly different origins. The human project begins with v. 3 and is expressed in the form of direct discourse. The duplication of such discourse—in vv. 3 and 4, in both cases with the expression "they said" highlighted by its placement at the beginning—makes it possible to distinguish two different aspects of the project. V. 5 signals a heightening of the action, with the narrator now introducing Yahweh as both actant (semiotic) and actor (literary). One suspects that such an appearance on the part of Yahweh marks a key moment in the story, creating in turn enormous suspense on the part of the reader: What will happen now? Yahweh's project—or, rather, anti-project—is also revealed by way of direct discourse in v. 7, as extensive as those of v. 5 and v. 6 combined. Between what Yahweh "sees" human beings as having done (v. 5) and what he himself decides to do (v. 7), one finds divine suspicion expressed regarding "human infinity" (v. 6). The very fact that such suspicion forms part of Yahweh's discourse proves quite significant. This is clearly a moment of enormous expectations, given the fact that a dénouement is announced. Such a dénouement is subsequently described by the narrator (v. 8). Once all this information has been given, the actions (or transformations, at the semiotic level) come to an end. V. 9—a verse whose absence would not be missed at all in the light of the two projects in question—functions as a necessary conclusion to the narrative as a whole, especially in terms of its character as "myth": the verse deals with the founding of Babylon, and it is important to read it as a counter-*Enuma Elish*.

The preceding introductory overview of the passage makes it possible to distinguish six brief sequential units in all:

1. Unity of Language and Habitat (vv. 1-2)

2. The Economic and Political Project (vv. 3-4)

3. Yahweh's Appearance (v. 5)

4. Yahweh's Anti-project (v. 6-7)

5. Dispersion (v. 8)

6. The Name of Babylon (v. 9)

DETAILED ANALYSIS OF THE TEXT

First Unit: Unity of Language and Habitat

(11:1) The whole earth had but one tongue and one language. (11:2) It so happened that, as they migrated from the east, they came upon a plain in the land of *Šin'ar*, and there they settled.[3]

The expression "the whole earth" at the beginning is a literary exaggeration: it is not the planet as a whole that is meant, only its inhabited area. Such a "logical" reading must give way, however, to a reading that is much more attentive to the symbolic level. The story commences by calling attention to a totality. There must be a reason for this. "The whole earth" has to do with the exclusivity of the one tongue. Why?

The actions begin in v. 2. Of the three verbs in question (migrated/came upon/settled), the last is clearly the most important, letting it be known that the migrants "from the east" did not simply traverse but actually settled on the plain that they had come upon. Moreover, the information concludes with a "there" that marks the place of settlement. Thus, v. 2 functions completely on the spatial level (seven words out of nine in Hebrew!), just as v. 1 does on the linguistic level. The plot begins to unfold.

The subject of the verbs is a general "they," which cannot be taken to refer to the descendants of Noah in chap. 10 on two grounds: first, it is impossible from a syntactical point of view; second, it does not make sense from a geographical point of view. The story thus resembles the trunk of a narrative sequence now lost. Indeed, it is better to acknowledge that the episode comes from a different literary context than that of 10:1-32, from which it can be differentiated above all in terms of what it has to say with regard to the origins of Babylon (see 10:10a). Given the importance of Babylon in exilic times (and, from a symbolical point of view, in postexilic times as well), one can understand the redactional presence of two foundational stories, since there is so much to be said about Babylon. Therefore, at this stage in the construction of the text, it is not necessary to determine who the "they" in question are but rather what it is that they do. In an indirect way, of course, the term does refer to the inhabitants of "the whole earth" in v. 1.

The expression "the land of *Šin'ar*" is not beyond resolution. It has already been mentioned in 10:10b, where it encompasses a number of famous cities, comprising an area equivalent to that of ancient "Sumer and Akkad," which would later become the territory of the Babylonian Empire. In fact, 10:11 distinguishes the area in question from the region to the north, where the Assyrian cities were to be found. While one could argue about the etymology of the term, one thing is clear: its correspondence to the *Šanhara* of the Hittite glyptics and the *Š-n-ğ-r* of the scarabs of Tutmosis III and Amenophis III, which designate Babylon without exception. A question does remain, however: why has the author employed such a rare term instead of the more common "Babylon"? The answer will be found within the story itself.

With vv. 1-2, then, the introduction needed by the narrator has been provided; the key developments will be narrated beginning with v. 3.

Second Unit: The Economic and Political Project

(11:3) Then, they said to one another, "Come, let us build bricks and bake them at the fire." They used the bricks for stones and the pitch for mortar. (11:4) Then, they said, "Come, let us build ourselves a city and a tower with its top in the heavens, and let us make thus a name for ourselves, so that we do not disperse over the face of the whole earth."[4]

The unit begins with the first instance of direct discourse, with the same "they" of v. 2 as subject. This discourse is in the form of dialogue. This is important, for it shows that humans do understand one another and thus can work together on a common project. The idea that comes immediately to the fore is economic in character: building *baked* bricks (there are unbaked bricks as well).

The story presupposes that the project was adopted by consensus and that it has been carried out. In fact, v. 3b simply records its execution, although from the point of view of an alien cultural horizon. In effect, in Canaan or Israel construction took place with stones and mortar (our "cement"), but in Mesopotamia, where stone is as scarce as wood, walls were made out of bricks, baked or unbaked, depending on the circumstances. To be sure, no one makes bricks with anything but construction in mind. Likewise, there is no talk of bricks or stones, pitch or mortar, except within the context of construction. Why does the text not say so? In the first place, to highlight what is being said and to leave for a later time the objective behind the construction in question. In the second place, and above all, to underline the importance of one language for communication as well as for the efficacy of the project. Within the story itself, which began with the theme of language, this is felt to be most relevant.

The second instance of direct discourse (v. 4) on the part of the "they"—who still remain unidentified—begins with the same exhortative interjection, "Come!" and a further verb of volition in the first person plural, like the two verbs of v. 3. The immediate objective is twofold: to build both a city and a very high tower. There is no question here of a "first time": mention has already been made in 4:17 of the first builder of a city, and there is a reference in 10:11-13—within the redaction of the present text—to Asur as the builder of four important cities. Quite simply, the theme is that of construction, already emphasized in v. 3—not the construction of houses for individuals, but rather the construction of a city and a tower.

The tower surely refers to the ziggurats, a common feature of the great cities of Babylon. Both cities and towers—one should note—have as their main referent the Gods (especially the tutelary God of the city) as well as the king. The term refers above all to the fortified sector of the city, the acropolis, where both the king and the administrative and religious apparatus of the city resided. The common people lived in the open city, protected only by the city walls.

There is no need to pursue the etymology of the word "tower" (*migdal*, from *gadôl*, "big"/"strong"), only the description offered by the text (the denotative level): the tower reaches the heavens (v. 4a). Is this simply a metaphor? It could very well be, and that in and of itself would be highly significant. The heavens represent, in effect, the abode of the Gods. One should think here not in terms of an assault upon the heavens, as a number of rabbinic texts proceed to interpret the passage, but rather as a "translation" by the text of the meaning behind the ziggurats, as revealed through their various names. Thus, for example, the ziggurat of Larsa was called *é-dur-an-ki* or "house of the union of heaven and earth," while that of Babylon itself was called *é-temen-an-ki* or "house of the foundation of heaven and earth." The ziggurat, therefore, stood for a mountain, which in turn represented, via its symbolic value of height, the abode of the Gods. Thus, every temple was looked upon as a mountain. In addition, archaeological as well as textual evidence clearly point to the enormous dimensions of these structures.

The motif of building a city and a tower reveals the ability of humans "to do things," functions as a source of pride, and grants as a result a sense of security. That is why the prophets speak of a tower (*migdal*) as a symbol of strength and pride (Isa 2:15 ["against every high tower, and against every fortified wall"]; 25:2-3; 30:25 ["on a day of the great slaughter, when the towers fall"]).

The rivalry between Yahweh and the Mesopotamian Gods is clearly established in Ps 78:69, following a reference to the mountain of Zion (v. 68b): "He built his sanctuary like the high heavens, like the earth, which he has founded forever." This is language typical of foundation myths of sanctuaries. In a similar vein, Canaanite cities are also described as "large and fortified up to heaven" (Deut 1:28), a comment placed on the lips of the Israelite scouts but repeated by Yahweh himself (Deut 9:1). If the sight of such cities had amazed the Israelites, one can easily imagine how the great fortifications and above all the great towers of the Mesopotamian plains would have impressed the exiles. The following description from the Book of Jeremiah, part of the great final oracle against that "enemy" city, no doubt conveys a good sense of what Babylon must have looked like: "Though Babylon should mount up to heaven, and though she should fortify her strong height, from me destroyers would come upon her, says the LORD" (51:53). The oracle seems like a response to the project of Gen 11:4.

A second objective signaled by v. 4 is directly dependent upon the first and is thus far more important in the story: through these two construction projects, the "they" wish to make a name for themselves. Within the story itself, the proposed projects have no defensive aim in mind; they serve rather as a manifestation of technical and cultural prowess, with obvious implications for the political and economic arena. The text focuses, therefore, on the ideological level—the creation of fame or renown by means of the feat accomplished. From the production of city and tower, therefore, the text shifts to the production of a name. This is a curious association of ideas. From this point on, moreover, the verb "to make" (*'aśah*) will function as a structuring lexeme for the remainder of the story. It was not previously employed with respect to the two projects of building bricks and building a tower and a city. Clearly, therefore, the making of a name for themselves is specifically highlighted thereby. Indeed, fame or renown as a result of great works of architecture constitutes a frequent motif in cuneiform and biblical texts, something to keep in mind for the interpretation of the story as a whole.

The "production" of the desired name will take place in two ways. First, through the very presence of the construction projects themselves, supposedly of lasting character. The accomplished feat results in fame—the production of a name. That, however, is not sufficient in and of itself, as the texts themselves show. Consequently, the identity of the builder is further and explicitly recorded, whether on the bricks, a stele, or even the foundation brick/stone. The present text, however, makes no mention of this latter mode of production of a name; it simply refers to the two projects in question, in itself a significant point.

V. 4b adds a sense of unexpected finality, hard to deduce from what precedes: "so that we do not disperse over the face of the whole earth." Something remains "unsaid" but is implied nonetheless. To begin with, the expression lets it be known that the dispersion is not at all wanted. To be sure, such a fixation on place should not be confronted with Yahweh's command to "be fruitful and multiply, and fill the earth" (Gen 9:1, 7). While such a reading may be present, it represents by no means the driving force behind a story of this sort. In fact, such a reading points to a different sort of message altogether, far more significant and relevant, as I shall point out below.

The dispersion is opposed to settling in one place, with the city as its center. The latter further symbolizes the concentration of power. Moreover, given what has already been established in v. 1, unity of language points to the feasibility of the works themselves (which presupposes a centralized organization) as well as the possibility of total and effective communication. From now on it is assumed that unity of language, essential for centralized power, is a benefit that must not be lost. No project would be feasible without normal communication by means of language. From a narrative point of view, that is, from the point of view of the composition of the story, the reference to v. 1 at this point is crucial, insofar as the latter introduces a key theme from the very beginning. It is the one language that makes possible the project of building a city and a tower (v. 3) as well as its execution (v. 4). It is this construction, moreover, that "produces" a name, fame or renown, insofar as it constitutes a great feat.

At the same time, the name acquired as a result of these great works of architecture (and others beyond these) functions as a cohesive force against dispersion—an ideological theme that functions as a narrative axe. Thus, the strength of the city is not only economic, political, cultural, and religious (everything is concentrated in it), but also ideological and, as such, appealing.

The "name" binds together, possesses a centripetal power. Such is the importance of the city in the historical experience of this time.

With v. 4 what the story has to say about human beings comes to an end; from now on, it is Yahweh who emerges as protagonist.

Third Unit: Yahweh's Appearance

(11:5) Yahweh came down to see the city and the tower that human beings had built.[5]

With this sentence the plot of the story reaches a decisive heightening. There is a sudden change in both setting and actors. The reader, as spectator, must shift accordingly and now witness the appearance of a new character.

To be sure, there is an ironic dimension to Yahweh's "descent," further sharpened by the motive in question, namely, his desire "to come down and see" the work of human beings. In effect, if the tower was supposed to reach up to the heavens, there would have been no need for Yahweh "to come down." As it is, he must displace himself so as to reach what lies far away. This giant project is thus at a good distance from Yahweh. There can be little doubt that irony is very much intended here.

V. 5b clearly records the fact of construction, an important element for understanding the story. The use of the perfect tense (*banû*) indicates a finished action. Therefore, it should not be translated as "they were building." The verse also manages to record in an indirect way the execution of the project mentioned in v. 4, a common feature of Hebrew narrative (cf., for example, Gen 1:26-27, where mention of the project is similarly followed by mention of its execution). In the light of such silence, one expects Yahweh himself to confirm the execution of the project on the basis of his own inspection.

One further element emphasized by the text, given its position at the end, is the subject behind the construction of city and tower—human beings (literally, "the sons of the human being"). The difference between the world of God and the world of human beings is affirmed thereby, so that the construction of the city and the tower that reaches up to the heavens is made to look as an act of impudence or excess on their part.

Fourth Unit: Yahweh's Anti-project

(11:6) Yahweh said, "Look, one people and one tongue for all, and this is but the beginning of their doings! Now, it will be impossible to prevent them from doing whatever they wish to do!" (11:7) "Come, let us go down and there confuse their tongue, in such a way that no one can understand what the other is saying."[6]

Yahweh's direct discourse begins with what seems at first sight a strange observation: does not Yahweh know what was said in v. 1 with respect to the "one tongue"? Indeed, the same expression is employed. Yet, it is not quite the same. In the first place, the observation no longer points to an original situation but rather to the consequences of such a situation. Yahweh "deduces" the unity of language after coming down to see the recently built city and tower (v. 5). In the process, the role of language is affirmed as an essential means of communication for any human enterprise. In the second place, the observation does record for the first time the unity of the group, defined as a people ('am). To be sure, the relationship between ethnicity and language constitutes a fundamental anthropological fact.

The word 'am does not appear in the classification of 10:5, 20, 31, 32 (clans/tongues/lands/nations), perhaps because of the different origins of the text in question. From this point of view, there is nothing particular about its use here. Still, everything that a text has to say contributes to its meaning. In this case the very novelty of the lexeme proves significant. Thus, for example, it is important to take note here of the relationship established between "people" and "tongue" and of its manifestation in social praxis. The Hebrew term conveys the sense of an intimate relationship, a relationship involving origins or kinship, a relationship among members of the group. This 'am, however, is impossible without unity of language, which makes for social and cultural identity. In addition, the combination of linguistic unity and "physical" unity make possible the accomplishment of extraordinary feats, such as that observed by Yahweh (v. 5b).

Up to this point, Yahweh speaks of what he has seen upon coming down from the heavens (v. 5), all of which could have been deduced from the story itself. The same phenomenon, with the same beginning particle, may be observed in Gen 3:22 (also J), as Yahweh proceeds to confirm what the narrative itself has already announced (3:5): "See, the man has become like one of us. . . ." In both cases, the confirmation of an act of human "excess" or hubris leads Yahweh to suspect further actions of a far more serious nature, whether it be the tasting of the fruit from the tree of life (in order to secure immortality) in Genesis 3, or something unspecified but presented in the gravest of terms and with a great deal of consternation, as is the case here in Genesis 11. In effect, the declaration, "and this is but the beginning of their doings," portrays what has already been accomplished as but a first step, rather than a final step calling for judgment. It is what could follow, therefore, that concerns Yahweh, insofar as he could lose control of the situation, as the second declaration makes perfectly clear: "Now, it will be impossible to prevent them from doing whatever they wish to do!" (v. 6b).

From the point of view of phraseology, the linguistic as well as conceptual parallel with Job 42:2 has often been noted (the only parallel), and it is worth recalling here. As the conclusion of the drama begins to draw near (with v. 6 the poetic text, the original poem, comes to an end), once Yahweh has revealed his greatness and power, Job responds with these words, so close to those of our text: "I know that you can do all things, and that no purpose of yours can be thwarted (w^{e}lo'- yibbaser mimm ka m^{e}zimmah)." While the idiomatic expression lo'- yibbaser mehem . . . yaz^{e}mû of Gen 11:6b is identical to that of Job 42:2, the equivalence in contexts is even more significant. In the light of his own experience, Job attributes to Yahweh unlimited power with regard to what Yahweh can do or intends to do (*zaman*). In Genesis 11, however, it is Yahweh himself who observes, having seen the construction of the city and the tower, that human beings are capable of carrying out whatever project they may conceive. In other words, human beings are capable of being "like God." They have already shown that such is the case (as in 3:22a, omniscience) and will in due time achieve their objective (as in 3:22b, acquisition of immortality). One can readily understand, therefore, Yahweh's profound consternation as well as Yahweh's choice of words, which in the Hebrew come across as slow, measured, worrisome.

What is it however that Yahweh actually fears that human beings will do? There is no mention of this in the text. The implication is that it will be something open-ended and without limits—simply, "doings." One should recall in this regard that the construction of the city and tower, described in technical terms both within the reference to the project as such (v. 3b) and to its execution (v. 5b), is interpreted as a "doing" within Yahweh's discourse. In other words, there will be a correspondence between what has already been done and what will be done in the future—"and this is but the beginning of their doings (*la'aśôt*)! Now, it will be impossible to prevent them from doing whatever they wish to do (*la'aśôt*)."

Could this be an example of the literary and theological motif of the envy of the Gods, as in Greek tragedy? What exactly is Yahweh afraid of? Gen 3:22 makes it clear that human beings must not attain immortality. In Gen 11:6b, however, the nature of this improper (rather than dangerous) project is not made explicit. A text as well put together as this one, so lean in its formulation, "knows" very well what it is that it wishes to say. Besides, the open-ended "doings" of v. 6b is quite suggestive, conveying all sorts of connotations. Such a "doing" has to be an infinite "doing." What amounted to omniscience and immortality in 3:22 now becomes omnipotence, the infinity of power—that which Job attributed to Yahweh alone. Yahweh's discourse thus prophesies endless acts of human "excess." As a result, something must be done to prevent this from happening, just as in 3:23-24 a way was found to keep human beings from having access to the tree of life. The decision taken by Yahweh is important and is formulated in terms of a self-exhortation: "Come, let us go down and there confuse their tongue" (v. 7a).

There is no need to discuss here whether the repetition of Yahweh's "descent," presented as a past event in v. 5a and as a future event in v. 7a, points to two different sources. It is rather a question of literary emphasis and common sense. God dwells "above" and, when he speaks, he does so from "above." There is no mention in the text that Yahweh, once having come down to "have a look," stayed around below for his various declarations and decisions. The matter is as simple as that. What is new in Yahweh's discourse is what he proposes to do in order to prevent the infinite "doings" of human beings. His decision, in effect, is nothing less than to confuse their language. For the third time, therefore, the theme of one tongue comes to the fore (vv. 1a, 6a), a key semantic axis in the story. For the redactor, this divine decision

points to the fundamental importance of language for every human "doing."
In other words, nothing can be achieved without mutual understanding by
way of language (v. 7b). As such, Yahweh's strategy proves most ingenious for
the undoing of any human project of great pretensions.

What has just been affirmed has a bearing on the story. The point is not to
suppress language, a decision that would render every human project impossible. Thus far, the text has spoken of only one great project—a project that
bears all the characteristics of unlimited power and that has been rendered
possible by both the concentration of all human beings in one place (presup-
posing the cooperation of all) and the use of the same language for communication, from the planning stages of the project (v. 4) through its execution (vv.
5b, 6a). It is precisely this sort of pretention to "divinity," to the exercise of
total power, that Yahweh wishes to undo through the confusion of language,
making any sort of mutual understanding for action impossible. As such, the
confusion of language is but a means to an end, which end becomes in turn the
essential point of the story.

From the point of view of intertextuality, one should note—especially since
it involves the same horizon of redactional production—the terminology
employed in Jer 51:11-12, part of an oracle against Babylon: ". . . his purpose
($m^ezimmatô$) concerning Babylon is to destroy it . . . for the Lord has both
planned ($zaman$) and done ($'aśah$) what he spoke concerning the inhabitants
($yoś^ebê$) of Babylon." The lexical and situational equivalencies as well as the
oppositions of agent subject and results are remarkable and point to a similar
horizon of concerns, arising no doubt from the actual experience of the historical Babylon on the part of the exiles.

From the point of view of the literary formulation of the divine decision,
three phraseological details should be noted, each of which resumes a previous
equivalence:

1. The second part of Yahweh's discourse (the anti-project, v. 7) begins with
the same formula used at the beginning of the human beings' second discourse: the exhortation, "Come!" followed by two verbs in the first person
plural:

"Come, let us build . . . let us make . . ." (v. 4a).

"Come, let us go down and confuse . . ." (v. 7a).

The linguistic equivalence becomes thereby an opposition in projects.

2. Literary analysis has noted the inverted assonance (phonetic chiasm) present between the $l^ebenîm$ (bricks) of the human project (v. 3a) and the nab^elah
(let us confuse) of the divine anti-project (v. 4).

3. The expression "one another" of v. 3a (the first occurrence of language
within the story itself) is repeated at the end of v. 7, within Yahweh's direct discourse, where it signifies the communicational non-occurrence of language.

One should note as well, as a point of perhaps secondary importance, the inverted sequence of the following elements: reciprocity of language/self-exhortation of humans (v. 3a) // self-exhortation of Yahweh (with the given assonance)/non-reciprocity of language (v. 7). Thus, just as one language serves to bring about a heroic project (v. 3a), so will the undoing of such a project come about as a result of a failure to communicate linguistically (v. 7).

In the end, this network of linguistic signifiers and signifieds points once again to the importance of communication by means of language, in the referential "event" of the text as much as in the text itself as present reality.

Fifth Unit: Dispersion

(11:8) And from there Yahweh dispersed them over the face of the whole earth. And they ceased building the city.[7]

One would expect, as is generally understood, the dispersion to be the direct result of the confusion in language, but that is not the case. Rather, it is Yahweh himself who is responsible for the dispersion. This point modifies the entire framework of the story.

In the first place, the execution of the divine decision of v. 7 is not narrated. One should recall in this regard that the execution of the project of v. 4, presupposed in v. 5, was not narrated either. Could the same situation apply here, so that the beginning of v. 8 presupposes the confusion of language? So it would seem. However, the meaning of the passage would then be altered: dispersion, carried out by means of the confusion in language, would no longer be the divine objective. Rather, the primary objective would then be to render impossible any great projects in the future, whether with regard to the building of cities and towers or anything else. All such projects require centralization through the power of one language. The text could have very well ended at this point.

V. 8, however, records a new and different intervention on the part of Yahweh, namely, the dispersion of human beings over the whole earth. This verse resumes and develops a theme parallel to that of language, the establishment of a fixed place, the "there" of vv. 2b and 7a: "from there" Yahweh scatters them in every direction (v. 8a). This is the spatial level, introduced in v. 2. The narrative is "woven" together thereby with the three semantic threads of language, space, and construction. The spatial motif, with the goal of the great human project as its climax (see v. 4b: "so that we do not disperse over the face of the whole earth"), now finds its anticlimax in v. 8. The failure of the human project as a whole is now placed in evidence. All that was proposed, all the effort involved, lies there as a symbol of frustration. While the text makes no mention of such frustration, it does form part of its metamessage, of its irony.

Everything is fine up to this point. With v. 8b, however, it seems as if the coherence of the story breaks down. Was it not the case, according to v. 5b, that humans "had built" the city and the tower? How can the text now say that they ceased building the city (no mention is made of the tower)? There are two ways to understand this observation:

First, the phrase could be read as a textual gloss, added by someone who failed to grasp the plot of the story. Two linguistic details should be noted: the accusative particle, not essential but common, is missing; there is no reference to the tower. According to this interpretation, v. 8b is superfluous and interrupts the sequence of thought of the original story.

Second, if the phrase does form part of the original text, it could be taken to mean that human beings "did not go on building the city." In effect, the construction of a city is a never-ending project, though not so the construction of a tower—hence, the omission of any mention of the tower in the text. Besides, the given construction of the tower is essential to the development of the plot, especially with regard to its climax—the realization on Yahweh's part that human beings are capable of carrying out any project (v. 6b). At the same time, the irony of Yahweh's "descent" to see the human feat is intensified as a result, since the tower was supposed to reach up to the heavens.

Rather than a gloss, therefore, the present form of the verse should be seen as correct, producing a deliberate sense-effect by means of disymmetry:

"Let us build ourselves a city and a tower" (v. 4a)

Yahweh comes down to see "the city and the tower" (v. 5a)

"And they ceased building the city" (v. 8b)

In the process, the tower acquires a special prominence. Its omission in v. 8b is due to its presence as a completed project that defies the heavens but that remains "there," lost, in the setting of the plain of Šin'ar, as a consequence of the dispersion. In conclusion, the text should be accepted in its present form, to be read from a literary perspective.

Sixth Unit: The Name of Babylon

(11:9) Therefore, he called it "Babel," because it was there that Yahweh confused the language of all the earth and from there that Yahweh dispersed them over the face of the whole earth.[8]

As previously noted, the story could have come to an end with v. 8. The "movement" of human beings as well as of the story itself, which began with v. 2, concludes with v. 8. Language has been thrown into confusion, and no other project is possible now. Humans have been dispersed, and the concentration of power at the service of megalomaniac interests has stopped. At the same time, the new conclusion of v. 9 does add a number of highly significant elements that respond to the essence of the story, as if the latter proceeded on different levels at one and the same time.

First, the formula "therefore" is typical of the etiological conclusions of myths. The original event narrated in the myth functions as the paradigm for present events or realities, whose meaning it seeks to explore. The original event also serves as an additional "explanation" for why the event in question is or is called as it is. Yet, one should keep in mind that this etiological dimension always remains subordinate with respect to the signifying dimension, unless the story itself highlights it, as is the case here. Then, it becomes another element of the signifying dimension expressed by way of the etiological dimension, as I shall explain below.

Second, in v. 9 there is only one transformation to be found, the naming of the city, with Yahweh as its subject. From a narrative point of view, this is an important detail. It is one thing to claim that this was the name given by popular tradition, another to claim that it was a divine imposition. Thus, in v. 9a the narrator recounts what Yahweh did (give the city a name), while in v. 9b the narrator continues with his own interpretation of this event. The two levels of discourse, constitutive of communication, must be kept separate. The text is very well constructed indeed, and there is no need to alter anything.

For a more profound understanding of this event, one would do well to recall the passage from the *Enuma Elish* (5.119-30) in which Marduk, proclaimed absolute king and sovereign by all the other Gods, addresses himself to them and announces the founding of Babylon as the chosen place for his own dwelling as well as for the assembly of all the Gods. In the face of this Mesopotamian tradition, Gen 11:9a constitutes a counterhegemonic affirmation, as a sociopolitical reading of the text would readily detect. This is by no means an innocent expression. Its meaning goes well beyond the etiological; indeed, the etiological dimension has been placed at the service of a countercultural message. Gen 11:1-9 thus represents a "counter-myth"—the biblical myth regarding the founding of Babylon, in which the signifiers and values of its Mesopotamian equivalents are deliberately inverted. The Babylon of the original myth is built by the Gods at Marduk's command, who proceeds to give it a name; the Babylon of the biblical myth is built by the first humans at their own initiative, but it is Yahweh who proceeds to bestow a fateful name upon it.

To be sure, there is more to the story than the fact that it is Yahweh rather than Marduk who gives Babylon its name. The name itself undergoes a substantial change in meaning. In point of fact, the historical name of the city signifies "gate-of-the-Gods," but the Babylonian myth of creation confers upon it the prestige of primordiality, associating it as it does with the cosmogony as well as with the word of Marduk himself. At the same time, the myth further implies that Babylon, which from a historical point of view emerges as an obscure city toward the beginning of the second millennium B.C.E., is as ancient as the cosmos itself.

In the face of this religious-cultural context, the naming of the city by Yahweh in v. 9 is fraught with irony and disdain. A different aspect of this irony can be observed in the linguistic play established between the following expressions:

"Let us . . . make a name (*šem*) for ourselves" (v. 4)

"He called it Babel" (*sᵉmah Babel*) and

"there . . . confused" (*šam balal*)

From the quest for a name-fame for itself, one comes to a name-confusion for the city under construction. It should go without saying that one cannot derive the term "Babel" from the verb *balal*, which means "to mix." It is simply impossible from a philological point of view. For that very same reason, therefore, either popular etymology, were such to be the case, or the myth's own unique etymology, a more probable scenario, proves far more attractive.

With respect to the redaction of v. 9, a twofold clarification of the name should be noted in terms of the events narrated within the story itself. On the one hand, the meaning "Babel = mixture" is connected with the confusion of language, which was part of Yahweh's purpose as revealed in his own discourse (v. 7b). Its execution, while not narrated as part of the story, appears as a given fact in the name bestowed on the city. For an interpretation of Gen 11:9 as a foundation myth for Babylon, such a meaning is central, linked as it is to the name of the city. On the other hand, the affirmation that follows, "and from there . . . Yahweh dispersed them," closely tied as it is to the name of Babylon, is also noteworthy. Besides, the motif of dispersion occurs at the end, just as it was the case in v. 4b. Is this due to the logic of the story (the dispersion as a result of the failure to communicate)? Is this the ultimate goal? Is it a secondary theme, complementary to the "linguistic" chaos of the builders? Is it an important theme at the level of redaction?

Perhaps there is one answer to all of these questions. The present story works with a variety of isotopies at the same time: linguistic, spatial, architectonic. The first of these, the linguistic, constitutes the semantic axe of the narration: it is found at the extremes (vv. 1 and 9) as well as in the center, indeed in both parts of Yahweh's discourse—both as confirmation of an event (v. 6a) and as sole objective of the divine action announced (vv. 7a and 7b). At the same time, the spatial isotopy, mostly geographical in nature, appears as an essential part of the story from the beginning (v. 2a). The one tongue as much as the one space make possible the construction of both city and tower.

Consequently, from the point of view of the overall coherence of the story, it is better to argue that the one tongue and the one location work together toward a third element, the display of power and fame (the "name"), which in this case is achieved through the construction of the city and the tower (vv. 3-4 + 5b), but which in the future could very well result in unimaginable deeds (v. 6b). Similarly, the dénouement of the story narrates how Yahweh attacks, to begin with, the unity of language (enunciated goal, v. 7), but then also how Yahweh frustrates the desire to remain "there," bringing about the dispersion of all (v. 8a), so that the city may not prosper ever again (v. 8b).

Going back to the formula at the conclusion of the myth, then, the name of "Babel" is explained in two ways: first, as "mixture/confusion (of language)" (v. 9a), by way of a quite suggestive etymology, far more literary than popular in nature; second, as a memorial to the fact that it was "from there" that

Yahweh dispersed everyone over the face of the whole earth (v. 9b). This expression "from there" (*missam*) at the conclusion of the myth is quite telling, insofar as it replaces "Babel," which, now, empty as it is, can no longer impose itself. The expression plays as well with the "name" (*šem*) of v. 4a, the primary objective of the joint human action. Such a desired "name" also remains empty. Indeed, if the builders have made a "name" for themselves, it is only the name of the city itself, which expresses the negation of every organized project.

It is clear, therefore, that Gen 11:1-9 has nothing to do with the emergence of the different languages of the earth. The confusion of language amounts to the negation of all communication, the primary function of language. Moreover, to argue that the main theme of the story concerns the diversity of peoples, as if this "myth of origins" brought to completion what Genesis 10 explained by way of genealogy, is to go beyond the text. The central theme is none other than the human lack of moderation, as symbolized by the description of the tower (v. 4a), the quest for a "name" as an ultimate goal (v. 4a), and Yahweh's suspicion regarding all human projects (v. 6b). These three references make up the semantic axe of the story, which in turn gathers all other motifs and themes.

GEN 11:1-9: GENERAL OBSERVATIONS

In the light of the preceding analysis of the text, a number of general observations are in order:

1. The text has come across repeatedly as structured in terms of small segments and tied together by means of multiple lexematic (some of which were pointed out in the introduction) as well as thematic relationships. The text as a whole, however, also reveals a structure, whether deliberate or not. To be sure, there have been a number of attempts to delineate such a structure. These are not opposed to one another as such but rather focus in each case on certain linguistic or conceptual elements rather than others. The proposed structure that follows is based on those literary and narratological aspects of the text highlighted in the course of the preceding analysis.

> a   the whole earth (a) one language (b) (v. 1)
> A
> b   land of *Šin'ar* (a) they settled (b) there (c) (v. 2)
> B   construction project: city and tower (vv. 3-4a)
> a   not to become dispersed
> C
> b   over the face of the whole earth (v. 4b)
> D   came down to see the construction (v. 5)
> "this is but the beginning of their doings" (v. 6a)
> X   "now it will be impossible to prevent them from doing whatever they wish to do" (v. 6b)
> D' let us come down to confuse their language (v. 7)
> a' He dispersed them

C'
   b' over the face of the whole earth (v. 8a)
B' they ceased building the city (v. 8b)
   a' he confused the language (b') of the whole earth (a') (v. 9a)
A'
   b' from there (c') he dispersed them (b') over the whole earth (a') (v. 9b)

As can be readily observed, the correspondences are perfect, but without excessive uniformity, whether as a result of the subinversions (signaled by way of small letters) in the symmetrical parallels or the variation in the two central motifs (construction and language) in B and B', in turn presented in inverse order with respect to vv. 1 and 2.

When carefully examined, one can see that all the motifs and themes that make up the narrative plot and that guide the communication at the pragmatic level come to the fore in this proposed structure. The placement of the center of the story at v. 6 (rather than at v. 5, as is customary in works that deal with the literary structure of the passage) allows one to see that the "point" of the story has to do with the undoing of possible human superprojects and not just the suspension of construction works in the city (v. 8b).

2. The analysis clearly shows that the story of Gen 11:1-9 has nothing to say with respect to the origins of human language. That is simply not its purpose; besides, the story has recourse to symbolic codes, such as that of monolinguism. In point of fact, the text makes no reference whatsoever to a diversity of tongues. "To mix/to confuse" (*balal*) is not the same as to diversify, to generate, to multiply. Such a theme is not raised at all in this passage. In this regard the terminology of chapter 10 is quite different, insofar as each genealogical summary makes reference to "separation/division" (*nifrᵉdû*, vv. 5, 31b) at a variety of levels. Moreover, the term *lasôn*, signifying one's own "language" or tongue (see 10:5, 20, 31, 32), does not recur at all. It is true that this is a different tradition than that of chapter 10, but even so in all five occurrences (vv. 1, 6a, 7a, 7b, 9a) the term *safah* denotes language as such, the act of communication, not the linguistic system we call "tongue."

3. "Dispersion" is not equivalent to the division of peoples in the "Table of the Nations." The verb *pûs* always conveys a negative sense with regard to reality and is never used with reference to any sort of organized activity. In other words, no diversity of peoples or nations comes about as a result of the dispersion feared by humans (v. 4b) and ordained by Yahweh (vv. 8 and 9b). On the contrary, the verb conveys the sense of "to scatter/to spread out/to disseminate" (as in the case noted above of v. 8b). Curiously enough, this is the same verb widely employed by the prophets, especially Ezekiel, in oracles of punishment or promise within the context of the exile. Thus, the people of Judah end up "dispersed = scattered" over all the nations, out of which they shall be "gathered together" once again. "Dispersion" has no constructive connotations; it denotes, rather, the loss of identity in a group that formerly constituted a unity.

The introduction of the division-of-peoples motif in this story has the counter-effect of drawing attention away from the path established by the text itself, which has to do with the dissolution of Babylon itself by means of the same weapon (the scattering over the whole earth) used by Babylon at the time of the destruction of Judah and especially of Jerusalem. That is the point of the story—the point behind this important myth regarding the founding and exile of Babylon.

In the light of the comments thus far, it would be quite incorrect to compare this story with that of chapter 10. In effect, the story has nothing to do with the division of humanity into tongues and peoples, a question that has already been addressed, but deals rather with a twofold strategy on the part of Yahweh: first, to undo the effectiveness of a megalomaniacal project already in operation; second, and above all, to prevent any other such projects from arising in the future. Such a conclusion bears an important hermeneutical strain for the perspective of the final text of the Pentateuch. To wit: the story makes the point that the same Babylon that drives the people of Judah into exile and "disperses" it over the whole face of the empire will, in turn, "be dispersed" by Yahweh. That is the metamessage of the myth.

At the level of biblical intertextuality, this story should be read alongside Isaiah 47, where one finds the same poetic and dramatic play at work with respect to the inversion of Babylon vis-à-vis Jerusalem, the two protagonist cities in postexilic biblical literature. Thus, the exile of Babylon plays an enormous role in Genesis 11, whether as a future possibility (v. 4b) or a present reality (vv. 8, 9b). This myth represents a foundational archetype that is also, at the same time, a prognosis regarding the final lot of Babylon, the oppressor of the Jews.

4. Within the same horizon of textual production, it is possible that the "city" may further connote an experience of oppression without parallel, drawing upon the memory of Egypt—where the children of Israel were forced to build two cities for Pharaoh (Exod 1:11); the experience of royal practices—especially those of Solomon (the building of the Temple, his palace, and a number of fortifications [1 Kgs 6-7, 9:15-19]); and all the suffering associated with Babylon itself—the city that conquered Jerusalem. Within such a referential historical framework, the city represents a symbol of the power amassed and enjoyed by the king, who has become an oppressor. Yahweh, the God of liberation, cannot dwell in such a city. His city, Mount Zion, remains his to the extent that righteousness dwells there. Otherwise, Mount Zion becomes like any other city: its God departs (Ezek 9:3; 10:4, 18; 11:23), should he prove unsuccessful in bringing about its purification (Isa 1:21-26).

5. Unity of language is a fundamental factor in every concentration of power. All such measures as the homogenization of practices, the centralization of the decision-making power, and the imposition of the dominant ideology have need of a univocal linguistic code. The will of the sovereign descends from the throne by means of a single channel, a controlled channel, that reaches all subjects in the same way. Such a context entails more than a universal tongue, in itself use-

ful in establishing communication with a multitude of peoples, each with its own local tongue. It also entails, through the use of such an essential resource, an attempt (a) to make uniform the culture, religion, and life of the nations; (b) to impose norms of behavior that make it "necessary" for such nations to acquire the products of the empire, deemed better than any autochthonous projects; and (c) to install the "normative" worldview, as was the case with the Latin language in ecclesiastical circles. In this way local languages are immediately marginalized and can ultimately be "submerged" either as a result of ideological compulsion (being ashamed of using them) or force. History is replete with examples of denigration or suffocation of aboriginal languages.

Consequently, Gen 11:1-9 problematizes the unity of language, from the point of view of human hubris or excess, as an instrument of oppression. Once again, the text has nothing to say with regard to the "many tongues," that is to say, with regard to the incredible cultural diversity represented by the different languages of humanity. Even if it did, however, as it has traditionally been interpreted, such plurality of languages would represent both punishment for the oppressor and blessing for the oppressed. Unity is bad; division, as an expression of diversified and enriching cultures at all levels, is positive. Nevertheless, interesting as such an interpretation may be, that, I repeat, is not the theme of this text. To be sure, the message as seen from this other point of view is quite valid: the one who dominates demands the use of a single language—supreme expression of the concentration of power. The narrative strongly points to any such unity of language as a dangerous thing, which God proceeds to undo.

CONCLUDING COMMENTS

In choosing a proper title for this passage, a title that would correspond to its content, I would argue for the following: "The Founding and Exile of Babylon." As a counter-myth, whose purpose it is to undo the ideological effects of the great Mesopotamian myth of the creation of Babylon (the *Enuma Elish*), the passage ridicules the great god Marduk and establishes the absolute pre-eminence of Yahweh. As such, the biblical myth conveys a message of hope not only to its original intended audience but also to us, who as a people oppressed become its addressees as well. The glory of empire always has its dark side. In sum, the narrative of Gen 11:1-9, when seen from the point of view of its original context of production, not only conveys enormous strength but is also quite helpful in generating new utopias.

By paying attention to the *whole* text and its sociopolitical context, I have unearthed in Gen 11:1-9 a meaning that is much more in keeping with the situation of the dispersed Judean people than those of traditional interpretations. In this story the tradition saw an "event"—strange indeed—or a legend, the kerygmatic function of which was not very clear. When read as a myth, however, the text takes on a different value altogether. It now refers to a foundational act—the origin of Babylon—seen from the perspective of those who were oppressed by that same city and empire. As such, the story should be recovered in catechesis and theology as well as in liturgy and preaching in connection with the many biblical texts that deal with examples of imperial praxis and the divine judgment that falls upon them. Far from being an isolated and folkloric story, therefore, Gen 11:1-9 emerges as a key text in the kerygmatic construction of the Pentateuch.[9] Needless to say, the ramifications of this approach to and use of the Bible for the practice of biblical studies are immense.

NOTES

1. For a more expansive presentation of this approach, see my *Exilio y sobrevivencia. Tradiciones contraculturales en el Pentateuco (Comentario de Génesis 4-11)* (Buenos Aires: Lumen, 1996).

2. Translator's Note: What follows is an English translation of the author's own translation into Spanish of the Hebrew text. Subsequently, in the detailed analysis of the text that follows, I provide in the case of each structural division the Spanish original in a note. All other translations of the Bible are taken from the New Revised Standard Version.

3. (11:1) Era toda la tierra una lengua y un habla única. (11:2) Sucedió que al emigrar ellos desde el oriente, encontraron una llanura en la tierra de *Šin'ar*, y se establecieron allí.

4. (11:3) Se dijeron entonces el uno al otro: "¡Vamos! Fabriquemos ladrillos y cozámoslos al fuego". Sirvió para ellos el ladrillo como piedra, y el asfalto sirvióles de argamasa. (11:4) Dijeron luego: "¡Vamos! Edifiquémosnos una ciudad y una torre cuya cúspide esté en el cielo, y hagámosnos así un nombre, no sea que nos dispersemos sobre la superficie de toda la tierra".

5. (11:5) Bajó Yavé a ver la ciudad y la torre que habían edificado los seres humanos.

6. (11:6) Dijo Yavé, "He aquí a un pueblo único, y una lengua única para todos ellos, ¡y éste es el comienzo de su hacer! Ahora, ¡no se les podrá impedir nada de lo que proyecten hacer! (11:7) ¡Vamos! Bajemos y confundamos allí su lengua, de tal modo que no escuche uno la lengua de su compañero".

7. (11:8) Y los dispersó Yavé de allí sobre la superficie de toda la tierra. Y dejaron de edificar la ciudad.

8. (11:9) Por eso llamó su nombre "Babel", porque allí confundió Yavé la lengua de toda la tierra, y de allí los dispersó Yavé sobre la superficie de toda la tierra.

9. For the coherence between this story and the message of the Pentateuch, see J. S. Croatto, "Algunas claves literarias y teológicas para entender el Pentateuco," *Estudios Bíblicos* 52 (1994) 167-94.

12

"Go Therefore and Make Disciples of All Nations" (Matt 28:19a)

A Postcolonial Perspective on Biblical Criticism and Pedagogy

Musa W. Dube

> Imperialism—a system of economic, political, and cultural force that disavows *borders* in order to extract desirable resources and exploit an alien people—has never strayed far away from a field of pedagogical imperatives, or what might be called an ideology of instruction. Christianity, Progress, Democracy, or whatever is the prevailing imperialist version of history demands of certain cultures, nations, or the "chosen" races that they subject those who fall radically short of the ideal state. Subject people are "savage," "infantile," "untutored," "backward," or simply "underdeveloped"; as the imperialist encounters them, a model of their "uplift" is always thus entailed.[1]
>
> —Jerry Phillips, "Educating the Savages"

The title of the present study invokes Matthew's text because of its imperative to disavow borders. The command not only instructs Christian readers to travel to all nations but also contains a "pedagogical imperative"—"*to make disciples of all nations*." Does such an imperative consider the consequences of trespassing? Does it make room for Christian travelers to be discipled by all nations, or is the discipling in question conceived solely in terms of a one-way traffic? The first question is well addressed by the gospel: prior to this command, the Matthean Jesus declares, "All authority in heaven and on earth has been given to me" (Matt 28:18b). In other words, Christian readers have been issued an unrestricted passport to enter all nations in obedience to their Lord, without any consultation whatsoever with any of the nations in question. The answer to the second question is not directly provided by the gospel. Nevertheless, the text clearly implies that Christian disciples have a duty to teach all nations, without any suggestion that they must also in turn learn from all nations. Consequently, if all nations are to be entered and "discipled"

224

by Christian teachers without any sort of reciprocal stance or attitude on the latter's part, do we not then find in the gospel an operative model of outsiders as infants to be "uplifted"?

These issues of traveling with authority, entering all nations, and teaching all nations are not at all peripheral to a postcolonial feminist, such as I, and her views on the future course and function of biblical criticism and pedagogy. As a postcolonial subject—that is to say, as someone whose history, economics, politics, culture, and encounter with the Bible are intricately interwoven with the Western imperialism of the eighteenth through the twentieth centuries—both the question of traveling and the ideology of instruction lie at the heart of my experience. Thus, my view of what direction and role biblical criticism should take in the future is inevitably informed by my encounter with imperialist domination, colonization, and neo-colonization as well as with the continued struggle for liberation. Indeed, I have been affected by imperialist travelers, and I, in turn, have become a dependent traveler.

INTRODUCTION: PERSONAL AND HISTORICAL TRAVELING

Personal Travels

The story of my traveling begins when my family had to migrate from Zimbabwe to Botswana. This was in the 1950s, when the village in which they lived, farmed, and grazed their livestock was suddenly declared the property of a white Rhodesian settler. All the occupants of that area were faced with two choices: either to remain in their homes and become servants of the white settler or to move to some dry, insufficient, and infertile lands, which were called "reserves." Resisting such resettlement and perhaps not believing that a foreign traveler could claim the land of their ancestors by simply saying a word, my family chose to remain in their home. It soon became quite clear that, on top of having to become servants of the new white master, they would be allowed to own up to only four cows, just enough for ploughing, as well as a small garden, nothing else. It was then that they decided to move to Botswana in search of land. Botswana, too, was a British colony at the time, but, given its harsh climate, its colonization had been undertaken primarily to preserve Cecil John Rhodes's dream of building a railway across the length of Africa, from the Cape to Cairo.

I have also engaged in some traveling of my own. I traveled from Botswana to the United Kingdom for my Master's degree in New Testament Studies and then from Botswana to the United States for my doctoral studies. Unlike the Matthean Christian readers, who travel with authority to teach all nations, or their imperialist counterparts in more recent centuries, who can lay claim to any land, I have traveled to these nations with no authority and restricted privileges. In the United Kingdom, for example, my fees were ten times those of students from the European Economic Community, even though I come from one of the so-called Commonwealth countries. Similarly, in the United States I held a visa that did not allow me to work, except when such work was directly related to my studies. While my type of travel may seem to be different and desirable, it remains firmly within the hegemonic structures of power: I traveled to the Christian nations to be "discipled" by them.[2] While metropolitan travelers journeyed to other nations to claim land, to teach, and to do business, I am not reciprocally entitled to any such privileges.[3] Later on, I shall return to these travels of mine and give some details of my classroom experiences for the good of those who are seeking new ways of teaching biblical criticism in a postcolonial era.

Historical Travels

My experience of travel, whether from the point of view of my family or of myself as an individual, further reflects my broader social location. As a Southern African citizen of Botswana, I have hosted and entertained renowned Christian travelers such as Robert Moffat and David Livingstone, who became the founders of what is known today as formal education and who were champions of colonization. Initially, the aim of formal education was to enable Africans to read the Bible, thereby training evangelists as well as teachers for the mission schools.[4] Subsequently, this missionary-founded education served to supply the colonial administration with clerks. From the beginning, therefore, formal education functioned as a structural instrument with which to wrench and wean individuals away from their so-called pagan culture, backward state, and primitive beliefs. Put differently, formal education became a powerful tool of colonization and ultimately its own form of imperialism.

From the point of view of feminist concerns, the introduction of a new system of economics, education, and religion clearly served to define a woman's place as secondary. Prior to colonization, most women in African societies were farmers and storytellers, with many holding prominent religious positions as well.[5] After colonization, however, a drastic change took place. To begin with, the new colonial economy converted most of the fertile lands of Africa into plantations that supplied Western industries with raw materials. Women continued as farmers, but only as producers of food for the home, staples not integrated into the international trade system. In addition, since formal education favored the training of males for the church and colonial offices, the exclusion of females meant that written literature would become the domain of males, relegating the role of women as storytellers to the private space of the home.[6] Likewise, while many African religions had female divine symbols and roles, the new Christian education systematically derogated these by enforcing Christian religion upon all students and thus training males to assume and enforce a strictly patriarchal Christian view of the Bible.[7]

The figure of David Livingstone proves quite telling in this regard. A missionary and a doctor, Livingstone not only became a celebrated explorer, botanist, ethnographer, geographer, and philanthropist but also fought against slavery.[8] Livingstone devoted his life to "opening up Africa" to "Christianity, commerce, and civilization."[9] This triple vision of his meant that for most

Africans Christianity was experienced as intricately bound together with structures of domination. Moreover, his myriad professions meant that imperialism was also experienced by Africans as a complex network involving a variety of disciplines and practices. As J. H. Mphemba points out, "First the white man brought the Bible. Then he brought the guns, then chains, then he built a jail, then he made the native pay tax."[10] Such an understanding of the role of the Bible in imperialism is further attested by the now common saying, "When the white man came he said to us, 'Let us pray.' After the prayer the white man had the land, and we had the Bible."[11]

In South Africa, for example, authoritative travelers, claiming to be the "chosen races" of God, proceeded to dispossess the indigenous people of their lands, livestock, and culture and to exploit their labor. Again, the choice was clear: the black populations of South Africa could either flee, become servants, or move to reserves, where land was dry, insufficient, and infertile. Here too, colonization, followed by the system of apartheid, was justified on the basis of the biblical text and solidified by means of an educational system that sought to keep the black population as servants. In fact, the model behind such authoritative travelers, who proceeded by dispossessing the natives and creating dependent travelers in Sub-Saharan Africa, goes back many centuries, to a time when the "slave trade exploited African labor power outside Africa to develop the West."[12] During the slave trade, theories of saving the souls of the African people through enslavement were also propounded and supported on the basis of the biblical text.[13]

Consequently, the history of the suffering and exploitation of Sub-Saharan Africa has been championed by readers of the Bible and has always involved a mixture of Western Christianity, Western commerce, and Western civilization. Thus, at the Berlin Conference of 1884, when the Western imperialist powers met to divide the map of Africa among themselves and to draw up a constitution on how to go about claiming the continent—without any consultation, of course, with the Africans themselves—Christian missionaries, as integral players in imperialism, were given special recognition. The constitution provided that "Christian missionaries, scientists, and explorers, with their followers, property and collections, shall likewise be objects of special protections."[14]

Today, the birth of a new South Africa marks the end of a century of negotiating and fighting for political liberation. Yet, African countries have emerged from their wars of independence to realize that Livingstone's master plan of Christianity, commerce, and civilization grounded imperialism on a much more complex foundation than that of political domination. In effect, the African economies and cultures have been converted into satellites of their former colonizers. As a result, the struggle for liberation seems to get ever more distant, as more and more countries become indebted to such institutions as the International Monetary Fund, the World Bank, and multinational corporations in the post-independence era. In other words, the economic and cultural domination of African countries by the Western countries is far from over.

As Ngungi wa Thiong'o points out, both "William Shakespeare and Jesus had brought light to the darkest Africa."[15] We are still confronting, therefore, the larger face of cultural and economic imperialism, with its many and complex networks. Shakespeare still reigns, as we continue to be identified with, to speak in, and to write in the languages of our former colonizers. The Bible also remains an undeniable element of our heritage from imperialism. So far, the bulk of our time has been consumed by the struggle for political independence—a struggle that called for us to "negotiate with the structures of violence,"[16] capitalizing on the themes of liberation within the Bible; now, however, the time has come to ponder the role and future of biblical criticism as postcolonial subjects.

Postcolonial Subjects

By "postcolonial subjects" I mean both the West and the Two-Thirds World, the former colonizer and the formerly colonized, the so-called developed and the allegedly underdeveloped, the North and the South. The term "postcolonial" indicates that we have all been thoroughly constructed by imperialism to perceive each other from a particular stance. As postcolonial subjects, therefore, we have to assess the various mechanisms underlying both past and present imperialism; as postcolonial subjects, moreover, we must also prevent its perpetuation by understanding past and present exploitation and by seeking new ways of encountering and respecting "the other." As I have argued above, for me and other postcolonial Sub-Saharan African subjects, the question of how the Bible is to be read within the quest for full liberation is central to the struggle against cultural and economic imperialism.

To be sure, biblical criticism is still largely defined by the centers of the West. However, as postcolonial subjects of Sub-Saharan Africa, I would argue that the future course and role of biblical criticism must be informed by our own *history*, our own experience, and our quest for cultural and economic liberation. In other words, the quest for the future direction and function of biblical criticism cannot be divorced from the fact that for Sub-Saharan Africa Christianity came as part of a package involving the institutions of Western commerce and civilization as well. As such, the coming of Christianity was accompanied by a structural process of pauperization, whereby our perceptions of reality and beauty were denied, and abetted by a variety of disciplines and practices.

Quite ironically, it is precisely our history of oppression and exploitation at the hands of the Western metropolitan centers that binds the West and the Sub-Saharan African experience. What happened in the past and what is now happening to the many struggling and exploited peoples of Sub-Saharan Africa is inseparable from the metropolitan centers of the West. As Edward Said argues, "Imperialism has consolidated the mixture of cultures and identities on a global scale" so that "no one today is purely one thing."[17] Therefore, imperialism as a category of analysis is as central for the West as it is for Sub-Saharan Africa and the rest of the Two-Thirds World, at least for those academicians willing to work for the course of human liberation.

Invitation to New and Different Travels

The preceding biographical and historical introduction has placed travel and travelers at the heart of domination and subordination in the Sub-Saharan African nations. I have invoked travel, first of all, because for most Sub-Saharan Africans the Bible was brought by travelers, who set up what is today called formal education and cleared the road for colonialism. I have further invoked travel as that dynamic that has brought many peoples, cultures, and lands together—a phenomenon that is far from declining, either now or in the future. Indeed, one of the major reasons why we have to address the course and role of biblical criticism and pedagogy is that traveling has turned the classroom into a much more complex entity than ever before, as individuals of different cultures, races, classes, genders, religions, and sexual orientations come together under the same roof. Thus, just as in the past the colonizers traveled to many countries and taught many nations their way of life—their religion, language, medicine, trade, architecture, commerce, way of dressing, and so forth—so today the colonized come to the imperial centers and, by their very presence in these centers, not only demand to be heard and to be included, but also raise questions regarding the methods, contents, and aims of biblical criticism in the world.

More significantly, I have also invoked travel not to argue against it nor to wish it away, but rather to invite readers to take new and different journeys, journeys that we must all undertake. While the imperialist journeys only served to create wounds and alienation, new and different journeys of the mind, the spirit, the heart, and the body are needed, this time to touch and to be touched, to heal and to be healed. The journeys of the past involved travelers who went forth to discover places that had already been discovered and to name rivers, mountains, and falls that had already been named. Such journeys involved those who taught but would not be taught and those who were listened to but would not listen. Such journeys involved those who truly traveled in the "dark continent," for they never saw anything there except darkness. Yet, it is not too late, if one is willing, to take new and different journeys: to listen, to hear, to see, to learn, to dialogue; to be taught, to be healed, and to be touched by those whom we have always by-passed.

In what follows, I will argue, first of all, that the Bible should be read as an imperialist text—a text that was used to subjugate other races and na-tions, men as well as women; a text that articulates an ideology of imperial-ism. I will then go on to argue that the view of the Bible as a text of liberation and resistance on the part of those races and nations who have suffered most from imperialism only attests to the pervasiveness of imperialism in the world. Finally, I shall examine some implications of the phenomenon of imperialism for biblical criticism and pedagogy. Throughout I will draw occasionally from my own travel experiences as a foreign, black woman and a postcolonial subject pursuing studies in the metropolitan centers of the West.

THE BIBLE AS AN IMPERIALIST TEXT

One of the most striking moments of my life took place when I went to consult one of my professors and told her that I was struggling with how to read the Bible in the light of its imperialist role in Sub-Saharan Africa. Her response was, "Yes, the Bible is a resistance text of the colonized and you must reclaim it from the imperialists." How truthful was her statement, for the whole of the New Testament was written by colonized Jews under Roman imperial occupation, and yet nothing could have been further from my own historical experience and convictions! For me, the Bible was a text of the conquerors, of imperialists and colonialists, who justified their actions by claiming a God-given right, as the histories of Africa, America, and Asia amply testify. On the basis of its historical use, therefore, the Bible has indeed functioned as an imperialist text.

If one defines an imperialist text as a text that encourages its readers to disavow borders, to enter any nation with authority, and to regard the occupants of such nations as untutored, then the Bible, and the New Testament in particular, clearly espouse an ideology that promotes and legitimizes imperialism. Again, the Matthean Jesus is very much to the point here: "All authority in heaven and on earth has been given to me. Go therefore and make disciples of all nations" (Matt 28:18b-19a); as commissioned servants, the disciples bear the unlimited authority of their master.

Yet Matthew was written among colonized Jews, suffering under the exploitation of the Roman Empire. Logically, therefore, one would expect it to be a text of resistance, aiming not only to preserve the autonomy of Jewish culture, including the right to worship God according to their own ways in their own land, but also to secure political and economic independence. However, by propounding a universal imperative of going forth unto all nations and teaching all nations, Matthew sets forth an agenda of disavowing borders not at all unlike that of imperial Rome. Like the Greek and Roman empires, therefore, which promoted their own cultural and religious practices among the subjugated, Matthew also espouses a Jesus who, in the way of other kings and emperors, sends forth his servants to establish an empire and to teach the subjugated to obey everything he has commanded (Matt 28:18-20).

How is this vision of Matthew related to the general struggle of the Jewish people, fighting for their right to worship and to live as they wished in their own land? Is he offering a solution that favors the oppressed Jewish nation or is he imitating the enemy? Does Matthew consider the fact that other nations, much like his own, would also resist the imposition of foreign culture and find it oppressive?

The basic issue, of course, is not whether Hellenistic or Roman culture was good or evil in itself. What makes any culture oppressive is its *imposition* on other cultures as a way of undermining their autonomy and imagination. Likewise, the problem with the command of the Matthean Jesus to disciple all nations, whether in the context of the Sermon on the Mount or of the gospel as a whole, is not that his words are not words of wisdom, but rather that the imperative to teach all nations—"*to obey everything that I have commanded you*" (Matt 28:20a)— constitutes an imposition that undermines the autonomy and culture of these other nations. Similarly, the reaction against the imperial domination of countries such as the United Kingdom, France, Portugal, Spain, Germany, or the United States is not because the language, religion, system of trade, form of government, or culture in question are not good in themselves, but rather because their imposition on others of so-called universal standards only serves to undermine the autonomy of such others.

One could respond, of course, that the Matthean command has to do with religion, not with economics or politics. As the historical sketch above readily shows, however, the line between religion, commerce, and civilization is quite thin, if not altogether nonexistent. In fact, from the point of view of Matthew's Jewish context, there was no distinction between politics, economics, and religion. While Matthew and his nation were fighting against economic exploitation and cultural imposition on the part of Rome, the vision that emerges out of the gospel is uncomfortably imperialist. One is inevitably compelled to ask as a result whether any literature produced by the oppressed and the colonized supports imperialism, and here the answer has to be in the affirmative.

Indeed, studies of the colonized show that they pass through a variety of stages: first, total compliance with the imperialist powers; second, partial collaboration characterized by revolts and negotiation for particular rights; finally, total rejection of imperialism.[18] Depending upon at which stage textual production occurs, the literature of the colonized may completely accept and praise imperialism, may collaborate with imperialism, or may totally reject imperialism. Now, a major characteristic of imperialism is its capacity to rule from a distance by sending a few settlers and occupants and using the elites of the subjugated nation as collaborators.[19] The effect of this strategy is to keep the face of the real enemy hidden, while planting divisions among the oppressed, who are likely to perceive the collaborating elites as the enemy. However, even when the real enemy is recognized, the oppressed still fight against the elites on account of their collaborative stance. Another strategy of imperialism is to create competition among various interest groups, who begin to vie for the favor of the empire against other competitors. Such a division of the oppressed is always to the advantage of the imperialist.

A number of these patterns are readily discernible in the Matthean Gospel. For example, Matthew represents one of many interest groups vying for the power to define reality in occupied Israel.[20] After the temple's destruction in 70 C.E., the need to determine who and what defined Jewish culture could not have been more acutely felt. That Matthew offered his own solution and was rejected is self-evident from his vitriolic rhetoric against the Pharisees (Matt 23), his winning rivals. Similarly, Matthew's contention for power, as in most occupied territories, is accompanied by a softer presentation of imperialist power. Thus, for example, the Matthean Pilate is absolved from the guilt of crucifying Jesus, while his wife is characterized as a divine instrument who receives dreams regarding the innocence of Jesus.[21] Such a portrayal of imperialist forces as benign resonates with Matthew's own version of imperialism, involving the entering and discipling of all nations. More importantly, such a relationship shows that any religious vision that espouses a universalist view will ultimately need the support of a political and economic system that clings to the same ideology.

I am using Matthew here as an example of the larger biblical text. It is true, to be sure, that most biblical texts were born within the context of Israel's struggle against a succession of empires, from the Babylonian to the Roman. Such a situation was not always successfully resisted.[22] Many times it had to be condoned, given the might of these empires, while at other times it was resisted and rejected. There were times as well when Israel itself behaved as an empire.[23] This prominence of imperialism in the formation of the biblical tradition means that in many ways imperialism also came to inform the thinking of those who offered resistance to it and hence was at times regarded as quite natural. Consequently, given its historical compatibility with the biblical tradition, imperialism lies at the bedrock of biblical thinking and remains equally powerful today.

While the Gospel of Matthew represents an example of imperialism from the New Testament, the story of the exodus from Egypt serves as a corresponding example from the Hebrew Bible. In the story of the exodus, the God of Israel who liberates his people from slavery and exploitation is celebrated. However, the act of claiming Canaan as a God-given land, when it was already occupied, can hardly be said to represent a story of liberation. At the heart of this story lies an imperialist ideology of domination, as confirmed by the much later claims of the Christian founding fathers of North America and the South African Dutch Boers to be a "chosen race" and the use of such claims to dispossess Native Americans and black South African peoples, respectively, of their lands. In sum, there can be little doubt that the Bible offers support for as well as resistance against imperialism, from both a textual and a historical perspective.[24]

THE BIBLE AS RESISTANCE TO IMPERIALISM?

A reader may wonder why I place such emphasis on the Bible as an imperialist text, given the fact that many groups—such as African Americans; Southern African blacks; Latin Americans—who have suffered from severe forms of imperialism have turned to the Bible for help and have found therein a God who takes sides with the poor. From such a perspective, the story of exodus is read as if the subsequent occupation of the land had not taken place. Commenting on this overtly selective reading, Renita Weems argues that it has nothing to do with lack of sophistication on the part of readers but rather "says more about the depth of human yearning for freedom."[25]

More importantly, such an overtly selective reading, a reading that proceeds by suppressing the oppressive aspects of the text, constitutes a political strategy whereby the oppressed can talk back to the hegemonic powers in the latter's own language, that is, in the language of the Bible. This is one of the strategies that the victims of imperialism have employed to appeal to the very depths of their oppressors' beliefs. This, however, does not mean that the subjugated are not aware that in so doing "they are negotiating with the structures of violence,"[26] nor does it mean that they are not aware that "the master's tools will never dismantle the master's house."[27] Such groups are acutely aware of the fact that "it is the final triumph of a system of domination when the dominated start singing its virtues."[28]

Thus, the "singing" of the liberating themes of the Bible by the subjugated should be seen as a part of their strategy for survival, as the grip of imperialism continues to tighten in the Western metropolitan centers and to make the liberation of the Two-Thirds World ever more distant. The subjugated are very much aware that such a strategy not only has limited results but also constitutes a double-edged sword, since it can be readily used by the oppressors to justify their belief that they have given the uncivilized a language, an education, and a civilization without which the latter would not be able to talk back to them. The very fact that the victims of imperialism have emerged speaking the language of the metropolis and professing to be Christians, when in many cases their own languages and religions continue to exist, does not at all invalidate my point regarding the pervasiveness of imperialism but rather serves as eloquent testimony to the degree to which imperialism has managed to impose a few universal standards on a world of difference.

At this point, I should like to reiterate my definition of what constitutes imperialism. Imperialism is characterized above all by its structural *imposition* of a few standards on a universal scale. This imposition does not meet "the other" as an equal subject, with dialogue and free exchange as a result. On the contrary, this imposition rests on a view of "the other" as a blank slate to be filled, whereby the rights of "the other" are structurally derogated and "the other" are rendered dependent. As Ngungi wa Thiong'o has put it, imperialism is a "cultural bomb" whose aim it is to:

> annihilate a people's belief in their names, in their languages, in their environment, in their heritage of struggle, in their unity, in their capacities and ultimately in themselves. It makes them see their past as one wasteland of non-achievement and it makes them want to distance themselves from that wasteland. It makes them want to identify with what is furthest removed from themselves; for instance other peoples' languages rather than their own.[29]

I have therefore used Matthew's command to travel, to enter, and to teach with authority as the title for this study in order to show that such a command does not seek "the other" as a subject with whom to engage in dialogue and exchange words of wisdom. In fact, since Christianity is primarily a mission-oriented religion with a claim to absolute and universal truth, there lies at its very heart an ideology of imperialism that seeks to subjugate others and that creates in the process a relationship of dependency between the tutors and the untutored.

By claiming that the Bible is an imperialist text, I do not undermine the strategy of claiming God's option for the poor, one of the strategies employed by the Two-Thirds World to plead with the structures of violence. Nevertheless, at this stage in our struggle for liberation, I should like to propose a different kind of strategy[30]—a strategy of postcolonial subjects, which calls upon both the dominator and the dominated to examine the matrix of past and present imperialism and to map ways in which they can speak as equal subjects who meet to exchange words of wisdom and life.

A number of Western biblical scholars have openly acknowledged the centrality of imperialism in Christianity. Wayne Meeks, for example, notes that Christianity did not only become the religion of the Roman empire but also became "unique in its imperial sponsorship."[31] He goes on to point out that these Christian "traditions are integral with the cultural identity of the West."[32] The latter point is also noted by Mary Ann Tolbert, when she writes that "for anyone raised in the Western society under the dominance of Judaism or Christianity, those religions and their sacred writings have profoundly affected the very categories by which experience is understood."[33] Likewise, Elisabeth Schüssler Fiorenza has argued that the formation of the Christian canon was informed by and aimed at the consolidation of the Roman empire and the church.[34] Consequently, the very collection and selection of the Christian texts sought to suppress difference by imposing a universal standard, that of the male-biased Christian canon.

That imperialism has informed the Christian texts, texts that have shaped the "cultural identity of the West," is without question. However, if these texts have informed and guided the West in its domination of the Two-Thirds World, how can postcolonial subjects—the former colonizer and the formerly colonized—speak to each other and teach these texts in the light of the experience of imperialism? In other words, what are the implications of acknowledging the centrality of imperialism in the Bible for the future direction and function of biblical criticism and pedagogy? In what follows I should like to offer some suggestions regarding how biblical criticism can be pursued and taught so that it confronts and counteracts imperialism. Such suggestions, however, can make a positive contribution only if individuals are willing to commit themselves to work in their various institutions for the liberation of all creation, going beyond the immediate interests of race, class, nation, gender, continent, and religion—in short, to engage in a biblical criticism that is "founded upon the affective experience of oppression rather than solely upon narrow definitions of essence."[35]

WHERE DO WE GO FROM HERE?
IMPLICATIONS OF IMPERIALISM FOR
BIBLICAL CRITICISM AND PEDAGOGY

At the present time, biblical criticism is still for the most part under the control of imperial centers such as the United Kingdom, France, Germany, and the United States. As the perpetrators of imperialism, the Western countries have long made the word "imperialism" itself anathema in their own vocabularies, using it only in connection with the former communist countries of Eastern

Europe. At the same time, literature departments in the West have bracketed imperialism as a category of analysis, despite its pervasiveness at the global level and the role of literature in fostering imperialism.[36] Such bracketing means that Western academicians have advanced literary methods and readings that continue to support and sustain imperial domination on the part of their respective countries.

A similar bracketing of imperialism in biblical criticism is noted by Emmanuel Martey:

> [Africans] have read European theologians and know how some of them opposed the violence of the two world wars. But none of these theologians, not even Karl Barth, despite his stance against naked aggression and violence of Nazi Germany, addressed the issue of colonial violence and military oppression against African people.[37]

At first sight, a direct connection between biblical criticism and imperialism may seem far-fetched. What does academic biblical discourse have to do with missionaries, television evangelization, churches, or governments? However, since biblical criticism is a discipline that is carried on by people who are members of churches, governments, and countries, such a relationship does indeed exist. Indeed, biblical criticism must acknowledge the fact that it has more or less served as "retainer" to these institutions and structures. One can ask, for example, how biblical criticism has countered the imperialist tendencies of the Western countries, either at present or in the past. If a clear stance cannot be mapped, one must go on to ask whether it is in keeping with the goals of biblical criticism to foster or endorse imperialism. If fostering imperialism is not compatible with the aims of biblical criticism, then imperialism as a category of analysis must be included in biblical pedagogy. Such a move should include critical analysis of its various manifestations: how imperialism inhabits institutions and relates to issues of race, gender, class, religion, and sexual orientation.

There is no biblical criticism without biblical critics. All biblical critics are situated in the world, and, as I have tried to show, it is a world that has been globally affected by the imperialist centers of the world. I have further argued that imperialism constitutes a complex network of academic disciplines and practices, in unison with Western commerce and civilization. If the Bible is indeed one of the major imperialist texts, what then becomes the responsibility of biblical critics in confronting this oppression? Biblical critics need to examine themselves individually regarding their stance toward imperialism and examine their relationship to the institutions and structures of imperialism, such as Western commerce and civilization. They need to ask themselves what they can do to counteract imperialism through their critical practice. To be sure, biblical critics, especially critics in metropolitan centers, can choose to ignore altogether these issues of imperialism and colonization. However, to ignore such issues is, in effect, to give them de facto support. On the other hand, biblical critics can choose to counteract imperialist domination by embarking on a critical practice that seeks to understand, expose, undermine, and arrest the imperialist forces of oppression and exploitation. What shape would such an inclusion of imperialism as a major category of analysis take in biblical pedagogy? What follows are a number of suggestions regarding how biblical studies can incorporate imperialism as a category of analysis within the discipline.

Biblical Criticism and Church Histories

Wayne Meeks has argued that a clear symptom of malaise in New Testament studies has been its isolation "from other kinds of historical scholarship—not only from secular study of the Roman Empire, but even from church history."[38] To be sure, a biblical criticism that remains so focused on the text and so divorced from the impact of the text on the world—for example, from the course of later church histories—has been instrumental in the bracketing of imperialism and other forms of oppression in the discipline. Yet, a look at the contents of Meeks' own work indicates that what he is actually advocating is the study of early church history. I would argue, however, that biblical criticism should be taught in conjunction with a variety of church histories. I do so because I believe that a concentration on the first centuries of the Christian church has allowed biblical critics to hide behind historical reconstructions of the early church and thus bypass altogether the central issues of our times.

Given the fact that the Bible has continued to lead many lives in different centuries, nations, and continents, biblical criticism should be taught in conjunction with the full range of church histories. Thus, for example, one can design courses that focus on biblical criticism and the colonial enterprise of the eighteenth through the twentieth centuries or on biblical criticism and African church histories in the nineteenth and twentieth centuries. Such different historical perspectives would allow critics to attain fresh and profound insights into the meaning and impact of these texts on the world. At present, the continued prioritization of early church history over all other church histories not only serves to shelter Western critics from confronting the imperialism of their own countries but also to silence the questions of the victims of imperialism.

Biblical Criticism and Other Canons

At the heart of Matthew's command to make disciples of all nations in obedience to Jesus' commands lies the imposition of a canon, a Christian canon, which proceeds by undermining the canons of those nations who are to be discipled. In other words, this command universalizes the Christian canon while undermining difference and diversity. Since canons are a deposit of culture, supposedly representing "the good and the beautiful" of any one nation's character, it follows that the suppression of other canons is oppressive and places the knowledge of subjugated groups, peoples, and nations in danger of being trivialized, misunderstood, or abandoned.[39] As a woman, I know that most canons marginalize women and represent for the most part the culture of the elites. As an African, I come from a tradition not of textual canons but rather oral canons. As a human being, I know that every society has a perception of reality and a standard of beauty that are a constant background to that society's culture. Thus, the notion of canon is closely tied to the identity of different cultures, and the exaltation of one canon over all others results in the imposition of a foreign standard of culture upon all humanity.

Since imperialism depends upon the suppression of other canons, and hence of diversity itself, one way of counteracting such oppression is for biblical criticism to become multicultural. Biblical criticism would have to be taught in conjunction with perceptions of the divine to be found in a variety of different groups, nations, and continents. To be sure, such an approach to biblical criticism will have to bear in mind that some perceptions of the divine are not textually oriented and that others, while textually oriented, do not have a dualistic demarcation between sacred and profane books. In such cases, works of art, symbols, proverbs, stories, songs, and words of wisdom may also form part of the canon of the group or nation in question.

What I am suggesting is a new approach to the history of religions. In the past the history of religions has operated from within an imperialist model, one of whose major aims it was to prove the superiority of the Christian tradition over all others. In addition, the study of other religions has tended to focus on what are usually called the "major" world religions, while excluding, for example, the religions of Africa and Native America. This exclusion of the religions of those who have suffered most at the hands of imperialism is in keeping with imperialist ideology, which denied all such religions their own perceptions of the divine. New ways of doing history of religions need to be configured, whose aims would be to underline and celebrate the fullness of diversity.

Canaan Banana has advocated a similar approach. Maintaining that the Bible has fostered many forms of oppression, Banana has argued:

> We must expand the frontiers of archeological research and excavation to encompass the entire universe. Religious shrines and traditions of the people of Asia, Africa, Europe, the Caribbean, and Latin America must surely be important sources of God's revelation. Nothing can be lost by studying how these peoples perceived and worshipped God in their own individual circumstances with the view of drawing from their rich heritage to broaden our understanding of God's activity in human history.[40]

Thus, Banana calls for revising, editing, and adding to the Bible, but above all, he argues, "we must start from the assumption that all creation is holy, an assumption which recognizes God's presence in all creation."[41]

Biblical Criticism and the Text

As a predominantly Western discourse, biblical criticism has tended to be text- and logocentric. Other cultures, however, have different ways of articulating their visions of life and perceptions of the divine. Pertinent here is the use of symbol, ritual, drama, poetry, and song—without a focus on text. The African continent, for example, is well known for its orality, but it is becoming clear that orality does not just mean illiteracy but rather the possession of different ways of articulating reality. Thus, social or religious discourse may be addressed in symbols, rituals, drama, poetry, and songs without any focus on text or even verbal articulation.[42] Many studies on the use of the Bible in the African Independent Churches show that, although the Bible is important, it is not engaged or used for its textual message but rather as a symbol of God's power.[43] This means, in effect, that issues of reading and struggling with the meaning of a written text are themselves the product of a particular cultural perspective, that of the West. Since issues of literacy and "educating the savages" were central to the strategy of colonization, there is a need to be much more self-critical regarding a text- and logocentric biblical criticism as well as to seek ways that do not privilege hegemonic forms of discourse.

Biblical Criticism and the New Methodological Shift

The traditional historical-critical approach was text-centered and emphasized an objective and neutral reader, whose aim it was to find the author's intended meaning and to understand the world behind the text. The new methodological shift, on the other hand, is reader-centered and interdisciplinary.[44] Sociocultural and literary approaches have shown that the biblical texts are both cultural constructs of their time and literary constructions of their authors, a fact which should alert us to any easy acceptance of these texts as containing exclusive and universal human standards. Reader-oriented theories have further shown that the meaning of a text lies not in the author's intended meaning but in the interchange between reader and text.

As such, this new methodological shift has described historical criticism as subjective and as representing the interests of its practitioners, European and North American white males. It has further exposed this way of reading as a way of imposing a universal standard, whereby all readers—regardless of gender, race, class, ethnicity, or national background—were expected to find the same meaning in the text. The shift, especially in terms of its reader-centered theories, has given way to the liberation of readers, allowing for differences among readers and enabling readers to insert their own questions and hold their ground.

At the same time, this new methodological shift does have its limits. To begin with, its theoretical orientation is largely of Western origin, and theory too is culturally bound.[45] In addition, as Stephen Moore has argued, in this shift readers have remained text-bound, still attempting to find the meaning in the text rather than creating such meaning freely and responsibly. Moore notes: "Reader theory in literary studies is a Pandora's box into which we infant literary critics of the Bible have barely began to peer. Opened more fully it might release something unsettling. . . ."[46] Moore's critique is enlightening, but in the end it too depends on Western standards for its conclusions. A look at African, Asian, and Latin American interpretations of the Bible clearly shows that the real reader in these contexts has been very much alive and that

Pandora's box has been glaringly open for quite some time now.[47] For this type of criticism, the question, "Is there a text in this class?" ceases to be a theoretical question. In effect, the biblical text becomes subordinated to the context, the culture, and the sociopolitical issues of readers, so that readers literally proceed to re-write the text. Moore's critique, therefore, fails to incorporate how Two-Thirds World readers have been reading.

Thus, if this new methodological shift wishes to avoid the imposition of a universal standard, it must acknowledge and take into account readers from the Two-Thirds World, who mix biblical stories with stories from their own continents—stories of poverty as well as stories of struggle against economic and cultural oppression. I would argue, therefore, that it is Africans, Asians, and Latin Americans, as those who celebrate diversity and confront imperialism, who are the real postcolonial readers. Indeed, their way of bringing other texts, contexts, and current struggles of exploitation and survival into biblical criticism shows that they have taken a stand against imperialism. In fact, many of the strategies I suggest in this essay can be readily learned from an analysis of Two-Thirds World criticism. Such a position implies that the new shift must become global by incorporating the criticism of the Two-Thirds World within its purview. I have argued that the Pandora's box of Two-Thirds World readers is glaringly open and that such readers are re-writing the text. Their readings may not be recognizable as biblical criticism, since they are openly theological, but then I believe that all historical as well as literary and cultural readings have been ultimately theological as well.

I should like to conclude by giving an example from my own studies in the United States on how the new shift can become global. On the one hand, I had a required course in New Testament methods, which presented a whole array of methods and theories regarding how the Bible could be read, ranging from traditional historical criticism to more recent literary and cultural criticism. The course provided the student with a variety of analytic methods. On the other hand, I took an elective course on global biblical hermeneutics, which exposed me to how different groups read the Bible and why. This latter course made me realize that most of what I had done in the course on methods was indeed enlightening, but of Western origin. It seems to me that, if we wish to counteract imperialism and move the new shift from a Western to a global level of discourse, a course on global biblical hermeneutics should be required as well.

Keeping the Focus: Biblical Criticism and Ethical Responsibility

One needs to ask, what is the major goal of biblical criticism and who is served by it? Is biblical criticism responsible only to its immediate institutions and structures, or does it have a global responsibility as well? Ulrich Luz has recently questioned the aims of the historical-critical approach and has called biblical criticism to responsibility. Pointing out that the Christian "text has produced untold suffering," Luz maintains that "the history of Christianity is, as we all know it, far from a history of love of enemies; examples to the contrary are numerous."[48] Thus, Luz argues that we cannot separate the Christian

texts from their "history of effects." Rather, he continues, "it is important to
see that the history of effects excludes the possibility of separating texts or
their interpretations from their historical consequences."[49] Thus, according to
Luz, "texts have power and cannot be separated from their consequences."[50]
This is a call to ethical commitment, with a twofold challenge to biblical critics: to confront such effects of the text as slavery, imperialism, colonialism,
neo-colonialism, anti-Semitism, homophobia, sexism, and racism; and to seek
ways of counteracting texts or interpretations that perpetuate any of these
forms of oppression.

As an outsider, I have found that in biblical criticism, ethical responsibility
has tended to focus on those evils that have occurred at the heart of the West,
while ignoring the historical effects having to do with the Two-Thirds World.[51]
In this paper I have called biblical criticism to recognize the global effects of the
biblical texts. To do so, one must always keep the following questions in mind:
Who is served by biblical criticism, and what does biblical criticism hope to
achieve? For questions such as these I find Edward Said's words quite to the
point: "Criticism must think of itself as life-enhancing and constitutively
opposed to every form of tyranny, domination, and abuse; its social goals are
noncoercive knowledge produced in the interests of human freedom."[52]

CONCLUDING COMMENTS:
FEMINISM, IMPERIALISM, AND BIBLICAL CRITICISM

While I was studying in the United Kingdom, I used to sit in seminars where I
was the only black and African student. As one might expect, we engaged the
text from a historical-critical perspective and thus as objective and disinterested readers. Most of the time, what the rest of the class observed provoked a
lot of discussion, while I found it boring and meaningless. At the same time,
the questions I raised were often met by the comment, "interesting," and followed by a brief silence, whereupon the class proceeded to other issues of the
text. Gradually, I began to regard my own questions as "eisegesis," as opposed
to the "exegesis" done by the rest of the class. As a result, I tried to be objective, neutral—to take things out of the text rather than to read them into the
text. Once again, however, I received the same response. I decided, therefore,
that I could no longer display my ignorance. I began to sit in long seminars
conspicuously silent, but boiling with anger for not voicing my own questions.
The dynamics of the method as well as the power relations at work—one has
to keep in mind that the British had been my former colonizers—seemed to
confirm what the colonizers had always said about us, namely, that the colonized were not sufficiently intelligent.

Fortunately, I had told my adviser that I was interested in studying about
issues of culture and women in the New Testament. Consequently, in the second
term we began to read a wide range of feminist theology and feminist interpretations of the Bible. We read, among others, Mary Daly, Rosemary Radford
Ruether, Letty M. Russell, Elisabeth Schüssler Fiorenza, Ann Loades, and
Ursula King. I could sit silent no longer. I began to speak out fearlessly. A num-

ber of particular statements struck home to me and came to define what I understood to be the meaning and goals of feminist biblical criticism: "Whatever diminishes or denies the full humanity of women must be presumed not to reflect the divine or an authentic relation to the divine";[53] "Until every woman is free, no woman is free"; and "The locus of divine revelation and grace is therefore not the Bible or tradition of a patriarchal church, but the ekklesia of women and the lives of women who live the option for our women selves."[54]

The reasons why such readings reinvigorated my interest and attention were clear. First, they addressed my interests as a woman. Second, they clearly stated the aims and goals of such criticism. Third, they proclaimed their allegiance not to the text as such but rather to the liberation of those struggling against oppression and exploitation. Fourth, they not only articulated a broad vision of the discipline but also were critical of any method that called for a disinterested and objective type of reader. In short, feminist biblical criticism advanced a very specific yet global vision of liberation: a commitment to the liberation of all people and an assault on all forms of oppression, even when supported by the sacred texts. In other words, the biblical text emerged as subordinate to the liberation of all creation.

Over the years feminist biblical criticism has grown in influence and sophistication. At the same time, however, I have become more and more disillusioned with it. As a postcolonial subject from Sub-Saharan African, I now see such criticism as representing by and large a challenge from within—a challenge to white male biblical critics to examine how their methods and objectives have contributed to the marginalization of women. I have also come to see such criticism as basically involving a lively conversation between different groups of feminists in the First World (e.g., white and African American; Jewish and Christian; Protestant and Catholic; liberals and conservatives; reformists and reconstructionists; revisionists and liberationists; the literary-minded and the historically minded). In such a conversation the concerns and experience of postcolonialism, of those outside the First World, remain at best secondary.[55]

Let me elaborate on this point. I have argued that postcolonialism has to do with the close linkage between the First World and the Two-Thirds World brought about by imperialism, which has successfully sought to enforce Western ideas and practices in all areas of life—be it commerce, religion, language, clothing, government, education, architecture, and so on—as universal standards. I have also argued that the very presence of people from the Two-Thirds World who speak English, French, Portuguese, or Spanish and profess to be Christian, while their own languages and religions have survived colonialism, constitutes eloquent testimony to the pervasiveness of imperialism. Again, I would emphasize in this regard that imperialism should be seen as a form of oppression characterized by the imposition of the values of the dominant on a worldwide scale, resulting in a relationship with "the other" where their perceptions of reality are devalued and they are seen as having to be taught the ways of the new civilization—to be "developed" and "Christianized." I have further argued that for the Two-Thirds World the Bible has functioned as one of the "master's tools," with which to inscribe a universal standard on a world of diversity. In other words, imperialist Christianity was by no means an encounter between subjects who engaged in a free exchange of words of life and wisdom. As such, I cannot but regard the goal of feminist biblical criticism, "to reclaim early Christian history" as its "own history and religious vision," as a goal that shares in the master's text. Such a goal can be achieved by reconstructing the presence and participation of women in the early church, but it cannot be liberating to those women who have experienced the master narrative as an assault on their own narratives.

Thus, the historical-reconstructionist approach, like the dominant historical-critical approach, goes behind the text and focuses on the first few centuries of the early church. This approach works to the exclusion of the modern and contemporary periods, in effect, that period of time that links together the biblical critics of the First and the Two-Thirds World. Such an approach has enabled feminist biblical criticism to bracket the role of the Bible in the promotion of imperialism during the eighteenth through the twentieth centuries. For example, Elisabeth Schüssler Fiorenza critiques the formation and selection of the Christian Testament as informed and impelled by the desire to consolidate the empire and hence to suppress the diversity of early Christianity, without at all dealing with how the Bible was used in the eighteenth through the twentieth centuries to suppress other religious traditions and undermine their perceptions of reality and the divine.

Likewise, the historical-reconstructionist approach has emphasized the role of women at the center of Christian history in terms of their contribution to the mission, in the face of a male authorship and scholarship that suppressed the presence of women. Once again, this has proved a great challenge to an androcentric scholarship and church and has given many women the courage to speak out and to take positions of leadership. However, such an approach has failed to analyze the ideology of the mission as such: does the mission approach "the other" as an equal subject or as an object of conversion? Indeed, my discussion of the Matthean mission text above has attempted to show that what the gospel propounds is an ideology of subjugation and subordination. From the experience of the so-called "mission fields," therefore, the failure of feminist biblical criticism to redefine the concept of mission, to see how difference can be encountered without the imposition of a universal standard, comes across just as imperialistic as the agenda of the metropolitan centers.

In fact, the recent feminist commentary on the Bible, *Searching the Scriptures*, shows how feminist biblical criticism is still conceived in terms of a challenge to white male scholars on the part of different First World feminists. Its exclusive focus on the Christian and Jewish canonical as well as extra-canonical texts—a body of texts that can hardly be separated from the Western domination of the Two-Thirds World—remains firmly within the imperialistic vision of raising one religious perspective as a universal standard. In other words, while earlier feminist statements had offered a vision in which priority was to be given to the liberation of women over the texts of Christianity and Judaism, such statements as the following seem to point in a different direction altogether:

Searching the Scriptures invites readers to move away from the prevalent feminist posture of either accepting or rejecting biblical texts on the whole to a careful critical assessment of and feminist engagement with ancient texts that challenge sociocultural stereotypes and produce a different cultural and religious imagination.[56]

While this invitation to focus on the master narratives and related texts is informed by new theories of multiple readings and is indeed liberating, it is also an indirect way of polishing the master's house to accommodate everybody, while the narratives of "the other" continue to be suppressed.[57]

At issue here is the fact that we are all inscribed, given its global reach and impact, within the historical experience of imperialism. Therefore, unless our critical practice takes deliberate measures to understand the mechanisms of past and present imperialisms—to understand the marriage of imperialism with issues of gender, race, class, religion, and sexual orientation—even the most liberationist of discourses will end up reinscribing the structures of violence and exploitation. If, however, feminist biblical criticism wishes to maintain its allegiance to the goal of liberation for all women and creation, as I still believe is the case, it will need to embark on new and different forms of travel.

Such travels should move us from an exclusive focus on one historical period, the fortress of the early church, to a concern for the many other histories of the Christian church; from one religious tradition to the other religious traditions of the world; from an approach that is text-oriented to an approach that makes room for symbols, ritual, art, songs, drama, and poetry. Such travels should also move us not only to read and listen to old stories but also to create new stories, as well as to keep the focus on the aims of our critical practice. Finally, such travels should move us as well from literary studies to cultural studies:[58] a study and critique of various religious cultures and texts, knowing full well that to focus on the Christian and Jewish literary constructions alone is to risk promoting and maintaining the culture of the dominant metropolitan centers at the expense of the cultural liberation of the Two-Thirds World.

NOTES

1. J. Phillips, "Educating the Savages," *Recasting the World: Writing After Colonialism,* ed. Jonathan White (Baltimore and London: The Johns Hopkins University Press, 1993) 26.

2. To be sure, a lot of metropolitan travelers have journeyed to our countries in order to engage in anthropological studies; however, the epistemological approach behind such learning remains hegemonic, insofar as it serves to prove the superiority of Western knowledge.

3. For different types of travelers, see Fernando F. Segovia, "Towards A Hermeneutic of the Diaspora," *Reading from This Place.* Volume 1: *Social Location and Biblical Interpretation in the United States,* ed. Fernando Segovia and Mary Ann Tolbert (Minneapolis: Fortress Press, 1995) 60-61.

4. According to the archival records, the Botswana initially understood the act of reading the Bible as "talking to a talking book." This suggests to me that they did not regard the Bible as either containing a meaning to be extracted or as having authority

over them. Rather, it would seem that they looked upon the Bible in terms of a conversation between text and reader, in the course of which they could agree, disagree, or compromise. In other words, readers were free to draw from their own experience and culture in talking back to the "talking book."

5. See E. J. Krige, *The Realm of a Rain Queen* (Oxford: Oxford University Press, 1947).

6. See Carol Davies and A. Graves, eds., *Ngambika: Studies of Women in African Literature* (Trenton: Africa World Press, 1986) 1-17.

7. This point is well illustrated in Ifi Amadiume, *Male Daughters, Female Husbands: Gender and Sex in an African Masociety* (London: Atlantic Highlands, 1987).

8. To be sure, behind Livingstone's commitment to put an end to slavery in the interior of Africa, there was a double standard, as is evident from his own words:

> My object in going into the country south of the desert was to instruct the natives in a knowledge of Christianity, but many circumstances prevented my living amongst them more than seven years, amongst which were considerations arising out of the slave system carried on by Dutch Boers. I resolved to go into the country beyond. . . ."

In other words, Livingstone was leaving Southern Africa to stop the slavery practiced by Arabs and African kings, because the Dutch Boers were enslaving black people! Cited in Norman E. Thomas, ed., *Classic Texts in Mission and World Christianity* (Maryknoll: Orbis Books, 1995) 67-68.

9. Timothy Holmes (*Journey to Livingstone: An Exploration of an Imperial Myth* [Edinburgh: Canongate Press, 1993] xv) quotes from Livingstone's secret letter to an influential colonial figure to show how there were also "ulterior motives" at work, largely ignored by previous writers:

> My objectives I may state that they have something more than meets of the eye. They are not merely exploratory, for I go with the intention of benefitting both the African and my own countryman. . . . I tell to none but such as you in whom I have confidence.

10. As cited by Basil Davidson, *Modern Africa: A Social and Political History* (London: Longman, 1994) 17.

11. Gerald West, *Biblical Hermeneutics of Liberation: Modes of Reading the Bible in South African Context* (Maryknoll: Orbis Books, 1991) 52.

12. Emmanuel Martey, *African Theology: Inculturation and Liberation* (Maryknoll: Orbis Books, 1993) 51.

13. See Katie G. Cannon, "Slave Ideology and Biblical Interpretation," *Interpretation for Liberation,* in *Semeia* 47; ed. Elisabeth Schüssler Fiorenza (Atlanta: Scholars Press, 1989) 9-23.

14. Louis L. Snyder, *The Imperialism Reader: Documents and Readings on Modern Expansionism* (New York: D. Van Nostrand Company, 1962) 211.

15. Ngungi wa Thiong'o, *Decolonizing the Mind: The Politics of Language* (London: James Curry, 1994) 91.

16. Gayatri Spivak, *The Post-colonial Critic* (New York: Routledge, 1990) 71.

17. E. Said, *Culture and Imperialism* (New York: Alfred A. Knoff, 1993) 336.

18. See Bill Ashcroft, Gareth Griffiths, and Helen Tiffin, eds., *The Empire Writes Back: Theory and Practice in Post-Colonial Literatures* (New York: Routledge, 1989) 4-6.

19. This strategy differs with various forms of colonization. For example, in the case of North and South America, Australia, Canada, and South Africa, colonialism was

marked by a massive number of settlers, who thus overcame the indigenous populations by way of sheer might and numbers.

20. See J. Andrew Overman, *Matthew's Gospel and Formative Judaism: The Social World of the Matthean Community* (Minneapolis: Fortress Press, 1990). Overman notes how the myth of Johanan's escape and his prediction of the next emperor is a way of seeking favor with the Roman imperial powers (38-43).

21. Compare also the story of the Roman centurion with that of the Canaanite woman (8:5-13; 15:21-28) as well as the story of the temple tax with that of the imperial tribute (17:24-27; 22:15-22).

22. See Richard A. Horsley, *Jesus and the Spiral of Violence: Popular Jewish Resistance in Roman Palestine* (Minneapolis: Fortress Press, 1993).

23. During the Hasmonean Kingdom (142-63 B.C.E.), the expansion of territory and enforcement of Judaism on the subjugated shows that Israel was no different from other imperial powers of the time (John E. Stambaugh and David Balch, *The New Testament in Its Social Environment* [Philadelphia: Westminster, 1986] 22-23).

24. Itumeleng J. Mosala (*Biblical Hermeneutics and Black Theology in South Africa* [Grand Rapids: William B. Eerdmans, 1989]) points out that "the biblical truth that God sides with the oppressed is only one of the biblical truths" and argues that "what one can do is to take sides in a struggle that is not confirmed by the whole struggle" (16, 27).

25. R. Weems, "Reading Her Way Through the Struggle: African American Women and the Bible," in *Stony the Road We Trod: African American Biblical Interpretation,* ed. Cain Hope Felder (Minneapolis: Fortress Press, 1991) 71.

26. Spivak, *The Post-colonial Critic,* 71.

27. Audre Lorde, *Sister Outsider* (Freedom: The Crossing Press, 1984) 112.

28. Thiong'o, *Decolonizing the Mind,* 20.

29. Ibid., 3.

30. See also Robert Allen Warrior ("A Native American Perspective: Canaanites, Cowboys, and Indians," *Voices from the Margin,* ed. R. S. Sugirtharajah [Maryknoll: Orbis Books, 1991]), who insists on reading from the perspective of the dispossessed Canaanites rather than that of the liberated Israelites and concludes by rejecting the use of the "master's tools": we "may be well advised this time not to listen to the outsiders with their promises of deliverance. We will perhaps do better to look elsewhere for our vision of justice, peace, and political sanity" (295).

31. W. A. Meeks, *The First Urban Christians: The Social World of the Apostle Paul* (New Haven: Yale University Press, 1983) 1.

32. Ibid.

33. M. A. Tolbert, "Defining the Problem: The Bible and Feminist Hermeneutics," *The Bible and Feminist Hermeneutics,* in *Semeia* 28; ed. M. A. Tolbert (Chico: Scholars Press, 1983) 120.

34. E. Schüssler Fiorenza, "Transgressing Canonical Boundaries," *Searching the Scriptures.* Volume 2: *A Feminist Commentary,* ed. E. Schüssler Fiorenza (New York: Crossroad, 1994) 1-14.

35. M. A. Tolbert, "The Politics and Poetics of Location," *Reading from This Place,* 1:313.

36. For an in-depth analysis of this thesis, see Said, *Culture and Imperialism.*

37. Martey, *African Theology,* 8.

38. Meeks, *First Urban Christians,* 1.

39. See Barbara Christian, "Whose Canon Is It Anyway?" *Issues in World Literature,* ed. Mary Caws, Patricia Laurence, and Sarah Bird Wright (New York: HarperCollins College Publishers, 1994) 17-22.

40. C. S. Banana, "The Case for a New Bible," *"Rewriting" the Bible: The Real Issues,* ed. J. L. Cox, I. Mukonyora, and F. J. Vestraelen (Gweru: Mambo Press, 1993) 21.

41. Ibid., 17.

42. Michael Taussig (*Shamanism, Colonialism, and the Wild Man* [Chicago: University of Chicago, 1987]) provides an interesting use of non-verbal discourse regarding colonial violence and healing among the Shamans of South America.

43. See the forthcoming issue of *Semeia* on *Reading the Bible with Ordinary Readers*, edited by Gerald West and myself.

44. For a clear, succinct summary of the new methodological shift, see F. F. Segovia, "'And They Began to Speak in Other Tongues': Competing Modes of Discourse in Contemporary Biblical Criticism," *Reading from This Place*, 1:1-32.

45. On this point, see Mark C. Taylor, "Unsettling Issues," *JAAR* 62 (1994) 949-63.

46. S. D. Moore, *Literary Criticism and the Gospels: The Theoretical Challenge* (New Haven: Yale University Press, 1989) 107. Further, according to Moore, one finds in biblical studies a moral to the effect that "real readers need not apply" (106), not even in reader-oriented criticism, where the reader in question is still said to be by and large "a repressed reader" (107).

47. See, among others, Virginia Fabella and Mercy Amba Oduyoye, eds., *With Passion and Compassion: Third World Women Doing Theology* (Maryknoll: Orbis Books, 1990); R. S. Sugirtharajah, ed., *Voices from the Margin: Interpreting the Bible in the Third World* (Maryknoll: Orbis Books, 1991); R. S. Sugirtharajah, ed., *Asian Faces of Jesus* (Maryknoll: Orbis Books, 1993); Ursula King, ed., *Feminist Theology from the Third World: A Reader* (Maryknoll: Orbis Books, 1994).

48. U. Luz, *Matthew in History: Interpretation, Influence, and Effects* (Minneapolis: Fortress Press, 1994) 33.

49. Ibid., 34.

50. Ibid., 33.

51. Luz's book is a good example: while he mentions anti-Semitism and the Holocaust, he says nothing about imperialism and colonialism.

52. E. W. Said, *The World, the Text and the Critic* (Cambridge: Harvard University Press, 1983) 29.

53. R. Radford Ruether, *Sexism and God Talk: Toward a Feminist Theology* (Boston: Beacon, 1983) 19.

54. E. Schüssler Fiorenza, "The Will to Choose and to Reject: Continuing our Critical Practice," *Feminist Interpretation of the Bible*, ed. Letty M. Russell (Philadelphia: Westminster, 1985) 127-128.

55. See, e.g., Amy-Jill Levine, *The Social and Ethnic Dimensions of Matthean Social History: Go Nowhere Among the Gentiles (Matt. 10:5b)* (Lewiston, NY: Edwin Mellen Press, 1988). Her reading of Matt 20:18-20 endorses universalism without problematizing its implications or assessing how it has affected the non-Western world. Her reading, however, is in conversation with First World Christians, whose celebration of the universalism of Christianity versus the particularism and legalism of Judaism has been instrumental in the evils of anti-Semitism.

56. E. Schüssler Fiorenza, "Transforming the Legacy of *The Woman's Bible*," *Searching the Scriptures*. Volume 1: *A Feminist Introduction*, ed. E. Schüssler Fiorenza (New York: Crossroad, 1993) 11.

57. See Kathleen O'Brien Wicker, "Teaching Feminist Studies in a Postcolonial Context," *Searching the Scriptures*, 1:367-80. While the use of woman as a universal category has been addressed, the use of Christianity as a universal standard largely remains unproblematized.

58. For this argument see Antony Easthope, *Literary into Cultural Studies* (New York: Routledge, 1991).

13

CROSS-TEXTUAL INTERPRETATION
AND ITS IMPLICATIONS
FOR BIBLICAL STUDIES

Archie C. C. Lee

It is a given in contemporary biblical studies that the texts of the Bible come from and reflect different social locations, cultural backgrounds, economic contexts, and political situations.[1] For contemporary biblical studies, therefore, in order to understand a text of the Bible, it is necessary to pay attention to its broad historical context, with questions such as the following in mind: Who put it into writing? For whom was it written? Why was it written? In *what* form and language? What resources were used? Questions such as these have been the concern of the historical-critical approach in biblical studies, and their corresponding answers have contributed to and shaped our understanding of the meaning of these texts. It has been the goal of historical criticism, therefore, to elucidate the history of the text.

More recently, however, biblical scholars have acknowledged the limitations of this approach, especially with regard to the fact that it presupposes an alleged objectivity on the part of the reader with regard to the text, established by means of a supposedly scientific method, and thus fails to take into account the vital interaction between the received text, the contemporary reader, and the act of reading in the process of interpretation.[2] As a result, the enormous impact of the social location, cultural background, economic context, and political situation of the reader on the process of interpretation has been completely ignored. Indeed, in the process the far-reaching influence of such factors as gender, race, and power on the reading of the Bible has been totally bypassed as well.

Thus, for example, within the discussion on biblical theology, it was believed that the biblical critic, through the use of historical criticism, could reconstruct the biblical world of the past, understand the "what was" of the text ("what the text meant"), and then proceed to apply the text to the "what is" of the present situation ("what the text means").[3] Yet, contemporary hermeneutics has shown that our reading and understanding of the past are deeply influenced not only by the presuppositions and biases of readers, but also by their contemporary sociopolitical and postmodern situations.[4] In effect, the social location of the interpreter is now seen as entering decisively into the process of interpretation. Such a "location," moreover, is further seen as encompassing the complicated questions of race and gender as well as economic and political relationships. As such, the concept of "location" actually involves, therefore, a "hybrid set of locations."[5] Consequently, literary critics now place much greater emphasis on readers, the response of readers to texts, and the act of reading as shaped by the interaction between reader and text.[6]

Biblical critics have come to realize, therefore, not only that the biblical text reflects different time periods but also that the views and interpretations of the Bible from different generations cannot be separated from their respective historical contexts. Thus, biblical studies in the West have been shaped by the social setting and historical background of different generations in the West, as they have tried to come to terms with the questions of their own age. For example, Rolf Rendtorff admits this very fact when he writes about the understanding of post-exilic Israel in modern German studies of the Old Testament.[7] Similarly, in a recent collection of essays, Walter Brueggemann takes very seriously the social dimension of both the biblical text and its interpretation.[8] More sharply still, feminist and liberation hermeneutics have constantly directed our attention to the social contexts out of which both the biblical texts and their interpretations come into being.[9]

BIBLICAL INTERPRETATION AND ASIAN REALITIES

Asian biblical scholars are certainly no exception in this regard. We have inherited the legacy of the biblical faith, the Christian doctrine handed down to us from the history of Western Christianity, and the tradition of contemporary Western biblical studies. At the same time, we remain very much rooted in Asia. On the one hand, we are located in the pluralist *social* realities of Asia. For example, given their experience of unjust political systems and an uneven distribution of wealth, the poor and oppressed of Asia have brought a completely different perspective to bear on the biblical text. Similarly, given their experience of suffering under oppressive and chauvinist patriarchal structures, Asian women have also contributed to the search for meaningful reading methods.[10] On the other hand, we are located as well in the pluralist *religious* realities of Asia. Indeed, Asia may be said to constitute a special region of the world in this regard, given the fact that it possesses a number of living religious traditions. These religions have prospered, closely associated as they are with the life and culture of the people. Their scriptures and classics have nurtured the life and spirit of numerous Asians. Thus, if Christian biblical scholars in Asia were to turn deliberately away from such realities and ignore the religious cultures of Asia and their corresponding traditions of textual interpretation, their Christian faith would never prove relevant to the concerns and needs of Asian peoples and, as a result, would never be able to contribute to and enrich the religious life and world of meaning of Asians.[11] For Asian biblical critics, therefore, there is an urgent need to search for and come up with principles and methods of biblical interpretation that are relevant to Asian contexts.[12]

ASIAN CHRISTIAN IDENTITY
AND CROSS-TEXTUAL INTERPRETATION

At the same time, however, when Asian Christians proceed to take equally seriously the Christian religion in which they believe and the religious culture that has shaped their lives, they experience a profound crisis of self-identity. We Asians live in two worlds, inherit two stories, and possess two texts: the world, story, and text of Christianity as well as the world, story, and text of the indigenous religious culture.

In the case of China, for example, the three religions present in Chinese culture—Confucianism, Buddhism, and Taoism—have left, in the course of their long history on Chinese soil, a profound imprint on the Chinese. On the one hand, these traditions constitute moral teachings, embodied in literature, language, customs, festivals, mythology, legends, stories, and folk religions; on the other hand, these traditions also convey a profound religious meaning, molding our perspective on life and our view of the world. By and large, therefore, Christianity represents a foreign element in Asian cultures, a "strange" and "unfamiliar" element, quite aside from the oppressive practices associated with colonialism and imperialism in the past. Thus, before the Christian faith appears on the scene, the self is characterized by traditional cultural values and precepts; then, after the encounter with Christianity, the result is a split self and a split world. Moreover, since the Christian faith demands an exclusive acceptance of the gospel at the expense of the local cultural heritage and involves a denigrating attitude toward all indigenous cultures, the new converts end up establishing separate compartments for these two conflicting worlds. For Chinese Christians, there is simply no easy way to be set free from this dilemma.

Yet, if we are to integrate within ourselves the encounter with and challenge of the "otherness" represented by Christianity, Asian biblical scholars must take equally seriously both our Asian cultural and religious heritage (Text A) and the Bible (Text B), instead of subjugating one "text" to the other or making one of these "texts" the absolute norm. Both Text A and Text B must be held in creative dialogue and interaction. One text has to be open to the claims and challenges of the other text in order for transformation to take place in a meaningful way. For Asian Christians the encounter of these two texts is not an option, nor is it an intellectual game in which one chooses to participate at will. Such an encounter forms part of the very experience of conversion to Christianity, a Christianity that has claimed absolute truth over all other "pagan" cultures and religions.[13] Consequently, both the sense of alienation and the crisis of identity involved in such a conversion need to be addressed and corrected by means of a cross-textual reading. The fundamental aim of this cross-textual reading is not simply to engage in the luxury of doing comparative studies, but rather to bring about an integrated self. Unless genuine crossings take place between these two texts within the self of Asian Christians, the self will remain disintegrated—a self torn between two worlds.

No matter the extent to which contemporary Chinese have appropriated Chinese culture, whether profoundly or artificially so, it is not at all easy to remain totally disassociated from Chinese spirituality or to transcend the confines of Chinese religious culture. Again, no matter how Chinese Christians have positioned themselves and committed themselves in life—a situation further complicated by the fact that the Chinese in mainland China, Taiwan, and Hong Kong appear to have different perspectives—the choice between the Christian religion and Chinese culture is not at all an easy one to make. While Christianity challenges us to deal with the complicities of the realities of Asian life at a cultural and religious level, Chinese culture presses us to reinterpret the Christian text and its traditional theology.

At the same time, the crisis brought about by the need to establish our self-identity and to determine our commitment in life provides us with an excellent opportunity to call ourselves back from despair and to regain a measure of hope and joy. Both Chinese culture and Christian faith possess their bright and dark sides, their positive and negative elements, their liberating and enslaving dimensions. Thus, whether we look upon the dark, negative, and enslaving elements in terms of inherent, oppressive elements against humanity or in terms of institutional and theological restrictions and biases coming from the tradition, such elements do not escape the judgment of serious biblical interpretation among contemporary Asian Christians. When this happens, the bright, positive, and liberating elements of Asian culture as well as Christian faith—that is to say, the part that is both human and enriching—can come to the fore. Having one text challenge the other, sharing the perspective of one text with that of the other, and attempting to integrate the two texts form the process of building a world of meaning which is both holistic and relevant to the context. Through this process the very acknowledgment of crisis can become the basis for developing our orientation and commitment as well as for reshaping our identity as Christian Asians. Such is the vision and objective of cross-textual hermeneutics, as I see it.[14]

I use the term "textual" here not only with reference to written texts—such as religious classics, literary traditions, and historical documents, but also to non-written texts—such as orally transmitted scriptural traditions[15] as well as social contexts, economic and political experiences, and life experiences. In other words, the pluralistic realities of Asia become the abundant text of Asian Christians. This text should be neither neglected nor underestimated. This multiple understanding of "text," which reflects the religiosity and spirituality of Asian people, provides the basic point of departure for cross-textual reading.

Presumably, the Christian text and the Chinese text are unrelated from a historical point of view, growing as they did out of very different cultural and historical contexts of their own. The task of cross-textual hermeneutics is thus very similar to that of critical theories in comparative literature, as Zhang Longxi describes it: "to transcend the limitation of a narrowly defined perspective and to expand our horizon by assimilating as much as possible what appears to be alien and belonging to the Other."[16] This encounter of the unfamiliar in the hermeneutical process, according to Longxi, will bring about an enrichment of experience and knowledge by means of a mutual engagement of the self and the other, what Hans-Georg Gadamer calls the "fusion of horizons." In such a process, the alien and the unfamiliar will eventually be absorbed with the familiar to become part of the engaging self. This is especially meaningful to Asian Christians, who have to come to terms with their double identity as both Asian and Christian. The two texts that are meaningful to the integrity of the self, the cultural text and the Christian text, must be integrated in a constant dialogue.

I use the term "cross" with such meanings as "interaction," "encounter," or "meeting" in mind, along the lines of crossing a river from one shore to the other.[17] Thus, besides placing two texts side-by-side, cross-textual interpretation also signifies the illumination of one text by the other, one point of view by the other. Through such encounters, new meanings can be discovered, meanings which might never be found by reading only one text. This is what I call "crossing." In fact, cross-textual interpretation does not stop with one crossing, for it envisions the possibility of many crossings, nor does it start from only one text and end up with another. The aim of such multiple crossings is not comparative studies as such but rather transformation and enrichment: the transformation of one's whole life, a process of self-discovery. The result in the end is an "enriched-transformed existence."[18]

By means of cross-textual interpretation not only will the foundation of Asian contextual theology be further consolidated, but also the vitality and spirituality of Asian Christians will become much more distinctive. This encounter among various contexts will provide resources thereby for coping with the social and political complexities of Asia and beyond as well as for making our societies more human. Asian Christianity will then be able to leave its own mark in the traditions of the ecumenical church and make its own contribution to both the Christian religion and humanity as a whole.

IMPLICATIONS FOR BIBLICAL INTERPRETATION AND BIBLICAL PEDAGOGY

The critical awareness of Asia as a religiously plural world inevitably awakens biblical scholars and theologians to the fact of a plurality of scriptures. For example, in the light of this particular aspect of the Asian scene vis-à-vis the West, Stanley Samartha, an Indian Christian scholar, writes with regard to one's approach to the understanding and interpretation of the biblical tradition:

> In the West the Church had to develop its hermeneutics in response to developments in science, philosophy and historiography and other secular movements. The Church in the West had no scriptures of other faiths to take into account. Therefore, its hermeneutics inevitably had to be a mono-scriptural hermeneutics. Today, however, Christians in a multi-religious world cannot ignore other scriptures that provide spiritual support and ethical guidance to millions of their adherents.[19]

To be sure, this situation regarding the plurality of scriptures in Asia has immense implications for biblical hermeneutics and biblical pedagogy. Indeed, it constitutes a profound challenge to traditional notions of canon/scripture, concepts of authority, and understandings of truth-claims.

First, biblical interpretation must go beyond a mono-scriptural hermeneutics. The need at present is for a cross-textual or cross-scriptural approach, an approach that not only allows the various scriptures to enter into dialogue with one another but also—and very importantly from the point of view of the identity and integrity of Asian Christians—facilitates the transformation of the scriptures in question. Indeed, recent efforts to rethink the notion of "scriptures" have been quite illuminating.[20] In this regard, insights from the encounter between and the transformation of Yahwist faith and Canaanite culture can prove very illuminating as well.[21] Our situation in Asia, however, is different from that of the Bible and must not be dominated by the triumphalist celebration of one religious conviction (Yahwism) over another (Baalism). In fact, there is need for further studies to re-address the imbalance of the biblical transformation, which has perhaps been shaped by a Judeo-Christian perspective and understanding.[22]

Second, hermeneutical methods adopted or developed in the religious traditions of Asia—as in the case of Hindu, Buddhist, Taoist, and Confucian hermeneutics—must be re-examined from the point of view of relevance to biblical pedagogy. Recent research along the line of comparative hermeneutics can shed new light on biblical studies.[23] In fact, there is a group of biblical scholars presently involved in a research project entitled "The Bible in the Context of Other Asian Scriptures."[24] The teaching of biblical studies in Asia will definitely take a different shape and be greatly enriched by this effort to take into account the scriptures of other living religions. Biblical studies must not be separated from the study of world religions and cultures; on the contrary, courses on other religions and cultures have to be incorporated into the curriculum of religious and theological studies. Not only must we study the religion and culture of the Ancient Near East and the Bible,[25] but also we must not neglect our own religious heritage and cultural traditions.

Finally, I should like to underline one last point in this task ahead of us. We need to review our understanding of syncretism and overcome our fear of it, before we can engage in fruitful cross-textual and cross-scriptural hermeneutics within a context of religious and cultural pluralism. After all, syncretism is regarded as a positive development and much encouraged in the history of most Asian religions.[26] In the end, all religions are syncretistic in one way or another, and neither the Christian faith nor the Bible is an exception in this regard.[27]

NOTES

1. On the social setting of biblical texts, see the works of Norman K. Gottwald, e.g., "Social Matrix and Canonical Shape," *Theology Today* 42 (1985-86) 307-21; and *The Hebrew Bible—A Socio-Literary Introduction* (Philadelphia: Fortress Press, 1985) chaps. 1-2. On the sociopolitical background of prophecy, see Robert Wilson, *Prophecy and Society in Ancient Israel* (Philadelphia: Fortress Press, 1980) chap. 1; Burke O. Long, "Social Dimensions of Prophetic Conflict," *Anthropological Perspectives on Old Testament Prophecy,* ed. Robert C. Culley and Thomas W. Overholt (Chico: Scholars Press, 1982) 31-60; Andrew Mayes, "Prophecy and Society in Israel," *Of Prophets' Visions and the Wisdom of Sages: Essays in Honour of R. Norman Whybray,* ed. Heather A. McKay and David J. A. Clines (Sheffield, JSOT Press, 1993) 25-42.

2. For a brief review of the development of the historical-critical method, see Rolf Knierim, "Criticism of Literary Features, Form, Tradition, and Redaction," *The Hebrew Bible and Its Modern Interpreters,* ed. Douglas A. Knight and Gene M. Tucker (Chico: Scholars Press, 1985) 124-65. For more recent developments, see Robert C. Culley, "Exploring New Directions," ibid., 167-200; and Rolf Rendtorff, "Between Historical Criticism and Holistic Interpretation: New Trends in Old Testament Exegesis," *Congress Volume: Jerusalem, 1986,* Supplements to Vetus Testamentum 40 (Leiden: E. J. Brill, 1988) 298-303.

3. The concepts "what the text meant" and "what the text means" are employed by Krister Stendahl ("Biblical Theology, Contemporary," *The Interpreter's Dictionary of the Bible,* 1:418-32) to characterize the task of biblical theology.

4. See the discussions of the Bible and Culture Collective in *The Postmodern Bible,* ed. George Aichele, et al. (New Haven and London: Yale University Press, 1995).

5. Ibid., 5.

6. See ibid., 20-69. See also Wolfgang Iser, *Prospecting: From Reader Response to Literary Anthropology* (Baltimore: The Johns Hopkins University Press, 1989) 31-41; *The Act of Reading: A Theory of Aesthetic Response* (Baltimore: The Johns Hopkins University Press, 1978).

7. R. Rendtorff, "The Image of Postexilic Israel in German Bible Scholarship," *Canon and Theology: Overtures to an Old Testament Theology,* trans. and ed. Margaret Kohl (Edinburgh: T. & T. Clark, 1994) 66-75.

8. W. Brueggemann, *A Social Reading of the Old Testament: Prophetic Approaches to Israel's Communal Life,* ed. Patrick D. Miller (Minneapolis: Fortress Press, 1994) 174-96.

9. See, e.g., Elisabeth Schüssler Fiorenza, *In Memory of Her* (New York: Crossroad, 1986); J. Severino Croatto, *Exodus: A Hermeneutics of Freedom* (Maryknoll: Orbis Books, 1987). See also Christopher Rowland and Mark Corner, *Liberating Exegesis: The Challenge of Liberation Theology to Biblical Studies* (Louisville: Westminster/John Knox Press, 1989).

10. See, e.g., the articles by biblical scholars of the Third World in R. S. Sugirtharajah, ed., *Voices from the Margin. Interpreting the Bible in the Third World,* 2nd ed. rev. (London: SPCK; Maryknoll: Orbis Books, 1995). For a summary of Asian biblical hermeneutics, see R. S. Sugirtharajah, "Introduction, and Some Thoughts on Asian Biblical Hermeneutics," in R. S. Sugirtharajah, ed., *Commitment, Context and Text. Examples of Asian Hermeneutics,* spec. issue of *Biblical Interpretation* 2 (1994) 251-63.

11. Stanley J. Samartha, "Scripture and Scriptures," *One Christ—Many Religions: Toward a Revised Christology* (Maryknoll: Orbis Books, 1991) 66-86.

12. For recent attempts to develop Asian ways of biblical interpretation, see the articles in the special issue of *Biblical Interpretation* mentioned in n. 10 above as well as the recent volume of Kwok Pui-lan, *Discovering the Bible in the Non-Biblical World* (Maryknoll: Orbis Books, 1995), which raises important and critical issues related to the task of hermeneutics in the Asian world.

13. On the hostility between the Christian religion and Chinese culture and religion, see Jacques Gernet, *China and the Christian Impact: A Conflict of Cultures* (Cambridge: Cambridge University Press; Paris: Éditions de la Maison des Sciences de l'Homme, 1985) 126-40.

14. For the basic principles behind cross-textual hermeneutics, see my "Biblical Interpretation in Asian Perspectives," *Asia Journal of Theology* 71 (1993) 35-39. For its application to Chinese creation myths, see my "Genesis 1 from the Perspective of a Chinese Creation Myth," *Understanding Poets and Prophets: Essays in Honour of George Wishart Anderson,* ed. A. Graeme Auld (Sheffield: JSOT Press, 1993) 186-98; and "The Chinese Creation Myth of Nu Kua and the Biblical Narrative in Genesis 1-11," *Biblical Interpretation* 2 (1994) 312-24.

15. See William A. Graham, *Beyond the Written Word: Oral Aspects of Scripture in the History of Religion* (Cambridge: Cambridge University Press, 1987).

16. Zhang Longxi, *The Tao and the Logos: Literary Hermeneutics: East and West* (Durham: Duke University Press, 1992) xiv.

17. I have been asked why I use "cross-textual" rather than "inter-textual." Two reasons come immediately to mind. First, in the Jewish rabbinical tradition of hermeneutics, the term "inter-textual" refers to the relationship between or among texts within the Bible. Thus, the rabbis think that the Hebrew Bible constitutes an organized whole. As such, it is not only consistent from beginning to end, but it also involves cross-referencing and hence cross-expansion in meaning. Second, contemporary biblical scholars have developed this idea even further, as they search for important historical links in literary forms and concepts between texts or chapters of the Bible. See, e.g., Michael Fishbane, *Text and Texture: Close Readings of Selected Biblical Texts* (New York: Schocken Books 1979); Daniel Boyarin, *Intertextuality and the Reading of Midrash* (Bloomington and Indianapolis: Indiana University Press, 1990); Danna Nolan Fewell, ed., *Reading Between Texts: Intertextuality and the Hebrew Bible* (Louisville: Westminster/John Knox Press, 1992).

18. For this term, see Richard Wentz, *The Contemplation of Otherness: The Critical Vision of Religion* (Macon: Mercer University Press, 1984) 13.

19. S. J. Samartha, *One Christ—Many Religions,* 67.

20. See, e.g., Frederik M. Denny and Rodney L. Taylor, ed., *The Holy Book in Comparative Perspective* (Columbia: University of South Carolina Press, 1985); Harold Coward, *Sacred Word and Sacred Text* (Maryknoll: Orbis Books, 1988); Miriam Levering, ed., *Rethinking Scripture: Essays from a Comparative Perspective* (Albany: State University of New York Press, 1989); Jean Holm, ed., *Sacred Writings* (London: Pinter Publishers, 1994).

21. For example, Tikva Frymer-Kensky (*In the Wake of the Goddesses: Women, Culture, and the Biblical Transformation of Pagan Myth* [New York: The Free Press, 1992]) has analyzed the transformation of Canaanite myth in the Bible from the perspective of fertility and sexuality.

22. Scholarly assertions regarding the distinctiveness and superiority of the Judeo-Christian religion over other religions have had a definite impact on the proper understanding of Judaism and Christianity. Sociological and anthropological theories have seldom been applied to either of these religions. See Howard Eilberg-Schwartz, *The Savage in Judaism: An Anthropology of Israelite Religion and Ancient Judaism* (Bloomington and Indianapolis: Indiana University Press, 1990) 1-66.

23. See, e.g., John B. Henderson, *Scripture, Canon, and Commentary: A Comparison of Confucian and Western Exegesis* (Princeton: Princeton University Press, 1991).

24. This project is under the coordination of the Programme for Theology and Cultures in Asia.

25. J. Andrew Dearman, *Religion and Culture in Ancient Israel* (Peabody, MA: Hendrickson Publishers, 1992).

26. On the phenomenon of syncretism in Chinese culture and religion, see Judith A. Berling, *The Syncretic Religion of Liu Chao-en* (New York: Columbia University Press, 1980).

27. See, e.g., Morton Smith, "The Survival of the Syncretistic Cult of Yahweh," *Palestinian Parties and Politics that Shaped the Old Testament,* 2nd ed. corr. (London: SCM Press, 1987) 62-74; Anton Wessels, "Biblical Presuppositions For and Against Syncretism," *Dialogue and Syncretism: An Interdisciplinary Approach,* ed. Jerald D. Gort, et al. (Grand Rapids: William B. Eerdmans, 1989) 52-65; Jonathan A. Goldstein, "Jewish Acceptance and Rejection of Hellenism," *Semites, Iranians, Greeks and Rome: Studies in their Interactions* (Atlanta: Scholars Press, 1990) 11-32.

I4

BIBLICAL EXEGESIS
AND ITS SHORTCOMINGS
IN THEOLOGICAL EDUCATION

Temba L. J. Mafico

The modern academic trend in divinity schools and seminaries is to approach the Bible through a variety of scientific methods, collectively known as biblical exegesis. Lately, however, many biblical scholars seem to regard the historical-critical method as having been superseded by the many methodological "-isms" of recent times—structuralist criticism, narrative criticism, rhetorical criticism, and so forth. To be sure, there are those who still regard the historical-critical method as among the very best tools biblical scholarship has to offer, ultimately more comprehensive in nature than the other methods and thus inclusive of them as well. At any rate, there is no doubt that biblical exegesis has become too academic, too complex, and too cumbersome. It has become so professional that doing research today has become an end in itself in seminaries and divinity schools. Indeed, as a result of paying more attention to method than to theology in and from the text, a number of scholars have apparently become confused with regard to the worth of their labors, even turning against one another's methodological approaches to the Bible.[1]

Looking at the story of creation in Genesis, for instance, the exegete not only must ask whether the story represents an objective historical reality or simply an ideological narrative created by the author, but also must grapple with the question of why the author or redactor devised this narrative as a vehicle for communicating a theological message with serious repercussions for the status of women in both society and the church. Exegesis thus concerns itself with both the relationship of biblical historiography to real facts and the message communicated by such historiography, whether factual or ideological, in light of the questions raised by the people of the time. The problem facing the exegete, therefore, has to do not only with how to separate history from story in a biblical narrative, but also with ascertaining what message the narrator was attempting to communicate. Such an enquiry naturally leads to an investigation of the social and political conditions prevailing at the time of composition.

Given the flaws in the way that biblical exegesis is presently being done, many students take the course in exegesis primarily because it is a core course required for graduation. Even though they pass the course, the majority of them end up having learned very little or nothing at all. Some will never even remember the exegetical method while preparing sermons during their ministry.

By approaching the Bible simply as literature and dwelling more on such issues as textual structure and rhetoric, biblical exegesis has, as a consequence, lost its real value as a tool for elucidating scripture in a way that highlights its theological and didactic message. The questions scholars are presently asking, discussing, and writing about are not of much relevance to the problems and questions with which people in the church, in real life, are grappling. This is not, of course, the first time that scholars have been criticized for being engaged in a futile academic service with no value to humanity. Søren Kierkegaard's criticism of the philosophers of his time and their philosophical approach to life remains an appropriate critique of biblical scholars today. Kierkegaard would have accused modern exegetes of having become like those who build enormous castles but continue to live in nearby shacks, rather than taking up residence within their own massive systematic buildings. He writes, "Spiritually speaking, the thought of a human being must serve as the building in which that human being lives; otherwise, everything turns topsy-turvy."[2] The exegetical method has, in effect, become topsy-turvy, insofar as it produces beautiful structures for the biblical texts but fails to show how such structures had an impact upon the contemporary communities with their theological message. Henri Mottu, commenting about the irrelevance of the theological education of his time in Europe, put it this way:

> The overriding characteristic of our theology is that it is without any relationship to the religion of the people. . . . It sails high above the earth, remote, like an eagle, and frightens people on its lonely flights. And finally does not even find its own nest.[3]

Likewise, contemporary biblical exegesis frightens students and provides no help for the task of theological communication within the church. For example, people wonder why the good suffer while the wicked prosper. To teach them only about the structure of the Book of Job, pointing out its similarities to other ancient Near Eastern texts, will by itself do nothing to comfort a person who is facing bereavement and unmerited suffering. It is only when, following the exegetical process, Job's enquiry is adapted and applied to contemporary situations that students begin to master adequately the method and rewards of the exegetical method. There are, to be sure, many current questions that exegesis must address. Thus, blacks would like to know whether there is any way that their presence in the Bible can be ascertained by biblical scholars. Similarly, women, concerned because many vehement male preachers strongly believe that women's inferiority to men is based on biblical texts such as Gen 2:18-23 or Eph 5:22-27, would like to know whether God created them inferior or equal to men. Exegesis should enable such preachers to realize that there is a contrasting creation story in Gen 1:26-28 in which man and woman are created simultaneously and are subsequently blessed to multiply and fill the earth.

My major objective in this study, an exegesis of Gen 2:18-3:19, is to show how biblical exegesis can function as a viable tool for theological teaching. The study will clarify how the two creation stories of Genesis were meant to communicate, albeit using different metaphors, a profound message by means of complementary rather than contradictory stories. My aim in this regard is to dispel any illusions to the effect that male chauvinism is in accordance with God's providence, since it is underscored in the story of creation in Genesis.

CREATION AND THE EQUALITY OF THE SEXES IN GEN 2:18–3:19

The story of the creation of humans raises intriguing and enigmatic problems. If the man was created from the dust of the ground (Gen 2:7), why was the woman formed from the "rib" or "side" (ṣēlāʻ) of hāʼādām[4] (3:21-22)? What did the second story of creation imply by portraying Yahweh ʼĔlōhîm as creating the woman in an unusual way?[5] Was the author's intention to reveal that the woman was inferior to the man? Such questions are highly significant, because many Christians interpret this text in such a way as to perpetuate the suppression of women in the church, at the workplace, and in the home. Again, my intention in this study is to exegete this story in such a way that it cannot be used deliberately or erroneously to undergird male chauvinism. I shall proceed as follows. First, I shall analyze the way in which the text was redacted, in order to suggest a reconstruction of the original story of the creation of humans. Then, I shall proceed with a linguistic analysis of key words used in the story that, in my opinion, have been seriously misinterpreted, beginning with the divine compound appellation Yahweh ʼĔlōhîm used in Gen 2:4b-3:24.

MARRIAGE IN ANCIENT AFRICAN TRADITION

I became interested in revisiting the story of the creation of humans in Gen 2:18-3:19 when I realized the parallels that it shares with ancient African traditional marriage customs and religious beliefs.[6] For example, in ancient Africa,[7] when a young man was of marriageable age and wanted to start his own family, he abandoned (ʻāzab) his parents' home and built a hut at the outskirts of the homestead. There he would spend most nights playing his musical instruments by the fire. The father would occasionally eavesdrop to listen to the music his son was playing.[8] Oftentimes, the music would include statements to the effect that he was tired of staying with his parents, that he was bored of being alone, and so forth. The father would then disclose this information to the aunts, who would in turn begin the process of searching for a woman who would become the young man's "companion" or "counterpart," i.e., one who is kᵉnegdô. The father, meanwhile, would begin to prepare a dowry for the marriage, either selling cattle or looking for cattle to present. When the right woman was finally found, she would be brought to the man to see how he would react toward her.[9] Normally, the man would trust the choice made for him, aware that it was the wish of his parents and aunts that he should have a woman who complemented him, a woman whom he would cherish for the rest of his married life. In other words, this woman became an 'ēzēr kᵉnegdô (a companion like his own mirror image; cf. Gen 3:18, 20).

A woman, on the other hand, did not leave the homestead as a sign of her readiness for marriage. She continued to live with her parents, doing the daily household chores. The mother would, however, listen to the songs her daughter would sing, while stamping mealies or grinding corn. If the songs were somber and reflected loneliness, the mother would report this matter to the aunts. The aunts would then begin courting a man who would be suitable as a counterpart to their niece. The man sought had to possess attributes that complemented those of the woman.[10] It is clear that in this African traditional practice it is the man who abandons his father and mother in search of a woman (cf. Gen 2:24).

Another cultural idiosyncrasy of ancient Africa was the strict separation of the roles played by men and women, husband and wife, in the governance of the family. The man was the chief breadwinner for the entire family: he was expected to hunt and fish to feed the family; he cut the wood to build the home and was responsible for defending both home and tribe; he was also a role model for the male children.[11] The woman, on the other hand, was responsible for the home: she took care of the children; she prepared and served food for the entire family; and she served as the role model for the daughters. She also taught the sons what they should expect of a good wife. On matters relating to food, its preparation and distribution, the husband had absolutely no say at all. He was expected to eat whatever his wife served him. This custom made me see the similarity with the creation of humans in Genesis, where the man eats the fruit that the woman serves him without asking any questions (Gen 3:6-7). It also led me to appreciate the respective divine curses of Gen 3:14b-19: the man would till the barren ground in order to feed his children; the woman would serve as childbearer.

REDACTIONAL NATURE OF GEN 2:18–3:29

There is clear evidence that the Yahwistic creation story is a redactional product and, as a result, quite confusing. To begin with, the clearest sign of redaction lies in the fact that, while the creation of humans is in prose, the exclamation of the man upon meeting the woman for the first time is in poetry.[12] Second, Gen 2:10-14, which gives an account of the rivers, appears to be an interpolation, insofar as these verses interrupt the flow of the creation of the human species.

Third, there is dittography with regard to the placing of humans in the garden. Thus, in 2:8b it is stated that "God planted the garden in the east in Eden, and there he put hā'ādām[13] whom he had formed." However, there is no explanation given as to why Yahweh made 'ādām or why God placed them[14] in the garden. Then, in 2:15 we read again: "Yahweh 'Ĕlōhîm took hā'ādām and put him in the garden of Eden. . . ." To keep the flow of the account, the redactor added the phrase "to till it and to guard (preserve) it." If šāmar means "to guard," the redactor does not explain how *hā'ādām* was to guard the garden. If, as the author probably meant to convey, *šāmar* means "to keep/preserve," then who performed this work subsequent to Yahweh's expulsion of *hā'ādām* from the garden? It is interesting to note that the duty of tilling the ground is analogous to the duty allotted to humans in the Babylonian creation story, the *Enuma Elish*,[15] according to which humans were created to till the ground for the feeding of the gods.[16]

Fourth, in 2:16 God provides an orchard from which humanity is to feed. Thus, *hā'ādām* is to eat of every tree that is pleasant to the sight and good for food. There are two trees in the first account: the tree of life and the tree of the knowledge good and evil.[17] No divine injunction is given to *hā'ādām* concerning the tree. In the second account, however, *hā'ādām* is warned that, should they eat of the tree of the knowledge good and evil, *môt tāmût*,[18] "you will surely die."

Finally, there is another problem with the text. The conversation between the serpent and the woman introduces other dimensions concerning the tree of the knowledge good and evil that were not originally disclosed to *hā'ādām* when God created them (vv. 8-9). For example, God does not give any command with regard to eating or not eating on the part of the humans from the tree of the knowledge good and evil or from the tree of life, both of which are in the midst of the garden (2:9).[19] In the second account, God commands *hā'ādām* not to eat the fruit of the tree of the knowledge good and evil (3:17). In 3:3 another dimension of the prohibition is disclosed. Not only are humans forbidden to eat its fruit, they are also forbidden to touch the fruit. The snake apparently lived in or had free access to the tree of the knowledge good and evil, which Yahweh 'Ělōhîm had forbidden humans to eat from and even to touch. Yahweh 'Ělōhîm does not disclose the reason why humans are to observe this stern prohibition, reinforced by a death threat as it is. It is intriguing that the snake should be aware of Yahweh 'Ělōhîm's inner secrets regarding the tree of the knowledge good and evil, while humans, in whom was found the breath (*rûᵃḥ*) of Yahweh, have no idea of the tree's secrets.

At any rate, there is no place in the earlier conversations where Yahweh commands humans not to touch the fruit of this tree. All that is said is that *hā'ādām* is to eat of every tree that is pleasant to the sight and good for food (2:9). It is natural to assume that when the woman saw that the tree was good for food and delightful to the eyes—the two criteria that Yahweh had laid down—she ate its fruit and, like a good partner, shared with her husband (Gen 3:6; cf. 2:9a). The phrase "the tree was to be desired to make one wise" is suspect, raising the possibility that it might have been added much later, as a way of shifting the blame for eating the forbidden fruit from *hā'ādām* in general to the woman.

Nowhere in Yahweh's speech are the esoteric attributes of the tree of the knowledge good and evil disclosed. In Gen 2:16-17 Yahweh 'Ělōhîm does not say that the tree of the knowledge good and evil would make humanity prudent or confer insight (*śkl*).[20] Rather, what Yahweh does say is that, if they eat of it, they will surely die. The serpent was aware that Yahweh 'Ělōhîm was plainly lying.[21] What would happen if *hā'ādām* ate the fruit of the tree of the knowledge good and evil is that they would both become wise. To prove this, the woman and the man eat the fruit and do not die. As the snake had predicted, both of them become wise, able to distinguish between what is good and what is evil. This is contrary to Yahweh 'Ĕlōhîm's solemn warning that they would surely die if they disobeyed the prohibition. One might even be tempted to assume that, since the snake had so much hidden knowledge of things and was more prudent than all the creatures that God had created, God did not give it a chance to defend itself before cursing it (Gen 3:14). Perhaps the serpent, in response to Yahweh's question, would have disclosed more secrets, a very embarrassing situation for Yahweh 'Ĕlōhîm.[22]

All these discrepancies lead us to the following conclusion. The original account of the creation of humans can only be reconstructed by isolating all the material interpolated into the story. The Yahwist has nicely framed the creation of the woman by means of the word "alone," placed at the beginning of the text, and the phrase "one flesh," which ends the narrative. In 2:18 the author reports that Yahweh did not find it good that *hā'ādām* should be alone (*leḇadô*). Following the separation of humanity into two sides of different sexes, the writer reveals that the male counterpart left his parents and cleaved once again to its female counterpart, with the two sides becoming, as it were, one flesh (*leḇāśār 'eḥād*). The Yahwist's literary style is very effective in showing the closeness and self-identity the man found in his wife. The author contrasted the man's reaction to the animals with his reaction to the woman whom Yahweh 'Ĕlōhîm brought before him. When all the excerpts of Yahweh's involvement with humans are placed together, the original text seems to have read as follows:

(7) Then Yahweh 'Ĕlōhîm formed a human being from the dust of the ground and breathed into his[23] nostrils the breath of life. Thus the human being became a living creature. (18) Then Yahweh 'Ĕlōhîm said, "It is not good for the human being to be alone. I will make a companion like his very self. (21) And thus Yahweh 'Ĕlōhîm put the human being into deep sleep, and while *hā'ādām* slept, God took one side and closed the flesh over the place. (22) Yahweh 'Ĕlōhîm then built up the side which was taken from the human being into a woman. He brought her to the male counterpart (23) and the man[24] exclaimed:

> "This one, finally, is bone from my bones,
> flesh from my flesh.
> To this one will be called woman,
> because from the man
> this one was taken."[25]

(24) That is why a man forsakes his father and mother and cleaves to his wife, and the two become one flesh. (25) Now the two were both naked, the man and his wife, but they were not ashamed.[26]

EXCURSUS: THE COMPOUND
DIVINE NAME YAHWEH 'ĔLŌHÎM

The compound divine name Yahweh 'Ĕlōhîm must be analyzed, given the fact that many scholars have been baffled by its unique usage in the Pentateuch. It appears only in this compound form in Gen 2:4b-3:24 and Exod 9:30. As Gordon J. Wenham remarks,

> The strangeness of the phenomenon has taxed the imagination of literary critics and exegetes alike, for whether one accepts the usual documentary analysis or not, the commentator must still explain why here the editor of his finely constructed tale has forsaken his usual policy of using one name or the other and instead uses both together.[27]

J. L'Hour further realizes that the redactional theories fail to account for this strange phenomenon.[28] Following the arguments of other scholars, L'Hour surmises that Yahweh 'Ĕlōhîm was used to show that God was both creator and Israel's covenant partner. He goes on,

> This would explain also why the serpent and the woman avoided the compound divine name in their conversation. The god they are talking about is malevolent, secretive, and concerned to restrict man: his character is so different from that of Yahweh 'Ĕlōhîm that the narrative pointedly avoids the name in the dialogue of 3:1-5.[29]

In any event, my position on the usage of Yahweh 'Ĕlōhîm is that the two names are in apposition to each other. Moreover, the divine compound name is not restricted to Gen 2:4b-3:24. It is used continuously throughout the Old Testament, with the element *'ĕlōhîm* found in construct chain, as in, e.g., *Yahweh 'ĕlōhê ṣᵉbā'ôt* (Yahweh, the gods of the armies), *Yahweh 'ĕlōhê yiśrā'ēl* (Yahweh, the gods of Israel), *Yahweh 'ĕlōhênū* (Yahweh our gods), *Yahweh 'ĕlōhêkem* (Yahweh, your gods), and so forth.

Before the Israelites became monotheistic, they were decidedly polytheistic, like all the other nations around them.[30] The term *'ĕlōhîm*, which is overwhelmingly interpreted as a proper noun throughout the Old Testament, was originally a generic noun that referred to the many deities worshiped by the Israelites from the patriarchal to the monarchical period. A more careful study of the early religion of Israel by itself, in complete isolation from later Israelite and Christian monotheism, shows that the Israelite leadership attempted, for political rather than religious reasons, to replace the tribal traditional belief in the *'ĕlōhîm* (gods) of the forebears with a belief in one supreme deity, Yahweh. Walter Eichrodt correctly points out that,

> From the time of the Exodus from Egypt onwards new elements were continually entering the tribal covenant union. Sometimes these were

Hebrews—the Joshua covenant of Josh 24 refers to such a case—sometimes foreign, especially among the southern tribes which had not been into Egypt. This explains why the twelve tribes are enumerated differently in Judg 5; Gen 49; and Deut 33.[31]

I would like to add that, when the new tribes joined the tribal league, they brought with them their *'ĕlōhê hā'ăbôt* (the gods of the fathers). Much effort was spent on selling Yahweh to these new tribes. The way in which Yahweh gained supremacy over the *'ĕlōhîm* is presented in mythical form, with Yahweh portrayed as triumphant over the forces of chaos,[32] a process analogous to the ascendancy of Marduk over the Mesopotamian pantheon.[33] This goal was cautiously achieved by incorporating the *'ĕlōhîm* of the forebears into Yahwism. When, finally, the Israelites accepted Yahweh as their supreme god, they did not in any way negate the existence and worship of their patron deities. Thus, B. Lang notes,

> The religion of Israel which we know only from the biblical polemics against idolatry is polytheistic. Yahweh was the national god, but not the only deity who was worshipped.... Via a minority-movement "for Yahweh alone" it initiated the cultic reform connected with the figure of king Josiah and Deuteronomy (623/22 B.C.). In the exile the monolatry was further developed into a monotheism which denied the existence of other gods. . . .[34]

In the patriarchal period the Israelites revered the *'ĕlōhîm* as the *'ĕlōhê hā'ăbôt*. These were individual deities with specific individual names: Abraham's patron deity bore the epithet *māgān*, "the Benefactor [of Abraham]" (Gen 15:1);[35] Isaac revered *paḥad yiṣḥāq*, "the Fear/Kinsman of Isaac" (Gen 31:42, 53);[36] and the epithet of Jacob's patron deity was *'ăbîr ya'ăqôb*, "the Bull of Jacob" (Gen 49:24; Ps 132:2, 5; Isa 49:26, 60:16).[37] Alt noticed that the religion of the patriarchs was very distinct from the later Israelite religious traditions. This, he pointed out, "becomes stronger as one continues to probe into the tradition of the God[s] of the Fathers," and added, "It seems that originally several distinct gods . . . must have existed side by side, before they were combined in the figure of the God[s] of the Fathers and identified with the God worshipped by Israel. . . ."[38]

Following the Israelite settlement in Canaan, most likely during the period of the monarchy, Yahweh and the *'ĕlōhîm* of the forebears coalesced, and the two appellations were identified as referring to the same deity, Yahweh.[39] Apparently, the introduction of Yahweh as the only God of Israel met with much resistance. There were some tribes, particularly those in the north, that did not abandon their gods in order to worship Yahweh alone. It is for this reason that, as soon as the united kingdom of Israel split, Jeroboam made two bulls, placing one at Bethel and the other at Dan. In dedicating them he said, "Behold your gods (*'ĕlōhêkā*) who brought you up from the land of Egypt."[40] As a result, the name Yahweh 'Ĕlōhîm, the same compound appellation used in Gen 2:4b-3:24, was adopted as a compromise name. The religious leaders of Israel devised the compound name to facilitate the adoption of Yahweh by all the tribes, particularly those who staunchly adhered to their *'ĕlōhê hā'ăbôt*. The identification of Yahweh with the "gods of the fathers" was politically motivated by the need to unite all the ethnic groups of Israel under the monarchy. Prior to this point, the tribes were divided by ethnic origin, belief in their respective *'ĕlōhê hā'ăbôt*, and dialectical differences.[41]

MEANING OF THE TERM 'ĀDĀM

The assumed priority of the man in the creation of humans, which has been used to justify male domination of women, is the result of a misunderstanding of the usage of the Hebrew term *'ādām*. This term was originally used as a collective generic term meaning "human beings," regardless of gender.[42] However, since the Hebrew verb would always be masculine, even if only one man were to be found in a group of many women, it is obvious that later translators would be misled in regarding *'ādām* as representing a man, as is particularly reflected in various Bible translations. This is also the only possible explanation for how *'ādām* came to be regarded as a proper name in the masculine gender.

The author's concern in this narrative is about the creation of humans and their relationship with both Yahweh 'Ĕlōhîm and other human beings. It is for this reason that the Yahwistic writer uses a neutral term, *'ādām*, for human beings as a species rather than *'îš* (man, husband) or *'îššâ* (woman, wife). The article *hā-* used with *'ādām* decisively points to the fact that the latter term was understood by the author as a generic term for humans and not as a proper noun referring exclusively to the male gender. Philologically, it is unusual for a proper name to be used with an article.[43]

Several questions arise when either *hā'ādām* or *'ādām* is regarded as a synonym for *'îš* or as a proper noun referring exclusively to the masculine gender in this text. First, if *'ādām* means "man," this would mean that God gave the injunction not to eat the fruit of the tree of the knowledge good and evil to the man before the woman was created. If that is the case, then why did the man not speak out against the woman's decision to eat the forbidden fruit? He should have been aware that she did not yet know about God's prohibition, and rightly so. Why did he simply receive the fruit without reminding the woman of God's prohibition? Obviously, the resultant picture of the man is not a very good one at all; on the other hand, the woman is revealed as more natural, curious, communicative, and progressive.[44] She was willing to argue with the serpent, while the man, on the other hand, proved docile, naive, even dumb, according to this text. At any rate, based on her conversation with the serpent, the woman knew about the command that God had given to *hā'ādām* (of whom she was a side) concerning the tree of the knowledge good and evil (Gen 2:16-17). While the term *'ādām/hā'ādām* is a generic term that refers to both men and women, it is the context in which it is used that determines whether it should be translated "humans" (man and woman), "man" (*'îš*), or "Adam."[45]

WAS 'ĀDĀM A HERMAPHRODITE?

Textual evidence forces one to assume that *'ādām* was, in all probability, a bisexual being, i.e., in the sense that he/she was male and female in one body. This bisexual human creature did not, therefore, have a counterpart. That is to say, *hā'ādām*, in this composite state, did not have a partner who was exactly like them (*kᵉnegdô*).[46] Hamilton appears to grasp this interpretation in his definition of *kᵉnegdô*. Thus, he points out, "The last part of v. 18 reads literally, 'I will make for him a helper as in front of him (or according to what is in front of him).'"[47] As far as intimacy was concerned, Yahweh 'Ĕlōhîm realized that humanity as a hermaphrodite was alone without an *'ēzēr kᵉnegdô*.

Thus, Yahweh 'Ĕlōhîm caused a deep sleep to come upon *hā'ādām* and took one side (*ṣēlā'*) to create the woman. In other words, Yahweh split the bisexual *'ādām*, separating the female side from the male side. Then, Yahweh closed the wound left on the male side by the excision of the woman from him. God then built the female side into a woman. Thus, *hā'ādām*, whether male or female, had an *'ēzēr kᵉnegdô*.[48]

It is interesting to find that the interpretation of *hā'ādām* as a hermaphrodite may be found in the rabbinic tradition. The Jewish (Tannaitic) tradition holds the same teaching. When God created *'ādām*, he was androgynous, i.e., bisexual. This tradition teaches that male and female came about when God took the side of a man and from that half God made a woman. In other words, a man or a woman is not a complete being by himself or herself. It is by their marriage that the original whole that God created is restored (Midrash Rabbah Gen 8:1).[49]

Turning to the prepositional phrase *kᵉnegdô*, it is clear that it is formed of the preposition *neged* with the prefix *kᵉ* (like, as) and the suffix *ô* (his). Frances Brown defines *neged* as follows: "what is conspicuous, or in front, opposite to."[50] This definition suits our argument, because it presents the woman as standing in front of the man in their relationship. It does not imply the inferiority of the woman to the man. Although she is different, she is equal to him. This depiction of the woman in her relation to the man is reminiscent of the relationship between Gilgamesh and Enkidu.[51] Gilgamesh was a unique person, two-thirds divine and one-third human. He brutally ruled the city of Uruk. Having suffered much from his tyranny, the people of Uruk entreated the gods to create one equal in strength to him. The great gods, the Igigi and the Anunnaki, approved the request and asked the divine creatress Aruru to make a counterpart to Gilgamesh:

> Thou, Aruru, didst create [the man];
> Create now his double, . . .
> When Aruru heard this,
> A double of Anu she conceived within her.
> Aruru washed her hands,
> Pinched off clay and cast it on the steppe.
> [On the steppe she created valiant Enkidu].[52]

Gilgamesh and Enkidu became inseparable friends, sharing good times and participating in adventure together until death did them part. Analogically, the woman Yahweh 'Ĕlōhîm created appears to have been the double of *hā'ādām*, who then became the man's companion and counterpart.

EQUALITY OF MAN AND WOMAN IN GENESIS

When God brought all the animals to humanity, there was not found an *'ēzēr kᵉnegdô*, "there was not found[53] a compatible partner (i.e., one like his own mirror image)" (Gen 2:20). By the names the man gave to these creatures, Yahweh 'Ĕlōhîm clearly realized that there was no affinity between them and the man. When God presented the woman who was built from the side of *hā'ādām*, in other words, from the very body of *hā'ādām*, the man quickly realized the affinity between him and the woman and exclaimed (2:23):

> "This one, finally, is bone from[54] my bones,
> flesh from my flesh.[55]
> To this one will be called woman,[56]
> because from the man
> this one was taken."

The redactor or narrator went on to state that, having found the woman, the man forsook or abandoned (*'āzab*) his father and mother and cleaved (*dābaq*), i.e., became stuck on to his wife.[57] By sticking together both became one flesh again, as formerly when both were simply *'ādām*. The vocabulary of both the narrative and the poem serves to reinforce the unique closeness that exists between the man and the woman, between husband and wife. This identity of the man and the woman is of two people who, although equal, were, nonetheless, opposite to each other.

SUMMARY

Our interpretation of *'ādām* explains a number of enigmatic questions relating to the creation of man and woman. To begin with, it answers the question as to how the woman knew about the tree of the knowledge good and evil, if Yahweh 'Ĕlōhîm had spoken only to the man. In addition, it also answers the question why the man did not object to the woman's offer of the forbidden fruit, if Yahweh had spoken to him alone, man to man. According to the Hebrew text, the man was standing right there next to the woman. Perhaps the man's culture was similar to African culture in that a man did not question his wife on matters concerning food. That the man was present when the woman was arguing with the snake is clear from the plural verbs in the second person that the snake used with reference to the man and the woman. This is also shown by the woman's response, which uses the verbs in the first person plural in order to include her husband and herself together. The text also betrays the presence of the man by the statement: "and she also gave to her husband who was with her (*'immāh*) and he ate" (Gen 3:6). By omitting the phrase *'immāh* in their translations, a number of biblical versions have greatly exacerbated the erroneous assumption that the woman was alone in the field when she met the snake.[58] This would mean that she then brought some of the fruit to the unassuming man, who ate in complete innocence.

It is clear that the Yahwist is portraying males in a very poor light in this story. For example, the man left his father and mother to become a slavish dependent to his wife. The man did not even lend support to his woman when she was trying to convince the snake of God's prohibition concerning the tree of the knowledge good and evil. He was uncommunicative, offering no opinion and no defense of the divine principles God had given him. He is of the attitude that whatever is good for the woman is also good enough for him. This is clear even in his response to God: "The woman whom you gave to be with me,[59] she gave me the fruit from the tree and I ate" (Gen 3:13). No response could be more unintelligent than this one. Finally, if this is the true state of the first male whom Yahweh created, then it is no wonder that God quickly realized that: "It is not good that the man should be alone; I will make a counterpart for him" (Gen 3:18). The man and the woman were equal because they were partners: bone from the same bone and flesh from the same flesh. Based on the preponderance of the textual evidence, to deny the equality of the sexes would mean affirming that the woman was superior to the man in intellectual development, creativity, and emotional stability. Analogical to ancient African tradition, it is the man who abandoned his father and mother in search of a woman who would become his counterpart, giving him rest and sleep. No longer does he stay all night playing musical instruments and agonizing over his loneliness.

CONCLUSION

In the story of the creation of man and woman, it is clear to a critical reader that the narrative is not based on actual history. There is no question that in this narrative ideology is being played against objectivity.[60] There are many similar folk stories in Africa, albeit with different moral lessons in mind. The biblical account of the creation of man and woman is intended to underscore the point that a man without a woman is alone, because he lacks a counterpart exactly like him but opposite to him (*'ēzer kᵉnegdô*). Whereas two men living together would always count as two individual men, a man and a woman living together become one flesh (*bāśār 'eḥād*). The redactor of this story stressed this important point by showing how a man would abandon his own parents once he had found a suitable woman as his counterpart. The narrator's goal was to show the profound relationship that exists between a man and a woman when they become husband and wife in an ideal marriage. This is one of the messages that issues out of the narrative of the creation of humans in Gen 2:18-27 and Gen 1:26-27. It can therefore be said that the narrators were not as much interested in historical accuracy as in the impact of their theological ideas for the communities of their time.

NOTES

1. See, e.g., I. Provan, "Ideologies, Literary and Critical Reflections on Recent Writing on the History of Israel," *JBL* 114 (1995) 585-606; T. L. Thompson, "A Neo-Albrightean School in History and Biblical Scholarship?" *JBL* 114 (1995) 683-698; P. R. Davies, "Methods and Madness: Some Remarks on Doing History with the Bible," *JBL* 114 (1995) 699-705.

2. S. Kierkegaard, *Pragmatism* (New York: Meridian Books, 1955) 27-28.

3. W. J. Hollenweger, "The Ecumenical Significance of Oral Christianity," *Ecumenical Review* 41 (1989) 264.

4. As will be shown below, the term *'ādām* should be generally interpreted as a generic word meaning simply "humanity" or "human beings" in most cases. Some contexts, however, require either "Adam" or "man." See C. Westermann, *Genesis 1-11* (Minneapolis: Augsburg Publishing House, 1987) 201-02; G. L. Wenham, *Genesis 1-5*, Word Biblical Commentary 1 (Waco, TX: Word Books, 1987) 32.

5. The time lapse between the creation of the man and that of the woman—a separation of fourteen verses!—makes it seem as if the woman was created as the result of an afterthought on the part of God. This textual arrangement reinforces the belief that the woman was created for the pleasure and comfort of the man.

6. The elderly people, as grandparents, often called the grandchildren together to tell them the stories of *kare kare* (of long, long ago). Some of the stories I still remember have to do with family life. Storytelling was the way of passing on oral tradition from generation to generation.

7. By "ancient Africa" I mean the period preceding the arrival of the white people in Africa. As in the Middle East, there are still people in Africa today who have preserved the traditional life of ancient Africa and have deliberately rejected Western civilization.

8. Ancient Africans (as well as most modern Africans) did not discuss sex with their children. However, sex matters could be discussed with aunts (excluding the mother's sisters, who were regarded as mothers), cousins, brothers, and peers.

9. Marriage was accepted by faith on both sides. It did not really matter much in ancient times whether a woman was beautiful or not, because the main purpose of marriage and sexual intercourse was not sexual gratification per se but rather raising a family. Enjoyment of sexual intercourse was regarded as a fringe benefit obtained through marriage.

10. There are some similarities in this tradition with the Hebrew practices during the time of Abraham. It is Abraham who sends his servant to look for a spouse for Isaac from among the mother's nieces. Isaac accepted the woman whom Eliezer found for him without asking questions.

11. If sons did not behave well, their unbecoming conduct was blamed on the father. Similarly, well-behaved daughters were credited to the mother's ability to teach by both word and example.

12. Against J. Wellhausen, Gunkel argued that the prose narratives in Genesis began as poetic traditions, often going back to high antiquity (*Legends of Genesis* [New York: Schocken Books, 1901] 2). The same phenomenon may be observed in African tradition, where many historical and etiological legends are being recovered from poetic hymns and ritual recitals; see, e.g., S. Feldman, *African Myths and Tales* (New York: Dell Publishing Co., 1963) 11.

13. Contra V. P. Hamilton (*The Book of Genesis, Chapters 1-17*, in The New International Commentary of the Old Testament [Grand Rapids: William B. Eerdmans, 1990] 160), who is baffled by P's use of *'ādām* as both a generic term (Gen 1:26-27) and a proper name (Gen 5:1). At any rate, I find that Hamilton's assertion that *'ādām* in Gen 5:1 is a proper name has no firm basis. How does he differentiate the usage of *'ādām* in Gen 1:26-27 from its later usage in Gen 5:1?

14. See Gen 1:26-27 and 5:1-2. The generic term *'ādām* is masculine. Hence it was natural for the original author to use a masculine personal pronoun, "he, him." However, since the term refers to both male and female, the author without warning used the plural pronoun "them." It is as plural that the term *'ādām* will be translated in this article.

15. See E. A. Speiser, "The Creation Epic," *Ancient Near Eastern Texts Relating to the Old Testament,* ed. J. B. Pritchard (Princeton: Princeton University Press, 1969) 68.

16. Ibid., Tablet VI:35-38.

17. According to Hebrew syntax, *hadda'at* is not in construct chain with *ṭôb wārā'.* Thus, the translation, "the tree of the knowledge of good and evil," is wrong, since it seriously distorts what was originally meant by the redactor. The phrase *'ēṣ hadda'at ṭôb wārā'* means "the tree of the knowledge good and evil." Obviously, *da'at* excludes its use as a bound form. This argument is corroborated by the fact that in Gen 3:22 Yahweh 'Ělōhîm consults the divine council to announce that *hā'ādām* has become like one of the divinities, *lāda'at ṭôb wārā',* "knowing good and evil." The expressions *hadda'at* and *lāda'at* are both in the same syntactical relationship with regard to *ṭôb wārā'.* Hamilton (*Genesis,* 160 n. 2) is correct in translating the *'ēṣ hadda'at ṭôb wārā'* as "the tree of the knowledge good and evil." As he points out (ibid., 162-63), "What we have is an infinite construct preceded by the definite article followed by two accusative nouns (or adjectives?)."

18. Here Yahweh 'Ělōhîm is speaking to *hā'ādām* before the separation of the female side. This also explains why the verb *tāmût* is in the masculine gender: it is in agreement with *hā'ādām.* Following the separation, the man and his wife are walking in the garden when they encounter the serpent. The serpent refers to them in the plural and the woman responds in kind. This clearly indicates that the man and the woman were in the garden together. In Gen 3:1 the snake addressed the couple using the phrase *tō'keˡlû.* As is the case in Hebrew, the verb will always be masculine if a male is included in a group of women, regardless of number. In her response (Gen 3:2) the woman uses the plural verb *nō'kal,* "we may eat," to include her husband. The rest of v. 3 is in plural form. I find this to be the most cogent view, supporting in turn the argument that both the man and the woman were present during the woman's encounter with the snake.

19. The preposition *beˡtôk* means "in the midst of" or "among" and not "in the center" of the garden, as it is frequently understood.

20. If *hā'ādām* was created as a fool, as the critical reading of the narrative would suggest, one wonders why the woman would have desired to be wise, since a fool never knows the distinction between wisdom and folly.

21. See D. R. G. Beattie, "What Is Genesis 2-3 About?" *Expository Times* 92 (1980/81) 490.

22. The snake did not deceive or beguile the couple. It told the truth and was punished for telling the truth, which in turn made both the man and the woman free from blinding stupor. It should be noted that their eyes become open because of the snake and not by God's grace.

23. The use of "his" does not necessarily refer to the masculine. In this verse it refers to the noun *hā'ādām,* which is masculine although it refers collectively to human beings.

24. The original male side appears to have retained the title *'ādām,* creating thereby the ambiguity between its two meanings of "humanity" and "man," a synonym of *'îš.*

25. If the man had been brought to the woman, she would have reacted in the same way as the man did, because, from her point of view, the man would have been taken from her.

26. Verses such as these raise suspicion that they were added at a later time by the redactor to stress the importance of marriage, as well as to show how strong conjugal bonds are or should be between man and woman.

27. Wenham, *Genesis 1-5,* 56.

28. J. L'Hour, "Yahweh Elohim," *Révue Biblique* 81 (1974) 524-56.

29. Ibid., 57.

30. I have fully discussed this topic in my, "The Divine Name Yahweh 'Ĕlōhîm and Israel's Polytheistic Monotheism," *Journal of Northwest Semitic Languages*, 22(1996) 155-73.

31. W. Eichrodt, *Theology of the Old Testament*, 2 vols. (Philadelphia: Westminster Press, 1959) 1:39 n. 2.

32. Exod 20:2; see also: Deut 5:6; 6:21b-25; 15:1-18, where in v. 2 Yahweh and the *'ĕlōhîm* are equated; Josh 24; and passim.

33. See A. Leo Oppenheim, trans., "Babylonian and Assyrian Historical Texts," *Ancient Near Eastern Texts*, 265. A succinct discussion of the parallels will help clarify the point. Marduk became the plenipotentiary deity because he defeated Tiamat, a goddess who, together with her military host, represented chaos. To honor him for his triumphant victory, the Igigi and the Anunnaki (the great gods) conferred upon him full authority and presented him the tablets of destiny. Once a year, during the Akitu festival, an eight-day celebration attended by the people of Babylon, Marduk's fifty names were recited. This religious myth was adopted for both religious and political reasons to explain how Babylon superseded Kish in importance. Kish had been regarded as a sacred place because it was there that kingship had been first lowered from heaven. The myth was also religious in that it legitimated the rise of Marduk as the plenipotentiary deity above the great gods of Mesopotamia, often referred to as his fathers.

34. B. Lang, "Zur Entstehung des biblischen Monotheism," *Theologische Quartalschrift* 166 (1968) 135. See also J. de Moor, *The Rise of Yahwism: The Roots of Israelite Monotheism*, Bibliotheca ephemeridum theologicarum lovaniensium 9 (Leuven: Leuven University Press, 1990) 3, especially n. 9. See also T. Mafico, "God's New Name Yahweh 'Ĕlōhîm and the Unification of Israel: A Challenge to Africans and African Americans," *Journal of the Interdenominational Theological Center* 23 (1995) 56-59.

35. F. M. Cross supports this interpretation on the grounds of parallelism. He sees *māgān* as parallel to *śkrk lk*, "your reward" (*Canaanite Myth and Hebrew Epic* [Cambridge: Harvard University Press, 1973] 4-5). See also F. W. Albright, *From the Stone Age to Christianity*, 2nd ed. (Baltimore: The Johns Hopkins University Press, 1946) 188-89, 327 n. 71; A. Alt, "The God of the Fathers," *Essays on Old Testament History and Religion* (New York: Doubleday, 1966) 23-38.

36. See Mafico, "God's New Name Yahweh 'Ĕlōhîm," 55 n. 10.

37. Names of animals in Ugaritic and Hebrew were used to refer to nobles, heroes, and lords; see H. L. Ginsberg, *The Legend of King Keret: A Canaanite Epic of the Bronze Age*, in Bulletin of the American Schools of Oriental Research Supplementary Series 2-3 (New Haven: American Schools of Oriental Research, 1946) 42. It should also be noted *'Ēl* is designated as *tōr* "bull" in A. Herdner, *Corpus des tablettes en cunéiformes alphabétiques découvertes à Ras Shamra-Ugarit de 1929 à 1939* (Paris: P. Geuthner, 1963) 5.5.18-19. This can be compared with Amos 4:1, where the rich women of Israel are referred to as "cows." See also F. M. Cross and D. N. Freedman, "The Song of Miriam," *Journal of Near Eastern Studies* 14 (1955) 237-50, for parallels in Exod 15:15, Isa 14:9, Ezek 17:13, and 2 Sam 1:19.

38. Alt, "The God of the Fathers," 38.

39. If the Israelites had originally worshipped one God, there would have been no need to try to convince them through repeated appeals like "Hear O Israel, Yahweh Our Gods (*Yahweh 'ĕlōhēnū*) is one Yahweh." For the different names by which Yahweh was called during the period when the *'ĕlōhîm* were being fused with Yahweh, see Mafico, "God's New Name Yahweh 'Ĕlōhîm," 57.

40. Exod 32:4; see 1 Kgs 12:28. I have clarified these texts in my article, "The Divine Name Yahweh 'Ĕlōhîm from an African Perspective," *Reading from This Place*. Volume 2: *Social Location and Biblical Interpretation in Global Perspective*, ed. F. F. Segovia and M. A. Tolbert (Philadelphia: Fortress Press, 1995) 26-29.

41. For example, the Ephramites pronounced the word "Shiboleth" as Siboleth, unlike the people of Gilead (Judg 12:6).

42. Contra Hamilton (*Genesis*, 159) who asserts that *hā'ādām* should be translated as "man," while *'ādām* without a definite article should be regarded as a proper name. C. Westermann (*Genesis 1-11* [Minneapolis: Augsburg Publishing House, 1984] 202) is unequivocal in stating that "*hā'ādām* in the Old Testament describes a human being without further qualification." See n. 13 above.

43. See Mafico, "The Divine Name Yahweh 'Ĕlōhîm," 29 n. 32.

44. Thus also S. Niditch, "Genesis," *The Woman's Bible Commentary*, ed. C. A. Newsom and S. H. Ringe (Louisville: Westminster/John Knox Press, 1992) 13-15. However, I am surprised by the fact that she assumes that the man was created prior to the woman, whom she assumes to have been created from the man's rib, literally.

45. For example, in Gen 3:8 and 17, *'ādām* is used as a synonym of *'îš*, but in Gen 1:26-27 and 5:1-2 *'ādām* refers to both male and female, even if it uses the masculine singular verb and possessive pronoun. See also Num 12:3 where *'îš* is only an individual among *'ādām* on the face of the earth.

46. This idea has been suggested by other scholars on the basis of the term "rib" or "side" (*ṣēlā'*), but they quickly go on to dismiss it in spite of the fact that Greek mythology and later Jewish (Tannaitic) tradition support it (Hamilton, *Genesis*, 178).

47. Ibid., 175. The idea of a bisexual being with a male and female side is also found in Greek mythology; see, e.g., Aristophanes's discourse on love in Plato's *Symposium* (189-93). Plato reveals that originally there were three kinds of human beings joined back to back, like Siamese triplets. Each of the triplets had full faculties of a complete human being. These types of creatures could be masculine, feminine, or bisexual. Because of their attempted rebellion, the supreme God, Zeus, split this creature into individual entities, either as two men, two women, or as man and woman. Acknowledging their remorse, Zeus rejoined the severed halves in such a way that they could copulate and increase their population.

48. The phrase is masculine to agree with the masculine *'ādām*; see n. 14 above.

49. It is amazing that Hamilton (*Genesis*, 178) dismisses the Greek and Jewish analogies and translations as going beyond the statements of Genesis. He sees this interpretation as reading into the text what is not there. Surely, as long as the text does not tell us unequivocally what is meant by the terms in question, no interpretation based on the context is presumptuous.

50. In F. Brown, et al., *A Hebrew and English Lexicon of the Old Testament* (Oxford: Clarendon Press, 1974) 616, the root *ngd* is defined as meaning, "to be conspicuous." In Arabic *nagada* means "to overcome, be apparent, be conspicuous," with the added connotation of being "courageous, effective and vigorous." In Hebrew the preposition *neged* means "in front of, in sight of, opposite to." It is much stronger than *lipnê*.

51. See Speiser, "The Creation Epic," Tablet III (v) 21-23; cf. Assyrian version, Tablet III (i) 1-6.

52. Ibid., Tablet III (v) 21-24.

53. The writer makes it clear that it is God who did not find a companion fit for the man. This is implied in the use of the passive voice: "there was not found." In other words, it is not the man who chose the woman; rather, it is God who gave the woman to the man as a counterpart and a companion.

54. The man expresses complete identity here. He realizes that the woman comes from his very bones. All that matters here is identity and equality, not primacy of the man and the subordination of the woman.

55. While *bāśār*, "flesh," represents weakness in the Old Testament and serves as the antonym of *'eṣem*, "bone," it is generally used in the Old Testament to indicate identity. In Gen 37:27 Joseph's brothers declare, "Joseph is our brother, our own flesh" (see Gen 29:14; Judg 9:2; 2 Sam 5:1; 19:13). This contradicts W. Brueggemann ("Of the Same Flesh

and Bone [Gen 2:23a]," *CBQ* 32 [1970] 532-42) who regards the words "bone" and "flesh" as representing a covenant formula.

56. Here again it is not the man who names the woman. If naming implies superiority of the namer over the named, then the woman was not inferior to the man, because she was not named by him. The writer uses the passive voice in this line, "This one will be called," not by man. All the man did was to acknowledge a fact, i.e., that the woman, unlike the animals, was identical to him.

57. Because the woman was better adjusted to living on the earth than the man, the redactor deliberately and unequivocally states that it is the man who abandoned his parents to find support from his own wife. In other words, the writer here is more concerned with the man looking for his separated half, and, as it seems, his better half.

58. The Revised Standard Version omitted '*immāh*. However, the New English and the New Revised Standard Version have rectified the meaning, but this correction comes much too late, given the irreparable damage that has already been done to the status of women in relation to so-called original sin. In the minds of many Christians, woman is a weaker sex because she wandered in the garden and fell victim to the snake's deceit. Her fall also led, subsequently, to the man's fall, so it is generally believed.

59. It should be noted that the man realized that the woman was given to be with the man, not to be dominated by the man. Otherwise the man would have said, "The woman whom you gave to serve me. . . ."

60. Contra Provan, "Ideologies," 587.

15

THE HERMENEUTICS OF LIBERATION

Theoretical Grounding
for the Communitarian Reading of the Bible

Pablo Richard

There is a movement at work today in the whole of Latin America and the Caribbean that has come to be known as the Communitarian Reading of the Bible. There are a number of other appellations for it as well, such as the Popular Reading of the Bible, the Pastoral Reading of the Bible, and the Latin American Reading of the Bible. Within this movement it is the people of God themselves who begin to read and to interpret the Bible directly, from within their own social, cultural, and spiritual location. Such a movement reveals a number of distinctive characteristics. First, it is an ecclesial movement, in the process of transforming the ecclesial base communities as well as all other grassroots organizations of the churches. Second, it is an ecumenical movement, lifting the Word of God as its highest authority, above and beyond all ecclesial and religious boundaries. Third, it is a movement that embodies at one and the same time a pedagogical process, a way of spirituality and holiness, and a spiritual force for the global transformation of society. While it is by no means a movement involving facile success and large crowds, it is nonetheless a movement that is growing rapidly and laying down solid foundations for a reconstruction of the Jesus movement in the twenty-first century and the third millennium.

The Hermeneutics of Liberation constitutes a systematic and critical theoretical orientation for this Communitarian Reading of the Bible. It is, as it were, a second act that follows upon the practice itself, the first act. Its aim is to provide legitimacy, direction, and theoretical consistency for this practice of biblical re-reading. Indeed, it is important to make theoretically explicit not only the paradigm changes, epistemological ruptures, hermeneutical presuppositions, and interpretive methods that lie behind the Communitarian Reading of the Bible, but also its overall coherence with the faith and the tradition of the churches as a whole. Without a proper hermeneutical theory, the Communitarian Reading

---

This is a translation by Fernando F. Segovia of the original manuscript in Spanish, "Hermenéutica de la Liberación: Teoría para una Lectura Comunitaria de la Biblia."

of the Bible runs the risk of becoming a simple popularization of the Bible or an inconsistent type of biblicism, subject to ready manipulation by any number of social movements or marginalization by the churches.

The Hermeneutics of Liberation represents much more than a contextualized hermeneutics or a hermeneutics with a social option or location. Both the Hermeneutics of Liberation as theory and the Communitarian Reading of the Bible as practice seek to create a *new hermeneutical space*, to be clearly distinguished from the hermeneutical space of the academy as well as the hermeneutical space of the liturgy and institutions of the churches. This new space is by no means in opposition to these other traditional hermeneutical spaces; it is simply different, although very much linked nonetheless to these other, already existing spaces.

This new communitarian hermeneutical space does not fundamentally call into question the traditional methods of biblical interpretation as such, only the spirit and goals with which these methods are practiced. The Communitarian Reading of the Bible radically questions as well the pedagogical practices at work in both biblical studies and biblical training. It calls into question a pedagogy that is elitist, authoritarian, and individualistic, opting instead for a communitarian, participatory, and liberating pedagogy. In fact, the pedagogical methods of popular education and liberating conscientization initially developed by that great pedagogue of the Third World, Paulo Freire, have been quite influential in the emergence of the Communitarian Reading of the Bible.[1] Quite influential as well have been the spirit and pedagogical methods behind Liberation Theology and the ecclesial base communities, with their traditional method of "seeing/acting/evaluating and celebrating."

For the Catholic world as such, two major documents concerning the Bible have been especially influential for the emergence and development of the Hermeneutics of Liberation: the Dogmatic Constitution on Divine Revelation (Dei Verbum) of the Second Vatican Council (November 18, 1965) and the recent document of the Pontifical Biblical Commission on The Interpretation of the Bible in the Church.[2] My own contribution in this study is both in continuity and in consonance with the magisterium of the Church.

THE HERMENEUTICS OF LIBERATION: HISTORICAL CONTEXT

The basic historical context for the Hermeneutics of Liberation within the present juncture of Latin America may be summarized in terms of a *reconstruction of civil society*, at the heart of which lies a *reconstruction of the Spirit*, for which a *reconstruction of the Sacred Scriptures* proves indispensable. In what follows I proceed to examine each of these three processes.

First, given the present context of Latin America, the *reconstruction of civil society* presents itself as a fundamental strategy. We are undergoing a displacement from political society to civil society, at the core of which lies no longer the taking of power, but the reconstruction of a new power. In the construction of this new power, culture, gender, and nature play a crucial role. Such factors emerge out of the new social movements, among which cultural movements, women's liberation movements, and ecological movements prove especially challenging. A new conscience is being born, whereby culture, gender, and nature are integrated into the more traditional economic and political dimensions. This reconstruction of civil society is regarded as a profound and long-lasting strategy: a reconstruction of society from below—a process of globalization from the grassroots—as the only way out of the present crisis of civilization in which we find ourselves.

Second, for this strategy of reconstructing civil society, the *reconstruction of the Spirit* becomes an urgent task. One witnesses today a significant resurgence of social movements with strong ethical, religious, and spiritual dimensions. At times, these movements prove ambiguous, bringing together a mixture of the authentic and the perverse. Thus, one finds spiritualist, fundamentalist, and sectarian tendencies; one also finds, however, an authentic reconstruction of the Spirit. Indeed, in these social movements as well as in the reconstruction of civil society described above, there is at work a positive re-evaluation of the spiritual and transcendent dimensions of the human being. At the very heart of these movements, therefore, there is a search for spiritual reconstruction—a union of Spirit with nature, with culture, with gender.

Finally, in the course of human history, an authentic religious dimension has always possessed a code, a canon, a norm, a sacred scripture. Consequently, a reconstruction of the Spirit proves fruitful and effective only if it involves a *reconstruction of the Sacred Scriptures*. In Latin America as well as in the Western Christian world, the Bible has been profoundly transformed by certain distorting paradigms of interpretation. Thus, one finds authoritarian, patriarchal, racist, fundamentalist, and historicist paradigms involved in a manipulation of the Bible. Similarly, one finds as well models of Christianity in which biblical interpretation is made subject to ecclesiastical and political interests, snuffing out the Spirit thereby and emptying the Word of God of all salvific and liberating value. As a result, both the reconstruction of civil society and the reconstruction of the Spirit are in need of a process for the reconstruction of the Sacred Scriptures. Such is precisely the aim of the Communitarian Reading of the Bible and the Hermeneutics of Liberation.

The insertion of the Communitarian Reading of the Bible into the broader context of the reconstruction of the Spirit and the reconstruction of civil society reveals, on the one hand, the very nature of this process and, on the other hand, accounts for the success and strength of this movement in Latin America. This movement is truly a response to a historical juncture. We are presently living through a profound crisis in the global system of domination. This very system is an expression of a more profound crisis involving modernity itself (as well as postmodernity, which is but an extension of the crisis of modernity: a modernity in extremis), a radical crisis of values, and perhaps even a global crisis of civilization. In the Third World political society finds itself in a state of devastation: the majority of people have no access to the political system; power itself becomes irrelevant (all is determined by the international financial system); and power is almost without exception corrupt. Within this context, the hope of the poor—and, from a theological perspective, the history of salvation—lies in the direction of the reconstruction of civil society. As mentioned above, such a reconstruction has to do with a long-range reconstruction of a new power—from below; from the social movements; from the new consciousness that includes the dimensions of culture, gender, and nature. Such a reconstruction is impossible without the Spirit, the fundamental strength of the poor and the marginalized. Such a reconstruction has nothing to do with a neoconservative or postmodern spiritualism, but rather calls for a rediscovery of the historical sources of our strength. The success and strength of the Communitarian Reading of the Bible have to do precisely with the fact that such a reading seeks to respond to this reconstruction of civil society and the Spirit. It is also within this historical process that the Hermeneutics of Liberation seeks to define its character and rationale.

CREATION OF A NEW HERMENEUTICAL SPACE

A "hermeneutical space" is an institutional *location*, in which a specific *subject* is identified, proper to that place and different from other subjects, who produces a concrete *interpretation* of the Bible, proper to that place and different from those emerging from other hermeneutical spaces. In the last ten years, the practice of the Communitarian Reading of the Bible has created its own hermeneutical space within society and the church. This space has been rendered legitimate as well as autonomous by the effectiveness and fruitfulness of the work itself in its interpretation of and witness to the Word of God. It is the goal, therefore, of the Hermeneutics of Liberation to provide a theoretical definition of this space already secured through the practice of communitarian reading. In this regard the creation of a theoretical space only serves to provide greater coherence and legitimacy to this already existing historical space.

Different Hermeneutical Spaces

There are two traditional hermeneutical spaces, both well-known and fully legitimated. The first of these is the *academic space*, as defined by theological schools, seminaries, and centers of study. Within this space the Bible is interpreted scientifically—according to the canons of the historical-critical method, the traditional literary methods, and the more recent methods that have recourse to the social sciences, such as sociology, cultural anthropology, and psychology. Within this space the subject of biblical interpretation is the expert—the exegete; the professor of Bible; the individual learned in the biblical sciences and related human sciences. The academic interpretation of the Bible is grounded in the correct use of scientific tools and the authority of the authors cited.

The second traditional and legitimated space is the *liturgico-institutional space* of the churches. This space has to do with the reading and interpretation of the Bible within both the context of the liturgy and the context of the normal exercise of the churches' teaching and magisterium. Within this space the Bible is interpreted according to the liturgical and teaching norms of the churches themselves. This space is supported by the work of academic exegesis, but is transformed according to the canons of the liturgy and the teaching of the faith in the context of the churches. To be sure, within the liturgical space the celebration of the Word is also carried out in community, but a community that properly follows the hermeneutical logic dictated by the liturgical order, with its calendar, canons, and norms. The subject of biblical interpretation within this hermeneutical space is the ordained minister or the lay person who has received the proper canonical mission to carry out his or her task.

These two spaces are, without question, legitimate and necessary. However, the Communitarian Reading of the Bible is giving rise to a new space, a third space, just as legitimate and necessary for a correct interpretation of and witness to the Word of God. Such a space we refer to, for now, as a *communitarian space*. It involves the reading and interpretation of the Bible in community, whether in the ecclesial base communities or in other ecclesial institutions or movements with a communitarian base. This interpretation of the Bible in community reveals different characteristics than those of either the academic or liturgico-institutional type of interpretation.

To begin with, the community represents a space for full participation—a space that not only includes those individuals who cannot take part in society (the poor; the marginalized; young people; women; and so forth), but also is present in those areas normally beyond the reach of the great institutions. In addition, the community further represents a space for solidarity and spirituality, for engagement in the task of liberation and the mission of evangelization. Finally, the community is also able to adapt itself more easily to the culture and religiosity of the people. Within this communitarian space the subject of interpretation is neither the expert nor the ordained minister, but the community itself. The community functions as an interpreting subject in the name of a greater subject, the people of God, inserted as it is within the civil society of its own historical context. Within the community one finds a communitarian reading and interpretation of the Bible that is participatory, creative, popular, pastoral; that takes seriously into consideration as well the cultural, gender, and ecological dimensions of the People of God.

In sum, one could say that the Communitarian Reading of the Bible creates its own hermeneutical logic "from below": from the perspective of civil society; of social and liberating movements; of the cultural and ethnic diversity of the people; of ecological movements and women's liberation movements; and, finally, of the sensus fidei of the People of God and the experience of faith in the interpretation and celebration of the Word of God in the ecclesial community, in consonance with the faith and tradition of the churches as a whole and under the guidance of the magisterium (recalling, lest we ever forget, that the magisterium itself "is not above the Word of God, but serves it...").[3]

While it is important to define these three hermeneutical spaces in theory as well as in practice, it is also important not to separate them from one another or set them in opposition to one another. In point of fact, these three spaces do come together in part. Thus, for example, there are academic spaces that identify with the liturgico-institutional space of the churches. In a similar vein, the base communities also represent a constitutive part of the churches: they form the church within the people—the church-as-people-of-God. Finally, it should be emphasized as well that the communitarian space has need of the other two spaces. Thus, the biblical interpretation carried out in the communities not only has recourse to the exegetical production of the academy, but also takes place within the tradition of the churches and under the guidance of the magisterium of the church. Such intercommunication and complementarity are partially achieved by way of the many workshops for biblical formation carried out by the pastoral agents in the communities, as well as by the close links established between the communities on the one hand and the pastoral centers and ecclesial institutions on the other. To be sure, the ideal is for these three spaces to complement one another and coincide with each other more and more, while each maintains the richness and specificity of its own respective hermeneutical logic.

The Spirit behind the Different Hermeneutical Spaces

Thus far, I have attempted to describe the basic relationships and differences among these three hermeneutical spaces. A further element now needs to be introduced as well: the spirit behind the biblical interpretation at work within each of these hermeneutical spaces. In theory, of course, it should be one and the same Spirit that guides and informs all three spaces, and, in point of fact, such is the case from time to time. However, attention must be paid as well to the possible and, unfortunately, rather frequent deviations from this ideal.

Oftentimes, for example, the spirit of the academy is the spirit of competition, of power, of prestige—the spirit of the marketplace, with a premium placed on individualism and curricular pride. Likewise, one may find in the churches the primacy of the institutional spirit, to the detriment of the Spirit who should guide in freedom the search for the Word of God. Thus, it is quite possible to find within the churches a trampling of this Spirit by way of institutional interests or an improper exercise of ecclesiastical power. Finally, within the communities themselves one may also find any number of spiritual deviations: theological manipulations; activism; a tendency toward historicism; a spirit of confrontation; a tendency toward self-marginalization. However, when the Communitarian Reading of the Bible is undertaken in the ecclesial base communities with a full sense of exegetical seriousness and ecclesial communion, then it is the Spirit who is normally in charge. The result is a biblical interpretation with Spirit: the Bible is interpreted in the same Spirit with which it was written. In the process, the Spirit of the community and of the People of God, which is none other than the same Spirit that gave birth to the Sacred Scriptures, is retrieved. Today, the communitarian space is by and large the privileged hermeneutical space for the work of the Spirit in the interpretation of the Bible.

Communitarian Reading: Different Levels

It is important for the communitarian hermeneutical space to be faithful to its internal communitarian and spiritual dimension as well as to its profound insertion within the historical and cultural reality of the People of God. At the same time, it is imperative that a proper exegetical and scientific task be carried out within this new hermeneutical space. Such exegetical work varies according to the different levels involved in the Communitarian Reading of the Bible. Three such levels can be readily identified, all profoundly linked to one another and possessing the same liberating hermeneutics.

First, there is the level of the masses. At this level, the re-reading of the Bible is undertaken by means of key texts transmitted either orally or in terms of pictures, drawings, symbols, songs, narratives, theatrical pieces, and so forth. Thereby a massive process of biblical re-reading is launched, within the context of the reconstruction of the Spirit and the reconstruction of civil society.

Then, there is the level of the ecclesial base communities (and other related groups). At this level, the re-reading of the Bible is carried out with a focus on the text itself, in a sustained and systematic fashion. At this level, furthermore, one already finds exegetical work as such, introduced by the pastoral agents who take part in various exercises of biblical formation specially designed for them. At this level the pedagogy at work is not at all of the impositional kind, but rather participatory and communitarian in nature.

Finally, there is the level of professional biblical interpretation. At this level, the re-reading of the Bible is undertaken in specialized centers of biblical formation and research, usually ecumenical and non-academic in character, dedicated exclusively to the service of the Communitarian Reading of the Bible and making use of a liberating hermeneutic. It is at this level, moreover, that exegetical work of a professional and scientific kind becomes indispensable. It would be wrong to think of the Communitarian Reading of the Bible as a spontaneous and subjective type of reading, far removed from all exegetical research. In fact, any spontaneous, populist, or historicist reading of the Bible is seen as ultimately disfiguring the Communitarian Reading. What is unique to the Hermeneutics of Liberation is neither ignorance nor the absence of exegetical research but rather the union of science and Spirit in the bosom of a community and under the aegis of a liberating pedagogy. Besides, it is this type of exegetical work, undertaken within our own hermeneutical space, that allows us to break with our dependency on the scientific biblical work of the academies in the First World. Such study allows us to benefit from the latter's findings, but with a keen sense of hermeneutical independence.

It is important to underline the fact that the exegetical work undertaken at the professional level of the Communitarian Reading of the Bible follows by and large the canons of traditional exegesis and remains faithful to the exegetical methods in vogue, while working out of its own communitarian space, quite different from both the academic space and the liturgico-institutional space. Such professional work is also in communion with a new historical subject: the poor people of God, which comes to expression in and through the base communities. Finally, and most importantly, such professional work operates with a different Spirit altogether.

The professional exegetes who work within the space created by the Hermeneutics of Liberation certainly read and study the great academic exegetes of the First World. Here, however, a distinction must frequently be made between the specific investigations carried out by the latter and the global result of such investigations. While there are many isolated elements of such research that can be of use to our own exegesis, we reject its global result—the context and the spirit in which such results are inscribed. We could say, metaphorically, that we make use of their bricks but not of the house constructed with such bricks. There are academic authors of the First World—such as Gerd Theissen, Wayne A. Meeks, or John Dominic Crossan—who have produced interesting as well as useful studies and observations, but the global result of their works proves alien and contrary to our own exegetical work. Such works come from other contexts, have other objectives, serve other interests, make use of a different market for their circulation and sale, and, most importantly, breathe a different spirit and culture. Again, we use their bricks but enter not into their houses. Our hermeneutical space is very different.

COMMUNITARIAN READING OF THE BIBLE AS A PROCESS OF TRANSFORMATION

The Communitarian Reading of the Bible is not only a process of interpretation but also a process for the transformation of individuals and communities.[4] The communities not only read and interpret the biblical texts, but also, and above all, discern the Word of God in them. The process of interpreting the Bible is but a means of discovering the living Word of God. It is necessary in this regard, therefore, to go beyond a certain type of intellectualism or rationalism (new forms of gnosticism), which ultimately reduce the process of biblical interpretation to a purely intellectual activity, bypassing altogether the ultimate goal of the Communitarian Reading, which is none other than a liberating encounter with the Word of God. As Paul writes, "For whatever was written in former days was written for our instruction, so that by steadfastness and by the encouragement of the scriptures we might have hope" (Rom 15:4). Or again, "All scripture is inspired by God and is useful for teaching, for reproof, for correction, and for training in righteousness" (2 Tim 3:16).

First, the Communitarian Reading of the Bible is a pedagogical process. In Latin America this type of reading has been developed in close relationship with the methodology of popular education. Emphasis is placed, therefore, on the creative pedagogical capacities of the community in the interpretation of the Bible. The community interprets the Bible, to be sure, but the Bible also interprets the community, insofar as it discerns, corrects, educates, strengthens, and matures the community. This Communitarian Reading is giving rise to stable and mature communities throughout Latin America. When the community, through its process of interpreting the Bible, can give witness regarding where God resides, what God is like, and what is God's will and word, it does so with authority, legitimacy, certainty, efficacy, and vigor.

To give the Bible to the People of God and to the community is to make it possible for them to transform themselves into a prophetic people and community, capable of giving witness to the Word of God. The process of Communitarian Reading thus constitutes a venue for the formation of lay people and pastoral agents (both men and women) possessed of authority and legitimacy, a development that in turn bestows upon them a great sense of maturity and autonomy in all their actions. At the same time, such maturity by no means signifies freedom from the authority of the Church, its tradition and magisterium, but rather a process of education and spiritual perfection that allows them to develop, with their own spirit and strength, their own specific vocation within the People of God.

Second, the Communitarian Reading of the Bible is a way of spirituality and sanctification. The Word of God that the community discovers has the power to transform the hearts of human beings, to bring about a change in modes of thinking and behavior, and to create a new practice and a new spirituality. The Communitarian Reading is thus a venue for a spirituality rooted in the history of salvation and the Word of God. The result is a spirituality that is solid and mature, historical and transformative, anti-idolatrous and liberating. When inserted into the tradition of the *lectio divina*—the systematic reading of the Bible from the perspective of prayer and faith—it becomes a venue for prayer as well.

Third, the Communitarian Reading of the Bible is a process of ecclesial reformation and transformation. As a pedagogical process and a way of spirituality and sanctification, such reading can only serve to unleash a process of ecclesial transformation. Indeed, wherever this type of reading is carried out in the churches, the result is a process for the actualization of the spiritual energy present in the People of God. Such a process is one of reformation from below, inspired by the Word of God, as Paul declared in his farewell to the Ephesian elders, "And now I commend you to God and to the message of his grace, a message that *is able to build you up* and to give you the inheritance among all who are sanctified" (Acts 20:32). The Communitarian Reading of the Bible thus gives way to a recovery of the church's identity, grounded in the history of its origins. In the process, the canon of the Scriptures is retrieved as a norm of faith and a criterion for the reformation of the church. To be sure, this process of ecclesial transformation is carried out with the support of the magisterium of the church and in communion with its authorities.

Finally, the Communitarian Reading of the Bible is the driving force behind a process of social, cultural, and religious transformation within civil society. As stated at the beginning of this study, the reconstruction of civil society, the reconstruction of the Spirit, and the reconstruction of the Sacred Scriptures form a continuous and closely linked process. Thus, civil society constitutes not only the original context for the pursuit of the Communitarian Reading of the Bible but also its point of destination, where the Word of God, acting through the community that interprets it and lives it, reveals the breadth of its liberating force and efficacy.

THE COMMUNITARIAN READING OF THE BIBLE AND THE CHANGE OF PARADIGMS IN BIBLICAL INTERPRETATION

The goal behind the Communitarian Reading of the Bible is not simply to work with new and liberating themes or to engage in biblical rereading solely for the sake of it; its objective, rather, is to bring about a transformation in the dominant paradigms of biblical interpretation. To accomplish such a task, it is absolutely necessary to bring together the work of professional exegesis and the

work of interpretation on the part of the base communities. In other words, it becomes necessary to bring together science and the Spirit, given the fact that the change of paradigms represents not only an intellectual task but also a change in ways of thinking as well as in spirituality. In effect, such a change in paradigms entails an ecclesial, social, and cultural transformation of global dimensions. Perhaps the best way to understand such a change in paradigms is by way of concrete examples.

1. With respect to the origins of Christianity and the New Testament, one finds the dominant paradigm of Christendom as formulated in the fourth century C.E. by Eusebius of Caesarea in his *Ecclesiastical History*. Eusebius sets out to write the "official history" of Christianity in order to legitimate the Constantinian model of the Church. Within this paradigm, Jesus emerges as the direct founder of the institutional church as it came to be later on. Moreover, an original unity of the Church is presented as its true model, while later diversity is characterized as a source of heresies. As a result, unity is associated with orthodoxy and diversity with heresy. From a historical point of view, however, such a construction is false. The fact is that there was diversity in Christianity from the very beginning and that it was unity that emerged out of the orthodoxy of diversity. Indeed, through its acceptance of so many diverse traditions and writings, the biblical canon consecrated diversity.

2. Another false paradigm involves a historicist reading of the Acts of the Apostles, with its reconstruction of the origins of Christianity in terms of the following theological and geographical design: from Jerusalem to Rome, through Antioch, Ephesus, and the other Pauline churches of the Aegean Sea. Within this paradigm, Galilee is completely bypassed, as is the expansion of Christianity to the south (the northern part of Africa) and the east.

3. A further example has to do with certain incorrect paradigms regarding the nature of ministry in the apostolic church. Again, later church situations are projected back into the apostolic origins of the Church, distorting thereby the beginnings of the process of church institutionalization. Thus, on the one hand, the hierarchical paradigm of bishops, presbyters, and deacons is accepted as directly apostolic. On the other hand, the church ministry of this period is described in terms of the sacerdotal and sacrificial model taken from the Jewish tradition of the Temple. Yet, it is widely accepted today that such a re-sacerdotalization and re-judaization of primitive Christianity dates from a much later time (the third and fourth centuries C.E.).

A very fruitful change of paradigms has taken place as well from the perspective of women in biblical interpretation. In effect, a comparative method involving the reconstruction of the conditions of women in the Jewish and Greco-Roman world, the rupture in this regard represented by the Jesus movement and the apostolic communities, and the later process of re-patriarchalization has served to de-structure patriarchal and authoritarian paradigms in biblical interpretation. As a result, the question of gender has emerged as a crucial theoretical orientation in the process of de-structuring and re-structuring the biblical traditions from the dominant paradigms into new paradigms—paradigms that make it possible to liberate the texts as well as the communities that read them from any type of patriarchy and authoritarianism.

A similar development has taken place from a cultural point of view. The use of the Book of Joshua to legitimate the colonial conquest of America, and the manipulation of the anti-idolatrous critique of the prophets to de-legitimate and oppress the autochthonous religions of these lands, are well-known. Eventually, a colonial hermeneutical paradigm was born, which ultimately emerged as dominant and which conquered and transformed the whole of the Bible. A Communitarian Reading of the Bible undertaken from the perspective of the Amerindian communities, along with the work of exegetes with a non-colonial vision of culture, has revealed the false character of such interpretive models. In the process, a new paradigm regarding Joshua has emerged, with a view of the book not as a model for conquest, but rather for the liberation of the land. Similarly, employing the paradigm of oppression/liberation, an intrinsic relationship has been established between idolatry and oppression as well as a fundamental opposition between the God of life and the idols of death. Further, the revelation of God present in these cultures has been rescued, and a new type of evangelization has been designed from the point of view of non-Western cultures. Such developments have made it possible to create new cultural and theological paradigms for the interpretation of the Bible that are neither colonialist nor eurocentric in nature.

Finally, a further development should be mentioned with regard to those historicist paradigms that exclude any consideration of nature from the realm of biblical interpretation. In this regard, the ecological movements have helped to change such models and to create new interpretive paradigms in which humanity and the world are seen as forming an essential part of the history of salvation.

NOTES

1. See, e.g., P. Freire, *The Pedagogy of the Oppressed* (New York: Herder & Herder, 1971).

2. "Dogmatic Constitution on Divine Revelation (Dei Verbum)," *Documents of Vatican II,* Walter M. Abbott, S.J., ed. (New York: Herder & Herder, 1966) 107-32; Pontifical Biblical Commission, "The Interpretation of the Bible in the Church," *Origins* 23:29 (January 6, 1994) 498-524.

3. "Dogmatic Constitution" #10 in Abbott, *Documents,* 118.

4. For further analysis of the Communitarian Reading of the Bible, see my "La Biblia y la memoria histórica de los pobres," *La fuerza espiritual de la Iglesia de los Pobres,* 2nd ed. (San José: Departamento Ecuménico de Investigaciones, 1988) 113-24; "Lectura Popular de la Biblia en América Latina: Hermenéutica de la liberación," *Revista de Interpretación Bíblica Latinoamericana* 1 (1988) 30-48; "1492: La violencia de Dios y el futuro del Cristianismo," *1492-1992, The Voice of the Victims,* in Concilium 1990/6; ed. Leonardo Boff and Virgil Elizondo (London: SCM Press; Philadelphia: Trinity Press International, 1990) 429-38; "Hermenéutica Bíblica India: Revelación de Dios en las religiones indígenas y en la Biblia (Después de 500 años de dominación)," *Revista de Interpretación Bíblica Latinoamericana* 11 (1992) 9-24; "Lectura de la Biblia en América Latina," *Vida, clamor, y esperanza. Aportes desde América Latina* (Bogotá: Ediciones Paulinas, 1992) 143-50; and "Crítica de la hermenéutica occidental y lectura popular de la Tradición: Hermenéutica del Espíritu," *Pasos* 49 (Sept.-Oct. 1993) 1-10.

16

BIBLICAL STUDIES IN INDIA

From Imperialistic Scholarship
to Postcolonial Interpretation

R. S. Sugirtharajah

What I would like to do in this paper is to explore how biblical studies were introduced in India and then to provide a modest proposal regarding the sort of contours biblical studies should develop in the future. Although I confine myself to India and Sri Lanka, the two countries with which I am familiar, I have no doubt that some of the issues I raise here will have some resonance in other parts of Asia. As I survey the discipline, I can identify two traditional modes of biblical studies in India. These can be categorized as "Orientalist" and "Anglicist." As a possibility for the future, I would like to propose a "Postcolonialist" mode of doing biblical studies. I will define these terms in the course of this study. The fact that these categories are yoked to imperialist periodization and couched in colonial terminology is itself a reminder and an indication that the Bible was seen as an ineluctable instrument of the Empire. Indeed, one of the devices employed to promote the Bible in India was to make propagandistic mileage out of the confession made by King George V that he himself read the Bible every day. This enabled missionaries of the time to market the Bible as "the book your Emperor reads."[1]

THE ORIENTALIST MODE:
INVENTING TRADITION

Biblical studies made inroads into India as part of what is now known as the "Orientalist" phase. Orientalism was the cultural policy advocated by colonialists as a way of promoting and reviving India's ancient linguistic, philosophical, and religious heritage. This policy was instrumental in excavating India's rich cultural past, and in the process it introduced Indians to the glories of their ancient heritage. It also elevated Sanskrit to a venerated status and ensured that the learning of it became indispensable for the natives. Orientalist policy was instigated partly out of the need to acquaint the rulers with the native way of life and partly as a way of effectively controlling and managing the Indian people.

Serampore College, India's first Protestant college, established in 1818 to instruct Asiatic Christian and other youth, emerged at a time when the Orientalist mode of constructing knowledge was being promoted by colonial administrators. One can detect shades of Orientalism in the very founding of the college. The college had as its policy to make provision for converted Christians to learn the ancient Indian shastras and Sanskrit, in addition to the Christian Scriptures. The "Prospectus" that the founders produced underlined this particular goal of the college:

> A College for Native Christian Youths, in which, while instructed in Scriptures, they shall be taught Sungskritu in the most efficient manner, and be made as fully acquainted with the philosophical doctrines which form the soul of Boudhist and Poumaic Systems, as are the learned in India themselves.[2]

Since its inception, therefore, the college was committed to creating a body of able native interpreters who would be enthused by the Christian message to act as evangelizing intermediaries between Christian texts and Hindu shastras. The same prospectus goes on to say, "If ever the gospel stands in India, it must *be native being opposed to native by demonstrating its excellence above all other systems.*"[3] The Orientalist rejuvenation of Indian culture provided an enormous impetus to the development of biblical interpretation in India. The Indian converts of the last century, following the path set by their erstwhile Hindu colleagues, were engaged in retrieving the neglected Indian classical texts rather than with the Western classical tradition, as the missionaries had expected.

Krishna Mohan Banerjea (1813-1885), a Bengali convert to the Christian faith, saw his task as that of showing interconnections between Vedic texts and biblical narratives. After his retirement from teaching theology at Bishop's College, Calcutta, Banerjea published a book entitled, *The Arian Witness: Or Testimony of Arian Scriptures in Corroboration of Biblical History and the Rudiments of Christian Doctrine, including Dissertations on the Original Home and Early Adventures of Indo-Arians* (Calcutta, 1875). In this and other writings Banerjea demonstrates the remarkable similarities between biblical and Vedic texts. He selects overlapping narrative segments such as the creation, the fall, and the flood from the great wealth of Vedic writings and compares them with passages from the Christian Scriptures. His intention is twofold: (1) to show that the Vedas come closer to the spirit of Christianity than do the Hebrew Scriptures; (2) to demonstrate that the pristine pure form of Hinduism found in the Vedas is identical with the Christian Scriptures, thus identifying contemporary Indian Christians as the spiritual heirs of Aryan Hindus. He writes:

> The fundamental principles of the Gospel were recognized, and acknowledged by ... the Brahmanical Aryans of India, and if the authors of the Vedas could by any possibility now return to the world, they would at once recognize the Indian Christians ... as their own descendants. ...[4]

Banerjea's conclusion is as follows:

> The Vedas confirm and illustrate Scripture traditions and Scripture facts. . . . Christianity fills up the vacuum—a most important vacuum—in the Vedic account of the sacrifice, by exhibiting the true Prajapati—the lamb slain from the foundation of the World.[5]

Banerjea's engagement with Vedic texts and biblical narratives was the affirmation, endorsement, and realization of the dream of the founders of Serampore College—that Christian natives would one day encounter native Hindus with their own textual tradition.

The Orientalist construction of a Golden Age of Indian civilization based on ancient Sanskritic texts and Sanskritic criticism continues to inform and influence Indian Christian biblical interpretation. Like the earliest Orientalists, some current biblical interpreters, including both Indians and expatriates, see the recovery of brahmanical tradition as a way of bringing to Indian Christians the truth of their own ancient heritage. The best examples of this current of thought are T. M. Manickam's *Dharma According to Manu and Moses*[6]; R. H. S. Boyd's *Khristadvaita: A Theology for India*[7]; and Swami Abhishiktananda's characterization of the Gospel of John as a Christian Upanishad.[8] In his investigation of Manusmrti and the Pentateuch, Manickam demonstrates that, in spite of the differences inherent in the two texts, both speak of human welfare and social ordering. Boyd's book is an attempt to work out a theology for India based on Romans but following the Sankritic *bhasya* or commentary tradition.

While these individuals were encouraging us to engage in comparative hermeneutics, others—such as Paul Gregorios, Thomas Manickam (again), Anand Amaladoss, and Sister Vandana—were making proposals for borrowing critical tools from Sanskritic literary tradition for the enhancement of Indian biblical hermeneutics as an alternative to the hegemonic Western strategies of interpretation. Gregorios urged Indians to recover the distinctive interpretative principles laid down by three Indian philosophical schools, the *Nyaya*, the *Vaisesika*, and *Sankhya*, while Manickam proposed a cross-cultural hermeneutics based on three Indian classical schools, *Mimamsa*, *Zyankarana*, and the Vedanatic school of Sankara, which developed their own methods to understand revelation. The recent call by Anand Amaladoss and Sister Vandana to revive the *dhvani* method of interpretation also falls within this Orientalist phase.

Anecdote One. In Rudyard Kipling's *Kim*, there is an old and wise Tibetan Lama. He is on his way to visit various Buddhist holy places. He meets with the English curator of a museum in Lahore. Astonished at how much the curator knows about his own religious tradition, the Lama regards him as the "Fountain of Wisdom," admits his own inadequacy, and says, "I know nothing." One of his desires now is to see for himself the River of the Arrow, where his Lord demonstrated his strength. He asks the curator:

> See, I am an old man! I ask with my head between thy feet, O Fountain of Wisdom. We know he drew the bow! We know the arrow fell! We know

the stream gushed! Where, then, is the River? My dream told me to find it.
So I came. I am here. But where is the River?[9]

I narrate this anecdote to demonstrate how Orientalism has created the notion
that it is Westerners who have mastery over our traditions and provide us with
both accurate description and proper explanation of it. Put differently, the
Sahibs know all.

THE ANGLICIST MODE:
INTRODUCING WESTERN TOOLS
TO SHAPE THE COLONIAL "OTHER"

Anglicism arose as an ideological program to counter Orientalism in colonial
India. It was a systematic attempt to replace indigenous texts and learning with
Western sciences and Western modes of thinking and to integrate the colonial
into the culture of the colonizer. Translated into biblical studies, it meant the
introduction of Western modes of biblical investigation in Indian theological
colleges. In practice, it meant two things in particular: (1) the importation of
Western reading techniques in the form of historical criticism and its allied disciplines; (2) the ushering in of biblical theology with its meta-themes—the Bible
as a theologically unified whole; the self-disclosure of God through historical
events; the distinctive character of biblical mentality, which differed from that
of its Hellenistic neighbors; and the unique features of biblical faith in contrast
to its Near Eastern environment. Anglicism also brought with it the "Modernist" ideas of belief in meta-narratives and objective reality, and narratives as
objects with determinate meaning, with its corresponding commitment to discover *the* meaning of the text.

I should like to use examples from "The Christian Students' Library," a vehicle for propagating Anglicism. This was a textbook series produced under the
aegis of the Senate of Serampore as recommended texts for Indian theological
students. These books had different color codes, and the blue cover designated
biblical studies. Although the general editors of the series made ambitious
claims that these volumes were written with Indian students in mind, most of
them pay scant regard to the immediate social, religious, and cultural contexts
of Indian students. They painstakingly situate the texts in their historical contexts and introduce students to the latest European biblical scholarship. For
instance, the commentary on the Psalms does not even mention India once, nor
does it discuss the rich and varied poetic devotional tradition that had been
developed in India over the years.[10] Almost all these books were written by
expatriate missionary teachers, some of whom had begun their missionary
careers in India before independence. These missionaries relied upon modernist
values to empower them as enlightened educators, but at the same time, in
inculcating these values, they helped to pave the way for the enslavement of
their Indian students. This is not the time to engage in a sustained evaluation of
these volumes and their specific historical and social contribution, but they do

cry for analysis, not only as cultural products of the time, but also in terms of the ideology they advanced and legitimized. Here I limit myself to an identification of their main features.

Characteristic Features

First, these volumes were relentless in their aim to propagate biblical faith as historical and objective, as opposed to Hinduism, which was seen as mythical and ahistorical. To establish such a claim, historical-critical tools were seen as an appropriate pedagogical instrument and an ally. The authors of these volumes learned their craft in England, Germany, and the United States and uncritically appropriated it and applied it to the Indian context. They were passionately evangelical in introducing the intricacies of this wonderful instrument. For example, Stanley Thoburn hailed it as a divine boon: "The scientific method is one of the greatest gifts that God has given to man, and none can deny the marvelous achievements that have come through its use."[11] The pedagogical use of historical analysis as a method of reading the Bible was the hermeneutical strategy used by these commentators to expose their students to the errors of their own shastras and the defects of their philosophical systems, while simultaneously enabling them to internalize the modernist virtues of objective certitude and determinacy. A historical consciousness was seen as a necessary virtue to sift fact from legend and as a way of establishing the factual basis of biblical faith. Listen to the words of Anthony Hanson:

> [W]e must be willing to have our Bible examined by any reasonable standard of historical criticism, because it is then that the character of Christianity founded on real historical events will stand out clearly.... On the other hand the events related in the Hindu scripture are found to be for the most part legend.[12]

The investigation of biblical narratives strictly in historical terms introduced what Kosuke Koyama calls a series of "non-crisis questions."

Anecdote Two. The Buddhist Parable of the Arrow[13] speaks about a man who has been wounded by a poisoned arrow. When his relatives arrange for a surgeon to pull out the arrow, the injured man will not let him. He first wants to know, Who shot the arrow? Which caste did he belong to? Whether he was a brahmin or of the warrior or the agricultural caste? He wants to know whether he was black, dark, or yellow. He wants to know whether the arrow was an ordinary one or of iron. In that crucial situation he is worried about these inconsequential questions. I narrate this story to show how in our biblical studies we were busily engaged in fruitless and trivial historical pursuits and never bothered to ask how they were related to questions closer to home. We agonized over the ending of Mark: where did the gospel end, at 16:8 or at 16:17? We racked our brains regarding where to put the punctuation mark in Romans 9:5. We tried to count how many letters Paul wrote to the Corinthians or how many visits he made to Jerusalem, since his accounts did not tally with those of Luke. Important as such questions are, they effectively turned our attention from the pressing social issues of the day.

In addition, along with biblical criticism, these volumes also introduced the biblical theology that reigned supreme at that time. This theology was shaped by a mosaic of different influences—the Protestant Reformed tradition, the Enlightenment, and the neo-orthodoxy of Karl Barth and Emil Brunner. These imported theologies were irrelevant at best and a distorting influence at worst. They dealt with European Protestant issues such as Law versus Grace, justification by faith or works, the Jesus of history versus the Christ of faith, and so forth. While castigating Indian idol worship as vain and superstitious, biblical theology introduced its own idol in the form of Rudolf Bultmann's demythologization. We were encouraged to fall prostrate before such an idol without pausing to think even for a moment that the whole program of demythologization was aimed at Europeans, who had lost a sense of awe and wonder and the feel for the numinous as a result of the scientific mode of thinking. Demythologization was seen as a transferable pedagogic strategy to illuminate the mental darkness of Indian minds and their superstitious ways.

Anecdote Three. Professor Hollenwager tells the story of John Mbiti, the first African to get a doctorate in Germany. When he went home, a great ceremony was organized to welcome him and honor his rare achievement. During the celebration a woman was brought before Mbiti. She was found to be possessed by a spirit. The elder there asked Mbiti to cast out the evil spirit. Mbiti said: "Well, you all know that I studied with Bultmann, and according to him there are no evil spirits. He has demythologized all." When they heard this, the people said, "What is the use of studying in Europe? Before you could heal. Now you can't." What this anecdote illustrates is how Western methods do not recognize the different worldviews and thinking modes of other people. Most of the commentators who were part of the Enlightenment paradigm saw their task as overcoming ignorance and celebrating reason and progress. For many Asian Christians the supernatural provides the foundation for their faith. They articulate their faith through dreams, visions, and healings. To devalue them or dismiss them as pagan and primitive is to relinquish our theological responsibility. Such an attitude raises the question of the role of scholarship and its accountability.

Lasting Legacies

As I look back now, I can readily identify at least six lasting legacies of these volumes:

1. First, they were responsible for what John Hull calls "Religionism," which he describes as follows:

> Adherence to a particular religion which involves the identity of the adherent so as to support tribalistic or nationalistic solidarity. The identity which is fostered by religionism depends upon rejection and exclu-

sion. We are better than they, we are orthodox, they are infidel. We are believers and they are unbelievers. We are right and they are wrong. The other is identified as the pagan, the heathen, the alien, the stranger, the invader, the one who threatens our way of life.[14]

What these volumes were trying to do was precisely this. They saw their task as improving the standards of "others," rectifying the morals of "others," and purifying the resources of "others." They were trying to din into students that biblical faith was superior and different, that there was no meeting point between it and Hinduism.

Thus, W. B. Harris, comparing Vedanta with Christian faith, tells the students: "These two types of religious experience, represented on the one hand by *Romans* and the other by Sankara, move in entirely opposite directions, meeting at no single point."[15] Then he goes on to show that Christian faith is personal as well as purposively historical and how God will bring history to a triumphant end, while arguing that Hinduism is impersonal, that its conception of time and history are unreal and cyclical, and that Hindus are caught in the endless cycle of karma-samsara. In other words, such exegetical comments reinscribe the notion that Hinduism is doctrinally vague and has no clear eschatological direction, whereas Christian faith is doctrinally exact and has a purposive history. Indeed, one of the things the writers of this series routinely remind their students is that Indians lack a sense of history. Wolfgang Roth tells his readers:

> In this regard a basic difference exists between the Jewish-Christian and Classical Hindu understanding of history. For biblical theology, history has ultimate significance because God acts in, with, and under historical events and so makes them the vehicle of his revelation, thus creating life, faith and fellowship. For classical Hinduism, history does not have ultimate significance.[16]

It is clear that these commentaries constantly extol the virtues of Christian salvation and simultaneously belittle a Hindu understanding of it. "Like Gnosticism," writes Maxwell R. Robinson, "Hinduism has no promise of universal redemption."[17] Likewise, he also reminds the students that, "We must not forget that there is this great difference between the Hindu and the Christian idea of a saint."[18]

These commentators also acted as watchdogs against the syncretic tendencies of Hinduism or, as Harold Moulton put it, the "all absorptive power of Hinduism."[19] They warn against any attempts at indigenization of the Christian faith. Commenting on 2 Timothy 1:14 about guarding the truth, Robinson writes: "In India the church has the peculiarly difficult task of seeking to interpret and present the Gospel. . . . There is the danger that the central truths of Christianity may become distorted in the process of trying to make them acceptable."[20] Lest the Christian church be swallowed up by Hinduism, the Christians must be vigilant in this hostile environment, as the early church was.[21] Roth upholds the example of the Old Testament, which "can serve today in the

Indian church as a safeguard in that it resists any dissolution of the Gospel into a timeless principle."[22] Religionism tends to produce stereotypes. These volumes helped to do that. Seeing oneself and one's enemy in terms of biblical stereotypes does not allow much scope for fresh dialogue and understanding.

2. The second legacy of these volumes was to reinforce the compartmentalization of theological studies. The categorization of theology—into dogmatic, moral, biblical, spiritual, and pastoral—emerged as a product of Western rationalism. The consequence of such an approach was fragmentation. This fragmentation takes place within the discipline and also across the disciplines. These volumes introduce a world of philological and lexical nuances, syntactical conundrums, and abstract historical facts. A feature of these commentaries is that they do line-by-line analysis of each pericope. They are excellent examples of historical-critical methods at work. But the trouble with this method, as we have all come to realize, is that it does not make any effort to integrate and is shy of asking theological questions.

Anecdote Four. The following excerpt is taken from a letter written by Julius Wellhausen, the Old Testament scholar, on April 5, 1882, to the Minister of Education, after deciding to change from the theology to the philosophy faculty:

> I became a theologian because I was interested in the scientific treatment of the Bible. It was in the course of time that I realized that a professor of theology has also the practical task of preparing the students for their ministry in the church. I realized that I was unable to meet this requirement. I am afraid to make the students rather incapable for their ministry.[23]

The point of the anecdote is clear, and I do not think that it requires any exegesis on my part. Linked with this fragmentation is the isolated setting in which biblical studies are undertaken. Biblical studies classes are seen as theological gulags, as if other sacred texts do not exist. For instance, in a class on the Gospel of John, the students are taught about the uniqueness of Jesus; then, when they find themselves in the Hinduism class, they find it confusing to read in the Gita that all paths lead to God. In other words, students are left with diverse and conflicting ideas, with no attempt made to integrate them.

Anecdote Five. There was a student who was puzzled by the conflicting messages he was hearing in his classes. In the Tamil class he was told by the Tamil teacher that a lunar eclipse was caused by *Rahu*, the solar king swallowing *Ketu*, the comet. But in the geography class he was told by the teacher that an eclipse was caused by the rotation of moon and earth. In a state of confusion, he went to the headmaster to find out what he should write in his examination. The headmaster told him that he should write what the geography teacher told him in the geography examination and what the Tamil teacher told him in the Tamil examination.[24] I narrate this anecdote to highlight the lack of an interdisciplinary and integrated approach in our theological education. The uncomfortable position into which students were placed when they appeared for theological examinations compounded the problem. "Compare the Christian understanding of incarnation with the Hindu understanding of Avatars"; "Write a critical essay on the merits of the Pauline concept of Grace and the demerits of the Saiva Siddthantha notion of Grace"; "Compare and contrast biblical and Hindu understanding of revelation"—such used to be the typical questions. The comparative nature of these questions forced students to commit themselves to critical judgments that went against the religious tolerance in which they had been born and brought up.

3. The third legacy of these volumes was to introduce alien hermeneutical practices and foreign thought patterns that effectively displaced indigenous ones. To begin with, biblical interpretation became a private, solitary activity. In India hermeneutics used to be a public activity undertaken by professional storytellers and singers. These volumes helped to introduce the notion that interpretation is a literary activity limited to an educated, literate class, thus effectively replacing existing modes of oral transmission. Interpretation in India used to be undertaken by a group of professional storytellers who would go around the villages and narrate, chant, and recite religious stories and poems, often accompanied by musicians and dancers.[25] Realizing the effectiveness of the method, the Indian Bible Society used to employ readers who would go around the villages to read the texts and would have face-to-face encounters with the local people.[26] Thus, hermeneutics was not a private affair but a public one, where villagers would gather to hear the Word afresh, not necessarily through reading but by listening and interacting. Faith, as Paul would have said, comes from hearing. But these commentaries changed the mode of interpretation by replacing a group of listeners with an individual reader.

4. The fourth legacy of these volumes was to replace the Indian narrative approach with the historical-critical approach. Indians tend to view texts as authorless narrative wholes, without any worry about their sources or the situation in which they were composed. For Indians, the text is only a medium and is not a means to understand the truth. It expresses emotive meaning, "feelings and attitudes rather than ideas, concepts, statements of universal truth."[27] In Indian hermeneutics, the text is seen for its beauty, grace, and emotive power. The task of interpretation for Indians is not engaging in exegesis but constructing new texts. No one struggles with the "Ur" text of the Ramanayana, but people come out with different tellings or versions to suit different contextual needs.[28] Studying from written texts was frowned upon. Recitation, repetition, and memorization were invariably preferred. In introducing the historical-critical approach, these volumes thus effectively eclipsed indigenous allegorical, symbolic, figurative, and metaphorical approaches. The narrative approach now in vogue in Western biblical circles vindicates the Indian approach to texts.

5. The fifth legacy of these volumes was to put aside natural theology and bring to the fore Karl Barth's notion of special revelation. The overwhelming hermeneutical hold of Barth on these commentators, and the bogey he created about natural theology, prevented them from acknowledging that there was an alternative mode of God's self-disclosure through natural and mundane life, a

mode with which Indians were familiar. By over-interpreting historical events such as the Exodus and the Christ-event, they under-interpreted the other dimensions of God's revelation through nature, cult, worship, and festivals.

6. Finally, these volumes were so saturated with Protestant evangelical issues such as sin, redemption, and the washing of blood that questions of dalits, women, and the indigenous people did not figure in their exegetical configurations. Robinson's comment that slaves should be encouraged to "keep their Christian witness clear by doing their best for those who employ them"[29] serves as an indicator of this ideological and theological stance.

In effect, what these volumes did was to produce an English-educated hermeneutical elite who cut themselves off from their own people. The volumes helped to create among them a homogeneity based on a powerful appropriation of Western interpretative methods and tools. Although Indian Christians came from different castes and classes, spoke different vernaculars, and identified with different ideological and theological positions, these texts helped to produce a homogeneous Christian identity. In the same way, Orientalists helped to locate them in an imagined community. The agenda for biblical studies was set by the major thrusts of Orientalist and Anglicist modes of interpretation. Thus, while Orientalism enabled Indian Christians to re-establish a relationship with their past and with their own community via a tradition invented by Europeans, Anglicism exposed them, through its insistence on a scientific approach to the Bible, to the ideas of the Enlightenment and modernity but failed to prepare them for the task for which they were training.

TOWARD POSTCOLONIAL CRITICISM

This is the story of biblical studies in India so far—though not necessarily the only or correct story. This is but my version of it. Others may come up with different analyses and different portrayals. I have narrated this in my own way as a stepping stone to the future. How then should biblical studies look? What is its future? Forecasting and prophesying is a tricky business. Like Amos, I am not a prophet nor a son of a prophet. I am only a brown-skinned, post-colonial cosmopolitan!

The two terms at the center of current hermeneutical discussion are "postmodernism" and "postcolonialism." Needless to say, both are contested terms. Both also have certain affinities. Nonetheless, postmodernism is still seen as Eurocentric in its theoretical and aesthetic emphases. Although there are attempts to collapse them into one and erase their differences, postcolonialism is emerging as a distinctive discourse of its own. The recognition of postcolonialism as a branch of cultural studies and the rapid emergence of a supporting literature are evidence of this.[30]

I imagine that postcoloniality will be the site where future biblical interpretation in India, or for that matter in Asia, will be worked out. It is the interpretation which will emerge from people who once were colonized by European powers, but now have some sort of political freedom, while continuing to live with burdens from the past and experiencing newer forms of economic and cultural neocolonialism. It will emerge from the economic, social, and cultural margins, where these are seen as "sites of survival," "fighting grounds," and sites of pilgrimage.[31] It will emerge among nations, communities, and groups that have been victims of the old imperialism, remain victims of the current process of globalization, and have been kept away from power throughout, only to achieve an identity that is nurtured and nourished by their own goals and aspirations. It will be a way of critiquing the universalist, totalizing forms of European interpretation.

What will distinguish it from Orientalist and Anglicist modes of interpretation is the conviction that the modernist values such models espoused, like objectivity and neutrality, are expressions of political, religious, and scholarly power. It will reject the myth of objective or neutral truth and will replace it with a perception of truth as mapped, constructed, and negotiated. Postcolonial criticism recognizes that interpreters have to be freed from traditional interpretative powers so that the voice of the voiceless may be heard. It will be manifest in terms of what Franz Fanon calls "fighting literature," "a revolutionary literature,"[32] as the authentic expression of people tired of exasperating attempts to assimilate and mimic the hegemonic Orientalist and Anglicist modes of interpretation. It will revalorize the hidden or occluded accounts of numerous groups—women, minorities, the disadvantaged, and the displaced. Unlike the Orientalist and Anglicist modes, it will not engage in the task of recovering the meaning of the text but will recognize a multiplicity of meanings. The retrieval and re-inscription of the past becomes a crucial hermeneutical activity. But unlike the Orientalist and Anglicist, postcolonial reading will negotiate the past differently, "not as a static fetished phase to be literally reproduced, but as fragmented sets of narrated memories and experiences as a basis on which to mobilize contemporary communities."[33]

Postcolonial criticism will have at least two distinguishing characteristics. The first of these will take its cue from Stuart Hall and look for what he calls oppositional or protest voices in the texts. He identifies four codes which current television discourse embodies—hegemonic, professional, negotiated, and protest or oppositional.[34] Biblical texts reflect all four codes and traditional interpretations generally fraternize with the first three. Postcolonialism will look for protest or oppositional voices in the texts.

For instance, the Parable of the Tenants (Mark 12:1-11; Matt 21:33-43; Luke 20:9-18) is usually read from an overly Christological perspective, or from the property owner's perspective, or from the perspective of allusions to the Hebrew Bible. Rarely is the parable read from the point of view of the people who were part of the audience. Most of the commentators erase the role of the people from the parable. There is no need for me to rehearse it. When one by one the tenants kill the messengers, the householder finally sends his son. He is also killed by them. Jesus asks, what will the owner do? He goes on to say that the owner will come and destroy those tenants and give the vineyard to others. When the people hear that the owner is going to destroy the tenants and give the land to others, their response is "God forbid" (Luke 20:16b).[35] They express shock, for they are heirs of Yahweh's allotment of the land whose inheritance has been stolen from them. People know that, once the land is gone, they not only lose the income, but are also at the mercy of the owner for new working arrangements. What postcolonial criticism will do is to bring to the front such marginal elements in the texts and in the process subvert the traditional meaning. It will engage in an archival exegesis as a way of rememorializing the narratives and voices which have been subjected to institutional forgetting.

The second mark of postcolonial reading will be to advocate a wider hermeneutical agenda that will place the study of sacred texts—Christian-Hindu, Christian-Buddhist, Christian-Confucian—within the intersecting histories that constitute them. It will replace the totalitarian and totalizing claims of biblical narratives with the claim that they have to be understood as the negotiated narrative strategies of a community and have to be read and heard along with other communally inspired sacred narratives. It will see these texts within an intertextual continuum embodying a multiplicity of perspectives. It will mean looking for the hermeneutical relations that these texts imply and inspire, resisting any attempts to subsume one under the other. The issue for us is how these diverse texts can help us account for our collective identities. The recent study of Matthew's missionary command alongside the Buddhist Mahavagga text by George Soares-Prabhu comes close to the postcolonial intertextual engagement I have in mind.[36] In this article, the other is celebrated without insisting on and fitting it into protocols set by missionary apologetics.

Anecdote Six. This final anecdote comes from *Gora*, a novel by Rabindranath Tagore written during colonial days. It is a story about the spiritual journey of the hero of the novel, Gora, which takes him to a fanatical belief in Vedic Hinduism as a panacea for India's ills, and from there on to his enlightenment, which comes through his foster mother, Sucharita. After his enlightenment he is in search of a new identity. He says,

> To-day I am really an Indian. In me there is no longer any opposition between Hindu, Mussalman and Christian. To-day every caste in India is my caste, food of all is my food . . . all these days I have been carrying about with me an unseen gulf of separation which I have never been able to cross over! Therefore in my mind there was a kind of void, which I tried by various devices to ignore. I tried to make that emptiness look more beautiful by decorating it with all kinds of artistic work. . . . Now that I have been delivered from those fruitless attempts at inventing such useless decorations I feel . . . that I am alive again.[37]

Then he goes on to ask for "the *mantram* of that deity who belongs to all, Hindu, Mussalman, Christian . . . alike—doors to whose temples are never closed to any person of any caste whatever."[38] In a postcolonial context, Gora would agree that what we need is not just a *mantram*, a sacred word, but *mantrams*, a multiplicity of sacred words, which are manifestly pluralistic and validated by many communities.

NOTES

1. James Moulton Roe, *A History of the British and Foreign Bible Society* (London: The British and Foreign Bible Society, 1965) 153.

2. See *College for the Instruction of Asiatic Christian and Other Youth in Eastern Literature and European Science* (Serampore: Serampore Press, 1818) 3.

3. Ibid., 5. Emphasis in source.

4. As cited in Kaj Baago, *Pioneers of Indigenous Christianity* (Madras: The Christian Literature Society, 1969) 14.

5. Ibid., 16.

6. (Bangalore: Dharmaran Publications, 1977).

7. (Madras, The Christian Literature Society, 1977).

8. S. Abhishiktananda, *Hindu-Christian Meeting Point: Within the Cave of the Heart* (Bombay: The Institute of Christian Culture, 1969) 85.

9. R. Kipling, *Kim* (Harmondsworth: Penguin, 1990 [1901]) 19.

10. A. P. Carleton, *How Shall I Study the Psalms?* The Christian Students' Library 8 (Madras: The Christian Literature Society, 1956).

11. S. Thoburn, *Old Testament Introduction*, The Christian Students' Library 24 (Madras: The Christian Literature Society, 1961) 34.

12. A. Hanson, *Jonah and Daniel: Introduction and Commentary*, The Christian Students' Library 9 (Madras: The Christian Literature Society, 1955) 4.

13. I owe this story to Kosuke Koyama.

14. J. Hull, "Editorial: The Transmission of Religious Prejudice," *British Journal of Religious Education* 14 (1992) 70.

15. W. B. Harris, *A Commentary on the Epistle of St. Paul to the Romans*, The Christian Students' Library 33 (Madras: The Christian Literature Society, 1964) 45.

16. W. Roth, *Old Testament Theology*, The Christian Students' Library 41 (Madras: The Christian Literature Society, 1968) 8.

17. M. R. Robinson, *A Commentary on the Pastoral Epistles*, The Christian Students' Library 27 (Madras: The Christian Literature Society, 1962) 168.

18. Ibid., 27.

19. H. K. Moulton, *The Acts of the Apostles: Introduction and Commentary*, The Christian Students' Library 12 (Madras: The Christian Literature Society, 1957) 49.

20. Robinson, *Pastoral Epistles*, 78-79.

21. Ibid., 168.

22. Roth, *Old Testament Theology*, 233.

23. As cited in Friedrich Huber, "Towards an Applicability-Aimed Exegesis," *Indian Journal of Theology* 29 (1980) 135.

24. I owe this story to Sam Amirtham.

25. Sisir Kumar Das, *A History of Indian Literature*. Volume VIII: *1800-1910. Western Impact: Indian Response* (New Delhi: Sahitya Akademi, 1991) 36-38.

26. See W. A. Smith, "A Historical Study of the Protestant Use of Bible for Evangelism in India," MRS thesis, Senate of Serampore, 1966, 52-53.

27. V. K. Chari, *Sanskrit Criticism* (Delhi: Motilal Banarsidass Publishers, 1990) 9.

28. See Paula Richman, ed., *Many Ramayanas: The Diversity of a Narrative Tradition in South Asia* (Berkeley: University of California, 1991).

29. Robinson, *Pastoral Epistles*, 61.

30. See, e.g., Patrick Williams and Laura Chrisman, ed., *Colonial Discourse and Post-Colonial Theory: A Reader* (Hemel Hempstead: Harvester Wheatsheaf, 1993); Bill Ashcroft, Gareth Griffiths, and Helen Tiffin, eds., *The Post-Colonial Studies Reader* (London: Routledge, 1995).

31. Trinh Minh-ha, *When the Moon Waxes Red: Representation, Gender, and Cultural Politics* (London: Routledge, 1991) 17.

32. F. Fanon, *The Wretched of the Earth* (Harmondsworth: Penguin, 1990 [1961]) 179.

33. Ella Shohat, "Notes on the Post-Colonial," *Social Text* 31/32 (1992) 109.

34. S. Hall, *Encoding and Decoding in the Television Discourse* (Birmingham: Centre for Cultural Studies, 1973) 16-19.

35. I am grateful to Itumeleng Mosala for pointing this out to me.

36. G. Soares-Prabhu, "Two Mission Commands: Interpretation of Matthew 28:16-20 in the Light of a Buddhist Text," *Biblical Interpretation* 2 (1994) 264-82.

37. R. Tagore, *Gora* (Madras: Macmillan, 1989 [1924]) 406.

38. Ibid., 407.

Part IV

BIBLICAL INTERPRETATION: PEDAGOGICAL PRACTICES

17

A RHETORICAL PARADIGM
FOR PEDAGOGY

Rebecca S. Chopp

Everyone seems to agree that theological education in the United States is in a time of great change. Some see it as a time of significant crisis. Others see it as a time of great opportunity, growth, and transformation. Whatever the evaluation, almost all agree upon a number of factors contributing to this time of change. In no privileged order we can list such influences as: the disestablishment of mainline churches; the influx of women and people of color in theological education; the entrance of second- and third-career students; the phenomenon of students not being raised in the church and needing catechetical instruction; the pluralism of Christianity; the pluralism of religion in America; the turn to postmodernism in culture; and the disappearance of disciplinary identity or cohesion in the academy. All this leaves those of us who teach in U.S. theological education not quite sure where to go for direction. Like juggling jello or herding cats, we are not sure how to give any direction to U.S. theological education.

In what could be called a typical academic way, we try to figure out the nature of theological education. If we can figure out the correct or ideal purpose of theological education, we may be able to form the appropriate mission statement and curriculum, or so the common reasoning seems to suggest. Some years ago, I was asked by the Lilly Endowment to evaluate a group of fairly recent books and articles on theological education. Nearly all of the pieces I evaluated followed this kind of ideational approach. Although many of the authors I read recognized that issues of cultural and global change (including who the subjects are of theological education) were fundamental, almost all bracketed such concerns to concentrate on the correct idea of what theological education ideally should be.

My curiosity stimulated, I decided to focus some research not on correct ideas, but on present and emergent practices of theological education, and how students use the practices within theological education. Knowing I could not research all students, I decided to try to do an initial investigation of the phenomenon of feminism and women in mainline U.S. theological education. I decided to follow instead what women (and men) were doing within feminist practices, understanding that these feminist practices are sometimes explicit in the school and sometimes exist more on the margins of the standard curriculum. (I concentrated on interviewing women and men involved in some kind of definable feminist practice, respecting the women who do not choose to participate in any definable feminist movement.) Interviewing countless women and some men, I discovered that women use theological education to write their own narratives, to form new mediating structures or ecclesial communities, and to offer a way of doing theology for the purposes of emancipatory praxis.[1]

I rather quickly realized that considering theological education from the perspective of faculty and administrators and from the perspective of students actually using theological education produce two quite different ways of seeing theological education. Faculty members talk about mission, nature, and purpose and try to craft a grand narrative of the unity of theological education. Students talk about identity, ministry, and spirituality and try to figure theological education out for themselves. Where the faculty and students meet together, however, is not generally in curriculum design or in individual appropriation of theological education but in classroom practices of teaching and learning. The space of and practices within pedagogy constitute the most dominant common place in theological education. Pedagogy as common place is the site of learning and teaching, community and fellowship, spirituality and scholarship. It is also rarely discussed in the discourses of theological education.

Pedagogy has to do with how we create the context of learning. Pedagogy in theological education has three basic forms: (1) the transmission of ordered learning; (2) the development of professional skills; and (3) individual therapeutic supervision. To a certain extent certain disciplines and courses have traditionally been associated with the respective forms. Ordered learning has often been associated with the "traditional" disciplines of Bible, theology, and history, as well as the more modern disciplines of sociology, economics, and psychology. Professional skills get associated with preaching, worship, church administration, and education. Sometimes skill-based techniques become the focus of the curriculum, while other times such techniques are considered applied learning in the practical arts of ministry. The individual/therapeutic supervision form of pedagogy has its home in pastoral care and field education. Although these are not one and the same, both tend to focus on individual learning, individual psycho-familial history, and becoming a wise or mature person.

All of these forms of pedagogy certainly are appropriate for theological education. Each of these forms has its good and bad styles. The pedagogical form of individual/ therapeutic supervision can be empowering to women who have not found their voice, or it can be a form of abusive, dictatorial confrontation. Ordered learning can be enlightening as tools of scholarship are given, or it can be deadening to any creative questioning as such tools are identified with learning itself. Professional skills can help persons know basic practices, or they can be used to turn ministry into a gimmick-based sales job.

What I am most interested in is another dimension of pedagogy where the focus becomes community formation and development. I am concerned with pedagogical issues of, by, and for community, both in terms of forming a classroom as a community of learning and shaping the purpose of learning in terms of building a religious community. Although ordered learning, professional skills, and individual therapeutic supervision are all necessary and important, none of them really touches on how to develop communities of religious practice.

Communities of religious practice are of great importance today. "Reading from this place" implies a kind of communal tradition or context. Most of us want to buttress up religious communities. Indeed, one of the few widespread commitments in U.S. theological scholarship is attentiveness to issues and forms of communal life. Feminists and liberationists speak of normative concerns for community and the need to move beyond the narcissistic individual. The proponents of narrative theology speak about cultural-linguistic communities, and the adherents of hermeneutical theologies talk about communities of interpretation. I cannot think of any U.S. theologian who champions Christianity as rooted in or for the individual. There is widespread agreement that the communal context is where we are from, where we are at present, and where we are going.

There is another important reason for my concern with pedagogy and community building/development that has to do with social location and the global context. As the essays in this volume demonstrate, there is a desperate need for the relating of the local and the global. My question is: how do we teach persons to develop/build community that is both attentive to local situation and in dialogue with global context? I am pursuing both a descriptive and a normative concern: descriptively, I want to focus on how we reflect upon and express community; normatively, I want to focus on building and developing Christian communities in global inclusivity.

I want to offer one way of thinking about a pedagogy that is attentive to social location, both in terms of a respectfulness for where students are and also a commitment to cultivating a kind of empathetic learning about others, including others of present and future as well as others represented through (or behind) historical documents. I will be suggesting a rhetorical understanding of pedagogy for community building. My goal is not to offer pedagogical techniques (which is usually the limits of discussion of pedagogy), but a rhetorical understanding of pedagogy based in and through certain key values. Because pedagogy is concrete—it happens in particular places—I want to begin with a pedagogical portrait around which to build my reflection.

PEDAGOGICAL PORTRAIT

The class in feminist theology was three hours long, with two-thirds of the time devoted to a critical reading of the assigned text for the session and the last third devoted to some kind of appropriation of the material. As I did every semester, I approached this first evening with a pedagogy based on textual explanation, critical analysis, and creative imagining ... and with a great deal of apprehension. What if we couldn't combine explanation, critique, and imaginative construction? Why didn't I direct all the discussion, by which I could quickly and easily keep control of the class and decide what was to be learned? Why try this balance of communal and individual learning, this combination of imaginative, aesthetic, and ordered cognitive learning?

We read Rosemary Radford Ruether's *Sexism and God-Talk*.[2] The class was struggling with naming the pain of patriarchy and with visualizing hope. It was obvious to the students that this twofold task of naming the depth of broken-ness while at the same time announcing new possibilities was a Christian enter-prise. This juxtaposition of brokenness and hope, of pain and new life, was what they had heard, in a variety of ways, throughout their Christian lives and certainly throughout most of their seminary education.

As we returned from break to participate in a student-led discussion section, we found the chairs placed in a circle. A wooden cross stood in the middle of the room. The women leading this part of the class session handed each of us a slip of paper as we entered and asked us to write down one specific experience of patriarchal oppression. As we sat in our circle around the cross, one by one we took turns naming each of these acts of patriarchy. Some women and men named experiences of individual pain, many of them acts of violence or acts of silencing. Others spoke about a woman or a man they loved who had been hurt by patriarchy, while still others named patriarchal acts affecting large groups of women. After each one read aloud the sin inscribed on the paper, she or he nailed the paper to the cross.

After a prayer, a table (altar) was uncovered. On it were all sorts of things. One by one we chose from this array, which included a kaleidoscope, a sand dollar, a bowl, a goddess image, a mask, an Indian doll, a Brazilian wood carv-ing, a glass statue, a wreath, a rock, a gourd, a shell. Then again we spoke, this time about new possibilities of God through the use of the symbols we had cho-sen. A woman spoke of the kaleidoscope as imaging the changing patterns of God in her life; another woman spoke of the fruit she had chosen as represent-ing life-giving forces in her experience; still another spoke of the wreath as a symbol of eternal, creative presence.

This educational/communal/liturgical event is often with me when I think about pedagogy as theological performance. By performance I mean how theol-ogy happens, the experience of it itself, the enactment of the words. That partic-ular night represents most of the changes and the opportunities in theological education. It stands as one night in a long process of reading a variety of texts, of arguing their points, of expressing the vision of the texts as well as our own vision. That night stands as one particular pedagogical symbol for me to the effect that the performance of theology occurred through everyone in the room.

The night also reflects my own theological, pedagogical, and social location. I am a feminist liberationist theologian who teaches in a large, mainline semi-nary. I teach and write theology as part of what I understand is an emergent movement of liberationist Christianity in the United States, a movement concerned with empowerment of new voices in the shaping of justice in the church, in the United States, and in the global context. As a theologian I con-sider my work to be about critical reflection on and conscious shaping of this movement, especially in terms of its employment of the symbolic grammar of Christianity.

TURNING TOWARD RHETORIC

I begin my understanding of pedagogy with three assumptions about the community in which pedagogy exists. First, pedagogy always already begins in the community of inquirers, both within and beyond the classroom. Heavily influenced by the pragmatists Charles Sanders Peirce and John Dewey, I understand all knowledge and learning to be inherently a communal activity first, and then a personal activity. Secondly, communities are real and concrete; they exist in time and space and have histories and futures. To build community and to talk about building community is to engage in the concreteness of time and space; any abstraction or theoretical reflection will be based within the concreteness of the community and communal reflection. Thirdly, communities exist in and through discourse, but also through bodies, feelings, knowledge, imagination, and relationships among people. Any understanding of community must include ritual as well as speech, fellowship as well as discussion. My pedagogical portraiture is focused on a ritual developed in the classroom for those participants to realize some of the material read and discussed. Such rituals function to bring diverse experiences together in a common space, not in order to make all experiences the same, but to enable the community to enjoy and in some sense perform the various diverse experiences. I cannot elaborate these assumptions about pedagogy and community in this essay; I refer readers to my book *Saving Work: Feminist Practices of Theological Education.*

Pedagogy, based on these assumptions and aimed toward community building is best understood through what some have called a rhetorical paradigm. In an essay entitled "Rhetoric, Pedagogy, and the Study of Religions," authors Richard Miller, Laurie Patton, and Stephen Webb define a rhetorical paradigm of pedagogy as one that views "teaching as a dialogical, local, and practical art."[3] While the authors of this provocative essay correctly identify a rhetorical paradigm as one that emphasizes deliberation, dialogue, and transformation, I want to stress the relationship between community and rhetoric. For to focus on community is, I think, to require a rhetorical pedagogy.

Rhetoric is the art of deliberation; it is concerned with determining life together in community. Especially in the Roman tradition, the tradition that influenced thinkers such as Augustine and Calvin, rhetoric is that form of understanding which is aimed at action. In this tradition, Don Compier suggests, textual inquiry serves action and not vice versa.[4]

Rhetoric judges what it is that ought to be done and thus requires attention to the relations of power, agency, and structure in a particular situation. Well suited to the contextuality of knowledge, rhetoric is also sensitive to moral persuasion within the community and in the larger pluralistic setting.

Philosophically, when pluralism is acknowledged and sure foundations cease to be sought after, rhetoric emerges as the way of deliberation. Rather than putting aside the struggles and dreams, beliefs and practices, involved in a particular situation, persons use these to explore the common ground to discover imaginative possibilities, to find new solutions, and to create new forms of life. Likewise, once the political construction of knowledge is accepted, rhetoric becomes the basis of self-conscious deliberation and transformation in community. In Terry Eagleton's words, "Rhetoric, in other words, precedes logic: grasping propositions is only possible in specific forms of social life."[5]

Rhetorical forms of argument attempt to name what is going on, to reveal distortion and corruption, to imagine possibilities out of present reality. The norms used in rhetorical argument will themselves be taken from the situation; that is, they will be material as compared to transcendental norms. To actually teach rhetorically is to engage the classroom in building possibilities for the future. The norms for the art of rhetoric are found in the authority of practical possibilities in the future. The following kinds of questions become central to deliberation:

• Who is speaking and from what location?

• Whose purpose does the discourse serve?

• What vision is produced through the practical possibilities imagined?

• In what way is this vision one of great social, personal, and planetary flourishing?

To think about pedagogy as a rhetorical practice, rather than primarily in the forms of instrumental, therapeutic, or ordered learning, is to emphasize the communal and the public aspects of deliberation. For not only do classroom participants (including the teacher) learn in and through community, a decidedly public character is also given to the deliberation. By public I mean that arguments and discourse are for public debate and that background theories such as cultural location, economic realities, and so on can be explicated at any point. As Richard B. Miller has suggested, the notion of the classroom itself is an ecology of public discourse:

> Central to this ecology is the notion, again from Aristotle, that dialectical reasoning is *dialogical*. That is to say, probable opinions must be "hammered out" from the preoccupations and judgements of public opinion. This creates the requirement for the instructor to establish a set of ongoing expectations according to which the classroom itself becomes a site of public discourse and debate. In order for the several sides of an issue to be weighed, "private" opinions demand expression. In the rhetorical paradigm, students are invited to make sense of their basic judgements in a moral space constituted by divergent points of view.[6]

One more point about a rhetorical paradigm needs to be made, and that is that it emphasizes the transformative potential of the classroom. For rhetoric is finally about deliberation and decision: it creates the space for us to decide that which could be other. And everyone, rhetorically speaking, is a potential subject for transformation.

I also want to underscore that the classroom is not just about discourse, though discourse is the ordinary medium of the classroom. Ritual, both those explicitly conceived, such as the one I portray above, and the anonymous rituals of beginning and ending class, how discussion takes place, how bodies are arranged, etc., all contribute to community and community building. A very common example of this is the difference sitting in a circle can make from sitting in rows for discussion. The physical arrangement can be as important as the words spoken. And time for creative appropriation or community-building exercises can all facilitate the rhetorical nature of education.

RHETORICAL-PEDAGOGICAL VALUES

But one cannot just instantly announce a shift to a rhetorical pedagogy. In order to move toward a rhetorical paradigm for the development of community, I have found it necessary to first encourage three fundamental values: justice, dialogue, and the imagination. These values become habits of classroom practice, they become valued ends in themselves, and they become the texture of community. Let me address each value in turn.

Justice

Central to concerns of global context and to building and developing local communities, justice becomes a kind of privileged value. Justice involves deliberation, representation, and construction within community. Justice means that everyone gets a voice in self-determination and has the resources necessary for communal and individual self-determination. Theological education should not just be about justice, it should be an exercise in justice. Justice, according to Iris Marion Young, names the very nature of conditions for community:

> For a norm to be just, everyone who follows it must in principle have an effective voice in its consideration and be able to agree to it without coercion. For a social condition to be just, it must enable all to meet their needs and exercise their freedom; thus justice requires that all be able to express their needs."[7]

In my own pedagogical practice, I think about rhetorical pedagogy in terms of developing what Elisabeth Schüssler Fiorenza has called an *ekklesia* as a counter-sphere of justice.[8] Schüssler Fiorenza invokes the term *ekklesia* to mark the difference between the church as a community of democratic participation, a communicative concept of justice, and the patriarchal church of an interlocking system of discrimination and subordination. In the *ekklesia*, neither women nor men speak as one group; rather different groups, individuals, and coalitions all have an opportunity to participate in the self-determination of community. The *ekklesia* names a different type of community than the patriarchal church, one constituted through justice rather than one which distributes justice as crumbs left from the table. Schüssler Fiorenza calls this a counter-public sphere, by which she means an oppositional space to the dominant public sphere in which the critique of patriarchy is generated and feminist visions and interests are articulated.

Although I do not see a classroom as a full sense of "church," I find Schüssler Fiorenza's concept of *ekklesia* extremely helpful as a correlative understanding: a classroom is about communicative, not distributive, justice; and as such it is about self-determination rather than discrimination and subordination. The classroom is also counter-public at least in terms of how deliberation and politics currently work in the United States. As a counter-public sphere the classroom attempts to have all voices empowered in the determination of the democratic community.

Sharon Welch has called for a form of education that she calls communicative ethics.[9] Welch argues that justice can be central only with the material and discursive relations between different groups. And this communicative ethic, as a basic shape of the educational process, is based on solidarity. Solidarity, according to Welch, includes both the granting of respect by different groups and, at the same time, recognition of the interdependency of different groups.

Education, thus, is not merely about justice, but it is itself an activity of justice. Education is a process of forming the necessary conditions for persons to know and be able to articulate their needs and for persons to learn the processes and ways of corporate life. From reading texts to performing rituals to debating competing positions, justice is not merely a product but a process of bringing the ethical and moral to bear upon the process of learning itself.

Dialogue

Dialogue has to do with real engagement with the other, with the ability to sustain empathetic communication. By empathetic communication I do not mean sympathy, the feeling of what another experience might feel to oneself. Rather, I mean empathy, the ability to imaginatively reconstruct another persons's reality, including how they might feel or experience that reality.

As Diana Tietjens Meyers has recently suggested, empathy really requires the ability to imaginatively conceive of what an experience or situation is like for the other.[10] Using one's own past experiences is important here, but cannot be the sole source for understanding other persons. Experiences of oppression, injustice, and marginalization are diverse. Empathy, according to Meyers, requires us to "mobilize our powers of attentive receptivity and analytic discernment."[11] Meyers contends: "Particularly when the other's background or circumstance are very different from one's own, empathy may require protracted observation and painstaking imaginative reconstruction of the minutiae of the other's viewpoint."[12]

Dialogue is not just about empathy, but about real material interaction. In a classroom situation such material interaction might be envisioned by the creation of dialogical spaces. In these spaces solidarity begins and freedom occurs. As Maxine Greene has suggested, "We might think of freedom as an opening of spaces as well as perspectives."[13] Education is a dialogical process of concrete encounter with others enacted through classes as well as through worship and committee. Education is about social interaction, and even reason within theological education is dialogical and communicative.

Conversation has become a key term for the analysis of reading and writing texts. David Tracy suggests that reading a text is like having a genuine conversation and must be distinguished from idle chatter, debate, confrontation, and gossip.[14] Tracy's model of conversation, which he adapts from Hans-Georg Gadamer, is defined by letting the subject matter take over, by forgetting one's own self, and letting understanding occur. Tracy's conversation model provides us with a way of placing understanding as not merely getting the facts in, but in a "disclosive" fashion. Conversation entails risk, an engagement that we will be changed, and thus conversation also entails transformation.

As a kind of model for dialogue that is itself a process of conversation, Tracy's notion gives us key ingredients: understanding, risk, and transformation. Yet in relation to the theme of justice, Tracy's model needs to be challenged at an essential point: the emphasis on forgetting one's self. Dialogue that attempts to abstract from concrete selves too often results in a privileging of a particular self who becomes the ideal model of conversation. Justice and the quest for emancipation require that dialogue be always among embodied and embedded selves who speak in their own voices and develop connections, including struggles and conflicts, within their actual context. As Peter Hodgson has suggested, "Dialogue, while related to conceptual or logical rationality, is always pressing toward discursive or communicative practices that have freedom as their telos; thus the dialogical and the emancipatory are very closely related."[15]

Imagination

With the stress on material as well as discursive practices leading to transformation and the struggle and desire for new visions of justice, imagination becomes a central pedagogical value. Imagination, the ability to think the new, is an act of survival. Yet the imagination is rarely explicit in the educational process and is usually relegated to a few small elective courses emphasizing how to use music in worship.

It is ironic, in some ways, that modern theology and theological education have paid so little explicit attention to imagination and methods of imaginative revisioning. Modern theology—in thinkers such as Karl Barth and Friedrich Schleiermacher, Paul Tillich and Karl Rahner, and the Niebuhr brothers—used imaginative revisioning to allow theology as the discourse of faith to survive the onslaught of modern rationality. Yet with the rare exception of thinkers such as Samuel Coleridge and Jonathan Edwards, the dimensions of imagination, beauty, and aesthetics were not emphasized as central to modern theological method.

In many forms of liberation theology, the imagination receives a great deal of attention. Feminist theologies tend to emphasize imagination, since recognizing the unrealized possibilities of a situation is central to feminist theological practice. Feminist theologies are thus replete with calls to the imagination, such as the one from Marjorie Procter-Smith, "Anamnesis for women requires the creation of feminist imagination, which permits women to appropriate the past and to envision the future."[16] Elisabeth Schüssler Fiorenza has suggested that an important step in biblical hermeneutics and in theological education is the creative visualization of the text. Sallie McFague, Rita Nakashima Brock, and Rosemary Radford Ruether have all modeled what it is to imagine new symbols and new meanings for symbols of God.

And, as my theological portraiture suggests, the imaginative aspect of discussion and ritual allows students to imagine transformation. Indeed, imagination is central to various tasks of rhetoric in the community, from the ability to imagine another person's feelings, embodiment, argument, to the ability to imagine new possibilities for community life, to the ability to really interpret a text from tradition. The value of imagination means that the process of education as well as the product of education includes a variety of styles and approaches. Active cultivation of the imagination is an important value and habit within the rhetorical paradigm of education.

CONCLUDING COMMENTS

In order to foster a pedagogy in and for community, I have suggested that theological educators, at least in the United States, might begin to think of a rhetorical paradigm. A rhetorical paradigm for pedagogy focuses on deliberation, transformation, and public arguments in community. Including discursive and non-discursive practices, such as ritual, a rhetorical paradigm builds community by developing habits and values of imagination, justice, and dialogue.

I am not suggesting that the rhetorical paradigm replace ordered learning, professional skills, or individual therapeutic supervision in theological education. In a longer essay, I might argue that the rhetorical paradigm should become the fundamental pedagogical paradigm within which the other three operate. But for now, I am content to argue that we need to supplement our present pedagogical practices with rhetorical pedagogy and its correlative fundamental values. Such a rhetorical paradigm will enable U.S. students and teachers to further the important task of developing local communities with global vision.

NOTES

1. Rebecca S. Chopp, *Saving Work: Feminist Practices of Theological Education* (Louisville: Westminster/John Knox, 1995).

2. R. Radford Ruether, *Sexism and God-Talk: Toward a Feminist Theology* (Boston: Beacon Press, 1983).

3. Richard B. Miller, Laurie L. Patton, and Stephen H. Webb, "Rhetoric, Pedagogy, and the Study of Religions," *Journal of the American Academy of Religion* 52 (1984) 820.

4. Don Compier, "Sin, Calvin, and the Rhetorical Tradition," diss., Emory University, 1991, 82.

5. Terry Eagleton, *Against the Grain: Selected Essays* (London: Verso, 1986) 169.

6. Miller, Patton, and Webb, "Rhetoric, Pedagogy, and the Study of Religions," 826-827.

7. I. Marion Young, *Justice and the Politics of Difference* (Princeton: Princeton University Press, 1990) 34.

8. E. Schüssler Fiorenza, *Bread Not Stone: The Challenge of Feminist Biblical Interpretation* (Boston: Beacon Press, 1986) 7.

9. S. Welch, "An Ethic of Solidarity and Difference," *Postmodernism, Feminism, and Cultural Politics: Redrawing Educational Boundaries,* ed. H. A. Giroux (Albany: State University of New York Press, 1991) 83-89.

10. D. Tietjens Meyers, *Subjection and Subjectivity: Psychoanalytic Feminism and Moral Philosophy* (New York and London: Routledge, 1994).

11. Ibid., 33.

12. Ibid.

13. M. Greene, *The Dialectic of Freedom* (New York: Teachers College Press, 1988) 5.

14. D. Tracy, *The Analogical Imagination: Christian Theology and the Culture of Pluralism* (New York: Crossroad, 1981).

15. P. Hodgson, *Winds of the Spirit: A Constructive Christian Theology* (Louisville: Westminster/John Knox, 1994) 99.

16. M. Procter-Smith, *In Her Own Rite: Constructing Feminist Liturgical Tradition* (Nashville: Abingdon Press, 1990) 37.

18

READING THE BIBLE
IN THE GLOBAL CONTEXT

Issues in Methodology and Pedagogy

Denise Dombkowski Hopkins,
Sharon H. Ringe, and Frederick C. Tiffany

Once upon a time, not so very long ago, within the academic community we thought we could speak of "critical biblical scholarship" and have a clear sense that we knew what that term encompassed. Anyone seeking to join the conversation could be socialized into that common world of discourse, thereby carefully circumscribing and prescribing the range of acceptable tolerance and the limits of permissible readings. But the particular and peculiar contours of that world were never really articulated. Even though it was the world of only a small minority of the earth's people, that minority held disproportionate power—especially the power to control access to the community of interpreters. The value system of that world appeared so "self-evident" that the cultural construct and its social location could remain invisible and unnamed. Unnamed, it appeared universal, even though it was not universal but merely hegemonic, representing the dominant social, economic, and cultural voice. Other voices communicating alternate critical interpretations (such as slave sermons and *The Woman's Bible*) were not admitted in the community of interpretation.

This paper grew out of the contributions and conversations of a team that shared in a project exploring issues of "The Bible in the Global Context." We express our appreciation to the Association for Theological Schools in the United States and Canada for the grant which supported this venture. Team participants were Denise Dombkowski Hopkins, David C. Hopkins, and Sharon H. Ringe (Wesley Theological Seminary, Washington, DC); Kathleen A. Farmer and Larry L. Welborn (United Theological Seminary, Dayton, OH); Frederick C. Tiffany and C. M. Kempton Hewitt (Methodist Theological School in Ohio, Delaware, OH). We offer this paper, developed as a communal project, to James A. Sanders, in the conviction that such shared work is a fitting extension of and tribute to his concern for the dynamics of community and canon.

Conversation about method and theological interpretation was considered to be the property of the academic guild. Such conversation took place within this framework of shared assumptions not only about the discipline itself, but also about the world in general and the values that made for meaningful life and thought. Agreed-upon questions of canon, text, philology, authorship, date, communities of origin and destination, and philosophical or religious background set the stage for hermeneutical discussions aimed at reaching agreement about the "meaning" of a text. Established methods (primarily historical-critical) governed the nature of inquiry. A common cultural lens focused the perspective. The drive was toward as high a degree as possible of clarity, certainty, and objectivity regarding one's historical analysis, and toward theological uniformity or at least systematization, grounded on that historical analysis, concerning the question of what God intended for humankind to be.

CHALLENGES TO CRITICAL CONSENSUS

Challenges to any reading might arise but always from within the contours of that known world of discourse. For example, in the early 1970s a chorus of voices proclaimed a crisis in biblical theology: biblical theology had lost its power to persuade, its prestige; biblical theologians found themselves unable to keep their arguments above criticism. The crisis encompassed the shift from theology as a descriptive discipline toward a more confessional theology of affirmation. When the Bible was employed to support that new theological project, the objectivity of the historical-critical method itself came under attack.

Instead of "objectivity," "passion" became the rallying cry for biblical theology in the 1980s: if one could not be objective, one needed to be passionate enough to do biblical theology. The search was for new ways to help people intersect with the Bible, building on such disciplines as the social sciences and aesthetics, fueled in many instances by passion and commitment as a common source of energy. What was felt to be lacking, however, was a set of agreed-upon criteria that would hold passion accountable.

More recently, the once pervasive historical-critical paradigm and the biblical theology built on that foundation have been challenged by literary methodologies. For some who practice these methodologies, the text itself becomes the meeting ground where the new consensus of meaning is to be discovered. For others the nature of text itself precludes finding meaning within the text. If no truth claim can be made for any reading, not only is consensus meaning not achievable, but dialogue itself has no value.

Such literary approaches, however, like the historical methods they would supplant or supplement, were honed in the universities (and seminaries held to the norm of the university) of Western Europe and North America. Within that context, one might acknowledge broad historical trends in Western intellectual history that would account for changing paradigms and emerging approaches, but there was still no need to identify the social location of any particular method—or to recognize the continuity of social location that gave shape to this intellectual history.

That hegemonic world, however, has begun to crack. Any number of philo-sophical, sociological, economic, and world-historical factors might be credited with beginning the dissolution of this single voice or (at most) close harmony of readings. A clear sign that such a shift has begun is the change in demographics within the academic community of biblical interpreters. Euro-American women have added their voices to those of the men of the dominant class and racial-eth-nic group. Women and men whose ancestral roots and/or present dwelling places are in Africa, Asia, and Latin America, along with indigenous peoples in such places as the Americas and Australia, have broken the easy harmony (and hegemony) of the First World. These changing demographics have added new perspectives to the conversation as well as new questions to the agenda of inves-tigation. Scholars whose gender, class, nationality, or racial-ethnic identity has placed them on the margins of the dominant society have begun to inquire into the experiences of their ancestors. They have asked about and begun to investi-gate the participation of these ancestors in the communities from and to which the biblical texts were written.

Interpreters are thus reading these texts through, within, and for the immedi-ate context of many and differing communities. Scholars are identifying the value assumptions that have guided the work of the academic guild and that have formed its readings. Gender, race, and class as categories of analysis have, in turn, led to the use of additional tools and methods, particularly those drawn from the social sciences and from various expressions of reader-response criticism, to probe the meanings and significance of texts. But, of course, these methods have also emerged from within and to a large extent have been shaped by the discourse of the university. To be sure, these new questions and new methods have elicited meanings and implications of texts that previously had not been recognized. Still the question remains: has the fundamental hegemony truly been broken?

ENDURANCE OF CRITICAL CONSENSUS

The new questions, concerns, and perspectives have been hedged in by the fact that the educational process for all professional interpreters of the Bible contin-ues to follow a common paradigm. Graduate education insists that each student demonstrate competence in the canons and methods of the recognized subdisci-plines and proficiency in the use of their prescribed tools. The price of admission to the conversation has been a willingness and an ability to communicate in the syntax of the dominant discourse. To be heard, the new agenda must be expressed in these terms. Furthermore, even if and when they can be so "appro-priately" expressed, such questions and concerns all too frequently are inter-jected as illuminating variations or interesting sidelights to the dominant project.

These perspectival shifts have, nevertheless, already made significant contri-butions to the educational process. Proponents of numerous new perspectives have become part of and have greatly enriched the conversation. In theological schools fascination with these new insights has generated an enthusiasm for multi-culturalism, in particular "globalization." It has become virtually mandatory to include readings from the Two-Thirds World as well as from African American, Asian American, Latino, Native American, and feminist scholars in bibliographies and course syllabi. But so far these voices remain largely muted. Their muffling—or worse still, co-optation—has happened in two ways. First, books and articles by such authors are found most often on the list of recommended readings. And if required, they are employed primarily to enhance the basic foundational project. They become colorful footnotes or addenda to a thesis that remains fundamentally unchanged. Or they are presented as examples of otherness, offering exotic new condiments to our rather bland diet. It is often only at the point of explicating the hermeneutics of a text that the interpretation is allowed to be flavored by these alternative perspectives, with their values of liberation and justice and their formulation of another history. They are not understood as contributing to the basic critical task. In fact, to gain hearing for the hermeneutic, the "critical work" must reflect methods recognized by practitioners of the dominant paradigm.

Here we find the second form of muting. Those interpreters who represent the perspectival shifts can do so only in the "Esperanto" of academic critical scholarship. Esperanto is by definition an artificial language without a specific community of origin; it is simply adopted as a common vehicle of communication in order to facilitate a particular task. Thus, it is an appropriate symbol for the universality and value-neutrality idealized in academic discourse. Measured against that ideal, the unique languages of the primary communities of the new interpreters from the margins are not valued—languages whose vocabulary and grammar provide the means for people who speak them to be historical subjects and not merely the objects of others' actions.

Nevertheless, these changes have not left the formerly dominant worldview untouched. The once easy hegemony no longer feels secure within itself. As new worlds of meaning are articulated, the peculiar and particular shape and the limited horizons of the old realm can no longer remain invisible. As interpreters acknowledge and articulate their own experiences, refusing to allow themselves to be defined by others, they have also articulated what has long been known to them, namely the distinctive social context of the dominant culture. The fiction of a hegemonic world whose particularity has been allowed to be invisible is giving way to the acknowledgment of diversity.

Even that recognition, however, does not necessarily signal a fundamental reorientation. Is "diversity" itself simply the newest attempt of the center to name and contain a hegemonic world? Is the new goal simply to expand the horizons of one's world in such a way that diversity can be subsumed within it? The world may have grown bigger, but it is still a single world, governed by the norms of modernity: uniformity, systematization, centralization, finality, universality, objectivity, and movement toward closure and agreement on meaning. Such an approach still allows for the assumption that a new "unity" can be achieved. Diversity is something to be managed and controlled—even eventually overcome. Following this scenario, the scholarly community will not be deterred in its search for a common language and a consensus interpretation.

TOWARD A NEW SHIFT IN DISCOURSE

There is another option that is unfolding before us. In this version of the story, the challenge facing the mutual and interactive formation of text and community is the movement from expanding perspectives within an accepted mode of discourse to a shift in the discourse itself. Such a reorientation will necessarily recast both methods of interpretation and theories of pedagogy—and our understanding of the relationship between them.

From a pedagogical viewpoint, this means that we must self-consciously model the affirmation of multiple readings in the classroom. This task will require from teachers active listening, attention to the classroom as a community of readers with individual processes of identification with a text, sensitivity to the tensions which emerge from the process of deconstruction of texts, and a pastoral presence to provide survival resources for the wilderness journey from deconstruction to new meaning.

Example: The Conquest/Settlement Narratives in the Hebrew Bible

As an example of the issues involved, we might look at the conquest or settlement narratives in the Hebrew Bible. Introductory textbooks and lectures will customarily note the various "data," such as archaeological findings, evidence in extra-biblical texts, and inconsistencies in the biblical references to Israel's entry into the land. These scholars will engage in their own analysis to draw their conclusions about how to read the texts. They will then identify dominant scholarly models of the reconstruction of Israel's "occupation of" or "rise to power in" the land, each of which attempts to account for the various data. Commonly noted are: (a) the conquest or military model; (b) the immigration, settlement, or gradual infiltration model; and (c) the social revolution or peasant revolt model. But upon hearing these explanations and the several theories, someone poses the perhaps rhetorical question, how can this be preached? How does one preach the three theories of the conquest? The question is really an effort to discern the relationship of this material to a community of interpretation.

The very posing of the question suggests one way in which historical analysis, for all that it offers, can be used in the process of a community re-shaping the canon. If enough "objective" ambiguity is created, it can allow one to presume to bracket such texts out of the canon, while awaiting resolution to the dilemmas that this form of critical analysis has created. It can focus the conversation virtually entirely on a debate between the theories. While such a debate can be very important, particularly when the best tools and principles of the disciplines are applied and followed, it is also important to remember that any historical or sociological research has its own social location.

The social context that gave rise to the peasant revolt model within academia has been acknowledged rather more frequently in the literature than has the social location of other theories. Since this model does not so easily fit the dominant ideology, its specific and peculiar outline emerges as a phenomenon that needs explanation. It is also possible that the very nature of sociological investigation makes one more sensitive to issues of social context. But all sociological and all historical research has its own specific social context. In the first place, every researcher functions within a particular social location, which will shape the perspectives and sensitivities of that interpreter, creating the lens through which information is filtered. But it is also important to remember that the disciplines themselves, their philosophical and methodological assumptions, their interests and horizons, will be shaped by the social location within which they have been developed. It is not simply a matter of determining which model best accounts for the data. One must also note which data have been admitted and which excluded, which models of research have been entertained and which have not even been imagined. In these ways communities are continually shaping the canon they read.

Attention to these issues is important not only for the historian or sociologist but also for those who will be informed by such work. While they may not "preach" the models, some model of historical understanding, articulated or not, will shape their interpretation of the texts. For example, to what extent is explication of text in terms of a "settlement model" shaped by the reader's social location within a context where the official histories portray the "settlement" of America and the gradual movement West? Or when a major focus is placed on the struggle between the religion of Israel and that (or those) of Canaan, how does that already shape the reading of this story by members of the dominant culture in the Americas or by representatives of the colonial regimes in Africa or by persons struggling to understand the Israeli-Palestinian conflict today?

The canon also shapes the community. That shaping occurs not only, or not even primarily, in terms of some original meaning of the text. The canon that shapes a community is the canon that has lived through a particular stream of history. It shapes the community as it has been successively received through the generations and taught anew by each generation. The canon continues to impact the community in the symbol system that was developed within the text and that continually grows out of and around that text. Thus the narrative of the conquest/settlement can shape the consciousness of a people in such a way that it can continue to live with a world orientation that allows it to rest easy with its own past, with its own narrative of settlement/conquest—and therefore to continue that past into the present and the future. And it allows people to do so even if they do not want to articulate the story. In fact, it may do so precisely in their silence—in their reluctance to articulate that story. Something is always being preached, if only in the void. The text does not lie inert, waiting for scholarly analysis and application to take on meaning. Is the issue in preaching these texts within and for the dominant culture really the ambiguity created by studying different models?

There are communities who have heard the conquest narrative preached at them and who have not received these words as liberating news. These communities have experienced the power of this text, as defined and appropriated by the dominant culture, as a canon that legitimizes an oppressive reality. This canon shapes the community as the community works out its response to the text. For example, members of the community may experience their suffering under that oppressive reality as having been given legitimacy by God. They might emerge as a community further beaten down by the perception of divine abandonment, or comforted by divine understanding and presence in the midst of their suffering, or empowered to change circumstances congruent with the text, but incongruent with the God in whom their faith is lodged.

In the process of being shaped by the canon, they shape it in turn, and this shaping of the canon takes place in the readings of multiple communities. This latter activity has gone largely unnoticed within the dominant culture of academia, obscuring the complexity of the interaction between canon and community. We are not simply talking about different angles of vision on the same event. We are talking about fundamentally different experiences. The canon of progress for one is the canon of oppression for another, and a community may well subvert the received canon in and because of its lived experiences. For example, if the predominant reading of the narratives of settlement/conquest has been used to legitimize the European conquest/settlement of the Americas, understanding those same narratives as referring to a peasants' revolt subverts the force of that canon.

First Example of Subversive Reading: Joshua 6

An example of a subversive reading of a text in the mutual shaping of canon and community occurred in an introductory Hebrew Bible class. There were eighty students in the class, about a fourth of whom were persons of color (mostly African Americans and some Koreans). A number were second-career students, bringing to their studies a wealth of experience in business and the professions as well as in the dynamics of family life and household management. The class had been studying the siege of Jericho in Joshua 6. On the seventh day of marching around the city, the people raise a great shout "and the wall fell down flat." Students protested that they could not preach the three or four theories identified above about Israel's emergence in Canaan, holy war as a tool of the later monarchy, or archaeological pictures of Jericho as an unfortified village in the 13th century B.C.E. They were correct, if that is all they intended to preach. Preach it literally or throw it away seemed on the surface to be the only choice. What afterlife does this text have in the local church?

An African-American woman raised her hand and shared that her church had used this text for the Sunday sermon and that that same evening the congregation had held a candlelight vigil in the neighborhood of the church. They all circled the neighborhood seven times with candles, singing "Joshua fought the battle of Jericho" in an attempt to say to the drug pushers, pimps, and addicts, "No more, you are not welcome here!" That Joshua passage gave healthy identity and hope to an inner-city congregation plagued by violence and drugs. In such a context the text itself makes its own social critique. In such a context the text celebrates its own power. To learn something of the life of this text with that particular African-American community opened new horizons of possibility.

That power is also its danger. Does one simply transfer this experience from that particular community to a community within the dominant culture? In celebrating this "conquering" power of the text, will persons of the dominant culture simply glory in the conquest of what they assume to be a commonly shared enemy? If so, the text can simply reinforce the comfort of the dominant culture with its own images and history of conquest. It could hinder recognition of that group's social location in this story told by the African-American woman. Sociologically, is the dominant culture more closely allied with the drug dealers or with African-American church community? For example, do the social structures of the dominant culture support the very presence of drugs in these marginal communities? To what extent do the religious values and institutions of the dominant culture also endorse such a "social policy"? Will members of the dominant culture experience the social critique which that text has brought to bear, not only upon this particular encircled community, but also upon the larger society that has given rise to it? If so, such analysis would pose another question: when the text sounds its trumpets, what walls will crumble within the social structures that support the marginalization of communities?

But there are yet other communities. In celebrating the power of this text to offer hope to a community that had felt itself assaulted by the drug culture—turning the tables and empowering this people to reclaim their own neighborhood—we must not close our ears to those voices that express their experience of abuse at the hands of this conquering text. The importance of this classroom example is that it demonstrates the power of the text to shape the life of a community. But that is precisely the point of its potential danger. Power can be misused. Power can be experienced as destructive. When the text sounds its trumpets, does interpretation also acknowledge those who hear it as an announcement of defeat and humiliation?

Is it also possible that some persons in those communities that have experienced defeat would hear clearly in the story told by the African-American woman that this conquest text is turning against the conquerors, conquerors who thought they had exclusive right to use the text in their own quest? Do we hear those who would explain that the story narrated in the classroom denies to the dominant community exclusive right to determine the canon?

It is not enough simply to hear such a story of interpretation from another community, from a different social location. The danger is that members of the dominant culture will hear that story only in the terms of their own understanding of social construct and their own social meanings. The story can be heard in such a context as good standing over against evil, as the church setting out to conquer immoral, destructive, pagan forces. Members of the dominant culture can easily self-identify with the forces of good, with the power of the church and the gospel. Would the teller of the story so identify the dominant culture? Would hearers of the story who have themselves experienced conquest at the hands of the dominant culture respond in like manner?

It is not enough that interpretations from other communities be admitted to the classroom, although that is an important step. It is also important that these interpretations be understood in the language and within the social constructs of the speaking community. If not, those voices will have been effectively muted. The classroom has become its own social location. In that context one must always ask who has the power to shape the reading and the hearing of texts. Do the interpreters finally speak for themselves, even if they come from many and different social settings? Does the agenda of the classroom finally cast all readings in the shape of the dominant paradigm? Or do we create the time and the space that will allow for the complexity of interactions between communities and canons—and within the context of a specific community of discourse, the classroom?

Such a shift will acknowledge that academia is itself a cultural context, though with its own diversity. Interpretation in the classroom will always have its own social context, including accepted methodologies, systems of credits and grades, and particular demographics. One must be as precise in identifying and giving attention to that context as to other social contexts. This necessitates looking critically at the ideologies functioning in all the differing perspectives brought to the table by the various student and faculty interpreters, in the texts that are chosen for study, and in the critical tools employed for that study. Each participant brings a particular personal and communal history to the table. Their various readings of the text will be informed by and related to those experiences. But the table gathering itself constitutes its own social context, defined by the "admissions" requirements—both stated and unstated—of such things as academic qualifications, linguistic abilities, financial means, and value assumptions. The table is also constituted with a professor or professors at its head, who will set parameters and who will finally determine grades.

To embrace this methodological shift will mean that the agenda of the center can no longer be the hegemonic goal of defining and redefining the globe. Instead, one must define one's own social context within that world and thereby open that world to challenge and to change. The danger, of course, is that one might simply define it and claim it. The alternative is for the center to recognize those voices that are missing and begin to listen for the margins. It will mean holding spaces at the table for the meaningful participation of those people and communities whose lack of specific academic or social credentials has been the means of excluding them. Interpreters who sit at the center, for reasons of gender, racial-ethnic group, class, or educational rank, would embrace an advocacy posture in solidarity with marginalized people and communities.

It may also mean changing the shape, the materials, and the location of the table. Around whose table do we gather? Who defines what constitutes an appropriate table? Such participation and advocacy will necessitate critical examination of the ideologies functioning in the various perspectives of interpreters, in the texts being studied, and in the critical tools themselves. In these terms, interpretation is the critical process by which texts are examined as performative instruments that convey relationship and meaning. Both the texts themselves and the processes of interpretation function to grant and to deny the right to be historical subjects as well as the right to specific material and non-material goods.

Such an agenda, of course, will not be easy. Not only must the multitude of voices be heard, but they must be heard as living voices within the particular worlds of their speakers. There must be space within the discourse for the hearer to be led into a different world. In so doing, one must learn to understand the boundaries of one's own world—even as one seeks to cross those boundaries. This will not happen quickly. This will not happen easily, particularly for those who have shared in the dominant culture. Our practice is that of colonizing and translating all other voices into the categories and grammar of our own language. It follows that both texts and interpretations function principally to convey meaning: to establish patterns of relationship among individual persons, groups of people, and institutions that are at heart expressions of power. Meaning-as-power is conveyed in the rhetoric of the texts themselves as vehicles of communication, in how they have functioned in the various communities that have received them, in who is invited or permitted to engage in the conversation about texts, in what methods of critical analysis are deemed legitimate, and in the ideologies embedded in all dimensions of the process. The key critical question to a text or an interpretation of a text is not "What does it mean?" but "Who benefits, and who loses?"

Second Example of Subversive Reading: Luke 15:11-32

The class was an introduction to the New Testament, demographically similar to the introductory Hebrew Bible class described above. As part of its study of the synoptic gospels, the class examined the parable of the "prodigal" son (Luke 15:11-32). They began by observing its context in Luke, as the last and most elaborate of three parables about "losts": a sheep, a coin, and at least one son. In each case, the loss leads to consternation (seen in avid searches in the first two parables and in the father's apparent vigil for the younger son's return), and the finding leads to rejoicing and celebration. The first of the parables—the lost sheep—is found in Matthew also, where it emphasizes the importance of not "losing" any who are part of the church. In Luke the three parables all respond to the grumbling of religious leaders who object to the company Jesus keeps: "This fellow welcomes sinners and eats with them" (15:2b). The emphasis thus seems to be on the joy of reconnecting with what has been lost.

That emphasis on joy confirms the traditional reading of the parable of the prodigal with which students were familiar: the gracious, loving father welcomes the son without even waiting for an apology for his disgraceful behavior. Similarly, we also are accepted by our loving Father-God, whatever our lives have been like, and we have only to celebrate God's limitless love that extends even to us. But a number of students were quick to point out that their lives had in fact not been as flamboyant and disdainful of their parents and family responsibilities as was the younger son's. They had in fact lived a life closer to that of the elder brother who always met responsibilities and who, if the truth be told, resented the notion that the "prodigals" would not get what they deserved but rather that God would exact no punishment for shortcomings but instead rejoice at their eleventh-hour return.

Attention to the dramatic form of the parable, with its concluding emphasis on the grudging response of the elder brother, helped to underline the common human responses evoked by the characters and their interaction. Exploration of the social world underlying the story uncovered additional implications. For instance, the request of the younger brother for his share of the inheritance needs to be seen against the legal conventions that would have entitled the younger of two brothers to one-third of the father's estate, in contrast to the older brother's two-thirds, but that would have limited him to receiving his inheritance only after the death of the father. His request for his share while the father still lived was an extraordinary and disrespectful act. More than simply wasting money in a lavish lifestyle, he defied the conventions on which the economic stability of the household and family was based. In contrast, the elder brother's obedient management of the estate exhibited respect for the fundamental social unit of family and household, and care for its economic well-being. When the father reinstated the younger son to the family he had left (with the symbols of robe, sandals, and signet ring), the obedient elder brother would be faced with again needing to divide the remaining estate with the "new" younger brother by the same two-to-one formula, but the result would be a material reduction in the wealth he might one day expect as a reward for faithful service.

Clearly the household envisioned in the parable is a wealthy one, where the estate was something to be reckoned with, including real estate, cattle, and servants. Within the limits of the parable, though, this household is a man's world. Students in the class were becoming accustomed to looking not only at the characters explicitly mentioned but also for absent characters and silent voices. Very quickly they noted the absence of any female characters in the story—a factor that has colluded in the common allegorical reading of the parable as a picture of the relationship between the loving heavenly "Father" and sinful "man." Nothing is said about the mother's reaction to or relationship with the two sons or whether the boys had any sisters.

A number of women spoke about their need to "translate" themselves into the story, or to render it general or abstract (as in the traditional allegory understood as a generic reading) in order to hear themselves addressed by it. The class talked about the difficulty of finding religious or spiritual issues explored only through the male world of inheritance laws and identity quests, and about the impact on modern readers of the "absent mother" of the family, in a time when the mother often represented the only consistent parental presence in the experience of many. They explored the dynamics of household and family structure among Luke's audience that would have enabled some to relate to such a story and made it difficult for others to have access to it then as well as now.

For the teacher it was gratifying to observe the students' growing sensitivity to such questions as who is absent as well as who is present and how hearers or readers of the story in the ancient world would have perceived what was taking place. It seemed that the conversation was drawing to a close, when an African-American woman spoke up: "I want to know about the servants." Being caught off guard, the teacher asked her to say more. She continued,

> I want to know about the servants. My mother has worked as a domestic worker all her life. Whenever the rich folks she works for give a party, my mother comes home exhausted. So I want to know, if this is a parable

about God's grace and love, where's the party for the servants? When do they get a chance to celebrate and enjoy God's blessings?

In more than twenty years of study of the Gospel of Luke, the teacher had never even thought to ask that question. Neither had most of the others in the class, and those who had (whose ancestors, for example, had been slaves or whose family members were also domestic workers) thought it was not an important question for the "real meaning" of the story. The woman's question provided the occasion to talk about a class analysis of the biblical writers and their communities as well as of interpreters and ourselves as interpreters. For example, Luke apparently could count on his readers to overlook the servants, just as have modern interpreters. They are mentioned as servants (NRSV, "slaves") only twice in the story, and on those occasions their role is simply to receive the order to prepare the feast for the family and guests to enjoy (15:22a, where the Greek word is *douloi*) and to provide information when asked (15:26-27, where the Greek word is *paidia*). Both roles leave unchallenged the servants' position at the beck and call of the householder and his family. The younger son is able to reflect with envy on the food they enjoy, in contrast with his own hunger in the distant country (15:17), but he does so by obscuring their status as slaves and referring to them as "hired hands" (*misthioi*).

The student's question became a significant teaching/learning moment because of the fresh light it cast on the parable —on how Luke had truncated the gospel by his cast of characters and by the class bias built into their roles, for example—and because it provided the opportunity to examine our own process of identifying "relevant" questions. Who decides what issues are appropriate to pursue and on what basis is such a decision made?

CONCLUDING COMMENT

That occasion raises important pedagogical issues, such as how such wisdom and insight can be tapped in the classroom. Relying on the grace of having a gutsy, "uppity" woman not afraid to ask the "impertinent" (in both senses) question cannot be the only alternative! How can the rich diversity of the community's wisdom find a more regular space in the teaching and learning process? Even more important, how can we celebrate the contributions of such diversity—and of the wisdom, insight, energy, and inspiration it generates—to the intricate rhythms of co-creation of canon and community?

19

CROSSING BORDERS

Biblical Studies
in a Trans-cultural World

Kathleen M. O'Connor

It was neither fascination with biblical languages nor interest in ancient history that attracted me to the field of biblical studies. What captured my imagination were meanings— literary, historical, and theological meanings—for today. As a product of the Roman Catholic biblical renewal movement that accompanied Vatican II, I have always cared about the question that arises after the disciplined work of exegesis is done, what I consider to be the goal of exegesis—the question of "So what?" What does this text mean for us, for our community, for the church, for the world? I care about the theological "appropriation" of biblical texts.[1]

BIBLICAL TEXTS AND CONTEMPORARY LIFE

Because of this interest, I searched for a graduate school that included biblical theology in its roster of sub-disciplines, with hopes that it would show me how to claim the scriptures for the struggles of everyday life. But biblical theology was looking for meaning in a different sense than I. Biblical theology was looking for system, for structures of unification in the biblical literature, for the Bible's center, and for the one great idea that would make the Bible's disparate voices whole. For me these were distant questions, abstractions from the scandalous specificity of texts. What I cared about were individual passages and books, and what they evoke about love and justice, life and death. I wanted to see how specific texts lead to enlightening connections, imaginative rebuildings; how they interact with cultures and open out to the future; how they speak of God. I did not want to tame the text; I wanted to release its fierce power.

In this quest for contemporary significance, historical-critical studies also disappointed me, because it stayed in the past. Edgar Krentz summarizes the goal of historical criticism as "the disciplined interrogation of sources to secure the maximal amount of verifiable information."[2] Concerned with the diachronic processes that gave rise to texts, seeking "scientific objectivity," it sought for an ancient "single meaning."[3] The characterization of historical criticism as concerned with a "single meaning" was probably never true in practice because there have always been competing interpretations of texts, achieved by employing different methods or by evaluating evidence differently within one method. But historical criticism explicitly kept ancient meaning at a distance, more or less sealed off from the modern world and the lives of interpreters, readers, believers. For scholars concerned with a text's connections with contemporary life, discovery of the ancient "religious meaning" was generally thought to provide adequate nourishment for theological and pastoral purposes.

From this perspective, historical criticism more or less banished contemporary appropriations to preachers and pastors, to persons lacking in rigor, to the biblically less-able. By contrast, biblical theology has been directly engaged with contemporary meanings but primarily in relation to systematic theology and modern philosophical and historical questions, not with appropriation of specific texts for contemporary readers.

Today, biblical commentators in various parts of the world are introducing radical shifts in methods of interpretation that not only take intense interest in the relation of biblical texts to the concrete realities of contemporary life, but also make dialogue with these realities the *raison d'être* for academic study of the Bible at all. I greet them with delight. The purpose of this essay is to describe some of these developments and to suggest a general framework for interpretation in our increasingly trans-cultural world—a framework that embraces appropriation of texts as a goal of interpretation. It is my thesis that the historical-critical method as a philosophy of interpretation is at an end, but that its legacy, a collection of tools and skills for interpretation, is as necessary as ever. As Elisabeth Schüssler Fiorenza asserts, however, this historical-critical heritage belongs in a "de-centered," servant position.[4] I begin by describing some of the challenges that postmodernism hurls at historical criticism. Then I turn to interpretations emerging around the globe that manifest these postmodernist developments and that reconfigure the practice of biblical studies. Finally, I describe a framework for interpretation and appropriation of texts that emerges from these challenges.

POSTMODERN SHIFTS UNDERMINING HISTORICAL CRITICISM

Various descriptions of postmodernism exist because, as Edgar McKnight[5] tells us, there are various definitions of modernism to which postmodernism is a reply.[6] Although I have no expertise in these matters, I cannot move forward in my work without taking some of these shifts into consideration even in the most preliminary manner. What is changing before our eyes includes our understanding of the role of interpreters, of the nature of texts, and of the functions of texts and interpretations.

Role of Interpreters

Contexts of interpreters/readers radically affect, some might say "afflict," interpretation. The border that sharply divided texts and interpreters no longer holds. This, of course, is nothing new. Long ago Rudolf Bultmann doubted the possibility of exegesis without *a priori* assumptions.[7] Although attention to context is not a new practice in biblical studies, recognition that interpreters themselves are context-dependent, perhaps even determined, is a notion that many of us are still absorbing. Only now is the context of the interpreter being consciously factored in as a major element affecting the results of interpretation. Today the question is, "How determinative are the contexts of interpreters for interpretation?"

Because we are drenched in our contexts, because our contexts are inescapable, every interpretation reflects more than the ancient text. It is by now a cliché among academics to observe that no interpretation is "objective" or context-free. David Clines asks whether interpretation should be free of the traces of its context,[8] but more properly the question is, "Is it possible for interpretation to be free of its context?" The work of the "new historicist" and cultural critic Stephen Greenblatt is built on the observation that "response to the past is inexplicably bound up with the present."[9] Scientific objectivity, in the sense that historical-criticism attempted it, is not achievable.[10] The shift toward reader-response and reception theories within biblical studies expresses the change of focus from the past of the text to the present of the reader.[11]

Before I ever heard of reader-oriented theories, I noticed, from my cat-bird seat on the faculty of a school of theology where the student body was markedly international, that economic, political, and cultural contexts of interpreters radically affect interpretation.[12] Students from Venezuela interpreted texts differently than students from Uganda, China, or New York City. I saw that contexts limit interpretations and that contexts illumine texts. But does this observation require the conclusion that texts are mere putty in the hands of readers? I return to this question below.

Nature of Texts

A second major challenge to historical criticism arises from the question, "What is a text?" or more precisely, "What can we find in a literary text?" Whereas historical criticism investigated multiple historical layers in texts, recognition has exploded upon us that texts and the language that composes them are multivalent, indeterminate, overflowing with "surplus of meaning," conscious and unconscious.[13]

Texts no longer appear as straightforward representations of past history. Instead, they emerge as negotiations and renegotiations of symbolic systems and prior interpretations, designed to address concrete circumstances of a particular community, but always saying more than they intend. Because texts are complex amalgamations of competing voices, no interpretation exhausts meaning.[14] In relating the element of indeterminacy that characterizes modern literary theory to biblical studies, Robert Morgan notes that the Bible's ability to mean "somewhat different things to different peoples . . . is a condition of its capacity to speak of God to different ages and cultures."[15]

Vincent Leitch summarizes current cultural criticism and literary theory regarding our changing understandings of the nature of texts. He observes that literary texts are "at once rhetorical, heteroglot, and intertextual."[16] By "intertextual," Leitch means not only that one written text is a reincarnation of previous written texts, à la Michael Fishbane,[17] but that all texts are "imbricated," rooted in, dependent upon, and speaking for their specific cultural contexts. Political, economic, and social contexts, therefore, both create the text and are encoded in it. Similarly, when Leitch says a text is "heteroglot," he means that it is shaped by language that pre-exists the author. Since language is socially inherited, it is both created by and expressive of culture and is, therefore, a multifaceted phenomenon. In this respect, a word means what it means, but it also means what it carries with it from the pre-existing life of the language and from the social, political, economic, and spiritual life of the community. Consequently, interpretations of texts will be multiple, perhaps inexhaustibly so. Leitch's description of texts as rhetorical leads to my third point.

Function of Texts and Interpretations

Biblical texts and interpretations have multiple functions. Besides providing possible insight into the past, biblical texts also behave rhetorically and symbolically. Biblical texts are rhetorical because they operate with persuasive intent, a fact long honored by rhetorical critics.[18] Because texts are embedded in "regimes of reason,"[19] that is, in the political, economic, social, and religious worlds that produced them, all texts serve the interests of their creators, just as all interpretations serve the interests of their producers. Recognition that texts and interpretation function rhetorically in service of power, of course, requires critical suspicion of both texts and interpretations.

Moreover, texts and interpretations have symbolic, metaphoric, and mythic functions; that is, they operate as arenas for "the practice of imagination."[20] Texts stimulate the imagination by means of suggestion and association, by image and metaphor.[21] From this perspective, historical aspects of texts are immensely important as the cultural home of symbols, but what is primary is the symbolic discourse, not the window on the past. When symbolic, mythic, and metaphoric functions receive priority in interpretation, biblical texts emerge as verbal art,[22] requiring a turn to poetics and aesthetics.[23]

These changes in the understanding of the role of interpreters, of texts, and of their functions have destabilized historical criticism as it has been theoretically described and typically practiced. Although historical criticism has valiantly served the churches in overcoming dogmatically driven interpretation,[24] historical criticism is no longer adequate for the needs of contemporary believers. That this is so is clearly evident in biblical studies as practiced among many communities of faith around the world.

GLOBAL BURGEONING OF BIBLICAL STUDIES

Developments outside the United States

Among the first to challenge the foundations of historical-critical studies were Latin American liberation theologians and interpreters working in *comunidades de base* (base communities). These include José Miranda, George Pixley, Fernando Belo, Elsa Tamez, Shigeyuki Nakanose, and others who interpret the Bible in the company of their communities as they confront physical and cultural annihilation from poverty, death squads, and state-sponsored terrorism.[25] They have discovered in the Bible a mirror of their struggles. The Bible blazes with hope and promise. It becomes for them a living word. It is "actualized" in their midst.

Carlos Mesters articulated the hermeneutical processes by which basic communities in Brazil "appropriated" the text.[26] He speaks of "pretext, text, and context" as three elements in a conversation that yields interpretation. For Mesters, "pretext" is the concrete situation that the community brings to the text. The "text" is both the scripture text and its ancient world. "Context" refers to the people's faith that brings the ancient text to life in their world. Mesters and other Latin American interpreters shift the starting point for biblical studies from the text to the concrete situation of the contemporary community. Interpreted from this perspective, the Exodus, for example, was no longer a book about "spiritual freedom" for all people, but an account of an enslaved people whose cry God heard. In such readings the text matters less as an account of historical events than for its symbolic power as a myth of origins, a vision of the justice that should prevail for slaves in a world where God hears the cry of the afflicted.[27]

But the Latin American outburst was only the beginning. In South Africa, an ecumenical group of theologians, pastors, and ministers issued *The Kairos Document*,[28] urging interpretation of texts from the perspective of victims in the South African system of apartheid. Their brief essay demonstrated the impact socioeconomic context has upon interpretations of texts as well as the pernicious rhetorical power of biblical texts used in support of a racist system. In the South African context, Old Testament scholar Ferdinand Deist urges biblical scholarship to indigenize, that is, to read the Bible against African traditional religions and African life, rewriting the Bible to free God from an ethnic preserve.[29]

Itumeleng Mosala insists that all theology and biblical study among South African blacks must begin with a hermeneutics of struggle, because struggle is the historical experience of that community.[30] Rather than abandon historical criticism, Mosala folds it into critical Marxism to help uncover redactional layers in the text of Micah. These layers, however, are not chronological strata of tradition or redaction, but literary traces that encode class struggle. Mosala excavates the text, hunting for liberating traditions of peasant communities that were subsequently overlaid by interests of the ruling classes. He uses tactics of historical criticism in a tour de force that replaces chronological questions with issues of class conflict. Although I do not find his criteria for distinguishing layers convincing, neither did I find Hans Walter Wolff's six-layered redaction of Amos to be unassailable.[31] My point here is that in the work of these South African interpreters the starting point of biblical interpretation is the concrete economic and political situation of the community and its African religious culture.

In Asia, circumstances of Christian communities are different and so, therefore, are the challenges to biblical studies. R. S. Sugirtharajah speaks of the "twin realities of the continent, religious plurality and economic poverty."[32] In many Asian countries, Christians form less than 1 percent of the total population.[33] They exist in cultures that already possess sacred texts far more ancient than Jewish Christian scriptures. They have long-established traditions of textual interpretation. They ask how Christians can interpret the Bible in Buddhist, Confucian, Shinto, Islamic, or Hindu countries.

One of the more articulate voices on these matters is that of Kwok Pui-lan,[34] a theologian from Hong Kong, who proposes that Christians include the religious texts of neighbors in their canon and employ methods of textual interpretation long used by Asian scholars. She urges a hermeneutics of "dialogical imagination" that combines the insights of biblical themes with other Asian myths, themes, and sacred texts. Again, the starting point for interpretation is not the text but the life of the reading community. In Asia, urgent questions facing faith communities concern neither historical reconstruction nor dogmatic purity. In Kwok's approach, historical questions, even formal, literary, and rhetorical ones, have little significance. The concern is for the interrelationship of a culture's symbol, myth, and ancient story with biblical texts.

Developments in the United States

Challenges to historical criticism are not restricted to other continents. Some of its leaders are biblical scholars working in the United States, including African Americans, Latinos or Hispanic Americans, feminists/womanists/mujeristas, and others. It is nearly impossible to keep up with the vast literature emerging from these perspectives. I mention here the work of only three.

Feminist biblical criticism has by now taken so many forms that it is difficult to characterize it. But in all its manifestations it begins with the diverse lives of women, not with the text. It is specifically engaged in a position of advocacy and attempts nowadays, at least, to avoid "totalizing" interpretations. Feminist scholars are concerned with the rhetorical functions of texts to oppress or liberate women and other peoples and with the symbolic power of texts to transform social structures. Recently, Elisabeth Schüssler Fiorenza has written of interpretation itself as a rhetorical strategy, a mode of praxis for the liberation of women.[35] Schüssler Fiorenza remains a steadfast disciple of historical criticism and historical reconstruction, but in her current work she claims that "historical scientific language is not scientific and descriptive but metaphorical and constructive."[36] Indeed, her reconstruction of early Christian origins as a "discipleship of equals"[37] functions rhetorically and symbolically as a new myth of origins for some Christians.

In a similar vein, African American biblical scholar Vincent Wimbush remarks that "every biblical reading must be recognized as, [sic] *culture-spe-cific.*"[38] For him "the question of *origins* is of minor importance—in isolation from concern about *function.*"[39] Biblical methods must be chosen "in terms of the people's history" and of how such methods could be of service in the people's present situation. Wimbush uses historical criticism in this task, but only in a sec-ondary position and in concert with a "cultural criticism" that seeks to analyze "symbolic referents" and to translate their meaning from one culture to another.

As a final example, the hermeneutical theory of Cuban-American Fernando Segovia emerges from the experiences of his own Hispanic American communi-ties.[40] As members of two cultural worlds, they are fully at home in neither and, in some respects, rejected by both, yet they are able to bridge both worlds lin-guistically and culturally. Segovia's biblical interpretation begins with the pain of marginalization of a people. It is consciously, pointedly, engaged in biblical studies as a strategy of liberation. It seeks to make critical readers of his com-munity, to break the text's power to oppress the community. It is, one might say, seeking to practice the gospel—to set people free.

Although only barely sketched here, the global burgeoning of biblical studies leaves the field in a different configuration than previously. What I wish to do now is to outline a methodological procedure of a direction, already underway, that decenters historical criticism and that sees critical actualization of the text as its goal.

A PROPOSAL FOR ACTUALIZATION OF TEXTS

The Beginning—Start with the Life of the Community

The explicit starting point of interpretation in the biblical approaches men-tioned above is contemporary life. By contemporary life I mean the particular situation of an interpreting community, not an abstract universal world. It could be argued, of course, that interpretation has always begun with the world of the interpreter. Much of Raymond Brown's groundbreaking work, for instance, arises from his location in Roman Catholicism, wherein ecclesial and doctrinal concerns inform his historical-critical investigations. But what I observe today is the conscious effort to begin with the concrete situation of a particular faith community. The implicit assumption of these approaches is that life itself is the text and, for many, the sacred place wherein divine and human meet.[41] Analysis of life, therefore, needs to be as rigorous and thoroughgoing as analysis of texts.

Biblical scholars cannot do this themselves; the task of crossing the borders between the study of ancient texts and the study of contemporary life is obvi-ously interdisciplinary. What is clear, however, is that to ignore the context of the interpreter and her community, to proceed as if the context does not matter or could be assumed to be universal humanity, is no longer intellectually credible. But not only that, efforts to "actualize" the text within local communities cannot be effective without rigorous attention to the multidimensional realities of that community's life, the hallowed place where human and divine meet.

In the methods of interpretation that I have described, context of interpretation is not defined as that of the individual interpreter. Instead, contexts are communal. In these works context refers to the circumstances of peoples whose lives share in experiences of subordination, poverty, and afflictions of many kinds. The biblical text becomes a partner in dialogue with their circumstances, sometimes shown to be a contributor, a weapon in their affliction; at other times discovered to be a mirror that reveals the true depth of their predicament, or gives hope for a transformed future. But it is the collective predicament that becomes the locus of revelation, the place of beginning, the primary site of authority—not the text.

The Middle—Text as Stranger[42]

Only after disciplined study of the contemporary context is it time to turn to study of the text. The obvious and not insignificant danger in this order of analysis, is, of course, that the world of the text will be conflated with or submerged into the world of the community. The text loses its voice by becoming a slave of its interpreters.[43] John Reumann warns that, if meaning comes from readers, the danger is "that everyone is confirmed in their own truth,"[44] or, I might add, their own untruth.

To prevent the collapse of the text into the readers' worlds, the text must be respected for what it is, a "stranger," "a socially and culturally conditioned other."[45] Since reading an ancient text is a trans-cultural process, a crossing of borders from the present to the past, the text must maintain its own integrity as would any partner in a cross-cultural conversation. Although recognition of the distance between the biblical text and the modern reader appears to be an unassailable contribution of historical criticism, even the notion of a text's integrity has come under attack in some forms of reader-response criticism. Edgar McKnight observes that an overly determined view of a text's integrity results in treating the text as an historical artifact. An understanding of integrity more suited to literature, McKnight suggests, would classify a text according to its genre and then allow readers to sort out a text's uniqueness in light of their own worlds.[46]

McKnight's suggestion seems insufficient, however, because texts are intertexts with other written works and with their worlds. To be respected as itself, the text requires disciplined, systematic study as an ancient literary document. Techniques and tools bequeathed by historical criticism as well as literary, sociological, and ideological criticisms—the entire panoply of methods can help us respect the text as stranger, as different from us in language, culture, worldview, and symbolic referent. Meir Sternberg is surely right in seeing value in both genesis-oriented and discourse-oriented approaches.[47]

In the methodological framework I am describing, however, these approaches do not hold pride of place. They serve by helping us interrogate, understand, and dialogue with the stranger, the text different from us. By allowing the text to hold its own in the dialogue, they enable conversation, but they do not control meaning. They do not provide one good approximation of the sense of the ancient scripture. Instead, they work like shafts of light that illumine parts of the stranger's world, language, and symbol system but leave other parts in obscurity. They help us cross borders but they do not control passage.

A text can no longer be viewed as admitting a primary, single meaning; it is best seen as discourse that creates a world of plural meanings and a "pluralism of symbolic universes."[48] Interpretation, therefore, must do more than try to uncover the original intention of either author or text, even if that were possible. Interpretation requires skills for interpreting poetic and cultural codes; it demands sensitivity to metaphor and symbolism; it needs sociological, anthropological, and cultural analysis. Indeed, interpretation calls upon the whole smorgasbord of methods available today.

The glimpses of the text and its world that we receive are unavoidably influenced, shaped, and decided—consciously and unconsciously—by the circumstances of the interpreters. In postmodern criticism, this is celebrated. Readers create meaning, but they do not do it alone. The text and its world participate as conversation partners when the text is granted an identity of its own.[49]

The End—Appropriation of Texts

In the past, practitioners of biblical studies have understood their task as the excavation of ancient texts to uncover their most original and, hence, authentic strata. That single-minded approach has been amply expanded to include literary, sociological, structuralist, anthropological, and even psychoanalytic analyses. In the emerging paradigm that I am describing, however, systematic analysis of the ancient text is only one-third of the work to be done. Listening to the text as stranger falls between investigation of contemporary context and an engaged return to that context. And that return may require art more than science, poets as much as historians, symbolists as well as linguists. I call this phase of the process of actualization the "retelling of the text." Its purpose is to provide theological resources to "remythologize" the world.

A principal reason the Bible has power from generation to generation is that it has the capacity as story, poem, symbol, and myth to change our vision of ourselves, of the deity, and of our place in the world.[50] Through its poetry, story, and symbolic visions, it captures imagination, emotion, and intelligence, providing us with vicarious experience that has the potential to change us. We enter the world of the text and let it enter ours. To actualize or appropriate a text, what seems to be required is a re-presentation or retelling that translates the text's symbolic, metaphorical power into specific modern contexts. The Bible itself, of course, is already a series of appropriating or actualizing acts that retrieve, retell, and re-enact other written and oral texts. In this way the Bible continually reconstitutes traditional stories and symbols for later communities.[51] As Robert Carroll describes events, "the Bible presupposes earlier literature, incorporates, tropes and retropes them in terms of its own construction before becoming the *Intertext*."[52]

Contemporary processes of retelling continue the biblical process insofar as they address particular communities with a shared set of presuppositions and translate the symbolic language of the Bible into a symbolic language of that community.[53] In such retellings the crucial ingredient is not historical insight, doctrinal or thematic proposition, legal prescription, or moral instruction, but rather the bursting to life of a text in the native idiom of a particular community.

Alicia Suskin Ostriker writes, "All myths central to a culture survive through a process of continual reinterpretation, satisfying the contradictory needs of individuals and of society for images and narratives of both continuity and transformation."[54] Culturally potent images get rearranged and recombined to sustain and to orient people in particular crises.[55] This creative process can refigure oppressive aspects of texts, foregrounding latent images from the peoples' perspectives, "and the entire story appears to change," or perhaps, says Ostriker, "We should say the story merely grows."[56] Retellings re-encode stories and re-image poems, bringing texts to life with intimacy and intensity in the language of the community. For such retellings to take seriously the text as stranger, I propose that we join R. S. Sugirtharajah in rejecting the "division of labor between the exegete and the expositor."[57]

The Center

The results of practicing biblical studies in the way I have outlined—beginning with the life of the community, conversing with the text as stranger, retelling the text in and with the community—would be multiple. As citizens of the United States, we might approach our task with a renewed humility toward the extent of our claims about a text. We might attempt to practice fidelity to our communities by asking specifically how texts address them and us. We might discover again how biblical texts shape us, limit us, and how they can be a light for our eyes and a lamp for our feet.

Such practice among exegetes of any denomination would require that we listen to our own communities and to communities from other parts of the world, giving more vitality to our own work and forcing us to acknowledge its particularity. Considering interpretations of other peoples, even trying them on for size, would illuminate what we have missed in a text.[58] Such a crossing of borders would, of course, further highlight issues of power already at play in evaluating and mediating between interpretations. The de-centering of historical criticism that I have described also decenters the exegete, the biblical scholar, and the academic community. What moves to the center of interpretation is the believing community.[59]

IN SEARCH OF A PEDAGOGY FOR CROSSING BORDERS

To teach biblical studies within such a framework obviously requires pedagogical practices and assumptions that extend beyond the classical lecture format. I am still searching for pedagogical clarity, but the experience of teaching an international population of Master of Arts and Master of Divinity students has had a lasting impact on me, even leading me to reappraise the field of biblical studies itself. Because my teaching had been influenced at first by the work of Paulo Freire,[60] and then later by that of Malcolm Knowles,[61] I attempted to employ dialogical and participatory methods of teaching and learning. I would set the text as a problem and invite students to investigate it, after I gave background lectures on the general historical conditions of the society from which the ancient text was thought to derive. I urged them to refrain from commentaries until after they had struggled with the text.

To help them work with the text, I taught the usual exegetical skills, such as how to divide the text into literary units, to look for narrative and character development, to find points of emphasis, repeated language, and to perform other literary analyses in search of the general thrust of the text. They were to arrive at a thesis statement that brought major elements of the text together. Then I encouraged them to connect the text to the historical, economic, and political circumstances in ancient Israel to the degree possible with our uncertain and incomplete knowledge. They were to speculate about how the text might have tried to influence its original readers, that is, to consider the text's rhetorical purposes. At last they would be ready to read commentaries.

Such preparation of the text transformed commentaries from the most boring genre known to humanity into challenging literature that often illuminated, challenged, corrected, or remained in opposition to student readings. Students then wrote brief exegetical papers for small group meetings where we discussed the text and tried to reach some consensus about its meaning. I was still operating with a one-meaning notion of texts. We never reached one meaning.

It was only after several years of these conversations that I began to realize the complicated nature of reading. Not only did students give various aspects of the texts differing weights in their interpretations (as do the commentaries), but they also began from different starting points in their own worlds. I am now attempting to employ a pedagogy that begins explicitly with students' contexts, urging them to describe their lives; socio-educational and socio-economic class; their relative privilege or its lack; their communal, religious, and ethnic backgrounds; their racial and gender identifications. I ask them to declare their loyalties to their communities by describing with whom they stand when they read. I warn them against reading for groups other than their own and against interpreting as if they lived in a vacuum.

Typically international and minority students are able to describe their contexts with more fluency than middle-class white citizens of the United States, who rarely have given reflection to the matter, with the exception of a few, usually women. When international and minority students are absent or present only in small numbers, I find it to be essential to provide readings from global and minority interpreters who are self-conscious about their worlds. This helps students from the dominant culture to become aware of the particularity of their worlds. The use of this literature serves another function as well. By providing models of contextualized biblical studies, it encourages all students, but particularly international, minority, and women students to find their voices and to claim the texts in their local communities.

In such a climate, to speak of the text as stranger serves as an apt analogy to describe the distances between the ancient text and the modern world. Students who have reflected on the particularity of their own historical contexts are primed to recognize the complexity of the process of reading ancient texts. To cross the borders to biblical texts, I attempt to teach skills of literary interpretation through actual practice on texts. I continue to ask students to investigate texts by staying away from commentaries until they have done their own work. Then I send them to the most divergent literature possible on that particular text, divergent in biblical methods and in cultural context. I try to include popular as well as scholarly interpretations. Sometimes we divide up the research tasks and report to each other, and I encourage students to work in culture or interest groups. I withhold my interpretations until I have heard and discussed theirs. Some resist, wanting to hear from the "expert" rather than doing their own work. But by doing their own analysis, they are in a position to disagree with me, to become aware of reasons for their own views, and to discover something no one else has seen in the text.

Finally, I invite students explicitly to appropriate the text for their reading community. The goal here is to describe what the text might say in their context. Must the text be resisted? Does it reinforce the status quo or provide a message of hope in the concrete circumstances of their world? Must the text be qualified or changed to speak to their people? I invite them to retell the text for their reading community, to write a midrash, to draw on symbolic language or images of the text and retrope them, or to reset the text in their community, providing a different ending or a new twist. Criteria for retelling the text include producing a creative result that emerges from the analysis of the text itself so that the retelling becomes an extension of or a conversation with the original text in the light of the students' reading community.

It is at this stage in the process of interpretation that differences among students become most apparent. A brief set of examples from my courses on the Book of Job may illustrate. A Peruvian student named Alida Tejada retold the story of Job as the story of the indigenous people of her country.[62] She saw in Job's suffering a symbolic account that evoked the suffering of her people. Amerindians of Peru not only lived in extreme poverty, having lost their land to the upper classes, but they also suffered from terrorist attacks by the Maoist group *Sendero Luminoso* (The Shining Path) who sought to destabilize the country by indiscriminate massacres. For Alida, Job represents her people, who hold steadfast in their suffering, who cry out for explanation and relief, but whose anger at God becomes an act of faith. But in Alida's retelling, the story closes without an ending. Restoration remains only a distant hope.

Alphonse Mirandu, a Tanzanian student, described the difficulties his tribal society confronted in attempting to understand and appropriate the book of Job. In his tribe of African Christians, it would be unthinkable to disregard the advice of friends and elders the way Job did, because friends and elders are sources of revelation in the community. Nor would an African Job go directly to God for help but would approach the deity through the intervention of the tribal chief and then of the spirits of the ancestors. Alphonse rewrote Job in the context of his tribe, attempting to engage the African traditional religion that formed the substrata of their Christian belief. Among the changes he made in the plot was to replace Elihu with the spirits of the ancestors who accompany the Tanzanian Job into the storm and help him "gird his loins like a strongman."

By contrast, white students from the United States most frequently appropriate the book by seeing Job as a heroic individual rather than a representative of the community. Often these appropriations portray Job as one who finds a voice over against the abusive and tyrannical deity they find in the whirlwind. Job becomes a kind of "SuperMensch" who goes on his way, alone but free. Others have discovered in the book a symbolic account of their own movement toward faith. One student retold the book by writing of the pain, humiliation, and finally of the freedom he found in facing his homosexuality. In his retelling, the friends became speakers for the tradition, the church, parents, and the wider society. But the storm that represented the chaos and confusion of his own life became a place of healing wherein he gained the truth and glimpsed the presence of the One beyond all names.

Such retellings can make biblical texts live in contemporary contexts by capturing the concrete realities of contemporary readers. The text is expanded by their lives, and their lives are challenged or uplifted by the stories that leave them no longer isolated in their pain. Such appropriations are capable of illuminating not only the ancient text but also the worlds of the multiple communities who today claim the text as sacred. They can bring the symbolic power of the text into conversation with the lives of real people. The final judge of the success of such retellings, of course, is not the professor but the reading community. This pedagogical practice, therefore, is responsible to communities outside the classroom and depends upon them for some of its raw material. To work well, such an interpretive biblical pedagogy needs voices from across borders so that dialogue among interpretations may occur. Without those voices, we may be in danger of returning the text to one single meaning.

The pedagogy for crossing borders that I have described decenters the professor, the expert, and the commentaries to place students at the center of a complex and multi-voiced conversation.[63] It seeks to engage students in serious analysis of their local realities, to provide them with skills and information for analyzing and engaging ancient literature, and to encourage artistic, creative, and critical appropriations that make the ancient stories ever new.

NOTES

1. "Actualization" of the text is the preferred term in a recent document of the Roman Catholic Pontifical Biblical Commission: "The Interpretation of the Bible in the Church," *Origins* 23:29 (January 6, 1994) 498-524. Either "appropriation" or "actualization" is better than the commonly used term, "application" of the text. "Application" implies that a biblical text may be applied to life like lipstick or a coat of paint. The process of interaction between text and life is far more complicated than applying one to the other. Robert Weiman ("Text, Author, Function and Society: Towards a Sociology of Representation and Appropriation in Modern Narrative," *Literary Theory Today*, ed. Peter Collier and Helga Geyer-Ryan [Ithaca: Cornell University Press, 1990] 91-106) prefers the German term

Aneignung because it does not involve the idea of ownership of property as does the English "appropriation" (94).

2. Edgar Krentz, *The Historical-Critical Method,* Guides to Biblical Scholarship (Philadelphia: Fortress Press, 1975) 6.

3. For descriptions of historical-critical methods, see ibid., 33-54; John R. Donahue, "Between Athens and Jerusalem: The Changing Shape of Catholic Biblical Scholarship," *Hermes and Athena: Biblical Exegesis and Philosophical Theology,* ed. Elenore Stump and Thomas P. Flint (Notre Dame: University of Notre Dame Press, 1993) 285-314.

4. E. Schüssler Fiorenza, "The Ethics of Biblical Interpretation: Decentering Biblical Scholarship," *Journal of Biblical Literature* 107 (1988) 3-17.

5. E. V. McKnight, *Postmodern Use of the Bible: The Emergence of Reader-Oriented Criticism* (Nashville: Abingdon Press, 1990).

6. For different descriptions of postmodernism, see Walter Brueggemann, *Texts Under Negotiation: The Bible and Postmodern Imagination,* ed. Patrick D. Miller (Minneapolis: Fortress Press, 1993); Claude Gaffre and Jean Pierre Jossua, "Editorial: Towards a Theological Interpretation of Modernity," *The Debate on Modernity,* ed. C. Gaffre and J. P. Jossua; *Concilium* 1992/6 (London: SCM, 1992) vii-xi; Mark Kline Taylor, *Remembering Esperanza: A Cultural-Political Theology for North American Praxis* (Maryknoll: Orbis Books, 1990) 23-45; Georgia Warnke, "Feminism and Hermeneutics," *Hypatia* 81 (1993) 81-98; Vincent B. Leitch, *Cultural Criticism, Literary Theory, Poststructuralism* (New York: Columbia University Press, 1992) xiii.

7. Robert Morgan with John Barton, *Biblical Interpretation,* Oxford Bible Series (Oxford: Oxford University Press, 1988) 257.

8. D. J. A. Clines, "Biblical Interpretation in an International Perspective," *Biblical Interpretation* 1 (1993) 67- 87.

9. S. Greenblatt, "Resonance and Wonder," *Literary Theory Today,* 77.

10. Leitch, *Cultural Criticism,* 83-93; Terry Eagleton, *Literary Theory: An Introduction* (Minneapolis: University of Minnesota Press, 1983) 14; Warnke, "Feminism and Hermeneutics," 83-84.

11. See Jane P. Tompkins, ed., *Reader-Response Criticism: From Formalism to Post-Structuralism* (Baltimore and London: The Johns Hopkins University Press, 1992); Sandra Schneiders, "The Bible and Feminism—Biblical Theology," *Freeing Theology: The Essentials of Theology in Feminist Perspective,* ed. Catherine Mowry LaCugna (San Francisco: Harper, 1993) 31-57.

12. The Maryknoll School of Theology, which closed in June 1995.

13. Paul Ricoeur, *Theology of Interpretation: Discourse and the Surplus of Meaning* (Fort Worth: Texas Christian University Press, 1976); Leitch, *Cultural Criticism,* 83-93; Eagleton, *Literary Theory*; Meir Sternberg, *The Poetics of Biblical Narrative: Ideological Literature and the Drama of Reading* (Bloomington: Indiana University Press, 1987).

14. See Elisabeth Schüssler Fiorenza, *But She Said: Feminist Practices of Biblical Interpretation* (Boston: Beacon, 1992).

15. Morgan, *Biblical Interpretation,* 257.

16. Leitch, *Cultural Criticism,* 39. See chaps. 3 and 4 for discussions of the nature of language and literature.

17. M. Fishbane, *Biblical Interpretation in Ancient Israel* (Oxford: Clarendon, 1985).

18. See Yehoshua Gitay, "Rhetorical Criticism," *To Each Its Own Meaning: An Introduction to Biblical Criticism and Their Application,* ed. Steven L. McKenzie and Stephen R. Haynes (Louisville: Westminster/John Knox Press, 1993) 135-49; John R. Donahue, "Between Athens and Jerusalem," 301-305; Phyllis Trible, *Rhetorical Criticism: Context, Method and the Book of Jonah,* Guides to Biblical Scholarship, Old Testament (Minneapolis: Fortress Press, 1994).

19. Leitch (*Cultural Criticism,* 1-13) substitutes this term for ideology and social formation.

20. So Garret Green, as cited in W. Brueggemann, *Texts Under Negotiation*, 14.

21. Frederick W. Dillistone, *The Power of Symbols in Religion and Culture* (New York: Crossroad, 1986).

22. A. R. Diamond and K. M. O'Connor, "Unfaithful Passions: Coding Women Coding Men in Jeremiah 2-3 (4:2)," *Biblical Interpretation*, forthcoming.

23. Robert Alter, *The Art of Biblical Narrative* (San Francisco: Basic Books, 1981) and *The Art of Biblical Poetry* (San Francisco: Basic Books, 1985); James L. Kugel, *The Idea of Biblical Poetry* (New Haven and London: Yale University Press, 1981); Sternberg, *Poetics*.

24. Donahue, "Between Jerusalem and Athens," 285-314.

25. J. Miranda, *Marx and the Bible: A Critique of the Philosophy of Oppression* (Maryknoll: Orbis Books, 1974); G. V. Pixley, *On Exodus: A Liberation Perspective* (Maryknoll: Orbis Books, 1989); E. Tamez, *The Scandalous Message of James* (New York: Crossroad, 1992); S. Nakanose, *Josiah's Passover: Sociology and the Liberating Bible* (Maryknoll: Orbis Books, 1993).

26. C. Mesters, *Defenseless Flower: A New Reading of the Bible* (Maryknoll: Orbis Books, 1989); and "'Listening to What the Spirit is Saying to the Churches': Popular Interpretation of the Bible in Brazil," *The Bible and Its Readers*, ed. Wim Beuken, Sean Freyne, and Anton Weiler; *Concilium* 1991/1 (London: SCM; Philadelphia: Trinity, 1991) 100-24.

27. J. Severino Croatto (*Exodus: A Hermeneutics of Freedom* [Maryknoll: Orbis Books, 1981] 12-30) calls the exodus a "vast reservoir of meaning."

28. *The Kairos Document: Challenge to the Church*, 2nd rev. ed. (Grand Rapids: William B. Eerdmans, 1987).

29. F. Deist, "South African Old Testament Studies and the Future," *Old Testament Essays* 5 (1992) 311-31.

30. I. J. Mosala, *Biblical Hermeneutics and Black Theology in South Africa* (Grand Rapids: William B. Eerdmans, 1991).

31. H. W. Wolff, *Joel and Amos*, Hermeneia (Philadelphia: Fortress Press, 1977).

32. R. S. Sugirtharajah, "The Bible and Its Asian Readers," *Biblical Interpretation* 1 (1993) 57.

33. Stanley J. Samartha, "The Asian Context: Sources and Trends," *Voices from the Margin: Interpreting the Bible in the Third World*, ed. R. S. Sugirtharajah (Maryknoll: Orbis Books, 1991) 36-49.

34. Kwok Pui-lan, "Discovering the Bible in the Non-Biblical World," *Interpretation for Liberation*, ed. Katie Geneva Cannon; *Semeia* 47 (Atlanta: Scholars Press, 1989) 25-42.

35. Schüssler Fiorenza, *But She Said*, 2-14.

36. Ibid., 82.

37. E. Schüssler Fiorenza, *In Memory of Her: A Feminist Theological Reconstruction of Christian Origins* (New York: Crossroad, 1983).

38. V. Wimbush, "Historical/Cultural Criticism as Liberation: A Proposal for an African American Biblical Hermeneutic," *Interpretation for Liberation*, 43-56.

39. Ibid., 44.

40. F. F. Segovia, "Toward a Hermeneutics of the Diaspora: A Hermeneutics of Otherness and Engagement," *Reading from This Place*. Volume One: *Social Location and Biblical Interpretation in the United States*, ed. F. F. Segovia and Mary Ann Tolbert (Minneapolis: Fortress Press, 1994) 57-73.

41. See Paul Dinter, *Beyond Naive Belief: The Bible and Adult Catholic Faith* (New York: Crossroad, 1994).

42. I have adopted the designation "stranger" from David Lochhead, *The Liberation of the Bible*, published by the Student Christian Movement of Canada and the World Student Christian Federation of North America, 1979. Segovia ("Toward a Hermeneutic of the Diaspora," 67) refers to the text as "Other" on analogy with the Hispanic cultural experience of themselves as "other."

43. Taylor, *Remembering Esperanza*, 26; Nakanose, *Josiah's Passover*, 2.

44. J. Reumann, "After Historical Criticism, What? Trends in Biblical Interpretation and Ecumenical, Interfaith Dialogues," *Journal of Ecumenical Studies* 29 (1992) 55-86.

45. Segovia, "Toward a Hermeneutic of the Diaspora," 68.

46. E. V. McKnight, "Reader Response Criticism," *To Each Its Own Meaning*, 197-219.

47. Sternberg, *Poetics*, 8.

48. Schüssler Fiorenza, "The Ethics of Biblical Interpretation," 14.

49. See Robert C. Culley and Robert B. Robinson, eds., *Textual Determinacy, Part I, Semeia* 62 (Atlanta: Scholars Press, 1993).

50. Walter Brueggemann makes this argument throughout his writings, most recently in *Texts under Negotiation*.

51. Bill Loader, "Biblical Perspectives on Issues of Multiculturalism and Inculturation," *Colloquium* 24 (1992) 3-13.

52. R. P. Carroll, "The Hebrew Bible as Literature—a Misprision?" *Studia Theologica* 4 (1993) 77-90.

53. Rabbi Jonathan Magonet, "The Biblical Roots of Jewish Identity: Exploring the Relativity of Exegesis," *Journal for the Study of the Old Testament* 54 (1992) 3-24. Jonathan Arac, ("The Struggle for the Cultural Heritage: Christina Stead Refunctions Charles Dickens and Mark Twain," *The New Historicism*, ed. H. Aram Veeser [New York and London: Routledge, 1989] 116-31) calls this process "refunctioning."

54. A. Suskin Ostriker, *Feminist Revision and the Bible*, Bucknell Lectures in Literary Theory (Oxford and Cambridge: Blackwell, 1993) 28.

55. Arac, "The Struggle," 124.

56. Ostriker, *Feminist Revision*, 29.

57. Sugirtharajah, "The Bible and Its Asian Readers," 64.

58. See Warnke, *Feminism and Hermeneutics*, 92.

59. The document of the Roman Catholic Pontifical Biblical Commission ("Interpretation of the Bible in the Church," 515) appears to recognize this shift, albeit not wholeheartedly, when it says that "sacred scripture is in dialogue with communities of believers."

60. P. Freire, *Pedagogy of the Oppressed* (New York: Seabury, 1970).

61. M. Knowles, *The Adult Learner: A Neglected Species* (Houston: Gulf Publishing, 1973).

62. A. Tejada wrote her version of the book of Job before the Peruvian theologian Gustavo Gutiérrez wrote his, entitled *On Job: God-Talk and the Suffering of the Innocent* (Maryknoll: Orbis Books, 1987).

63. See Ira Shor, *Empowering Education: Critical Teaching for Social Change* (Chicago: University of Chicago Press, 1992).

20

WEAVING A NEW WEB
OF CREATIVE REMEMBERING

Elaine M. Wainwright

Anger and tenderness:
the spider's genius
to spin and weave in the same action
from her own body, anywhere—
even from a broken web.[1]

These words and the many images they evoke—images of weaving, spinning, spiraling, shaping, and making the new, the fragile, the strong, even from the broken and the inadequate—are significant as a starting point for a consideration of how a feminist social location has an impact on biblical studies in particular and theological education generally. One of the most significant changes feminists have introduced into these areas in recent years has been a recognition of the importance of and an engagement in the symbolic, the imaginative, the creative, and the recreative in any theological undertaking.[2] It is indeed fitting, therefore, that a discussion of these areas into the twenty-first century be undertaken in dialogue with the images, metaphors, and symbols that are enabling many to envisage the transformed future toward which our present engagement seems to be drawing us.

WEAVER WOMEN ...

In light of the multifaceted nature of feminist discussions during the last decade and of postmodern critiques of totalizing theories, it is necessary to situate the feminist approach characterizing my own location within the variety of feminisms that have emerged. I do not wish here to enter the debate of essentialism or non-essentialism,[3] of gender or difference as key analytical categories.[4] Rather, I will simply locate the position taken within this debate by those types of feminism distinguished by their political or liberationist stance.[5] In this, I "cast my lot" with those women who seek to "reconstitute the world,"[6] weaving a new future for humanity even from the broken web of the past, shaping paths for nomadic wanderers through the wilderness of our inherited culture.[7]

One of the key characteristics of political feminism is that it has as its goal a transformation of society and of church or religious institutions within that society beyond what has variously been named as patriarchy or kyriarchy. In the early days of contemporary feminism, the broken web called patriarchy was characterized generally as the rule of the fathers.[8] Within feminist biblical studies, Elisabeth Schüssler Fiorenza has refined this broad notion by drawing attention to the "interlocking structures of domination" that constitute patriarchy, and she has recently supplemented the notion of "patriarchy" (the rule of the fathers) with that of "kyriarchy" (the rule of elite males).[9] In the Australian context, Rosemary Pringle, influenced by the postmodern critique of universals, asks whether overarching analytical categories such as patriarchy (or no doubt kyriarchy) serve to focus our analysis sufficiently in any particular situation.[10]

However general or specific the analysis, an awareness has grown in recent decades of the multidimensional nature of kyriarchal oppressions that find expression in forms of domination, oppression, and discrimination based on race, class, ethnicity, sexual orientation, and religious affiliation as well as gender.[11] The feminist approach in which I am engaged is, therefore, a critical one and seeks to allow these key analytical categories of gender, class, race, and religion to weave in and out of any analysis, any interpretation.

... FROM A BROKEN WEB

One of the most searing insights that feminist studies have brought to biblical studies is the radical recognition of the lack of "innocence" of text, context, and reader.[12] For myself as a white, educated, middle-class, Australian woman, it was the genderization of context, text, and reader that first became visible. This recognition of the profound and pervasive effect of ideology based on gender enabled me to understand a little more the racial, ethnic, religious, and sexual ideologies encoded in the text and its interpretations down through the centuries, as these have been articulated by those women and men whose lives they have touched most profoundly.[13] I recognize, however, that such deeply ingrained ideologies are not changed easily, as I grapple with the racism inherent in my Australian consciousness and the anti-Judaism that has characterized almost my entire formation within the Christian tradition—the anti-Judaism that permeates its foundational documents, the Christian scriptures.[14]

The critique offered by those doubly and triply marginalized by race, class, ethnicity, or gender has brought many feminists, especially those who are white and within the Western tradition, to a recognition of our own embeddedness within kyriarchal structures and their power dynamics. Teresa de Lauretis and Rosi Braidotti both acknowledge our situatedness within the ideology supporting kyriarchy and yet are aware that our analyses of patriarchy/kyriarchy place us on the edge seeking to move beyond it toward the subjectivity of the feminist female.[15]

The category of "difference" closely related to the above has received significant attention within recent feminist critical theory.[16] Braidotti has set out very clearly the way in which this notion has functioned as an analytical category: difference *between* women and men; difference *among* women in their cultural, racial, class, religious, and gender specificities; and difference *within* each woman.[17] She envisages the feminist project as an epistemological and political movement in which differing social locations will focus these aspects of "difference" in varied ways, both deconstructively and reconstructively. She concludes her essay with the hope that "our differences can engender embodied, situated forms of accountability, of story-telling, of map-reading,"[18] a project which could well be descriptive of the feminist biblical interpretation that seeks to undertake story-tellings and map-readings toward a transformed future.

The sociocultural locations of feminist interpreters must therefore be considered in their multidimensionality. The significance of social location, which has characterized contemporary feminisms because of the ever-increasing awareness that all discourse, knowledge, and truth claims are culturally conditioned and historically limited, has, more recently, become one of the hallmarks of postmodernism.[19] Malestream postmodernism has been characterized by relativism and abandonment of theory. In the face of this development, however, feminists are making more carefully nuanced claims for the significance of what Donna Haraway calls "situated knowledges" in the context of feminist political agency.[20] Linda Alcoff and Rita Felski link this feminist agency or subjectivity to social location in an interactive way, providing thereby a model for feminist rhetorical biblical studies.[21] As Felski states:

> [T]he relationship between structure and agency is dynamic, not static; human beings do not simply reproduce existing structures in the process of action and communication, but in turn modify those structures even as they are shaped by them . . . structural determinants both influence and are themselves influenced by social action and interaction.[22]

This introduces the aspect of ethical responsibility into the discussion of sociocultural location.[23] Both theory and application of that theory, while influenced by embeddedness within kyriarchal structures and a positioning of ourselves on the edge of them and in critique of them, also have the power to influence and to change those structures. Each biblical interpreter is being challenged in the present to be consciously aware of the rhetorical effect of what are proposed as supposedly value-neutral or historical propositions regarding meaning. It is necessary to uncover what genderized, ethnic, and socio-economic maps texts constructed for their original recipients, and what type of mappings or story-tellings they effect today.

For instance, to present an insightful interpretation of the four "original" beatitudes as contextualized in the possible rejection of the son—who embraced the reign of God movement by his family and kinship group—without any attention to the genderization of such an interpretation, in either the first-century context being constructed by the interpreter, or the context of a contemporary audience, seems to fail to address the ethics of biblical interpretation.[24] It assumes only male participation in the reign of God movement without addressing any of the implications of participation on the part of women. It fails to address both genderization in the honor/shame system on which it is constructed and the possibility of women's resistance within such a system, as suggested by the data being provided by both feminist biblical and historical studies. Even more importantly, failure to address the rhetorical function of such an interpretation in the context of its contemporary articulation, and doing so in the male-exclusive language that the interpretation presupposes, serves to perpetuate the exclusion of women from both the first-century and contemporary constructions of the biblical world. Unfortunately, an example such as the above is not an isolated aberration but significantly commonplace.

In light of the above, what can be or what might we dream or envisage as the web we could weave for a biblical criticism that would transform both religious and political structures into a new and different future, characterized by justice and the integrity of the whole of creation?

... TO SPIN AND WEAVE

First, a feminist social location calls for a shift in paradigm or paradigms in relation to the Bible itself. Elisabeth Schüssler Fiorenza called for such a shift as early as 1979.[25] The call remains urgent. The Bible can no longer be considered a source of archetypal or universal truths free from all sociocultural conditioning and encoding or merely a historical document that can be studied from a value-neutral, objective position. Rather, it must be seen as a rhetorical document, a document or collection of documents or texts produced in particular contexts by those with the power and resources to do so, in order to shape the consciousness of those receiving the text or to map visions or world views in particular ways.[26] Present-day interpreters are, therefore, engaged in the making of meaning as were first-century writers and readers/hearers; hence their interpretations create new stories, new maps that function rhetorically in a variety of settings—academic and theological halls, Bible study groups, churches, and homes around the globe. Scholars may image or model such an understanding of the text in a variety of ways—as prototype, as spiral, as web being woven and rewoven, as mapping and remapping. Some of these models have already emerged as a result of liberationist, feminist, African-American, Asian, African, ecological, and other contemporary perspectives. Others will follow, as biblical scholars take more account of social location and its effect. Such paradigm shifts will, however, have significant outcomes.

No longer can it be assumed that the supposedly value-neutral objective scholar, using tools such as historical criticism or social scientific criticism, can provide "truth" or "meaning" independent of engagement. Rather, a recognition of the engagement of both the original author and audience, as well as of contemporary biblical scholars and their audience, will develop an awareness that interpretation and hence theology is an ongoing undertaking, never completed and always perspectival. Such an understanding will validate a variety of methodological approaches that will uncover different aspects of the text and its function in context, enabling a variety of perspectives on "truth" and "meaning" to emerge and to be tested in the contemporary theological enterprise. In this way, no one method or perspective will obtain against which all others will be tested or against which they must struggle to define themselves for recognition. Rather, as Sandra Schneiders suggests, "the interpretive project begins with the proper formulation of the questions one wishes to ask of the text."[27] Such questions will be determined by the variety of social locations from which interpreters emerge and in which their interpretations will have an effect; and these same questions will, on the other hand, lead to a variety of methodological choices and combinations of choices. In this way biblical interpretation may indeed become the "dance" that Elisabeth Schüssler Fiorenza envisages, moving gracefully between author, text, reader, and context by way of a variety of steps that a methodologically rich repertoire offers.

The feminist approach in its multidimensionality has brought to the fore an awareness that needs much more attention in biblical studies, namely, the differing functions of *descriptive* and *prescriptive* texts and how these are used in the reconstruction of early Christianity or the world behind and of the text. The recognition that the Corinthian texts regarding the veiling of women for prayer and their being silenced in the assembly are prescriptive texts raises significant questions regarding women's participation in prayer and the assembly that evoked such texts.[28] Similarly, Clarice Martin has demonstrated that certain texts about slaves may have been prescriptive rather than descriptive of the lives of those in bondage.[29] Significant sociological and historical data has also been uncovered by those approaching the text and its context from a variety of contemporary perspectives, and this needs to be taken into account by all scholars. This will ensure that the dominant narrative is not considered the only narrative but that attention is given to the underside of the narrative, to those voices silenced or rendered almost invisible by the prescriptive texts, so that the dominant narrative is presumed to be both descriptive and prescriptive. This has been particularly demonstrated in relation to the gospel narratives in a way which ought to be taken seriously in future biblical scholarship.[30]

Recognition of multidimensionality also means that historical reconstruction will be challenged to take account of the differences in the community or communities of reception, which feminist and other liberationist perspectives are bringing to the fore. No longer will it be possible to posit monolithic communities or groups called Johannine, Matthean, or the like. Feminist studies have challenged such reconstructions in relation to women's reception of texts and their participation in the construction of both texts and traditions. Thus, greater recognition of ethnic differences, socio-economic and status differences, as well as differences in literacy and learning—to name but a few—will give rise to different receptions or interpretations of a text within the broad community of reception, revealing a much more nuanced reconstruction of those communities.

It is this insight that has emerged as a significant interpretive factor in my own current project of reading the character of Jesus in the Matthean narrative. When one allows the variety of perspectives that would have existed in the complex communities of the first century to have an impact on interpretation, it is no longer possible to argue for *the* central title or metaphor used for Jesus.[31] What becomes clear instead is that certain traditions were becoming more dominant while others were being silenced. That which links the myth and metaphor of Sophia with Jesus in Matthew's gospel would be one such example of the latter silencing of a tradition.[32] One can imagine that those for whom a tradition was significant would not see its disappearance without some resistance, and it becomes clearer that some alternative traditions were still being developed by the variety of households constituting the Matthean community until the time of compilation of the gospel narrative as a unified work. A feminist perspective on such resistance, together with the knowledge of certain countercultural movements among some Jewish and Graeco-Roman women of the first century,[33] directs attention to the counterstory or the story which can still be heard from the underside of the dominant narrative, especially in relation to women's traditions and women's participation in the traditioning process, their remembering of Jesus. In this regard it is not only the feminist principle of "difference" that has informed my biblical studies, but also that of resistance as articulated by such feminist scholars as ethicist Hilde Lindemann Nelson who addresses the question of counterstory as:

> a story that contributes to the moral self-definition of its teller by undermining a dominant story, undoing it and retelling it in such a way as to invite new interpretations and conclusions. Counterstories can be told anywhere, but particularly when told within chosen communities, they permit their tellers to reenter, as full citizens, the communities of place whose goods have been only imperfectly available to its marginalized members.[34]

I became aware of this voice from the underside or counterstory in my initial reading of Matthew's gospel from a feminist perspective, one in which the focus was on the female characters of that text.[35] Dialogue with feminist critical theory and its influence on a number of disciplines has also enabled me to articulate the theoretical framework for a reading of the male character Jesus, giving particular attention to the voices of women and men on the margins of the Jewish-Christian community, which was itself seen as dissident or resistant within the wider Jewish communities of its location.[36]

Drawing on the paradigm of the Bible as prototype enables an analysis of the many ways the first-century Christian communities developed traditions around Jesus and the reign of God movement, traditions that challenge monolithic interpretations by the contemporary communities of reception of the text. Different interpretations will need to be brokered in relation to their rhetorical effect within the communities of reception and the map-makings they accomplish. Biblical study undertaken within the arena of theological education is engaged study and, as such, participates in ongoing storytellings, ongoing mappings and remappings; in this regard, therefore, a feminist social location would provide a challenge to theological education.

... IN THE ART OF CREATIVE REMEMBERING

From the above interweaving of feminist critical theory and currents in feminist biblical interpretation, I have been influenced to see both the doing of biblical studies and the teaching of biblical studies within the context of theological education as an art of creative remembering. It is this art that enables the voices of the silenced and the marginalized to re-emerge, to be re-membered, and to enter the theological process in which they were once engaged. In the development of my own teaching during recent years, I have found that both courses and workshops in feminist interpretation of scripture have provided the most fertile ground for the exploration of the imaginative reconstruction of the first-century biblical world and of the stories of women's participation in that world. This exploration has enabled me as scholar/teacher and the students as biblical interpreters to construct images of the biblical world that were inclusive of gender differences, ethnicity, religious affiliations, and sociocultural locations. We have heard the voices of women—Jewish women, Graeco-Roman women, daughters of Sophia, worshipers of Isis, slaves, female participants in the reign of God movement, women leaders in synagogue and emerging *ekklesia*. They have peopled the world of the biblical story together with the men whose stories and whose voices dominate the narrative and hence the religious imagination.

More recently, I gained courage from my own research and from the experience of the creative remembering that I saw unfolding within the more explicitly feminist contexts to invite students in a course in Matthew's gospel to engage in the art of creative remembering as an element in their interpretation of that gospel. The class was constituted as a Matthean group that consisted of a variety of different reading communities—those Jewish communities that were faithful to the law and those influenced by emerging Pauline Christianity along a more "law-free" trajectory. Others included those predominantly Jewish households that were structured according to the *collegia* model and hence were more egalitarian than others, those of a strong Hellenistic Jewish background, and those whose background was Greek or Roman.

During the course, students were invited to read the entire Matthean story and the smaller weekly assigned sections from within the imaginative space of their first-century reading location. This entailed some initial work in developing a cohesive picture of this space and sharing the different spaces being created with the entire class. Workshop times within the course entailed discussions of texts within these reading location groups and from time to time a brief presentation of insights to the larger group. In this way, students virtually entered into the reality of the different sociocultural contexts and perspectives. They immersed themselves in these perspectives, learning how they would have shaped the construction of the narrative in a predominantly oral/aural culture, and how they would have profoundly influenced the reception of the text and its shaping of the life of the households that participated in the ongoing reign of God movement whose story was being told.

Such an approach engaged the imagination and creativity, the creative remembering of participants, as they sought ways of drawing others in the class into the world they were discovering. Some students chose to write their weekly response paper in this creative mode, and I include an example here:

The continuing story of a first-century Jewish Woman—I am restless and disturbed. Remember how I heard of the wisdom of Jesus and how I was looking forward to this week's meeting at Simon's house to hear of his power? Well, power he certainly has. The nine stories they told today show Jesus has unrestricted power over demons, he controls the elements of nature and he cures those who are blind, dumb or ill—he even has power over death! I have always liked hearing the stories told about miracle workers, but I've never before heard of one person being able to call on so much power in so many different ways. The thing is, Jesus showed up the Pharisees of his day. Jesus acted with mercy and compassion but in doing so he broke the laws. Not all the laws mind you, those who were healed were told to obey the Law and show the priests so they could re-enter society. . . . It's as if he's challenging the Pharisees. . . . I know my family would be upset by that, our family honour is built on the law, that is quite disturbing. But there were also stories about women that both excite and scare me. It's the same feeling I had when I realised the links women have with Jesus. I am beginning to believe that I can share directly in God's reign—I don't have to rely on the male head of my household as broker with God. Simon's wife, Hannah, told the group a short story about Jesus healing Peter's mother-in-law. Even though she may have been unclean, Jesus saw her, touched her, and made her well. She hadn't even asked for help. . . . Other stories helped me to realise what it meant to be a follower of Jesus—they said straight out that followers had to leave their own houses and families. But what will happen if I do? How could I exist out of my son's house? What would have happened if my father had left us to follow Jesus? No wonder the followers of Jesus are considered different and don't fit in with the other Jewish people in our town. Oh, this is so hard, but his wisdom and his power draw me. . . .

I nearly decided not to go back, but there were other stories that showed that people who approached Jesus with faith in Jesus were healed and saved. That was all that was needed. No sacrifice, no mediator. Just faith. It seems that Jesus can do these miraculous things because of the faith of the supplicant. Do I have this faith? I want to be transformed like them. I'll go back.[37]

Another group concluded the entire course with a launch of the Matthean scroll, drawing together aspects of the gospel story and its construction and reception as encountered throughout the course.

This course did, I think, enable students to engage in the construction of the Matthean story of Jesus in all its complexity and ambiguity. They saw that this gospel's theology, its story-telling, its map-making, was constituted within diversity, controversy, and even polemic. They were able to explore the rhetorical effect of such story-telling and theologizing in a way that invited them to be much more self-reflective personally. They were able to reflect on their contemporary reading locations in relation to the story-telling, the map-making, that we engage in as we re-tell, re-member the Matthean story of Jesus today. My own contribution to the conclusion of the course was a further invitation to this reflection:

I am the voice of the women of the Matthean Community—not all of them because you know as I do that prophetic change is never easy and not all can undertake the painful transition. I am the voice of those women who discovered something new in the reign of God movement, something stirred in our lives, we were changed and we were empowered to keep that change alive.

I weep now, weep and lament as I see you reading our community's story of Jesus through the kyriarchal lens of the final narrator/redactor. This group was gradually replacing the more egalitarian spirit and praxis of our *collegia* type gatherings in the homes of those women and men who emerged as our leaders with the *ekklesia* style, which, as they would have us believe, demanded male-only participants as in the city structure and a male leader.

Look at our stories—encased within the patriarchal frame of a patriarchal genealogy and a kyriarchal commissioning of eleven males! Look what happened to *Mary's* story. We had chosen those powerful foremothers—Tamar, Rahab, Ruth, and Bathsheba—to point to the way Mary's role in the birth of Jesus subverted patriarchal family structures, and what happens? She is silenced and lost in a story about Joseph.

Just imagine if her story had been told as we often told it, how it would have led to centuries of women's leadership rather than their submission. And those other stories which empowered us for leadership in our house churches—how could our traditioning, our story-telling be so changed! *Mary Magdalene* whom we know as a leader among the apostles, why is she not named among the apostles, why is she not present at the final commissioning when her teaching role in those years after the death of Jesus was known by all. At least they could not blot out our memory of her as first witness to the empty tomb, first to be commissioned to proclaim the resurrection, and first to encounter the risen Jesus. And she is not alone, Mary of Nazara accompanies her.

And look at *Petra's* story! Her name has been erased, she becomes Simon's mother-in-law, as if she needed the position of Simon to give her authenticity. She was one of many who became discipled to Jesus; she was one of the prophetic reign of God community who participated in the development of the movement. The story we told about her call was very significant in the development of our own ministry, a ministry which was similar to that of Simon/Peter and the others—but who would guess that from the story you have received. If you look carefully, however, you will see traces of our story-telling, the form of the story is still that which we developed.

And let us not forget *Justa*. Her story was one that authenticated our sharing in the making of the tradition and in leading the community in worship. We received it as a story of a woman who challenged Jesus across ethnic and gender boundaries. You would not believe—or perhaps you would—the struggle which surrounded the telling of that story. So many wanted to save Jesus' honor, Jesus' image at the expense of Justa but we held firm. We continued to raise our voices as hers each time the story was being told. We ensured that she had a voice and that it voiced the tradition, voiced the challenge. We did not succeed in keeping her name but our voices were raised as hers so that she could not be silenced. (I've heard tell, though, that another community in Asia Minor has eliminated her story altogether. That perhaps speaks loudly of that community's attitude to women and women's ministry and participation.) Our final narrators did, however, succeed in erasing her name, making her instead an anachronism—Canaanite!

And finally *Christa*, the anointing woman. Her story captures so many of our traditions as women, and we know too from our sisters in Palestine something of the shaping of her story. It was indeed their story, their making sense of the death of Jesus which began the shaping of this story. It is, therefore, one which is dear to us but not just for those reasons. Christa is a woman of action, a woman of passion at the heart of, participating in the passion of Jesus as we do, carrying out the *diakonia* with the one most in need, the least as our great parable tells us. Hers is a *diakonia* of friendship and of companionship. She gives as she has received. She is a woman of passion become compassion, and the very intimacy of her action places us at the heart of the story of Jesus and empowers us to continue her ministry today. Her story will continue to be told in memory of her, in memory of them (her Palestinian sisters), in memory of us.

But you have not remembered. You have not always told the gospel story in memory of her and of her sisters. And it is for this that I weep and have wept painfully down through the centuries. But now I see a glimmer of hope. Our stories are being unearthed again, brought to light. You cannot proclaim the gospel again only through a kyriarchal lens. You must allow our voices to be heard, our names to be proclaimed, and our traditioning of Jesus and the reign of God movement to find a voice. You must tell our stories to our memories so that they contribute to the memory of Jesus, just as we contributed to the shaping of that memory. If you continue to tell her tale in memory of her, their tales in memory of them, then I no longer need weep but can rejoice that biblical communities today may be communities of justice and freedom for all and that they and their story, in turn, will be told to their memory.

CONCLUSION

The interpretation of the biblical story in today's world for today's people does require a "spider's genius"—the ability to spin and weave even from the broken web of the story as we have received it from our ancestors. A feminist reading site has provided me with some of the insights and the tools to do this. My hope is that this perspective together with others will enable the weaving of a new web of justice and integrity for all.

NOTES

1. Adrienne Rich, "Integrity," quoted in Catherine Keller, *From a Broken Web: Separation, Sexism, and Self* (Boston: Beacon Press, 1986) vi.

2. For example, Rebecca Chopp names one chapter of her recent book (*Saving Work: Feminist Practices of Theological Education* [Louisville: Westminster/John Knox Press, 1995]) "The Warming Quilt of God" (72-96), drawing on what has become a significant feminist image. Similarly, Elisabeth Schüssler Fiorenza addresses the "dance" of interpretation in *But She Said: Feminist Practices of Biblical Interpretation* (Boston: Beacon Press, 1992) 9-10.

3. For a detailed discussion, see Diana Fuss, *Essentially Speaking: Feminism, Nature and Difference* (New York and London: Routledge, 1989); idem., "'Essentially Speaking': Luce Irigaray's Language of Essence," *Hypatia* 3 (1989) 62-80.

4. For an excellent overview of recent discussions in feminist theory, both European and North American, see Rosi Braidotti, *Patterns of Dissonance*, trans. Elizabeth Guild (New York: Routledge, 1991). For a location of these discussions within the context of postmodernism, see the essays in Linda J. Nicholson, ed., *Feminism/Postmodernism* (New York and London: Routledge, 1990).

5. Within theological feminism, this approach has been theoretically articulated most comprehensively by Elisabeth Schüssler Fiorenza. See, for example: "Transforming the Legacy of The Woman's Bible," in *Searching the Scriptures*. Volume 1: *A Feminist Introduction,* ed. Elisabeth Schüssler Fiorenza (New York: Crossroad, 1993) 1-24; *But She Said*; and *Discipleship of Equals: A Critical Feminist Ekklesia-ology of Liberation* (New York: Crossroad, 1993). In the realm of critical theory, I find this position presented most convincingly by Rosi Braidotti in *Patterns of Dissonance*. This position is also very similar to that defined by Rebecca Chopp as "prophetic feminism" in "Situating the Structure: Prophetic Feminism and Theological Education," *Shifting Boundaries: Contextual Approaches to the Structure of Theological Education,* ed. Barbara G. Wheeler and Edward Farley (Louisville: Westminster/John Knox Press, 1991) 67-90.

6. Adrienne Rich, "Natural Resources," *Dream of a Common Language: Poems 1974-1977* (New York and London: W. W. Norton, 1978) 67.

7. Rosi Braidotti (*Nomadic Subjects: Embodiment and Sexual Difference in Contemporary Feminist Theory* [New York: Columbia University Press, 1994]) develops the metaphor of "nomadism" or the notion of "nomadic subjects" as "a theoretical figuration for contemporary subjectivity."

8. See the now-famous phrase of Adrienne Rich (*Of Woman Born: Motherhood as Experience and Institution* [New York: Norton, 1976] 57): "patriarchy is the power of the fathers. . . ."

9. Schüssler Fiorenza, *But She Said*, 8. For her more extensive analysis of systemic kyriarchy, see also "Justa—Constructing Common Ground: To Speak in Public: A Feminist Political Hermeneutics," *But She Said*.

10. Rosemary Pringle, "Destabilising Patriarchy," *Transitions: New Australian Feminisms,* ed. Barbara Caine and Rosemary Pringle (Sydney: Allen & Unwin, 1995) 198-211.

11. Such awareness has arisen as a result of the critique of the hegemony of white middle-class feminism by women of color from different parts of the globe. Their voices are

heard in many different ways. In Australia, for example, challenges have come: (a) from migrant women: Sennie Masian, "The Profile of Filipino Woman—Not Read, Seen or Heard," *National Women's Conference 1990 Proceedings* (Canberra: Write People, 1990) 182-184; and (b) from indigenous Australian women: Anne Pattel-Gray, *Through Aboriginal Eyes: The Cry from the Wilderness* (Geneva: WCC Publications, 1991) and "Not Yet Tiddas," *Freedom and Entrapment: Women Thinking Theology,* ed. Maryanne Confoy, Dorothy A. Lee, and Joan Nowotny (North Blackburn: Dove, 1995) 165-192. The challenge is personal and political in Audre Lorde's open letter to Mary Daly in *Sister Outsider: Essays and Speeches* (New York: The Crossing Press, 1984) 66-71. See also Chandra Talpade Mohanty ("Feminist Encounters: Locating the Politics of Experience," *Destabilising Theory: Contemporary Feminist Debates,* ed. Michele Barrett and Anne Phillips [Stanford: Stanford University Press, 1992] 74-92) for a theoretical articulation of the necessity to deal with the difference within feminist discourses. Judith Butler ("Gender Trouble, Feminist Theory, and Psychoanalytic Discourse," *Feminism/Postmodernism,* 324-40) problematizes the word "woman" as a transcendental category within feminist discourse, and Judith Plaskow has, for many years now, consistently challenged Christian women regarding the anti-Judaism within their Christian feminist theologies. For a most recent articulation of her position, see "Anti-Judaism in Feminist Christian Interpretation," *Searching the Scriptures,* 1:117-129.

12. Chopp ("Prophetic Feminism," 82) names this recognition an awareness of "the fallible assumptions of discourse."

13. See, for example, Kwok Pui-lan, *Discovering the Bible in the Non-Biblical World* (Maryknoll: Orbis Books, 1995); Itumeleng J. Mosala, *Biblical Hermeneutics and Black Theology in South Africa* (Grand Rapids: William B. Eerdmans, 1989); and Cain Hope Felder, ed., *Stony the Road We Trod: African American Biblical Interpretation* (Minneapolis: Fortress Press, 1991).

14. A very significant publication that seeks to address this issue is that of the Council of Christians and Jews (Victoria), entitled "Rightly Explaining the Word of Truth," and with the following subtitle: "Guidelines for Christian Clergy and Teachers in their use of the New Testament with reference to the New Testament's presentation of Jews and Judaism."

15. T. de Lauretis, *Technologies of Gender* (Bloomington: Indiana University Press, 1986), in particular ix-x, 1-30; Braidotti, *Nomadic Subjects,* especially her chapter on "Sexual Difference as a Nomadic Political Project," 146-172; see also Morny Joy, "Feminism and the Self," *Theory and Psychology* 3 (1993) 275-302.

16. See Joan W. Scott, "Deconstructing Equality-Versus-Difference: Or, the Uses of Poststructuralist Theory for Feminism," *Feminist Studies* 14 (1988) 33-50.

17. Braidotti, *Nomadic Subjects,* 158-172.

18. Ibid., 172.

19. Judith Newton ("History as Usual?: Feminism and the 'New Historicism'," *Cultural Critique* 9 [1988] 87-121) argues that many of the postmodern assumptions characterizing the "new historicism" have been drawn, unacknowledged, from feminist theory.

20. See D. Haraway, "Situated Knowledges: The Science Question in Feminism and the Privilege of Partial Perspective," *Feminist Studies* 14 (1988) 575-99; Nancy Fraser and Linda J. Nicholson, "Social Criticism without Philosophy: An Encounter between Feminism and Postmodernism," *Feminism/Postmodernism,* 19-38; and Nancy Hartsock ("Postmodernism and Political Change: Issues for Feminist Theory," *Cultural Critique* 14 [1989-1990] 15- 33), who speaks of the "epistemologies of marked subjectivities" to characterize those that grow out of experiences of domination. Elspeth Probyn ("Travels in the Postmodern: Making Sense of the Local," *Feminism/Postmodernism,* 176-189) distinguishes between local, locale, and location and warns against location becoming a confined space that restricts questions and perspectives, bracketing out the concerns of those from different sites.

21. L. Alcoff, "Cultural Feminism versus Post-structuralism: The Identity Crisis in Feminist Theory," *Signs* 13 (1988) 428-438; and R. Felski, *Beyond Feminist Aesthetics: Feminist Literary and Social Change* (Cambridge: Harvard University Press, 1989) 55-75.

22. Felski, *Feminist Aesthetics*, 55. See also Mary Gerhart, *Genre Choices, Gender Questions*, Oklahoma Project for Discourse and Theory (Norman and London: University of Oklahoma Press, 1992) 34-43, and the hermeneutical spiral theory of interpretation involving genre choices and gender questions. She says that "each loop is only a part of the process of interpretation, and the individual reader is both acted upon and acting."

23. Elisabeth Schüssler Fiorenza addressed this issue in her presidential address to the Society of Biblical Literature ("The Ethics of Interpretation: De-Centering Biblical Scholarship," *Journal of Biblical Literature* 107 [1988] 3-17) and has kept it alive in her writings since then. See also Daniel Patte's recent publication, *Ethics of Biblical Interpretation: A Reevaluation* (Louisville: Westminster/John Knox Press, 1995), which addresses the question of ethical responsibility in biblical interpretation from the perspective of male Euro-American exegetes.

24. I use this example since it is one that I encountered recently and that helped to clarify further for me this issue in biblical interpretation.

25. E. Schüssler Fiorenza, "'For the Sake of our Salvation . . .': Biblical Interpretation as Theological Task," *Sin, Salvation and the Spirit*, ed. D. Durken (Collegeville: The Liturgical Press, 1979) 21-39.

26. Chopp ("Prophetic Feminism," 82-83) addresses the significance of the rhetorical in theological hermeneutics and defines it as the "relation of text to social practices," which "underscores the persuasiveness of discourse in both the text and its interpretations."

27. S. Schneiders, *The Revelatory Text: Interpreting the New Testament as Sacred Scripture* (San Francisco: Harper, 1991) 152.

28. See Antoinette Clark Wire, *The Corinthian Women Prophets: A Reconstruction through Paul's Rhetoric* (Minneapolis: Fortress Press, 1990) 116-134.

29. C. J. Martin, "The Haustafeln (Household Codes) in African American Biblical Interpretation: 'Free Slaves' and 'Subordinate Women,'" *Stony the Road We Trod*, 206-231.

30. See, for example: (a) On Mark: Monika Fander, *Die Stellung der Frau im Markusevangelium: Unter besonderer Berücksichtigung kultur- und religionsgeschichtlicher Hintergründe* (Altenberge: Telos, 1990); and Hisako Kinukawa, *Women and Jesus in Mark: A Japanese Feminist Perspective* (Maryknoll: Orbis Books, 1994). (b) On Matthew: Elaine Wainwright, *Towards a Feminist Critical Reading of the Gospel according to Matthew*, Beihefte *zur Zeitschrift für die neutestamentliche Wissenschaft* 60 (New York-Berlin: de Gruyter, 1991). (c) On Luke: Turid Karlsen Seim, *The Double Message: Patterns of Gender in Luke-Acts. Studies of the New Testament and Its World* (Edinburgh: T & T Clark, 1994).

31. Jack Dean Kingsbury has argued consistently for "Son of God" as the central metaphor in the Matthean narrative, regardless of which method he has used. See, e.g., *Matthew: Structure, Christology, Kingdom* (London: SPCK, 1973) and "The Figure of Jesus in Matthew's Story: A Literary-Critical Probe," *Journal for the Study of the New Testament* 21 (1984) 3-36.

32. See Celia Deutsch, "Wisdom in Matthew: Transformation of a Symbol," *Novum Testamentum* 32 (1990) 13-47 and *Hidden Wisdom and the Easy Yoke: Wisdom, Torah and Discipleship in Matthew 11.25-30*, Journal for the Study of the New Testament Supplementary Series 18 (Sheffield: JSOT Press, 1987). See also Russell Pregeant, "The Wisdom Passages in Matthew's Story," *SBL 1990 Seminar Papers*, ed. David J. Lull (Atlanta: Scholars Press, 1990) 469-493.

33. The works of Ross S. Kraemer (*Maenads, Martyrs, Matrons, Monastics: A Sourcebook on Women's Religions in the Greco-Roman World* [Philadelphia: Fortress Press,

1988]) and Mary R. Lefkowitz and Maureen B. Fant (*Women's Life in Greece and Rome: A Sourcebook in Translation,* 2nd ed. [Baltimore: Johns Hopkins University Press, 1992]) are but two examples of a feminist historiography that is providing insights into the lives of women in the Graeco-Roman world in the time of the late Greek Empire and early Roman Empire.

34. H. Lindemann Nelson, "Resistance and Insubordination," *Hypatia* 10 (1995) 23-40.

35. See *Towards a Feminist Critical Reading* and "The Gospel of Matthew," *Searching the Scriptures*. Volume 2: *A Feminist Commentary,* ed. Elisabeth Schüssler Fiorenza (New York: Crossroad, 1994) 635-677.

36. See Anthony Saldarini, *Matthew's Christian-Jewish Community* (Chicago and London: University of Chicago Press, 1994).

37. One of a series of such reflections completed by Valerie Hoare whose reading community was a Jewish household faithful to the law.

2 1

LESSONS FOR NORTH AMERICA
FROM A THIRD-WORLD SEMINARY

Antoinette Clark Wire

When I first asked if I could spend some time as a visiting scholar at Nanjing Union Theological Seminary in east-central China (where my parents had studied Chinese from 1925 to 1927), it was 1981. They wrote back cordially that they had just enrolled their first class of students in twenty years and were unfortunately too busy to welcome a visiting scholar. Later, in the course of subsequent visits, I was to learn of their recent history. This history and these visits have led me in turn to reflect on the character of theological education as practiced in developing countries, such as China, in contrast to the kind of theological education at work in my own context of North America. In the present study, therefore, I should like to offer a few of these reflections.

TRAVAILS OF THEOLOGICAL EDUCATION IN CHINA

After the Communist victory of Mao Tse-tung over the Nationalist forces of Chiang Kai-shek in 1949 and the outbreak of the Korean War in 1950 (1950-1953) had cut the umbilical cord that funded Chinese churches from abroad, all Protestant seminaries in China consolidated in 1952 into one institution, located at the Nanjing Union Theological Seminary. The president of the seminary wrote at the time of his excitement as small groups of faculty and students from the entire theological spectrum walked in the gate carrying everything they owned, unannounced and exhausted after days of train travel from points all over China. In the decade or so that followed this merger (1952–mid-1960s), Nanjing Union Theological Seminary proceeded to train many of the people who today occupy key positions of leadership in the Chinese church, offering a combined historical and fundamental curriculum that was meant to serve the needs of such a broad range of faculty and students.

From a political point of view, these were the early, heady years after liberation, when a new government was testing out reforms in every area of social life, including the gradual collectivization of the land and the institutions of the wealthy. From a theological point of view, a number of Christians saw such developments in terms of Armageddon, the end of the world. Other Christians questioned the pessimism of departing missionaries and started to reread the Bible in a new way, preaching a gospel that emphasized God's concern for the whole people, as well as Jesus' special defense of the poor and the outcast to the point of death. This early version of Liberation Theology, coming as it did more than a decade before its emergence in Latin America in the 1970s, was eventually derailed by developments in the political scene. On the one hand, power fell increasingly into the hands of extremist elements, who intensified the denunciation of opponents and the policy of forced industrialization. On the other hand, famine without recovery in the early 1960s led to widespread desperation and ultimately to the Great Cultural Revolution of 1966-1976. In the course of this upheaval churches, mosques, and temples were confiscated for financial purposes, all seminaries were closed, and religious, intellectual, and even party leaders were publicly ridiculed and imprisoned.

When Nanjing Seminary admitted its first new class almost two decades later, after the restoration of religious freedom in 1981, the campus had long served as housing quarters for the Red Guard, and all trees small enough to be cut down had disappeared for fuel. The enthusiastic new students were housed eight to a small room, with such activities as cooking and dining taking place in a makeshift shed. The members of this first class of 1981 have by now, after graduate study both at Nanjing and abroad, taken over many of the administrative and teaching duties in the dozen new regional and provincial seminaries that have since emerged across the country. To be sure, Nanjing Seminary remains the center of this network of theological schools as a result of its competitive entrance exams, its internationally trained faculty, and its graduate program. As such, the school can provide a strong focus for my own reflections as an outsider regarding what theological education in North America can learn from its counterparts in developing countries, such as China.

Let me say from the start that I reject the view that these largely college-level programs in a socialist society are so different from ours that there is nothing we can learn from them and transfer to our own situation. At the same time, however, I believe that we are likely to misunderstand at every point what we do see, and hence these reflections of mine can serve at best as a stimulus to further learning. I shall try to keep my comments as concrete and personal as possible in order to highlight how much they represent readings of the situation at Nanjing Seminary from the point of view of my own place and time as a woman teaching New Testament Studies at San Francisco Theological Seminary, within the Graduate Theological Union, in 1996.

REFLECTIONS ON THEOLOGICAL EDUCATION IN CHINA

The brief history outlined above should immediately alert us to any quick parallels between the two contexts in question. In fact, how many of our schools in North America have died and been resurrected? Thus, the celebration that took place on the thirty-fifth anniversary of the consolidation of seminaries (1987) represented a genuine thanksgiving to God for life, while the recent events commemorating the fortieth anniversary of this event (1992) gathered alums from all over the country to rejoice. Is there any way that the traumas our schools undergo—and which are most often experienced as another round of belt-tightening, loss of people, and sour disposition—might be recognized as threats from our own social world that we have marvelously withstood, so that our continuing life might be received as life from God?

Perhaps a closer analogy can be drawn to the first decade of Nanjing Seminary after the merger of 1952. At that time, an institution with a distinguished and honorable history and a deep purse suddenly became penniless and was berated for its past dependence on outsiders. While many drifted away, a few faculty and students from a variety of different worlds found a strategy for working together when there was little choice. Surely this had something to do with the ability of the Chinese church after the Cultural Revolution to drop denominations and practice different traditions within a single church. To what extent are our denominational schools nurturers of division, unwitting or not? Do our consortia effectively draw our churches into a different future? We argue that church unity is a matter for church representatives to decide and for us to follow, but in fact many aspects of theological education could be so organized as to intensify ecumenical experience, especially as financial stringencies force us to economize. When we choose cooperation with other schools in our registration and library systems, rather than in common worship and integrated teaching of Bible and church history, we are leaving to the next generation the hard steps necessary for a mutual respect based on knowledge rather than mere tolerance.

On my next sabbatical leave, in 1987, I was able to spend a term in Nanjing doing research at the seminary library, walking a mile from Nanjing University, where housing and food service for visiting scholars had by then become available. As it turned out, the religion faculty at the university, who served as my advisors in the study of recent Christian biblical interpretation in China, were also members of the faculty at the seminary, an arrangement developed after the Cultural Revolution in spite of the fact that seminaries and their degrees have no academic recognition in China. In the course of my stay, I was able to interview seminary faculty, was welcomed at their 7:30 A.M. chapel services, and was assisted in obtaining student lunch tickets, all of which allowed me to meet people and observe their life in common.

Commonality of Life

Four dimensions of seminary life at Nanjing come readily to mind as a result of this experience:

First, what I found most striking was the extent to which such life was a *common* life. A key factor behind this commonality of life is the fact that everyone who works and studies at the seminary lives there. At that time, students were housed in a large new building, senior faculty in apartment buildings, and junior faculty and staff still in old houses with one room per family. The new buildings were erected as a result of a remarkable cooperative arrangement with contiguous businesses, which had money but no land and which agreed to put up two buildings on the edge of seminary property and cede one to the seminary in return for use of the land. After the Cultural Revolution, the seminary had been returned more land than it needed but had no money for construction. In such ways the seminary functions as a work unit within the Chinese economy, surrounded by other units such as factories, schools, and businesses, each of which includes housing—in other words, a series of company towns.

Second, everyone has more time than money on their hands. Since they seldom have the resources for entertainment as understood in our society (e.g., movies, theater, dining out, travel, special events involving an admission price), people go walking on campus in the evening, stand and talk, or ride bicycles to the park. A new book is something special, as is a new person. Because life is not so full, the pace is slower and, I would add, people get to know each other better.

Third, given the great scarcity of higher education in China, students are willing to delay marriage and live in crowded conditions with a programmed schedule in order to receive advanced training.

Finally, these students and faculty form part of a very marginal religious group, the Christian church—most of them by family heritage and some by conversion—and have a common commitment to spread the gospel of God's love in Christ for the benefit of their people.

In effect, such factors make the Chinese seminary seem much more like a monastery, especially in terms of discipline and its spartan way of life. To be sure, with the course of time, circumstances have changed somewhat: for example, physical exercises to the sound of a loudspeaker at 10 A.M. have in recent years been replaced by intense games of ping pong or basketball after supper or Tai Chi late at night; similarly, meals now include some protein as well. Still, it is within the seminary community itself that all members of the community conduct the whole of their lives. This means that eating can lead into long conversations on any topic, that chapel services and special lectures are attended by all, and that even babies and retirees show up to see any special functions, such as the graduating students' variety show, a traveling troupe of Thai actors, or a visiting choir of American gospel singers.

The contrast with our campuses here is quite striking. North American individualism means that faculty and students often live off-campus and reserve their primary allegiances for their families and their jobs, fitting the courses they are giving or taking into the cracks in their schedules. As professional schools, seminaries have significant clout in guarding the entrance to future jobs, but at the same time they arrange it so that students can go through the required professional hoops on their own schedules, without having to enter into a long-term community discipline. This may be because such a community simply cannot be constructed on the basis of time bytes due from paid faculty and staff but would actually require the kind of commitment we are loath to give.

Although we do not have a culture conducive to such community and cannot easily build it against the stream, we do know that primary learning is communal and that many students do crave it. In the light of the present competition for students, Protestant seminaries will no doubt eventually put into practice a variety of models along these lines. Some will begin to offer a monastic-style education, with community residence and spiritual practices required of all teachers and students. Other seminaries will design more limited time frames in which to do this, offering perhaps highly structured six-week terms for intense community integration, worship, and reading of the Bible at the beginning of seminary life or the academic year. Nanjing Seminary offers a third possibility, assigning one faculty member to each entering class in order to shepherd them through their religious development until they graduate, an arrangement that results in the busiest years of that particular faculty member's career. Still other seminaries, following a model with good precedent, will set aside a particular day of the week for worship and common life, which day becomes thereby the locus for community. Of course, in seminaries that day can hardly be Sunday, and thus the practice is cultivated only with great persistence. Whatever the plan may be, it is clear that the common hunger-satisfying meal and the Lord's Meal are central in realizing Christian community.

Local Churches and Seminaries

At the same time, I should also point out, at Nanjing the "place" of seminary students is not so much the school as such but the communities that sent them and to which they shall return as leaders. For example, during several two-month research stays in the new guest rooms at Nanjing Seminary in 1990, 1992, and 1994, I was able to observe successive groups of students arrive on campus and return to their churches. In effect, unless a student is recommended for graduate study or transfers to the church of a spouse (to whom he or she is often married on the day before graduation at a common ceremony for several couples), students return to their local churches to serve as pastors or to nearby churches with even greater need. In addition, one Wednesday night a month students meet informally with others from their province to sing the familiar local songs, talk about news, and pray for the churches back home. Indeed, one student told me that, after the standard summer month working in his home church, a delegation had begged him not to go back to finish his studies; they said, "You already know so much more than we do. Stay with us. We are dying of thirst."

Twenty years without church gatherings or seminaries, followed by thousands, even millions, of new baptisms, means that most churches have no pastor as well as no building. As a result, lay people preach fervently. Provincial church leaders organize training sessions, and Nanjing Seminary produces a curriculum of study, a quarterly journal, and a series of sermons and commentaries; but in the end this only makes the participants want more. In 1990 a group of fifty such lay leaders, in their thirties and forties, from Henan Province, were sent to Nanjing Seminary for a year's study of the Bible. Leaving the library at ten or eleven at night, I would see many of them sitting in their classroom reading their Bibles for the next day's lesson. One woman in the group, who was teaching Tai Chi, talked about her husband and daughter, whom she got to see only once during the year when the school gave everyone train tickets home for the spring festival. Another woman was introduced to me as the only high-school graduate in the group. By the following year, 1991, Christians in Henan Province had organized their own seminary in Luoyang, which they then proceeded to move in 1992 to Zhengzhou, the capital of the province.

Following a similar process, seminaries have sprung up in many provincial capitals, gradually raising their admissions standards and bringing in graduate-level students from Nanjing Seminary to supplement local pastors as teachers. After graduation each spring, representatives of all seminaries come to Nanjing as the Theological Education Commission of the China Christian Council to set common policies, coordinate their work, and plan curriculum for the following year. Many of these schools have been waiting for years to get land outside their cities to build more adequate facilities. However, since land is distributed by the government and use for religious purposes does not have priority, churches are often forced to shoehorn entire local seminaries of fifty or seventy-five students into small church facilities. At the same time, the new market economy has put pressure on churches to develop stores or other businesses to cover rent and wages, with one seminary turning its cafeteria into a public restaurant as a way of improving the students' diet. As the national seminary, Nanjing is more financially secure, but it also operates in concert with these other schools and shares this innovative spirit fueled by the great needs of the church for leaders.

By way of contrast, conditions in church-seminary relations in North America are characterized by a shortage of positions for graduates, as many churches contract in size. Yet, the financial bind is similar to that in China, though for different reasons, and the need for strong leaders remains just as great here as it does there. Is there a chance that we could learn some of the entrepreneurial spirit with which they introduce new programs? Could we look for the kind of people in recruitment, ministry, placement, and church-seminary relations that would be willing to take more risks to try new things? Are people in tent-making ministries getting attention? Are there seminaries making concerted efforts in lay education? What are students being taught about economizing and economic development for a new age? In such a professionalized society, are we making adequate use of our recently retired people who, with a year in seminary, might do innovative ministries at low cost? What is our responsibility to young adults who are not churchgoers in their parents' sense and not likely to become such? The overall question is how to meet the leadership needs of the church so that it can be a light in the world and what each seminary can do to test new options with this aim in mind.

Study and Worship

Finally, I come to the area of study and worship, the heart of a seminary's life. Here Nanjing Seminary is hampered by the limited previous education on the part of the students, and thus it must supplement their high-school diplomas with lectures in history and philosophy at a general level, as well as with beginning work in Bible and church history, for the first two years. Then, in the second two years, these subjects are in turn supplemented by theology, preaching, and English, and more recently by pastoral care as well. The graduate (M.Div.) level involves three further years of advanced work, including lectures on

Christian theologians and movements, as well as individual research leading to a thesis in an area of particular interest.

From a logistical point of view, the students stay in the one room assigned to their class while the professors rotate, with increasing time periods for library study at advanced levels. Before the graduate level, methods of study are less emphasized than is content, and students demonstrate their comprehension both by way of discussion and written work, although there are also efforts by some teachers to generate critical thinking. The amount of reading required seems to be less than that expected in our liberal arts colleges and seminaries, but this seems to be not only because good written resources in Chinese are still rather limited, but also because the teacher's own interpretation, as presented in oral lectures, is taken very seriously. Field work includes such activities as ongoing assistance at one of the churches in Nanjing, trips to local places of historical significance, and, often after the third year, an extended trip by the class to another region or province to learn about issues in the churches there.

Seminary worship is integrated with study, with younger students leading worship in the evening and older students (and faculty) in the morning. Such worship reflects recent study and incorporates their own spirituality in both preaching and music. Sermons are most often didactic in nature, providing a model of life from a biblical passage and illustrating it with examples from daily experience. Obviously, many of the students have had previous opportunities to preach, and they speak with clear voices and conviction to the instruction of the community.

In these areas one finds further contrasts with our seminaries, both in terms of subject matter and approach. Although I have had less experience sitting in on classes than in chapel, in both places I have observed two elements at work from which we could particularly profit in our seminaries:

The first is a high respect for knowledge, as demonstrated by the eagerness to have a teacher and to be disciplined in learning until one's entire life comes to reflect a tested morality. This attitude may derive from the Chinese philosophical tradition, according to which an educated person would apprentice himself (and now herself) to a great teacher, until the teaching is absorbed into practice, and one is able to teach others in turn. Within such a context, teaching and learning are seen as skills, as if some martial art of life were being passed on. In such a context, moreover, theoretical and practical knowledge are not separated, mutual respect is regarded as essential for teaching and learning, and everything is directed toward proper conduct in a social setting.

Perhaps there are parallel models for learning in Western experience, but I have not watched them in practice. Could the Christian tradition be taught as such a "practical knowledge" in our seminaries? How would we tune into it from our different backgrounds, which value either "knowledge for its own sake" or, more recently, novelty more than tradition? Is the kind of mutual respect that such learning implies possible in our culture? Could we accept every sermon and lecture we hear as grist for our mill of learning the right way to live? More to the point, have we the patience to learn anything that takes so much time and practice?

The second element can be more briefly described. Learning in their setting is communal. Even though individuals must take their own entrance exams, once they become part of the community, they all make every effort to help one another. Competition is not stressed, and the assumption is that the group can do everything together. Therefore, the level of anxiety is low. This is not only of help in the task of thinking and learning, but also allows people to develop in a supportive environment. Again, this may be very hard to import into a society where excellence is seen as being at the top, number one. Yet, better learning would definitely be one of the results of developing such community life in a seminary, and sensitivity to this might help to marshall the teaching faculty to support a greater sense of mutual commitment.

CHINESE BIBLICAL INTERPRETATION

In closing I should like to describe something of the character of Chinese biblical interpretation generated at Nanjing Seminary. I return to where I began, to the period of the 1950s, when remnants of faculty and students were arriving from all over China to constitute a united seminary in this place. Although faculty and students in Nanjing today continue to work at contextual hermeneutics, they readily concede that the groundwork for a distinctive Chinese biblical interpretation was laid in those early years by the few teachers and pastors who dared to re-read the Bible in light of China's new claim to responsibility for its own history. I have focused my research, more fully introduced in a recent article in *Biblical Interpretation*,[1] on the new picture of Jesus that emerged at the time in such journals as *Tian Feng* and the *Nanjing Theological Review*.

The method in these early and tumultuous years was simply to retell the biblical story in such a way as to reveal its relevance to a new society and show the humble and yet significant role of Christians within such a society. This approach was grounded on the insight that Jesus was God's human image, demonstrating thereby that God had not given up on the human project but was working to complete and perfect it. In spite of human sin, therefore, there could be no grounds for pessimism, because God was present in human form. Consequently, it was the duty of Christians to challenge themselves as well as the whole human race to—to use a traditional Chinese phrase—*zhang da cheng ren*, "to grow up and become human beings." Thus, stories from both Old and New Testaments pressed people to claim healing power and divine gifts in order to shape the future for the benefit of all. Such emphasis stood in sharp contrast to the widespread missionary pietism that had taught God's rescue of individuals from an evil world.

During this early period, Jesus' life also functioned as the grounds for prophetic witness against oppression of the poor, of women, and of the sick. Particular emphasis was placed on gospel stories that highlighted the hypocrisy of religious leaders who considered themselves justified and looked down on such non-believers as the good Samaritan, who were redressing the wrongs of society. This strategy was clearly aimed as a mirror for those who had once formed the Christian elite, who thought of themselves as the source of all good and of others as the source of evil. By way of contrast, Jesus was seen as identifying with the common people as well as with the country at large. Thus, it was argued, Jesus lived with and taught these people and died because of his solidarity with them at the hands of the foreign occupation forces. Not only the gospel narratives of his life and death, but also wise sayings from throughout the scriptures were cited to affirm full commitment to human history—"God loved the world" (see John 3:16); "All good comes from God" (see Jas 1:17)—and God's people were identified not so much by what they said but by what they did, so that "whoever does the will of God is my brother and sister and mother" (Mark 3:35).

Finally, Jesus' resurrection was perceived as a recognition story by people who experienced the living Christ where they expected the dead Jesus. Thus, whether it was the story of Mary Magdalene or that of Peter or that of the disciples from Emmaus that was recounted, they did so not so much as people reciting a well-known and predictable tradition, but rather as people who found themselves facing in their own society and churches a very unexpected presence of Christ. In the midst of confusion, they found that their faith was not dead but alive, challenging them to become the new people demanded by the times.

Theologically, this point was developed by means of a dynamic view of God's Spirit. In contrast to the common view that the Spirit was reserved for the few who believed and were baptized, they found in the Bible that the life-giving Spirit was already present before creation, giving birth to the entire world. They saw this Spirit as active throughout the history of Israel and the history of the church, in the struggle to free peoples from oppression as well as in the birth and nurture of each new generation. So God's Spirit was by no means seen as the privileged possession of an inner circle, but rather as free from all institutional boundaries, calling Christians to risk involvement in new ventures.

Finally, it was emphasized that God's kingdom could not be identified with this new era of China but had to be discerned in each situation, since God's Spirit surprises people with life and hope. Such beliefs led in turn to praise of a God whose love for the world is beyond human understanding. The preceding comments represent but a glimpse at the sort of biblical interpretation that was being carried out in Nanjing in the 1950s, at the very beginnings of China's independent and soon-unified church. In the more difficult times to follow, the church was faced with the difficult task of working out new discernments, but its basic allegiance to the people of China remained grounded throughout on strong biblical foundations.

CONCLUDING COMMENTS

In the end, to be sure, this exercise in learning about theological education from a seminary in China is limited by my own view of that situation as an outsider. Its strength, however, comes from my insider's view of our context in North America and my urgency to have done with our cautious and defensive ways in the face of change. Could we imagine a time some years from now when our seminaries have branched out in different ways to meet the needs of their students and the communities they will serve, so that theological education is no longer a monolithic but rather a multidirectional enterprise? Who can help us see the options? Perhaps schools in places where survival has required people to be flexible and innovative, schools such as Nanjing Union Theological Seminary, have something special to contribute in this regard. If so, then we need to begin to ask questions of them, to listen carefully to what they have to say to us, and to try new things in our own context of theological education.

NOTE

1. Antoinette Wire, "Chinese Biblical Interpretation since Mid-Century," *Biblical Interpretation* 4 (1996) 101-23.

Contributors

Paulo Fernando Carneiro de Andrade, Pontifícia Universidade Católica do Rio de Janeiro, Rio de Janeiro, Brazil

Rebecca S. Chopp, Candler School of Theology, Emory University, Atlanta, Georgia

J. Severino Croatto, Instituto Superior Evangélico de Estudios Teológicos, Buenos Aires, Argentina

Denise Dombkowski Hopkins, Wesley Theological Seminary, Washington, D.C.

Musa W. Dube, Department of Religion, University of Botswana, Gaborone, Botswana

Francisco García-Treto, Department of Religion, Trinity University, San Antonio, Texas

Peter C. Hodgson, the Divinity School, Vanderbilt University, Nashville, Tennessee

Joseph C. Hough, Jr., the Divinity School, Vanderbilt University, Nashville, Tennessee

Kwok Pui-lan, Episcopal Divinity School, Cambridge, Massachusetts

Archie C. C. Lee, Department of Religion, Chung Chi College, The Chinese University of Hong Kong, Hong Kong

Temba L. J. Mafico, Interdenominational Theological Center, Atlanta, Georgia

Kathleen M. O'Connor, Columbia Theological Seminary, Atlanta, Georgia

Pablo Richard, Departamento Ecuménico de Investigaciones, San José, Costa Rica

Sharon H. Ringe, Wesley Theological Seminary, Washington, D.C.

Jean-Pierre Ruiz, Department of Theology and Religious Studies, St. John's University, Jamaica, New York

Fernando F. Segovia, the Divinity School, Vanderbilt University, Nashville, Tennessee

R. S. Sugirtharajah, Selly Oak Colleges, Birmingham, United Kingdom.

Mark Lewis Taylor, Princeton Theological Seminary, Princeton, New Jersey

Frederick C. Tiffany, Methodist Theological School in Ohio, Delaware, Ohio

Mary Ann Tolbert, Pacific School of Religion, Berkeley, California

Elaine M. Wainwright, Catholic Theological College, Banyo, Queensland, Australia

Vincent L. Wimbush, Union Theological Seminary, New York, New York

Antoinette Clark Wire, San Francisco Theological Seminary, San Anselmo, California

INDEX